HUMANISM AND THE RISE OF SCIENCE
IN TUDOR ENGLAND

Humanism and the rise of science in Tudor England

Antonia McLean

Heinemann · London

Heinemann Educational Books Ltd.
LONDON EDINBURGH MELBOURNE TORONTO
AUCKLAND SINGAPORE JOHANNESBURG
HONG KONG NAIROBI IBADAN KUALA LUMPUR

ISBN 0 435 32560 4

First published 1972

Published by Heinemann Educational Books Ltd,
48 Charles Street, London W1X 8AH
Printed and bound in Great Britain
by Morrison & Gibb Ltd, London and Edinburgh

To Ruari; and for David, Andrew and Catriona

Preface

During the sixteenth century England reached a turning point. This book is an attempt to show, in particular, how the expansion of knowledge brought about by the invention of printing resulted in an intellectual breakthrough. The use of printed books and the growth of the private library were not, however, the only causes of the startling advance in ideas and technology; the whole Humanist movement, with its emphasis on the participation of laymen in intellectual life, created a climate of opinion in which new ideas could evolve and flourish; while the expansion of education acted as a further stimulant. The intellectual ferment characteristic of the second half of the sixteenth century was a direct result of all these factors, and took many forms, of which science was only one. But in science the period was truly revolutionary, for it laid the basis for advances in mathematics, geography, physics, and the natural sciences which culminated in Newton. John Dee and Leonard and Thomas Digges, working on theories put forward by Roger Bacon in the thirteenth century, were using some form of telescope before 1571; William Gilbert defined the magnetic theory of the earth; Thomas Harriot's mathematical work directly anticipated Snell and Descartes. For succeeding centuries, the impact and originality of these advances cannot be over-estimated. Although it is only one aspect of the Tudor Renaissance, it is the area least examined and least familiar to students.

My thanks are due for all the help and encouragement I have received, but especially to my husband and to Professor May McKisack who has had nothing to do with the book but who first taught me history: to Judith and Elizabeth Eccleshare, Dr Richard Hunt, Dr Talbot and the staff of the Wellcome Library, Mr J. V. Pepper, Mr Michael Preston, Mr and Mrs George Goyder, Dr Anne Whiteman, Miss J. O'Hara May for the use of her thesis, the staff of the St Bride's Library, Miss Backhouse at the British Museum, Miss Sharp and the staff of the London Library, and finally to Miss F. Jardine and Mrs Herald for the typescript.

Contents

List of Illustrations

1. The impact of printing

It is well to observe the force and effect and consequences of discoveries. These are to be seen nowhere more conspicuously than in those three which were unknown to the ancients, and of which the origin though recent is obscure; namely printing, gunpowder and the magnet. For these three have changed the whole face and state of things throughout the world; the first in literature, the second in warfare, and the third in navigation; whence have followed innumerable changes; insomuch that no empire, no sect, no star seems to have exerted greater power and influence in human affairs than these mechanical inventions.[1]

History is the study of change in civilisations, first of all in time, but also in conditions. The political, social and economic background to any period is of vital importance, but as Bacon observed in his own time, technological changes may equal or even surpass all other forces in their effect on man. The publication of the *Oxford History of Technology* has made it possible for this type of influence to be studied in some detail and the significance of Bacon's mechanical inventions has at last been recognised.[2] All Bacon's three examples are important, but in the fifteenth and sixteenth centuries the most widespread and profound in its effect was the rediscovery of printing. For the period saw increasing political and economic stability, a steady growth of literacy among laymen, and the development of a new ideology at once secular and individualistic. By about 1450 Western Europe had in fact reached a take-off point – a stage where all that was needed was some mechanism to accelerate the rate of change. The decisive factor – the catalyst – was not the discovery of America, which passed almost unnoticed, nor the new learning; nor growing centralisation of political power; but the exploitation of a new mechanical process – the printing press.

The origins of printing

Printing is the ability to repeat significant images on chosen surfaces by mechanical means. Its essential characteristic is its repeatability. Until the nineteenth century the mechanical means was either a single block of wood,

[1]Francis Bacon, *Novum Organum*, Aphorism 129.
[2]Edited by C. Singer, E. J. Holmyard, A. R. Hall, T. I. Williams, *Oxford History of Technology*, OUP 1954, 4 vols.

metal or stone, or some form of movable type. Block printing was known in Europe from ancient times (e.g. in textile printing) and the rolling of inscribed seals along clay or wax tablets can be regarded as a form of printing, but until there was a receptive surface capable of being manufactured in quantity there was no economic advantage in the use of any method of printing for books, since scribes, whether slaves or monks, working from dictation in a scriptorium could produce editions of up to a thousand copies without much difficulty. As long as parchment or vellum were the only available receptive surfaces a single folio volume of two hundred leaves required the skins of a hundred sheep, or the equivalent in calves or goats.[1]

The supply of raw material alone set a limit to the number of books in circulation and there was no incentive to develop alternative methods of production.[2]

Printing as a method of book production was not initially a European invention. Like Bacon's other examples, gunpowder and the magnet, it originated in ancient China. In China, paper was manufactured from the end of the first century AD by pulping and drying the bark of trees, vegetable fibres and rags. The earliest known fragments were found in 1931 in a ruin of the Han dynasty near Kharathoto in the modern Ning-hsia province together with wooden manuscripts dated between 89 and 98 AD. The official date of its invention in Chinese records is 105 AD. By the fifth century paper had replaced silk, slips of wood, or bamboo as the normal writing material throughout China, and improvements, such as sizing the surface either with a glue made from lichen or with starch, had been made.[3] Paper travelled to Europe along the trade routes of central Asia and in the wake of conquest. In the eighth century the Arabs overran part of Chinese Turkestan and learnt the secret of paper making from their captives. By the ninth century it was in production at Samarkand, Baghdad, Damascus, and in South-East Arabia. It rapidly displaced papyrus as a writing material in the near East.[4] By the twelfth century paper was reaching Europe by two main routes: from Damascus via Constantinople, and from North Africa to Sicily. The earliest known paper document in Europe is a deed of King Roger of Sicily dated 1109, but it was probably imported into southern

[1]The Codex Siniaticus produced during the fourth century AD was written on both calf and goat skin, each spread using the skin of one animal. It originally probably consisted of about 730 leaves, of which 390 have survived. See British Museum pamphlet, *The Codex Siniaticus and the Codex Alexandrinsus*, 1951, pp 11-12.
[2]See M. Plant, *The English Book Trade*, George Allen and Unwin 1939, p17.
[3]This early use of bamboo strips is the probable reason why Chinese script runs vertically up and down the page.
[4]A letter dated between 883 and 895 found in Egypt and now in the Erzherzog Collection in Vienna, ends with the apology 'pardon the papyrus' indicating that paper was already fashionable for normal correspondence. T. F. Carter, *The Invention of Printing and its Spread Westwards*, revised by L. C. Goodrich, Ronald Press, New York 1955, p136.

Spain from the tenth century.[1] By 1221 paper was sufficiently widespread for the Emperor Frederick II to ban its use in official documents. The diffusion of the secret of paper manufacture was rather slower. From Egypt it passed along North Africa to Morocco and from there to Moorish Spain. The first known paper mill in Europe was established at Xativa in 1150; the first mill outside the Arab world was founded in France in 1157 by Jean Montgolfier at Vidalon near the Pyrenees.[2] In 1276 the first Italian paper mill was set up at Montefano, and in the following century Italy outstripped Spain and Damascus as the main source of European supply.[3] Germany did not begin to manufacture paper until the end of the fourteenth century. England had no mill until the end of the fifteenth.

No such clear connection between East and West exists for the introduction of printing. In China and the Far East block printing and printing from movable type were both in use by the fifteenth century. Block printing developed first, the impetus coming from the emphasis on reduplication of prayer texts in both Taoist and Buddhist religions. By 768 AD the technique was so far advanced that the Empress Shotoku of Japan could print a million charms to ensure a long life.[4] The use of the block print was twofold: it could ensure multiplication, and it could be used to fix an authoritative text. Traditionally the invention of printing for books dates from the tenth century, when between 932–953 AD the official printing of the Confucian classics from wood was undertaken by Chinese scholars under the direction of the Prime Minister Fêng Tao, but the technique was already in existence and the earliest examples of books printed from wood blocks date from the eighth and ninth centuries. The earliest surviving printed scroll was discovered in 1967 in the wall of a temple built in 751 AD in Kyongu, South Korea. The Kyongu scroll antedates the famous Diamond Sutra of Wang Chieh which was printed in 868 AD and found by Sir Aurel Stein in Turkestan.[5]

The invention of movable type, which also existed in medieval China and Korea, was a later development than the block print and evolved out of it. The earliest record is of a ceramic type invented by a craftsman Pi Shêng between 1041–1048. The type was set in a resinous base which could be heated to loosen it. Pi Shêng's invention was not immediately followed up (although

---

[1]T. F. Carter, *The Invention of Printing*, p248. An interesting manuscript of 1129 from the convent of San Gilos has alternate pages of paper and parchment. The paper probably originated in Spain, see T. F. Carter, *The Invention of Printing*, p139.

[2]There is a tradition that Montgolfier had been captured on Crusade and had worked as a slave in a paper mill in Damascus. Dard Hunter, *Paper Making: The History and Technique of an Ancient Craft*, Cresset Press 1947, p473.

[3]T. F. Carter, *The Invention of Printing*, p137.

[4]T. F. Carter, *The Invention of Printing*, Chapter 7.

[5]For the Kyongu find see *The New York Times*, February 15, 1967. The Diamond Sutra is now in the British Museum.

experiments were made in casting tin type) largely because of the difficulty of inking the type face. Early in the fourteenth century movable type was being cut in wood (thus avoiding the ink problem), the wooden pieces being trimmed to exactly the same size and held in place by bamboo strips. The characters were divided into rhyme groups, the only possible method of classification in a non-alphabetic script. The type-setter sat between two revolving tables, one containing the more usual characters, the other the less usual. By turning either table he could select the type required.[1] A fount of such wooden type has been found at Tun-huang in Turkestan, but interestingly enough, although Uigur is an alphabetic language, the type consists of words, not of characters, and is clearly derived from the Chinese ideographic script. In the thirteenth century the *casting* of bronze type in sand moulds was developed in Korea. In 1390 the casting of a fount of metal type was undertaken at the orders of the government, and during the fifteenth century eight separate founts of metal type were cast under official sponsorship. Korea continued to use movable type consistently until 1580, and intermittently until the nineteenth century. In modern times it has had to be re-introduced from the West. Although printing from movable type was known in China and Japan, it never replaced printing from wooden blocks largely because the virtue of printing was seen as a process of *exact* re-duplication on a large scale: the use of movable type increased the likelihood of textual error.

Two other forms of the block print in the Far East are of vital importance to the study of the discovery and evolution of printing in Europe: the printed playing card, and paper money. The use of playing cards probably originated in China and may have been linked to the practice of divination and the drawing of lots. They developed parallel to the block print and references to 'sheet dice' are found before the end of the Tang Dynasty.[2] The origin of paper money is also obscure, but it was being used in China in a limited fashion as a form of credit in the early years of the seventh century, and came into use as a currency in the tenth century. In spite of rapid inflation during the fall of the Sung, the idea of a printed paper currency was taken over by the Mongols and used by them during their period of power in the thirteenth and fourteenth centuries. It is this paper currency which was reported by Marco Polo and other European travellers to the East. Marco Polo wrote:

> All these pieces of paper are issued with so much solemnity and authority as if they were of pure gold or silver; and on every piece a variety of officials, whose duty it is, have to write their names, and to put their seals. And when all is prepared duly, the chief officer deputed by the Khan smears the Seal

[1] A full description of the making and use of wooden moveable type under the Mongols in 1313 was written by a man called Wang Chen and is printed in T. F. Carter, *The Invention of Printing*, pp213-7.
[2] T. F. Carter, *The Invention of Printing*, Chapter 19.

entrusted to him with vermilion and impresses it on the paper so that the form of the Seal remains printed on it in red; the Money is then authentic. Any one forging it would be punished with death. And the Khan causes every year to be made a vast quantity of this money, which costs him nothing, that it must equal in amount all the treasure in the World.[1]

The extraordinary thing is that with printing techniques virtually perfected and extensively used throughout the Far East, so little information reached Europe. The most obvious explanation, and part at least of the answer, lies in the spread of the Moslem religion across the trade routes to China. The Moslem world was prepared to accept paper and in fact brought it to Europe. They did not accept the use of print. For religious reasons the printing of the Koran was regarded as blasphemy. Even today it cannot be printed from movable type in a Moslem country. In 1727 it was officially laid down by Sultan Ahmed III that the Koran rested upon written tradition and must be handed down in no other way. It was with the greatest difficulty that the printing press established itself at all in Moslem lands.[2] The only exception is the find, among the mass of paper documents found near Crocodilopolis which are now in the Erzherzog Collection in Vienna, of fifty fragments of paper printed in Egypt. From the form of the script they can be dated as ranging from 900 to 1350 and they consist of religious texts from the Koran, prayers and charms. The method used is similar to that of China, i.e. the paper was pressed on the block, not vice-versa as in most textile printing. The fact that block printing was being carried on in Egypt, an Arab country, at the time of the Crusades is now certain, but how widespread was the activity and how influential is unknown. There is no reference to printing in Arab literature and in general it was neither accepted nor used. The important fact is that the great trading nation of the Arabs with their extensive links with both Europe and the Far East refused as a matter of religious principle to accept printing techniques, and effectively closed the way to Europe. The Islamic barrier was clearly one of the main reasons for the separate evolution of print in East and West, but cannot be the whole answer, because there is clear evidence that by the fourteenth century Europe had heard of the existence of paper money and the method of production of such money was essentially the same as block printing for books. It is also clear that playing cards reached Europe in the late fourteenth century and that their use and consequently their production spread rapidly. The other half of the answer must lie in Europe: in the fact that there was not yet sufficient literacy, and

[1]Currency notes from the late fourteenth century were found in Peking during the Boxer Rising. They are a foot by eight inches, printed on slate coloured paper with the amount shown in the text and in pictures of piles of coins. They are printed in black and over sealed in red.

[2]There were abortive efforts to establish a press at Constantinople in the eighteenth century. The first press was set up in Cairo in 1825. See T. F. Carter, *The Invention of Printing*, Chapter 15.

therefore not sufficient demand to act as incentive to the production of books by a mechanical process.

Both the knowledge of paper money and the introduction of playing cards into Europe took place when for a century the rise of Mongol power in Central Asia broke through the Islamic barrier and opened for a century direct contact between East and West. During the thirteenth century the Empire of Jenghis Khan and his successors stretched from the Euphrates to the Pacific, included large parts of southern Russia and penetrated for short periods into Poland and Hungary. Once unity of administration followed conquest, trade expanded and with it the possibility of cultural interchange. The Mongols were the natural allies of the Crusaders against the Saracen. Embassies as well as merchants went to the Mongol capital and the extraordinary cosmopolitan nature of the Mongol Court is indicated by the fact that in the middle of the thirteenth century the goldsmith to the Khan was a Frenchman, his seal cutter a Russian and a number of Europeans including one Englishman were living at Kara Korum. A Christian Mission was sent in 1294 and significantly one of its first actions was a translation of the New Testament into Tartar. These men as well as merchants and travellers must have come into contact with printing and with printed books.

It is just after the collapse of Mongol power at the end of the fourteenth century that block prints appear in Europe. The easiest to trace and to date are playing cards. These first appear throughout Western Europe in the last decades of the fourteenth century. By 1397 games were so excessive in Paris that an edict was passed in an attempt to regulate them. The clergy were forbidden to play in 1404. By 1441 the card *printing* industry was sufficiently well established in Venice for there to be an edict protecting the manufacturers from outside competition. The wording of this edict is significant for it clearly links the production of playing cards with the other early form of block printing in Europe, the production of religious prints.

> Whereas, the art and mystery of making cards and printed figures which is in use in Venice, has fallen into decay . . . Let it be ordained that . . . in future, no work of the said art that is printed or painted on cloth or paper, that is to say altarpieces, or images, or playing cards, or any other thing that may be made by the said art, either by painting or by printing, shall be allowed to be imported into this city.[1]

The religious block print developed parallel to the production of playing cards but its origin is more complex. Block printing by various methods had been used for textile printing in both Europe and Asia, so that the principle of transferring colour from an engraved block was known, but in textile printing it was normal to use two blocks one pressed against the other with the material in between, whereas in block printing on paper only one block was used. It

[1]Quoted in T. F. Carter, *The Invention of Printing*, p191.

seems probable from the basic similarity of technique that the main influence behind the use of block printing in Europe was from Asia, and that the penetration of Eastern Europe by the Mongols and the increased connections with the Far East during the period of Mongol domination were more important than any indigenous tradition within Europe itself. In fact early European block prints present distinct affinities with the early Taoist and Buddhist prayer charms. They were all religious in subject and were a sort of elementary mass production for common people unable to afford hand painted pictures. The earliest dated block print (1423) is of St Christopher and carries two lines of text. Its purpose, like the early charms of the East, was protective. These religious prints of the early fifteenth century are important because they lead directly to the block book. It was only necessary for the few lines of script cut beneath the first prints to expand into a short explanatory text for there to be the material for a short book.

Whereas the connection between the highly developed block printing techniques of the Far East and Europe, if tenuous, is virtually certain, there is no such direct connection in the case of movable type. It is one of the extraordinary facts of history that so little precise information of the achievements of Eastern Asia reached Europe that in effect the whole process and application of the technologies concerned had to be done again. The differences between ideographic and alphabetical scripts, the respect for the perfect accuracy of the block print in reproducing text which was dominant in Asia, the total hostility of Islam to printing of any kind, the collapse of the overland route to China in the fourteenth century, all played their part, and it was in Europe rather than in the older civilisation of China that the real technological 'break-through' in printing was to occur.

Printing in Europe

Two factors made the invention of printing in Europe possible. The first was the introduction of paper in the twelfth century; the second was the spread of literacy in the fifteenth. By 1400 a mechanical process had been developed capable of producing paper (a 'receptive surface') in quantity, and once the block print was in commercial use for the first time in Europe, the printing of books became a practical economic possibility. The essential skills were all in existence. Metal workers and jewellers were aware of the different properties of molten alloys. The techniques of precise engraving and of the use of moulds had been mastered. The screw press was familiar from its use in winemaking and in the domestic linen press. It needed only the catalyst of increased demand for books to fuse them together. As the century progressed it became increasingly clear that this demand was urgent. The printing press was not a fortuitous phenomenon. It came in response to a need when circumstances were exactly

1. Woodcut of St. Christopher, 1423. *(By courtesy of St. Bride Printing Library)*

right for its development. The production of paper and its use in manuscripts was increasing, and the literate public was expanding, and expanding moreover downwards in the social scale to include men who could not afford the price of handwritten books on paper, much less on vellum. In response to this demand the multiplication of texts became an accepted trade. Professional scribes were employed by the wealthy and by booksellers like Vespasiano di Bisticci, while in Northern Europe the Brethren of the Common Life produced theological works in quantity.[1]

Under these pressures, and with the basic materials now available, it is not surprising that a number of experiments in printing techniques, with a view to increased production, should appear in Europe at about the same time. The earliest to do so was the application of wood block printing (already in use in Southern Europe for textiles and playing cards) to texts. Even before the fourteenth century the outline of the great illuminated initials in manuscripts had occasionally been printed from a carved wood or metal block, and during the last part of the fourteenth century simple religious pictures for domestic use were being printed onto paper from wood blocks in Germany and the Low Countries.[2] The process was soon extended to the production of religious books, consisting of pictures with a few lines of text. These so-called 'block books' of the fifteenth century were found only in Germany and Holland, and are probably connected with the Brethren of the Common Life and their attempts to spread religion among the laity. It is obvious that the process, while suitable for illustrations, had severe limitations when applied to a page of text. It was an entirely separate development from the invention of the movable types, although it arose at the same time in response to the same stimulus. It existed alongside, and was eventually replaced by, printing from movable type.

The invention which really revolutionised the production of books was the discovery of a method of casting the individual letters of the alphabet in metal. What is interesting is that it is clear that attempts to do this were being made independently by metallurgical craftsmen in various parts of Europe. A Bohemian goldsmith Procopius Waldfogel is known to have been working in Avignon with some form of metal type, and similar claims have been made for craftsmen in Bruges and Bologna. The Dutchman Laurens Coster was trying along the same lines, and fragments printed from movable type, but of uncertain date, are now in the Museum at Haarlem. The evidence for priority however remains inconclusive for no complete printed work is known from any of these areas.

It remains definite that the first commercially successful printing process from movable metal type was developed at Mainz. The traditional 'inventor' was the goldsmith Johann Gutenberg. This may in fact be correct, since it

[1]S. H. Steinberg, *Five Hundred Years of Printing*, Faber and Faber 1959, p25.
[2]L. Febvre and H. J. Martin, *L'Apparition du Livre*, Editions Albin Michel, Paris 1958, p53.

seems probable that Gutenberg began working on some form of printing while still in Strasbourg in the 1430s, which antedates both Waldfogel and Coster. One of his partners, Andreas Heilmann, owned a paper mill, and there are references to 'printing materials' in a lawsuit of 1436. But the fact that printing expanded so rapidly in Mainz, (there were already several separate presses working 1450–1455) opens up the possibility that the actual invention may have been a corporate rather than an individual effort.[1]

In any event, the middle years of the fifteenth century saw the solution of the three basic problems of typographic printing, the manufacture of the type, the ink, and the press. The most essential of these was the method of casting the type using a variable-width mould and perfectly struck matrices. In this way metal letters of uniform size and exact shape could be produced, which could be fitted together to make up a page, and then separated and rearranged to make another. The process involved cutting each individual letter in relief on *steel* as a 'punch', which was then struck on a softer metal to make a 'matrix' into which was poured a molten alloy which when set formed the type. The alloy was a problem in itself, since the metal had to flow easily into the mould, set quickly without deformity (i.e., be non-porous), expand on cooling and be hard. One point in favour of Gutenberg's claim is that the mixture of metals finally used – lead with traces of tin and antimony to harden it – is similar to an alloy used by Gutenberg as a goldsmith when mass producing cheap cast mirrors in Strasbourg. Once the complex problem of casting the type was out of the way, the next difficulty was the ink, for the traditional water-based inks would not adhere smoothly to metal, and it was necessary to evolve an oil-based ink in order to achieve a clear crisp impression. Finally a method had to be found of pressing the metal type onto the 'receptive surface' of the paper. For this, the early printers probably adapted, by the introduction of the lever instead of the screw, either the domestic linen press or the agricultural wine press, although there are still a number of unsolved problems remaining. It is not known for instance exactly how small travelling printers carried on their craft.[2] But the press of the sixteenth century once fully developed remained virtually unchanged until the nineteenth.[3]

Printing is a highly complex process and its invention combined the scattered techniques of engraving, metallurgy, block printing and paper and ink manufacture, and fused them all into a completely new technology, which itself

[1]L. Febvre and H. J. Martin, *L'Apparition du Livre*, p71.
[2]For this see L. Febvre and H. J. Martin, *L'Apparition du Livre*, pp85–93.
[3]At this point metal replaced wood in the construction of the hand press, e.g. The Stanhope Press; and cylinder and rotary presses were developed thus making mass production easier. *The Times* was printed on a steam-driven cylinder press in 1814. The original hand press is now virtually obsolete and mechanical and photographic methods are used for type-setting. Certain methods of large-scale printing are already controlled by computers.

'introduced into Europe, more than three centuries ahead of its general adoption by industry, the "theory of interchangeable parts" which is the basis of modern manufacturing techniques'.[1]

If Gutenberg was really the 'inventor of printing' he was undoubtedly a man of genius. It is just possible that his inventive vision may have been greater still. In 1455 during the printing of the great 42-line bible, Gutenberg's financial backer Johannes Fust suddenly foreclosed on his partner and took over the firm which then continued as Fust and Schoeffer. Gutenberg's workmen and materials were dispersed, and this financial disaster of 1455 has contributed to an interesting piece of modern research which has opened up the possibility that Gutenberg was even more original than has hitherto been supposed. In his book *Gutenberg and the Master of the Playing Cards,* Hellmut Lehmann-Haupt has put forward the theory that Gutenberg may have been aiming at reproducing not only letterpress, but also the illuminated borders of manuscript books by mechanical means. There are striking similarities in decoration, particularly in flowers and animals, between a number of works all produced in or around Mainz between 1450 and 1460. One is the *Giant Bible of Mainz,* which is a manuscript completed about 1453 (now in Washington); another is the *Schiede Bible* one of the 42-line bibles of Gutenberg and Fust, completed between 1452 and 1456 (now in Princeton); and the most unusual is a set of playing cards from copper engravings with animal and flower suits by the anonymous 'Master of the Playing Cards' and dated by Lehmann-Haupt to 1453–4. The most probable explanation (since the similarities are too remarkable to be mere coincidence) is a common source or model book of the type known to have been used at the time, but Lehmann-Haupt also suggests that the extraordinary similarity between the *Schiede Bible* decorations and the Playing Cards indicates that Gutenberg may have been experimenting with copper engraving himself – a process quite distinct from relief printing from type. 'A new concept of Gutenberg's creative dream is emerging. There remains little doubt that he envisaged the typographical reproduction in colour of the medieval liturgical manuscripts current in his time. The engravings of the Master of the Playing Cards it seems, were not created *a priori* for a card game but as technical stepping stones toward the multiple reproduction of miniatures. Only when Gutenberg's financial disaster closed the Mainz workshop to him were these engravings utilized commercially for the production of playing cards.'[2] The engraved plates according to this theory were made for the Gutenberg bible and then adapted for other uses after the break up of the original firm – an explanation made more probable by the fact that the borders of the *Schiede Bible* are unfinished. Lehmann-Haupt in fact advances the theory that 'Gutenberg at

[1]S. H. Steinberg, *Five Hundred Years of Printing,* p27.
[2]H. Lehmann-Haupt, *Gutenberg and the Master of the Playing Cards,* Yale University Press 1966, p3.

Quod cu audisset dauid:descendit in presidiu.Philisthijm autem venientes diffussi sunt in valle raphaim.Et cõ= suluit dauid dñm dicens.Si ascendã ad philisthijm·et si dabis eos i manu mea?Et dixit dñs ad dauid.Ascende: qa tradens dabo philisthijm in manu tua.Venit ergo dauid ad baalphara= sim:et percussit eos ibi et dixit.Diuisit dñs inimicos meos corã me:sicut di= uidunt aque.Propterea vocatũ e no= men loci illi⁹ baalpharasim.Et reliq= runt ibi sculptilia sua:q tulit dauid et viri ei⁹. Et addiderunt adhuc philisthi= im ut ascenderent:et diffussi sũt i valle raphaim.Cõsuluit autẽ dauid dñm. Si ascendã cõtra philisteos:⁊ trada= eos in manus meas?Qui rñdit. Nõ ascendas cõtra eos sed gira post tergũ eorũ:⁊ venies ad eos exaduso pirorũ. Et cũ audieris sonitũ clamoris gra= dientis i cacumine piror tũc inibis pliũ: qa tũc egredietr dñs ãte faciẽ tuã:ut p=

2. Part of Gutenberg's 42-line bible, printed in Mainz, 1455. *(By courtesy of St. Bride Printing Library)*

an unknown moment in his career, began to make small single plates engraved in copper. Later at an equally unknown moment, he must have realised that he could not pursue these experiments further. *Nolens volens* he released the plates. His copper engraver – in other words the Master of the Playing Cards – looked for an opportunity to employ his printing material in an economically productive way. He decided to utilize the already existing intaglio plates to print a set of playing cards.'[1] It is a plausible and fascinating idea, and an unexpected bonus from Gutenberg's bankruptcy in 1455.

These interconnections between Gutenberg and the early printers of Mainz with copper engraving and manuscript illumination and decoration underlines the fact that the earliest books were simply intended to be reproductions of manuscript texts by a quicker and therefore more economic process. They were not regarded as something essentially different. It was not immediately understood that what had happened 'was not just an improved kind of writing. It was the abandonment of one method of book production for another'.[2] In fact as Dr Curt Buhler has pointed out some fifteenth century manuscripts are copied from early printed books so that for a time the two methods existed side by side.[3] Professional scribes continued to produce manuscripts for the collector; and on occasions lacunae or missing leaves in incunabula were completed by hand thus producing a sort of hybrid of a manuscript and printed book.[4] Incunabula were often sent round in sheets packed in barrels, and then bound locally. Sheets sometimes got lost, and letters survive between booksellers and printers about this.[5] An analogous fact is that about thirty copies of the 42-line Bible were printed on vellum, in spite of the fact that it needed 10,000 calf skins to produce them.

The growing demand for books

The demand for books which had initially called the process into existence, made its expansion inevitable. The invention of printing was essentially an invention of mass-production. Without sufficient demand, it would have been uneconomic; without the raw material of paper, it was useless. The two technologies of printing and paper-making expanded together. The paper mills of the fifteenth century soon found themselves unable to meet the increased demand, and new mills spread into northern Europe wherever conditions were suitable. The first English press was set up by Caxton in 1476, the first known

[1]H.Lehmann-Haupt, *Gutenberg and the Master of the Playing Cards*, p72.
[2]B. Farringdon, *Francis Bacon. Philosopher of Industrial Science*, Lawrence and Wishart 1951, p447.
[3]Curt F. Buhler, *The Fifteenth Century Book*, University of Pennysylvania Press 1960, p16.
[4]Curt F. Buhler, *The Fifteenth Century Book*, p46.
[5]I owe this information to A. G. Thomas, Esq.

English paper mill, that of James Tate, followed it in 1496.[1] The quantitative effect of printing is a vital one, for it was this which made possible the explosion of ideas in the sixteenth century. It is one of the reasons why the theories of the humanists and the teachings of Luther were transformed into the Reformation, and it lies behind the revolution in scientific thought after 1550. Wyclif and Hus had remained parochial, the work of the 'Merton School' of mathematicians in fourteenth century Oxford was largely forgotten, but the printing press made the sixteenth century a fertile breeding ground for intellectual experiment, and one of the seminal periods of European thought.

The sack of Mainz in 1462 hastened the spread of printing, for it scattered the workmen and technicians throughout Europe, especially to Italy. By 1480 there were printing presses in more than 110 towns, of which 50 were in Italy, 30 in Germany, 8 each in Holland and in Spain, 5 in both Belgium and Switzerland, 4 in England, 2 in Bohemia, and 1 in Poland. By 1500 the total number of towns with presses had risen to 286. The number of actual books printed is more difficult to calculate with accuracy, but even approximate figures are staggering enough. The probable population of Western Europe at the close of the fifteenth century was in the region of 100 million people yet by 1500 35,000 editions of between 10,000 and 15,000 different texts had been issued from the printing presses. An edition varied from 300 copies to as many as 3000, but the average run was 1000 copies per edition, this makes a probable total of at least 20 million individual printed books in circulation by 1500. In the sixteenth century the numbers increased rapidly, so that between 1500 and 1600 it has been estimated by Febvre and Martin that between 150,000 and 200,000 editions were printed making a total of 200 million books during the century.[2]

This rapid expansion of printing in the late fifteenth and early sixteenth century in turn stimulated the evolution and diversification of type. The invention of printing imposed upon typography the immense task of fashioning types in metal whose shapes should approximate as closely as possible to pen made letters familiar for centuries to writers and readers of manuscript books. The prodigious energy of the first printers brought into existence between the year of the invention and the close of the fifteenth century hundreds of founts of type based directly or indirectly upon manuscript hands and like them

[1]Tate's mill failed; and although spasmodic attempts were made to establish a paper industry in this country they were not successful until the end of the seventeenth century, for the simple reason that there was no linen industry to supply enough linen rags for the manufacture of white paper. Most English printers imported their paper from France or the Low Countries. The situation was changed by the wars with France in the eighteenth century, the expansion of the linen industry, and the immigration of Huguenot technicians after the Revocation of the Edict of Nantes. See D. C. Coleman, *The British Papermaking Industry*, Clarendon Press 1958; and Christopher Hill, *Reformation to Industrial Revolution*, Weidenfeld and Nicolson 1967, p380.

[2]L. Febvre and H. J. Martin, *L'Apparition du Livre*, pp396-7.

varying with their provenance.[1] The local scripts of France, Spain, Italy and Germany all therefore produced distinct 'families' of type: D. B. Updike's famous book on *Printing Types* is divided into regional groups for this reason.[2]

The migration of the first printers from Mainz had therefore the important result of bringing them into contact with a wider variety of scripts on which to base their types. This had particular importance in Italy where humanistic influence was strong and where a hand based on a revived Carolingian miniscule rather than the angular heavy 'black letter' was prevalent.[3]

As more type faces were cut they divided into two main streams, those derived from the 'textus quadratus' hand which became loosely known as 'gothic' or 'black letter'; and those which developed from the humanistic scripts which became known as 'anticha' or 'roman'. Both main varieties were in existence in Germany and Italy by 1467. By the beginning of the sixteenth century a third variety, 'italic', based on the condensed slanting cursive hand used by the humanist scribes had also been cut. Italic, which could be combined with 'roman' or 'black letter' or used on its own, had the advantage that it was condensed and like 'gothic' could get more words to the page than the more open 'roman' face. Initially there was no conflict between the various forms. The great early typecutters such as Nicolas Jensen are known to have cut both 'gothic' and 'roman' founts.[4] The type-face used on any particular occasion was determined either by the manuscript hand current in the area, as in the Mainz Bibles, or by the character and contents of the book printed. 'Anticha' or 'roman' faces were thought appropriate to classical and humanist texts; 'black letter' was used for legal or liturgical works; and the batarde or semi-cursive types of the 'gothic' family were considered suitable for romances and vernacular writings.[5] Froben in Basle printed the works of Erasmus in 'roman', 'italic' and 'greek' founts, and the Bible in 'black letter'.

Yet during the sixteenth century 'roman' and 'italic' type gained over 'black letter' and its derivatives, and by the seventeenth century had virtually replaced it in every country except Germany. There were many inter-connecting reasons for this: the emergence of the printed book as a thing distinct and different from a manuscript; the spread of humanism and the expansion of a

---

[1] Stanley Morison, *German Incunabula in the British Museum*, Victor Gollancz 1928.

[2] D. B. Updike, *Printing Types: their History, Forms and Use*, Harvard University Press 1922, 2 vols.

[3] In an interesting article in *The Library*, New Series Vol. XXIV Nos 1-2, June-Sept 1943 on 'Early humanistic script and the first Roman type', Stanley Morison has traced in detail the influence of the great fifteenth century Italian calligraphers such as Niccolo de Niccoli, Antonio di Maro and Poggio on the early type face cut by the German printers Sweynheym and Pannartz from their refuge in the monastery of Subiaco in 1465.

[4] D. B. Updike, *Printing Types*, Vol. 1, p74.

[5] Stanley Morison, *Black Letter Text*, CUP 1942, p29.

IVNII IVVENALIS AQVINA TIS SATYRA PRIMA.

EMPER EGO AVDITOR
tantum?nunquám ne reponam
V exatus toties rauci theseide
Codri?
I mpune ergo mihi recitauerit ille
togatas?

H ic elegos?impune diem consumpserit ingens
T elephus?aut summi plena iam margine libri
S criptus, et in tergo nec dum finitus, Orestes?
N ota magis nulli domus est sua, quam mihi lucus
M artis, et aeoliis uicinum rupibus antrum
V ulcani. Quid agant uenti, quas torqueat umbras
A eacus, unde alius furtiuae deuehat aurum
P elliculae, quantas iaculetur Monychus ornos,
F rontonis platani, conuulsáq; marmora clamant
S emper, et assiduo ruptae lectore columnae.
E xpectes eadem a summo, minimóq; poeta.
E t nos ergo manum ferulae subduximus, et nos
C onsilium dedimus Syllae, priuatus ut altum
D ormiret·stulta est clementia, cum tot ubique
V atibus occurras, periturae parcere chartae·

3. Aldine italic, slightly enlarged, Venice, 1501. (*By courtesy of St. Bride Printing Library*)

lay reading public who bought books for entertainment and pleasure, thus increasing the demand for classical and contemporary works; the superlative quality of the early 'roman' and 'italic' founts cut in Italy by the Frenchman, Nicolas Jensen, and the Italian Franscesco Riabolini or Griffio. Printers responded to demand, and the demand was increasingly biased towards types derived from the humanistic script. Another important factor was that the 'roman' and 'italic' founts were in themselves more flexible, particularly in their capacity to combine upper and lower case letters (i.e., capitals and ordinary print), and 'roman' could be used together with 'italic' adding emphasis to certain words or passages, or separately. The influence of the early printers in Italy was also important. In response to the demand in their area, which was mainly in humanistic and classical works, the presses of Erhard Ratdolt and Aldus Manutius produced books of such quality that they have had a lasting influence on European typography.

The career of Aldus is of particular significance. Before the end of the fifteenth century he had realised the potentialities of the new medium. He can claim to be the first printer-publisher; he produced books in small format – virtually pocket editions – which were no longer trying to be anything but printed books. The Aldine 16mo books were in reality a sort of Venetian Everyman's Library, and are comparable in relation to other books of their own time to the paperback editions of today.[1] The importance of Venice in this breakthrough of the printed book is outstanding. Between 1495 and 1497 out of a total of 1,821 editions printed 447 appeared in Venice, and 150 presses were operating there at the end of the fifteenth century.[2] Since in the main the clients of the early Italian printers were humanists, the main demand was for books in 'roman' or 'italic'. The example of Froben illustrates that it was consumer demand, and the character of the text, which determined the type used, rather than a deliberate policy on the part of early printers. Printers were in business for economic not for aesthetic reasons.

By the beginning of the sixteenth century Greek and Hebrew founts had been cut thus opening up the Greek classics and the Bible in their original form to scholars. Although the production of manuscripts for private circulation continued until the seventeenth century, the scribes were gradually superseded (and absorbed) by the new technology, and printing became an art in its own right. In the sixteenth century the centre of excellence in both printing and type design shifted from Italy to France where the direct patronage of the monarchy assured the early printers of the protection of royal power. This in turn also advanced the spread of the 'roman' type face, since Geofroy Tory of Bourges, the first French printer to be given the title of *imprimeur du roi*, was a strenuous advocate of 'roman' type. He was then followed by the Estiennes,

[1] D. B. Updike, *Printing Types*, Vol. I, p127.
[2] S. H. Steinberg, *Five Hundred Years of Printing*, p56.

¶ *Agaricum.*

Garicum vt fungus naſcitur in arbor
glandiferæ præſertim arbores hoc fe
phorum quoq; prouenit colore candi
gus albus,odoratus,antidotis efficax,
ribus naſcens,noƈe relucens.Signum
nebris decerpitur.Dioſcorides autho
caudicibus naſci,quadam putrilagine
eſſe ſtirpis cuiuſdam exiſtiment.Quib
telligitur ſimilis laſerpitio,textu raro
ficie minus compaƈa.Duo genera conſtituunt. fœminam,qua
mari,reƈo venarum diſcurſu, peƈinatim digeſto:mas rotund
quaqueuorſum,& cōcretu ſuo ſpiſſior.Vtriq; guſtus initio dulc

4. Roman type from Ruel's *De Natura Stirpium,* De Colines, Paris, 1536.

father and son, and Simon de Colines, who were all scholar printers of the highest order, and who were all influenced by Italian design.

In all this England lagged behind. Printing, introduced by Caxton in 1476, remained curiously parochial. Caxton himself learnt the trade in Cologne and the Netherlands, and his type faces were derived from the 'black letter' and 'bâtarde' founts used in Germany and the Low Countries. Even after Caxton's death the trend continued. Most of the early printers in England were foreign. Wynkyn de Worde, Caxton's foreman and successor, came from Alsace, Richard Pynson was a Norman. Although Pynson has the distinction of printing the first book in 'roman' type in England (the *Oratio* of Richard Pace in 1518) and Wynkyn de Worde followed with Whittington's *Syntax* in 'roman' in 1520, these remained isolated examples. The dominant influence in English printing in the sixteenth century was French, but the founts imported were versions of the 'textus quadratus' slightly rounder than the German form but nevertheless 'black letter'.[1] 'Black letter' remained dominant in England until the second half of the sixteenth century, but at that point England followed most other European countries and gradually adopted 'roman' type. Possibly the first book in English to be printed in 'roman' was appropriately enough Robert Recorde's *Castle of Knowledge* which appeared in 1556. The fact that it was a mathematical text book written in the vernacular underlines the theory put forward by several scholars that the triumph of 'roman' over 'gothic' was not purely a matter of legibility or convenience, but an aspect of the whole intellectual revolution of the sixteenth century. 'What dies out is not the "gothic" character, it is the literature to which it was properly applied. As medicine changes from Rhases to Veselius, law from Bartolus to Cujas, so the "Revival of Learning" changed the philosophical books which men wanted to read from Duns Scotus and Occam to Cicero and Erasmus, and ultimately to Montaigne and Francis Bacon. The prevalence of Roman type is not a "technical advance"; it is an attitude of mind.'[2] This is certainly an interesting idea but leaves the problem of the survival of 'black letter' in Germany unsolved, unless it is argued that the disturbed political and religious situations made innovation difficult, or that the survival of 'black letter' somehow became a matter of national prestige. The distinctive character of German art and architecture offers a possible analogy.

From the first, the printing of books was an economic venture, and it has remained so ever since. Books were printed in order to be sold, and any printer who failed to realise this speedily went bankrupt. Considerable capital, in paper, machinery, and wages was locked up in each edition, and even the marketing of books was a problem, for they were heavy and difficult to transport. Initially marketing was done in two main ways. Individual travellers or book

[1] Stanley Morison, *Black Letter Text*, p29.
[2] E. P. Goldschmidt, *The Printed Book of the Renaissance*, CUP 1950, p26, and Stanley Morison, *Black Letter Text*, p30.

The descrypcyon of Englande.

floweth at these thre Ryuers/ʒ departeth
the thre prouynces of the ylande/as it we
re the thre kyngdomes ysonder. The thre
partes ben Loegria/Cambria/ and Nor
thumbria/that is myddle Englande/wa
les/ʒ Northumberlande ¶ R. This na=
me Temse semeth made one name of two
names of two Ryuers that be Tame and
yse/for the Ryuer of Tame renneth besy
des Dorchestre and falleth in yse/therfore
all ỹ Ryuer fro the fyrst heed vnto the eest
see is named Tampse or Temse. Temse
begynneth besyde Tetbury/ that is thre
myle by northe Malmesbury. There the
Temse spryngeth of a welle that renneth
eestwarde and passeth the Fosse/ʒ depar=
teth Gloucestre shyre ʒ wylshyre/and dra
weth with hym many other welles ʒ stre
mes/and wexeth great at Grecestre/and
passeth forth thã towarde Hampton and
so forth by Oxenforde/by wallynforde/by
Redynge/and by London. ¶ Wilhelmus
de pon.ca.ii. At ỹ hauen of Sandwytche
it falleth into the eest see/and holdeth his
name. xl. myle beyonde London/ʒ depar
teth in some place Kent ʒ Essex/ westsex
and mercia/that is as it were a great de=
le of myddell Englande. ¶ R. Seuerne is
a Ryuer of Brytayne ʒ is called Haberne
in brytyssh/and hath that name Haberne

5. Page from Higden's *Polychronicon*, Wynkyn de Worde, London, 1515. *(By courtesy of St. Bride Printing Library)*

pedlars could carry samples from place to place. This method became particularly important when questions of censorship or evasion of government controls was involved, as in the distribution of Lollard and reforming texts in England,[1] or in France, where between 1540 and 1550 Geneva became the centre of a network connected with a group of booksellers and printers in Lyon.[2] This method of distribution eventually became linked with the various clandestine presses both Protestant and Catholic throughout Europe. The second method was at the great international book fairs which developed at the end of the fifteenth century – Frankfurt, Lyon, Medina del Campo, and Leipzig, were all important book marketing centres. Payment was either by direct barter or exchange of editions, or by bills of exchange. Before long, catalogues were issued by printers and publishers giving the titles of their books available. As long as Latin remained an international language, the book fair was a perfectly logical and efficient way of marketing, but from the early years of the seventeenth century onward Latin gave way steadily before the rise of vernacular literature.[3] At the Frankfurt book fair, from 1566–70, out of 344 books, 118 were in German, and 226 in Latin; from 1601–5, out of 1,334, 422 were in German, 813 in Latin; but by the end of the century books in German were in the majority. But prior to 1500, 77 per cent of all books were in Latin, 7 per cent in Italian, 5–6 per cent in German, 4–5 per cent in French, and 1 per cent in Flemish. When the titles are grouped in categories, 45 per cent of the texts were religious, 30 per cent were literary classics, or medieval romances, 10 per cent were concerned with law, and 10 per cent were scientific or pseudo-scientific, (e.g. almanacs).[4] Febvre and Martin have shown from a comparative analysis of the numbers of religious and secular books printed in Paris between 1500 and 1559 that there was a marked decline in religious texts.[5] But no clear conclusion can be drawn from these particular figures which reflect local conditions of censorship and politics. A more detailed analysis of books printed in England between 1480 and 1640 is given by Edith L. Klotz in the *Huntington Library Quarterly* 1938.[6] In this analysis, the categories of books are more detailed and are done in ten yearly intervals. Religion and philosophical works remain in the majority accounting for 1,562 out of a total of 3,530 titles; History, Sociology, and Science all increase from 2 titles in 1480 to 30 in 1640, political works increase from 1 in 1490 to 78 in 1640; and literary works from 14 in 1500 to 156 in 1640. A more recent general analysis of English books is to

[1] A. G. Dickens, *The English Reformation*, Batsford 1964, pp28–9.
[2] L. Febvre and H. J. Martin, *L'Apparition du Livre*, p456.
[3] Statistics for the Frankfurt fair are given by L. Febvre and H. J. Martin, *L'Apparition du Livre*, p353.
[4] L. Febvre and H. J. Martin, *L'Apparition du Livre*, p378; S. H. Steinberg, *Five Hundred Years of Printing*, p84.
[5] L. Febvre and H. J. Martin, *L'Apparition du Livre*, p400.
[6] See Appendix A and *Huntington Library Quarterly* 1938, p417.

be found in H. S. Bennett's *English Books and Readers* in two volumes 1475–1557, and 1557–1603. He points out that of 103 titles known to have been printed by Caxton, 56 were religious, while the next largest section was poetry and literature.[1] Another point which emerges clearly from Bennett's study is the number and importance of works published in English and translated into English during the period.[2]

Impact of books on society

The effect of the introduction of printing into Europe was profound, but it was not immediate. The type of books printed, and their appearance, was very much the same as the type of book turned out by the 'scriptoria' of the same period. Printing did not therefore in the first instance alter the cultural background of Europe. In fact to a certain extent it may initially have limited it. Febvre and Martin have pointed out that the expense involved in printing made selection inevitable, so that although more copies of a given text were available, the range of texts was narrower and reflected the editorial judgement of the printer-publisher and the taste of the age.[3] As a result, a number of important medieval texts, the letters of Héloise and Abélard for example, were not printed until the seventeenth century or later. In the same way the imaginary travels of Sir John Mandeville were preferred to the authentic account by Peter Martyr of the voyages of Columbus. Printing certainly facilitated learning and diffused knowledge, but the knowledge tended to be traditional, and there is no evidence that, except in religion, printing hastened the spread of new ideas until at least the middle of the sixteenth century. In fact the printing of medieval scientific texts possibly delayed the acceptance of the new observational theories of men such as Copernicus and Gilbert.[4] Copernicus' *De Revolutionibus Orbium Coelestium*, originally published in 1543, had to wait over twenty years for a reprint.

Although the printed book itself started by being an international force, from the very beginning the forces of disruption and the rise of the vernacular were implicit in the mass production of books. While Latin remained an

[1]H. S. Bennett, *English Books and Readers 1475-1603*, CUP 1952, Vol I, p17.
[2]H. S. Bennett, *English Books and Readers*, see the list of translations into English between 1475-1560, Vol I, p277-319.
[3]L. Febvre and H. J. Martin, *L'Apparition du Livre*, p394: 'Et l'apparition de l'imprimerie dans ce sens peut être tenue pour étape vers l'apparition d'une civilisation de masse et de standardisation'.
[4]L. Febvre and H. J. Martin, *L'Apparition du Livre*, p420: 'Ainsi, l'imprimerie facilita peut-être dans certains domaines le travail des savants. Mais, au total, on peut penser qu'elle contribua nullement à hâter l'adoption de théories ou de connaissances nouvelles. Au contraire, vulgarisant certaines notions depuis longtemps acquises, enracinant de vieux préjugés – ou des erreurs séduisantes – elle semble avoir opposé une force d'inertie à bien des nouveautés.'

It liketh me to shelle by subtil songe with slacke & delitable solline of strenges/holle that nature mighti-ly enclineth & slittich the gouernement of thinges/and by suche lalles she puruepable kepeth the grete worlde.& holl she byndinch restreyneth al thingis by a londe that maye not le unlouden/al le it so that the lions of the coiltrepe of chere leuen the fair cheynes & taken metes of the handes of folke that yeuen it hem.and dreden her sturdy maistres of whiche they le wonte to suffre letinges/if that her horrible molthes ben bledde, that is to seyn of lestes deuoured.her corage of tyme passed that hath ben idle & rested repaireth agein.& they woxen greuously & remembren on her nature/ andy slaken her neckis from her cheynes unloude/andy her maistre first to torn with blody teth.assapeth the woode wratthes of hem.that is to seyne they freten her maister/& the Jangeling birde that singith on the hye brauches/that is to seyne in the wode.& after is enclosed in a strait cage al thaugh the pleyng besinesse of men, yeue hem honyed drinkes & large metes with swete studie/yet natheles yf thilke byrde skipping out of her strait cage.seeth the agre-ble shadolles of the woodes/she defouleth with her fete her mete yshadde/& seketh on morninch only the wode & thy-terith desiring the wode with her swete koyse/the perdy of a tre that is haled adoune by myghty strength folleth redi-

6. The Flemish *bâtarde* type used by Caxton for Boethius, translated by Chaucer, London, 1478. (*By courtesy of St. Bride Printing Library*)

international language books could carry ideas across frontiers and create opinions which transcended nationalism. The works of Erasmus did precisely this. But as the century progressed and the circle of literacy widened, authors could no longer count on a general understanding of Latin and began to write in their own language. This use of the vernacular in the printed book itself fractured the international community of scholars. At the very outset of printing in England Caxton in his Prologue to the second edition of *The Game and Playe of the Chesse* in 1483 justified his translation of the text into English 'to thende that somme which have not seen it ne understonde frenssh ne latyn. I delybered in my self to translate it in to our maternal tonge'.[1] Printers and booksellers were constantly trying to enlarge their public, and at the same time the new availability of books itself increased a taste for reading among classes such as women, which had hitherto been only partially literate. By the middle of the sixteenth century the proportion of books in the vernacular steadily increased throughout Europe. 'In Germany, up to 1517 . . . the yearly output of books in the German language averaged 40; in 1519 it was 111, in 1521 it reached 211, in 1522, 347, in 1525, 498'.[2] The ultimate effect of printing was undoubtedly to stimulate and to crystallise (e.g. to fix spelling and grammar) national languages. In some instances, for example Welsh and Basque, it may even have ensured the survival of a minority tongue.[3] The greatest single influence was naturally the Bible. 'By 1500, 30 Bible translations had already been printed in vernacular versions (mostly in German) compared with 100 Latin versions of the Vulgate. After 1522 every European nation received the Scriptures in its mother tongue.'[4] But as a direct consequence of this development of national languages and literature, the international unity of European culture was broken. The difficulty of communicating scientific and intellectual ideas across the language barrier led to fragmentation of knowledge along nationalist lines, which our own age is now trying to overcome. Only within the Catholic Church did Latin retain its old predominance.

Bacon was right. In the long run printing transformed the society which had called it into existence. But it did not achieve this by simply multiplying the number of books. Once invented, the technology of printing started a chain reaction. The advent of the printed book produced in considerable numbers, in small format and at reduced costs, changed the whole conception of reading. In the age of manuscript books, reading was essentially a corporate activity, and

[1] W. J. B. Crotch, *The Prologues and Epilogues of William Caxton*, EETS 1928, p12.
[2] S. H. Steinberg, *Five Hundred Years of Printing*, p87.
[3] S. H. Steinberg, *Five Hundred Years of Printing*, pp85–6.
[4] The Netherlands in 1523 (N.T.) and in 1525 (O.T.), England in 1524 (Tindale's N.T.) and in 1535 (Coverdale's Bible), Denmark in 1524 and 1535, Iceland in 1540 (N.T.) and 1584, Hungary in 1541, Spain and Croatia in 1543, Finland 1548–52, Poland 1552–3, the Slovenes in 1557–82, the Rumanians in 1561–3, the Lithuanians in 1579–90, the Czechs in 1579–93. S. H. Steinberg, *Five Hundred Years of Printing*, pp87–8.

reading even in solitude was probably reading aloud. In early manuscripts punctuation and even divisions between words are often absent: they were not in fact necessary. But with the portable cheap printed book, reading became an individual activity, pursued silently and in isolation. This produced two obvious results: it reinforced the growing individuality of man by allowing him to select and absorb information and ideas by himself, and as a direct effect, divergent interpretations of written texts increased. At the same time, by a sort of reaction, the printed text itself was often given an increased validity, which gave the written word in effect a false authority. This was particularly true of religious texts.[1]

By an ironical paradox printing not only stimulated individual creative thought, it also intensified the rise of nationalism and increased the power of the state. The mass production techniques of the printing press put a powerful weapon in the hands of any government, which could be used to break down internal barriers, such as those of dialect, as well as to indoctrinate people with a sense of corporate identity. Propaganda, as well as the ordinary day to day administration, were both strengthened by the use of the press. It was equally potent in the hands of an opposition. The control of the press was a problem which inescapably faced all sixteenth century governments.

In England the control of printed books was initially in the hands of the ecclesiastical authorities. The importing or printing of books could only be done under licence from the Archbishop of Canterbury or the Bishop of London and early printers such as Wynkyn de Worde or Thomas Berthelet found themselves in trouble for failing to observe the regulations in 1525 and 1526. But the continuing evasion of the regulations and the smuggling of prohibited books, such as Tyndale's *New Testament*, from abroad created an entirely new situation which was aggravated by the divorce of Catherine of Aragon. Henry tackled the problem by re-inforcing the control of the church by the power of the State. In 1529 the first list of prohibited books was issued by the government and in 1538 an attempt was made by proclamation to establish censorship over secular writings as well as those considered heretical by the church. The power of the Council and Star Chamber was added to that of the ecclesiastical Courts. At the same time the crown extended its power over the printers themselves by granting specific privileges to certain individuals. The imprint 'cum privilegio' is first found on a book in 1518 and licences to print certain particular types of book such as grammars, law books, or the extremely lucrative religious texts created what were virtual monopolies within the industry under royal control. The coveted position of printer to the King is first found under Henry VII and evolves steadily as the importance of the new medium was gradually understood by the authorities.[2] In the reign of Edward VI a policy

[1]See Marshall McLuhan, *The Gutenberg Galaxy*, Routledge and Kegan Paul 1962.
[2]In addition to the publication in print of ordinances and government proclamations this

of blanket suppression of a particular type of book, resulted in destruction on a large scale.

Mary's reign was a turning point in the history of government censorship in England. For the first time the press was used extensively and with effect against the central government. The result was to 'raise the question of censorship in its acutest form'.[1] The secret presses of Mary's reign can be divided into those functioning in England and those operating from the Continent. The secret English presses are particularly difficult to trace with precision because not unnaturally they adopted the use of the false colophon, and their publications purport to emanate 'in Rome before the Castel S. Angel, at the signe of St Peter' and other similar unlikely places. Identification is only possible by investigation of peculiarities of type and paper. There was certainly a centre at Ipswich and probably more than one press in London. The London publications are all rather crude and uneven in execution suggesting the work of amateurs using any type they could lay hands on. In defiance of all the efforts of the government, they kept up a steady flow of propaganda and occasionally even produced full length works such as the *Lamentations of Ladie Jane Grey*.

The presses on the Continent were more widespread and even more dangerous. Some of the most important printers of the previous decade, for instance Richard Grafton (the King's printer under Edward and a leading London merchant), Hugh Singleton and John Day, all eventually went into exile and were all concerned in publishing abroad. There were important centres at Geneva, Basle, and Strasburg, but the chief centre both for printing and distribution was probably Emden. It had trade links with the East Coast cloth areas which could be used for distribution, and presses already existed there. Emden saw the publication of Cranmer's *Defensione*, and the works of Ponet and Becon. In the same way the French monarchy, anxious to promote as much trouble in England as possible, allowed a press to operate from Rouen, where Michael Wood produced a translation of Gardiner's *De Vera Obedientia*; and books were smuggled across the Channel from ports such as Dieppe.[2]

The finance for these presses probably came from two sources. Wealthy exiles were able to draw money from their estates and property in England (hence the importance of quashing the bill against this in the Parliament of

privilege included the publication of authorised propaganda and some religious texts. For further reading see the following: F. S. Siebert, *Freedom of the Press in England,* University of Illinois 1952; H. S. Bennett, *English Books and Readers 1475-1557*; S. H. Steinberg, *Five Hundred Years of Printing*; P. M. Handover, *Printing in London,* George Allen and Unwin 1960, Ch.III.

[1]D. M. Loades, 'The Press under the Earlier Tudors', *Cambridge Bibliographical Society,* 1964, p29.

[2]For the theory that there may have been a press in Dublin see H. R. Plomer, *The Library,* 1910.

1555); and merchants and gentry in England subscribed secretly and sent the money overseas. 'The subscribers in England naturally took great care to conceal their actions but it is probable that a number of those prominent in the next reign, including Cecil himself, were among them.'[1] It is also perhaps significant that there was no attempt to organise a campaign of counter-propaganda in defence of the royal policy.

Mary's reaction, or rather that of her government, to this threat to her rule, was efficient if not altogether effective, and remained the official method of controlling the press until the removal of most forms of censorship in the late seventeenth century. In 1557 she granted a charter of incorporation to the Stationers' Company, and then gave it the task of disciplining its own members in the interest of the government. The ninety-seven freemen of the company were granted the monopoly of printing and bookselling throughout the country; at the same time they were empowered to search the premises of all printers and confiscate and burn any unauthorised printing found. The Stationers' could imprison the offender, levy a fine of up to 100 shillings and as a last resort break the press and deface the type. These powers could be used to protect printers from unauthorised pirating as well as to enforce the censorship laws. The University presses were outside the scope of the company, and its activities were confined to London, but in effect this meant a virtual control of all licensed printers since no official provincial printers existed at this time. A further Act in 1586 confirmed these privileges.[2]

The incorporation of the Stationers' Company and its use as a means of controlling the press is an interesting example of a typically Tudor solution to an administrative problem. With no standing army and no really efficient civil service the practical alternative was to combine profit with support for the government. The Stationers' would have been incorporated in any case during the sixteenth century since the increase in demand for books and for printed publications had made them both wealthy and influential. The advanced techniques required by the craft and the heavy capital outlay necessary restricted its practitioners to a relatively small number of experts creating an ideal environment for both government control and exploitation. Alongside the development of censorship there emerged the use of the press to enforce royal authority. It is clear no Tudor government could afford to believe in the freedom of the press, and that uncontrolled presses survived as a mark of inefficiency rather than of tolerance.

Free or not, the effect of printing on society was profound. The strengthening of the individualism already inherent in Renaissance thought was one of the factors behind the intellectual leap forward which separates the seventeenth century from the fifteenth. The other is the expansion of education, which,

[1] D. M. Loades, 'The Press under the Earlier Tudors', p40.
[2] H. S. Bennett, *English Books and Readers*, Vol II, Ch III.

while it arose from a complex social demand stimulated by humanist thought, was made possible only by the multiplication of books.

In an attempt to elucidate the working of this intellectual change in England, it has been necessary to include early humanist thought, and the ideas of scholars and intellectuals in the first half of the century, since these are important indications of the ways in which the new learning was evolving in England, and led on to the expansion of education in the middle years. The rise of Tudor science would have been impossible without this expansion of education and developed out of it, but the initial stimulus to scientific advance was economic: the need for new trade routes led directly to the mathematical lectures of the Muscovy Company and the researches of Dr Dee and his circle: the dissolution of the monasteries produced improved surveying techniques. But, once launched, scientific research gathered its own momentum. The experiments of Dee and Digges with perspective glasses, Harriot's advanced work on optics, neither originated in, nor contributed to, financial gain. The naturalists did not identify species for money. The spread of ideas, the improved methods of education, the use of books, in turn produced a new and more accurate outlook. There is a direct link between the philological scholarship of the humanists and the increased precision of the scientists, and between both and the impact of the printed word. The advance of science was part of a many-sided intellectual movement produced by the use of print. If this book has concentrated on it to the exclusion of advances in literary and allied fields, it is because it is a less well-known path, and because any alteration in fundamental concepts of the natural world affects all other changes in thought.

2. Early humanism in England

Humanism is a convenient and general term for a new approach to learning which led eventually to a new view of society. It is this last fact which gives this movement in European thought such importance. For if the 'rise of the gentry' contributed to the permanence of the Reformation in England, the 'rise of the literate laity' may be said to have partly caused it.[1] *compare with Elton.*

Medieval origins

Humanism originated not as a reaction against medieval learning, but as a *accommodated* growth and development within it. It involved a revival of classical studies based on a more critical approach to existing texts, but this was reinforced by the discovery of more accurate manuscripts, and even of hitherto unknown texts. These discoveries widened the dimensions of learning by the introduction of new ideas, and the revival of the study of Greek. This introduction of new methods and new thought inevitably produced a more flexible and less dogmatic approach to knowledge than that of the medieval schoolmen, and ultimately involved new methods of teaching, and a new approach to education. Humanism expanded. It started as a trickle, produced a river powerful but still *Interesting* confined within its banks, then a flood which for a short time carried all before *analogy* it, until finally the main force having been spent, it remained like a delta with a number of divergent channels all joining the sea in a new age. What is obvious is that it was impossible for there to be a revival of learning based on a study of the classical writers of antiquity without men becoming aware of the implications of what they read. The assimilation of the moral and political theories of the Greek philosophers, and of the social and ethical assumptions implicit, for example, in the speeches and writings of Cicero, led inevitably to a conception of man as a rational and socially conscious being in his own right; and this alteration in mental outlook gave further impetus to the education of the laity and to the idea that the layman had an essential part to play in society. As a direct result of this second factor the use of the vernacular developed as a means of communication between educated men. The really significant feature of all these changes was however that the humanistic movement which began as a purely intellectual revival among scholars rapidly developed political and

[1]Margaret Aston, unpublished article on 'Books and Belief in the Later Middle Ages', Papers presented to *Past and Present* Conference on Popular Religion 1966.

later religious overtones which eventually altered its whole character, and which ultimately gravely weakened the medieval church and medieval society.

It has been pointed out that the revival of 'pure' classical Latin and the concentration on style characteristic of early humanist scholars was a reaction against the monopoly of learning by clerics, and that this explains another characteristic of later humanism, the insistence on simplicity and direct understanding of religion. Dr McConica suggests that: 'The violent animus of the humanists and reformers in this epoch against scholastic writing, about which they commonly had very little real information, must be seen at least in part, as objection to a theology which had become the exclusive monopoly of a clerical élite. The emphasis on good Latin was itself an expression of laicism, since it automatically repudiated the specialised language of the schools and emphasised the clarity of discourse between educated laymen sharing the cultural heritage of the classics.'[1] Whatever the reasons, the idea of a literate and increasingly cultivated laity is essential to the correct understanding of the intellectual developments of the fifteenth century.

In England, the reign of Richard II marked a cultural turning point. It is the period when English finally superseded French as the language of official and legal business and of the Court.[2] There was a sudden increase of vernacular literature. A whole school of poetry for example developed in Northern Europe and England. It was the age of Wyclif, Langland, Gower and Chaucer. Chaucer is particularly interesting not only because he wrote in English, but because he illustrates the new forces at work in society. He was more than the greatest poet of his age, he was a layman high in Court service, and powerful in local government. He was a J.P., and member for Kent in the Parliament of 1386. He travelled on diplomatic missions to France and Italy. In fact it was in this way that he came into contact with the new movement in European thought, and added a knowledge of Dante, Boccaccio and Petrarch as well as the French romances to his traditional learning.[3]

England was fortunate in having a specialised centre of lay learning in the legal training offered by the Inns of Court. In the Common Law, England possessed a body of knowledge unique in Europe, and powerful in the state. One has only to look at the importance of common lawyers in Parliament from the fourteenth century onwards, to the writings of Fortescue and to the increasing definition of the spheres of law in the fifteenth century, to realise the immense importance of this specialised group of trained laymen. Their influence on the whole outlook of the politically important section of society was immense, and above all it was a secular influence. 'It is difficult to exaggerate the role of common lawyers in the development of anti-clericalism . . .

[1] J. K. McConica, *English Humanists and Reformation Politics*, Clarendon Press 1965, p18.
[2] H. S. Bennett, *English Books and Readers 1475-1557*, p7.
[3] M. McKisack, *The Fourteenth Century*, Clarendon Press 1959, pp529-32.

The judges figured prominently among those who attacked the church courts and clerical privilege in the crisis of 1515 . . . The numerous gentry who went up to the Inns of Court, thus moved into the worlds of advanced ideas in the heart of the metropolis.'[1] Even in general education it would be inaccurate to assume that learning and literacy were confined to clerics. Literacy was a test of admission to the guilds, and there were borough schools in certain areas such as Hull where the control of the school was in the hands of local men.[2] As early as 1406, a Statute of Labourers extended (in theory at least) the right of rudimentary education to all: 'Every man or woman of what state or condition that he be, shall be free to set their son or daughter to take learning at any school that pleaseth them within the realm.'[3] The parish clerk was expected to teach if necessary, and itinerant schoolmasters of various sorts, not always clerical, could and did establish themselves even in areas controlled by the church. Ecclesiastical control of teaching could be challenged and the case taken to the secular courts. In fact, a struggle developed which, though on a small scale, Dr. Simon describes as 'endemic' in the fifteenth century.[4]

Nevertheless it was through the Church and by clerics that the new approach to learning and new standards of scholarship first reached this country. Dr. Weiss has shown that beginning with Poggio Bracciolini, who came over at the invitation of Cardinal Beaufort in 1417 and spent four uncomfortable years in the vain hope of finding rare classical manuscripts in the English monastic libraries, a steady stream of able churchmen travelled to and from the Papal Chancery and the Italian centres of learning to England. Officials such as Piero del Monte, who was papal tax collector from 1435 to 1440, both influenced leading men in England, and on their return to Italy often acted as agents in the collection of books. At the same time important English clerics and aspiring scholars travelled in increasing numbers to Italy. The universities of Padua and Bologna, the school of Guarino di Verona at Ferrara, the Platonic Academy in Florence, the Papal Chancery, all acted as focal points for English students abroad.

The first Englishman to speak and read classical Greek with fluency was Robert Flemmyng who studied under Guarino, compiled a Graeco-Latin dictionary, and wrote Latin poetry in a villa in Tivoli. An Englishman, John Free, gave Guarino's funeral oration, and was famed for his scholarship even in Italy. Before his early death in 1465 Free had not only become one of the leading Greek scholars of his age but had graduated in medicine and civil law.[5] Influential laymen like John Tiptoft Earl of Worcester could spend some years

[1] A. G. Dickens, *Lollards and Protestants in the Diocese of York*, OUP 1959, p14.
[2] Joan Simon, *Education and Society in Tudor England*, CUP 1966, p6 et seq.
[3] Quoted in Joan Simon, *Education and Society*, p24.
[4] Joan Simon, *Education and Society*, p21.
[5] R. Weiss, *Humanism in England during the Fifteenth Century*, Basil Blackwell 1941, p111-2.

studying in Italy, and finally with Grocyn, Linacre and Colet the English educational renaissance may be said to have begun. But even by the middle of the fifteenth century a new type of intellectual administrator can be seen in England, and improved standards of Latinity and paleography were making their appearance in diplomatic and official correspondence.

The fifteenth century episcopate is well worth investigation. It provided a steady stream of able administrators who were also highly qualified scholars, often trained in Italy. Thomas Bekynton, who rose in Humphrey of Gloucester's household to become Bishop of Bath and Wells, Secretary to Henry VI, and ultimately Keeper of the Privy Seal, and Adam de Moleyns, Bishop of Chichester who was lynched at Portsmouth in 1450, are examples from the middle period; Bishops Morton and Fox under Henry VII, from the end. A few, such as William Grey Bishop of Ely, and George Neville, the younger brother of Warwick the Kingmaker, who became Bishop of Exeter and ultimately in 1465 Archbishop of York, collected important libraries and acted as patrons of learning and scholarship. At least one, Reginald Pecock Bishop of St. Asaph in 1444 and then of Chichester from 1450 until his disgrace in 1457, had real importance as a thinker considerably in advance of his time. Pecock tried to defend the Church against the Lollards by the use of reason, rather than the authority of the Scriptures. His major work *The Repressor of over much blaming of the Clergy* was written in English which is significant in itself. He had a critical approach to texts, and queried the authenticity of the Apostles' Creed; he even wrote a new version and revised the Ten Commandments. Not surprisingly he was eventually accused of heresy himself, deprived of his bishopric in 1457 and forced to recant.[1]

The efforts of individual scholars, the efficiency and erudition of the episcopate, and the direct connection with Italy are not in themselves enough to explain the change in intellectual climate which took place in fifteenth century England. It is necessary to look as well to the great collection of books and manuscripts which were accumulated by a few influential people, and which in part at least found their way into the College and University libraries of Oxford and Cambridge, and thus directly influenced the next generation of scholars. Even if Oxford's statement that Humphrey of Gloucester's books had made learning possible for the first time in the University was an unctuous exaggeration[2], the effect of his donation, and of others during this period, was tremendous, simply because their libraries contained texts never available

---

[1]For Pecock's views see E. F. Jacob, *The Fifteenth Century*, Clarendon Press 1961, p684; R. Pecock, *The Repressor of over much blaming of the Clergy*, ed. Chuchill Babington, Rolls Series 1860, Introduction.

[2]'Previously there had been it is true a University of Oxford: but study there was none, for there were no books: now however through your gifts, we too can discern the secrets of learning.' Quoted in H. Maynard Smith, *Pre-Reformation England*, Macmillan 1938.

before. Even a superficial glance at a list of books collected by these patrons makes it clear that they all have one thing in common: they all contain a number of important Greek works either in the original Greek or translated into Latin, including the newly discovered dialogues of Plato. For the first time at Oxford, and to a lesser degree at Cambridge (which was not quite so lucky in the extent of its benefactions) the ideas and teachings of the Greek philosophers were accessible.

Of these private libraries the most important and the most varied in content was that of Humphrey Duke of Gloucester, uncle to Henry VI. Humphrey was a princely patron with wide contacts; papal officials, bishops, travelling diplomatists were all used by him to search for manuscripts. He employed Italians such as Frulovisi and Beccaria as secretaries, and in addition commissioned works direct from important humanist scholars in Italy. In his service Frulovisi wrote his *Vita Henrici Quinti*, and Humphrey was so impressed by Leonardo Bruni's translation of Aristotle's *Ethics* that he asked him to follow it with the *Politics*. In the same way he patronised Pier Candido Decembrio who dedicated his translation of Plato's *Republic* to the Duke, and sent him a beautifully bound copy in 1443. Besides these Humphrey is known to have possessed a copy of Plato's *Phaedrus* and possibly other dialogues translated into Latin, Plutarch's *Lives*, a Latin *Ptolemy*, all that was then known of Livy, Caesar's *De Bello Gallico*, Suetonius' *De Vita Caesarum*, Pliny's *Letters*, Vitruvius *On Architecture*, Varro's *De Lingua Latina* and Apuleius *The Golden Ass*.[1] He also had a selection of Italian and French books, including a French translation of the *Decameron*, Dante's *Commedia* and some Petrarch. From his own time, Duke Humphrey had Del Monte's *De Vitiorum et Virtutum inter se differentia*, Poggio's *De Avaritia* and Bruni's *Isagogicon*. A substantial part of this library was donated to Oxford during the lifetime of the Duke where a portion of it still remains. A section was acquired by King's College, Cambridge after his death.

Another important library was collected by William Grey, Bishop of Ely. His main interest was theology, but his books also included some important classical texts, Aristotle's *Politics* and *Ethics*, some of Plato's dialogues, Valla's *Thucydides*, and Plutarch's *De Virtute et Vitio*, Lucian's *De Amicitia* and the natural history of the elder Pliny. He also possessed an early printed *Josephus*.[2] The bulk of Grey's Library went to his old college Balliol, but a small portion went to Peterhouse, Cambridge.

The scholar Robert Flemmyng also gave his books to an Oxford college, in this case Lincoln. His library was smaller than Grey's, but is interesting because it contained a few important early texts in the original Greek, including St. Paul's *Epistles*, and an *Acts of the Apostles*. Flemmyng was unusual in that

[1] For details see R. Weiss, *Humanism in England*, p62 et seq.
[2] R. Weiss, *Humanism in England*, p92 et seq.

he also collected poetry and among his books were the *Commediae* of Plautus, and a commentary on Virgil.

The last really significant library is that of the layman, John Tiptoft Earl of Worcester. Tiptoft was one of the most unusual Englishmen of his century and his library is for this reason of great interest. His collection of books, intended for Oxford and Cambridge was scattered at his death, and only a portion remains (in places as far apart as Copenhagen and Madrid). But it is possible to deduce that he had a representative collection of works by scholars of his own day, many of whom he had met in Italy, and that he probably introduced into England the first copies of Lucretius' *De Rerum Natura* (now in the Bodleian), Tacitus' *Dialogus de Oratoribus*, and Suetonius' *De Grammaticus et Rhetoribus*. Tiptoft also had two early printed Bibles, imported from Cologne in 1468.[1] Tiptoft's versatility and learning however transcended merely collecting books. He made a number of translations into English of Latin works, including Cicero's *De Senectute*, and *De Amicitia*, and Caesar's references to Britain. He himself wrote a romance based on Buonacorso de Montemagno's *De Nobilitate*, where two lovers plead their virtues before the Senate, and the definition of true nobility is based not on birth, but on education, manners, and public service. The *Declaration of Noblesse*, printed by Caxton, was one of the earliest examples in English of the new humanist lay ideal.[2]

Early English humanism

The final phase of the early development of humanism in England was the sudden spread of the teaching of Greek in the last quarter of the fifteenth century. This was partly due to the presence in England of a number of Greeks such as Emmanuel of Constantinople, and partly due to the interest of a number of important men like William Sellyng Prior of Christ Church Canterbury and John Ankwyll, headmaster of the newly extended Magdalen College School at Oxford. While the Universities proper, apart from accepting books, lagged behind in the reception of new methods of classical study, Sellyng made Canterbury a centre of learning, and Ankwyll revolutionised the teaching of Greek and Latin with his book *Compendium Totius Grammaticae*. It was at Magdalen College School that the headmasters of the next generation, William Horman of Eton and William Lily, first High Master of St Pauls, were trained, and it could claim as pupils, Grocyn, possibly Colet, Wolsey, Dr. Edward Wotton, Tyndale and probably Sir Thomas More.[3]

At this point humanistic studies in England reached a turning point. The

---

[1] R. Weiss, *Humanism in England*, p117 et seq.
[2] R. J. Mitchell, *John Tiptoft*, Longman 1938, pp175-85.
[3] For Colet see Sears Jayne, *John Colet and Marsilio Ficino*, OUP 1963, p14; and R. S. Stanier, *Magdalen College School*, Basil Blackwell 1958, Ch. 3. Later pupils include Lawrence Humfrey, William Camden and probably Richard Hooker.

position just prior to Henry VII's accession can be summed up as follows: a growing number of scholars had learnt Greek; classical texts had been collected and now existed both in University and College libraries and in the hands of private men; attempts had been made to compile dictionaries and new methods of teaching grammar had been introduced. Nevertheless in the opinion of Dr. Weiss at this stage humanism proper did not exist in England. In his view, English humanism differed fundamentally from the Italian because it did not replace scholasticism as a cultural system but merely improved classical learning and added a knowledge of Greek. 'The evidence that has reached us suggests that very few, if any, perceived the fundamental difference between scholasticism and humanism. All they saw was that the Italians were particularly proficient in Greek and Latin letters, but this they regarded as a normal development of medieval scholarship rather than as the result of a reaction . . . The wider intellectual issues raised by Italian humanism evaded them, and beyond its mechanical side they failed as a whole to understand it . . .'[1] On the surface English humanism remained still fragmented, individualistic and mostly in the hands of clerics.

This view now needs a certain amount of modification. Professor McConica argues that in the sixteenth century at any rate, English thought was intimately bound up with developments on the Continent, and cannot be viewed in isolation.[2] It is probable that this rather broader conception of the problem should be extended to cover at least the last two decades of the fifteenth century. Although English humanism in this period differed from that of Italy in that it was initially more religious and less openly secular, this was largely the result of particular influences. In general the two movements were inextricably connected. They derived their impetus from the same sources, but interpreted them differently. It is arguable that the key to the change in mental climate which becomes apparent in the early sixteenth century in England, is to a large extent derived from the absorption and transmission of the philosophical ideas of Plato. To a certain extent this fusion of Platonic and Christian thought liberalised and freed the whole conception of religion, and as long as it was maintained, the effect persisted. But in the synthesis of Platonic and Christian ideas so carefully constructed by members of the Florentine Academy such as Marsilio Ficino and Pico della Mirandola there existed an inner tension which rendered it unstable. It had to reach a more liberal, even a more secular position, or revert to mysticism and even to obscurantism. The whole cultural thought of the Renaissance has been described as facing at the end of the fifteenth century 'an inescapable crisis in its destiny; it had to decide whether to go back to Savonarola or forward to Machiavelli, to Cesare Borgia, to Giordano Bruno'.[3]

[1] R. Weiss, *Humanism in England*, p180.
[2] J. K. McConica, *English Humanists and Reformation Politics*, p6.
[3] Ernst Cassirer, *The Platonic Renaissance in England*, trans. James E. Pettegrove, Nelson 1953.

English scholars could not escape the dilemma any more than those on the Continent, and their attempts to solve it lie at the root of the development of English humanism and its distinctive contribution to European thought. It persisted into the seventeenth century when the Cambridge Platonists offered in their turn an opposition to the empirical philosophy of their day which was both a challenge and a stimulus to scientific rationalism.[1] In the twentieth century the same conflict persists in the present confrontation between the mechanistic and moral interpretations of man and the universe.

Grocyn

In the late fifteenth century, the key link figures between the Italian and English Renaissance are Grocyn, Linacre and Colet. In a way they illustrate the progressive urgency of the need to come to terms with the implications of the new learning. Grocyn was hardly conscious of the problem and remained a brilliant scholar; Linacre sidetracked it by concentrating on science; only Colet really faced the issue, and can be said to have been deeply influenced by Plato. But they all in varying ways introduced new elements of Greek thought into England. Grocyn was born in 1442 and died in 1519. He visited Italy in 1488 and was there at the same time as Linacre with whom he founded a lasting friendship. He studied Greek at Florence under Politian and Chalcondylas, but he never seems to have become a strong Platonist and was once reported as saying that the difference between Aristotle and Plato was that Aristotle lived in a world of science and Plato one of myths. But although Grocyn remained to a certain extent medieval in outlook, he contributed to the spread of Greek learning in England by his public lectures in Oxford, and by his scientific approach to textual criticism which resulted in his famous lecture in 1501, when following Valla he disproved the authenticity of the works of Dionysius the Areopagite. Grocyn has left no written works which have survived. His importance therefore is largely personal, in the fact that he was the first Englishman to teach Greek publicly, and in his influence on his circle of friends. It has to be inferred rather than proved.

Linacre

Linacre also was hardly a Platonist, although he spent part of his time in Italy in Florence at the centre of Platonic studies, and was patronised by the Medici family. But he made his own distinctive contribution to English humanism. He was born about 1460 and lived until 1524. He is interesting because he is the first English Renaissance scientist. He became a practising physician and eventually first President of the College of Physicians. He may have been a pupil of Prior William Sellyng at Christ Church Canterbury and possibly went with him to Italy in 1487. At any rate Linacre remained in Italy till 1499, and

[1] For this whole development see Ernst Cassirer, *The Platonic Renaissance*.

during this period he studied Greek like Grocyn in Florence. In 1489 he went
to Rome, and at this point his career took a completely different course. Whilst
in Rome he became the friend of a scholar called Hermolaus Barbarus whose
great interest was the study of early scientific texts. Influenced by him, Linacre
studied medicine at Padua and graduated as a doctor in 1496. Linacre was
fortunate in his timing for two reasons: the first accurate Greek texts of Galen
were published in Italy in 1500 and with this medical studies entered a new
phase, for the printing of an accurate text of Galen was the first step to the
destruction of his theories; secondly, they were printed and published in Venice
by Aldus Manutius, and Linacre became closely associated with the printer and
lived in his house for several years. Linacre's first translations from the Greek
were printed there in 1501. Linacre returned to England therefore with a
double reputation as a Greek scholar and as a scientist. The next ten years of
his life are obscure, but were probably spent in the practice of medicine and
possibly occasionally lecturing. He was also translating scientific texts like
Proclus' *De Sphaera* from Greek to Latin. He began but did not finish a translation of Aristotle's *Physics* and *Meteorologica,* but he did succeed in making
available to doctors six books of Galen. He lectured on Aristotle, and wrote two
successful books on Latin grammar and construction. He has been described as
'one of the first Englishmen to master the Greek language, and to make serious
use of his knowledge'[1]. On the accession of Henry VIII, Linacre began a career
at Court, and became the first President of the College of Physicians in 1518.
Like Grocyn he was a close friend of Colet, and in turn these men all directly
influenced Thomas More and Erasmus[2].

Colet

Of all these three early English humanists Colet is particularly difficult to
interpret. This is precisely because he illustrates most clearly the particular
twist English humanistic thought gave to the ideas then current in Europe.
Colet was deeply influenced during his stay in Italy and subsequently at Oxford,
by the Platonic philosophy of the Florentine Academy, and found himself
ultimately caught in the difficulties inherent in the reception of Platonic ideas
into Christian theology. On the one hand Colet was narrow even puritanical
in his outlook, personally austere – a man who regarded the world as evil, and
who could advise his hearers at Oxford to confine their reading to Christian
works:

Those books alone ought to be read, in which there is a salutary flavour of

[1]Fritz Caspari, *Humanism and the Social Order in Tudor England*, University of Chicago
Press 1954, p24.
[2]For the main points of this account of Linacre's life see Sir George Clark, *A History of the
Royal College of Physicians*, Clarendon Press 1964, Vol.I Ch.3.

Christ, in which Christ is set forth for us to feed on. Those books in which Christ is not found are but a table of devils. Do not become readers of philosophers, companions of devils . . .[1]

When Colet founded St. Paul's he banned logic from the curriculum, since it appealed to reason alone. This deep-rooted prejudice against the teaching of philosophy in English schools has persisted to this day. This rigid attitude has led some modern historians to regard Colet as essentially reactionary.[2] It led the German historian W. F. Schirmer to label the whole of early English humanism as 'pedagogic-theological' and to see in it the origins and roots of English puritanism.[3] It is perhaps interesting to note that Colet only learnt Greek late in life, and was dependent upon translations in his formative years.[4]

But this is not the whole of Colet, his other aspect is more complex and more elusive – but far more influential. He was the friend and teacher of More. He may well have reorientated the whole of Erasmus's thought, for in the opinion of one authority at the time of his meeting with Colet in 1499, the bent of Erasmus's mind was still undetermined. 'The meeting with Colet changed Erasmus's desultory occupation with theological studies into a firm and lasting resolve to make their pursuit the object of his life . . .'[5] He founded St. Paul's School, and placed it under lay and not clerical control, and in his final statutes for the school, he advocates a wide classical education. 'I would they were taught always in good literature, both Latin and Greek, and good authors such as have the very Roman eloquence joined with wisdom, especially Christian authors that wrote their wisdom in clear chaste Latin'. Colet began a revolution in English educational methods which was to have momentous consequences. 'Colet set out to place learning at the service of living, to present it as a means of preparing the individual to live well himself, and to do good in society . . . he set an essentially new educational aim.'[6]

The dichotomy in Colet's thought between 'puritanism' and 'humanism' has given rise to considerable debate and lies behind the parallel discussion on the exact nature of Colet's contribution to protestantism in England. Colet himself was charged with heresy during his lifetime, although the charge was dropped, and like other humanist reformers he was outspoken in his condemnation of the current abuses of the Church. Recently Professor Leland Miles has investigated the protestant content in Colet's theology in some detail and has concluded (somewhat inconclusively) that his

[1]Quoted in Sears Jayne, *John Colet and Marsilio Ficino*, p38.
[2]H. Maynard Smith, *Pre-Reformation England*, p452.
[3]See Fritz Caspari, *Humanism and the Social Order*, p22.
[4]Sears Jayne, *John Colet and Marsilio Ficino*, p48.
[5]P. Duhamel, 'The Oxford Lectures of John Colet', *Journal of the History of Ideas*, 1953, p506.
[6]Joan Simon, *Education and Society in Tudor England*, p80.

thought 'does not fall wholly within either Catholic or Protestant tradition. Indeed the accumulated evidence . . . surely establishes beyond all reasonable doubt that Dean Colet is best interpreted as a transitional figure . . .'[1] The key to the interpretation of Colet probably lies in the way in which he absorbed and transmuted the ideas of the Platonic Academy in Florence and fused them with his own genuine religious conviction.[2] In his lectures on the Pauline Epistles given at Oxford after his return from Italy during 1496-1499 Colet undoubtedly started a new tradition of Biblical interpretation in England, one in which the Bible was not fragmented into formal investigation or buried in textual criticism, but is regarded as 'a book . . . designed to effect a revival and reformation of life.'[3] The recent discovery in the library of All Souls College, Oxford of a copy of Marsilio Ficino's *Epistolae* with marginalia in Colet's hand and copies made by Colet of two letters addressed to him by Ficino, together with his own reply, has thrown considerable light on the way Colet's thoughts developed during this crucial period. Marsilio Ficino was head of the Platonic Academy in Florence from 1473 to 1494 and the *Epistolae* was in fact a collection of essays and letters on philosophical questions and treatises on theological subjects. Although it is clear from the correspondence that Colet and Ficino never actually met, Colet was clearly deeply influenced by Ficino during the period of the Oxford lectures. The whole question has been examined in detail by Mr. Sears Jayne in a book based on the newly discovered volume in which he prints the entire marginalia and the three letters.[4] In his opinion Colet went through two phases, one in which the Neo-platonic and Platonic approach was important, and a later stage in which he reverted to a narrower and more theological approach. 'Colet had apparently a good deal of enthusiasm for Platonism during the middle twenty years of his life, but very little during the last twenty. Platonism was only a tributary to the main stream of Colet's thought colouring its waters for a short distance and then disappearing'.[5] Ficino's thought remained profoundly secular, and his whole approach to religion tended to break the monopolistic and rigid tendencies of conventional catholicism.

It is perhaps the very diversity of the manner of worship as decreed by God, which radiates a marvellous charm throughout the Universe. For as the rule

---

[1]Leland Miles, *John Colet and the Platonic Tradition*, George Allen and Unwin 1962, p213. Leland Miles has an interesting tabular comparison of Protestant and Catholic views in Colet's works, p212.
[2]Leland Miles had pointed out that there is an important philosophic distinction between Plato's own philosophy, Neo-platonism, and the Florentine Platonists. Leland Miles, *John Colet and the Platonic Tradition*, pxiii.
[3]Ernst Cassirer, *The Platonic Renaissance in England*, p13.
[4]Sears Jayne, *John Colet and Marsilio Ficino*.
[5]Sears Jayne, *John Colet and Marsilio Ficino*, p39.

of Heaven, it is more important to be actually worshipped than to be worshipped by this or that gesture . . . He would rather be worshipped in any manner, be it ever so absurd, so long as it is human, than not to be worshipped at all on account of pride.[1]

At the end of the fifteenth century, as in our own, accepted beliefs were in a state of flux. Ficino's words would in any case have been dynamic, but in the context of his own time, they were dynamite. Even though to a large extent Colet rejected or at least transmuted a considerable proportion of Ficino's ideas, he could not remain unaffected by them. Ficino's view of religion was essentially intellectual, Colet's was theological and he distrusted the intellect, and substituted the more practical faith and works. To Colet it was sufficient that men should love God, not necessary that they should know Him. But the influence of Ficino and the Neo-platonists, suppressed and hidden, remained at work. In the final analysis, Colet, like More and Erasmus, remained within the formal framework of the Catholic Church while infusing it with a new spirit. Nevertheless, Colet's dilemma does illustrate an important problem, and in his view is an example of a more general change permeating the whole of English thought at this time. As Sears Jayne points out Colet lectured at Oxford (and read the *Epistolae*) 'just at a time when a powerful new dynamic was beginning to put pressure on traditional Christianity. Just as Christianity in the eighteenth century had to shift gears to adjust to deism, in the nineteenth century to evolutionism, and in the twentieth century to existentialism, so in the fifteenth century England had to adjust to a revival of Hellenism . . .' Colet arrived in Oxford just in time to participate in the process of accommodation, a process which may be called the Tudor Hellenisation of Christianity.

'It is this process which links Colet . . . to More, Erasmus, Grocyn and Linacre. The most important thing that these men had in common was not their reform instincts or their Latin scholarship, but their Greek studies; instead of calling them "Oxford Reformers" or "Oxford Humanists", one ought rather to call them "Oxford Hellenists". Their distinctive contribution to English culture was the Tudor Hellenisation of Christianity'.[2]

Mr. Sears Jayne makes an important point; for, as the quotation from Ficino shows, the Hellenisation of Christianity was a dangerous process, and acted as a solvent on existing institutions. The teaching of these English Hellenists had a wider importance than their impact on religion. They changed the whole cultural background of their age, and unleashed forces which ultimately altered both State and Church.

---

[1]Ficino, *De Christiana Religione*, quoted in Cassirer, *John Colet and the Platonic Tradition*, p15.
[2]Sears Jayne, *John Colet and Marsilio Ficino*, pp40–41.

3. Patronage and the new learning

Although it is clear that the geographical position of England made it inevitable that intellectually and politically her development would differ from the rest of Europe, the importance of the continuous links between England and the Continent is now becoming apparent. It is no longer possible to think of the intellectual revival in England as parochial, scholastic and inward looking (although superficially these characteristics do exist), its roots have been shown to lie deeper; in the diplomatic exchanges with foreign courts; in the fruitful links with Italy through the church and the peripatetic élite; and the connections with the Low Countries through the more mundane medium of trade. The movement for reform was not confined to the new Hellenist intellectuals, but existed also in the stubborn tradition of independent religious thought centred outside the church, and permeating the humbler rather than the politically influential sections of society.

There is also a new emphasis on the continuity of the movement within itself, and here England is in marked contrast to the rest of Europe. From its inception in the late fourteenth century the English intellectual revival in its various forms, though occasionally checked, was never entirely destroyed. The religious wars and internecine feuds which disrupted and drove underground the more liberal and moderate ideas of the continental humanists, by a combination of fortunate and fortuitous circumstances never became endemic in England. The foundations laid by Colet, Linacre, Erasmus and Elyot in the opening years of the century, stood enlarged and expanded at the end. Political pressure, though it existed, never reached the point of crisis where ideas had to be formalised into total rigidity. More important still, the increasing internal prosperity of the country and the marked increase in individual wealth in certain sections of society was itself a decisive factor in ensuring the survival of the humanist ethic, for the new approach to learning created in its turn a new movement in education, and the men so educated siphoned back the same ideas into the next generation.

This fact is of crucial importance when assessing the real forces of change in sixteenth century England, for the expansion of educational facilities which resulted from the combined forces of private charity and official policy, helped to transform society from one where the main purpose of education was entry into the church to one where the end envisaged was partly secular. Government interference was a permanent factor. It has been argued that the key feature of the educational changes in the 1530s was the way in which university reform was sponsored by the state.[1] The two Regius Professorships, the royal foundations of Christ Church Oxford and Trinity College Cambridge, the whole evolution of the college system, were all a means of extending government control. Yet, at the same time, the increasing participation of the landowning and mercantile classes both as recipients and benefactors, acted as a counterpoise to the power of the state. Alone among the countries of Western Europe, in England the influence and ideas current early in the sixteenth century enjoyed an uninterrupted evolution.

The destruction of Erasmian humanism on the Continent was the result of social unrest.[2] In England, although at the time of the Pilgrimage of Grace there were signs of reaction, the relative social and political stability permitted the continued liberalisation of education and thought. On the Continent the Erasmian élite was eventually destroyed in the tide and countertide of Reformation and Reaction, in England they survived. When 'Erasmianism' reappeared in Europe it took on a different form, for example the Jansenist movement in France in the seventeenth century.[3] In England it remained on the surface, and what was initially essentially an intellectual movement evolved by the simple process of educating a new generation of human beings – the raw material of historical change – who translated theory into practice, and what was more important, into government, thereby altering society itself and affecting all aspects of Church and State. But because the essential characteristic of the human mind is its diversity, and because one of the results of the revolution of printing was to interiorize knowledge, the effects of humanism when translated into action were far from uniform. This explains the contrasting careers of the early intellectuals. Erasmus could remain uncommitted except on paper, but his close friend Thomas More could not. It is this which gives such significance to the life of More. He is the first clear example of Erasmus' 'Christian layman', and his arguments in Book I of *Utopia* for and against becoming 'un homme engagé' and entering politics remain to this day a classic expression of the dilemma faced by a man of humanitarian and liberal principles on becoming the servant of, and therefore committed to, an authoritarian regime.[4]

The diffusion of learning in England, though continuous can be divided into phases. The early movement belongs to the fifteenth century. The second which lasted until the break with Rome was a seminal period, when (although it was

[1]H. Kearney, *Scholars and Gentlemen: Universities and Society in Pre-Industrial Britain, 1500–1700*, Faber and Faber 1970, p35.
[2]H. Trevor Roper, *Desiderius Erasmus: Collected Essays*, OUP 1957.
[3]For an interesting experiment in the liberal education of girls under the patronage of Louis XIV, see Nancy Mitford, 'St. Cyr', *History Today*, January 1965.
[4]They make an interesting comparison with the same problem discussed more fully in the recent novel about the Communist regime in Rumania *Incognito* by Pietri Diumitri, Collins 1967.

cross-fertilised by Erasmus) 'humanism' in England began to show independent characteristics of its own. It shed its theological scholasticism, such as it was, it widened its horizons, and became more dynamic. It gained a permanent foothold in the educational system of the country with the founding of St. Paul's, and in the universities with the establishment of Christ's and St. John's at Cambridge, and of Corpus Christi and Cardinal College at Oxford, together with a series of new professorships. It saw the production of More's *Utopia,* and of Sir Thomas Elyot's book of less originality but of more practical importance, *The Governour.* The third period covers the middle years of the sixteenth century when the whole educational and social system was changed by the religious crisis, the dispersal of the abbey lands, and the secularisation of education. It included the inevitable rethinking of the ideas underlying government, the nature of obedience, the limits of sovereignty. It was the time when the men and women who were to dominate the final years of the century were educated. It thus laid the foundations for the fourth period, the age of Elizabeth, when in a burst of intellectual splendour the humanism of the sixteenth century reached its culmination.[1]

Broad divisions of this sort are convenient, but they can also be misleading. Intellectual movements are by their nature continuous and a more recent view suggests that there was no abrupt break in the last years of the reign of Henry VIII and that the patronage and employment of humanist intellectuals continued and even increased in the final years of Henry VIII, particularly in the protestant group round Cranmer and Queen Catherine Parr. While it is undeniable that turning points occurred, the process of intellectual expansion continued uninterrupted. It was an evolutionary not a metamorphic process.

Patronage and the 'new learning'

It becomes therefore more constructive and more rewarding to study the methods of diffusion – the means and media through which the new intellectual ideas penetrated society. As the use of the printing press increased, methods of communication became at once more individual and more diffuse, and knowledge and ideas could spread under their own momentum. But initially the spread of the 'new learning' was promoted by direct and individual patronage – apparent throughout the fifteenth century but increasingly significant and widespread under the Tudors.

At the centre was the Court, and here the earliest important influence was that of the mother of Henry VII, Lady Margaret Beaufort, who was 'the principal bridge between the humanism of the Yorkist Court and that of the new age.'[2] She still retained the theological bias of the initial period of the movement in

[1] F. Caspari, *Humanism and the Social Order,* Ch. 1.
[2] J. K. McConica, *English Humanists,* p55.

England, but her foundations point the way to the 'Erasmian' expansion of the
1520s. She continued the Yorkist patronage of Caxton, and his successor Wynkyn
de Worde printed at her request both Hylton's *Scala Perfectionis*[1] and Atkinson's
translation of à Kempis *Imitation of Christ*. On a less pietistic level, she secured
the publication of a translation of Brandt's *Ship of Fools*. Her real importance
lies however in the expansion of education. She sponsored a Court school, and
founded the Lady Margaret Professorships of Divinity at Oxford and Cambridge,
and the Lady Margaret Preacherships (providing for six sermons annually in
Hereford, Cambridge, East Anglia, and London) in an attempt to fill the serious
gap between educated and uneducated clergy.[2] With the help of her chaplain
John Fisher (Chancellor of Cambridge from 1503 and Bishop of Rochester) she
endowed two colleges at Cambridge, Christ's and St. John's. They both had
a theological bias and were intended for the better education, and therefore
reform, of the secular clergy. Her endowments were completed by Fisher after
her death. Her direct patronage of education was therefore impressive – but
her indirect influence was equally pervasive. She gave benefactions to the great
monastic houses of Syon, Shene and Greenwich, all of which were noted for
their integrity of life and humanist connections. Her household was a centre for
able men and advanced ideas. One of her chaplains Christopher Urswyke, a
civil lawyer and diplomatist, was a friend of Erasmus and had two sermons by
Luther among his considerable collection of books.[3] Lady Margaret's influence
and endowments were clearly consistently on the side of the new liberal movement within the church, and while they remained religious rather than secular,
they were outward looking and humanist, never scholastic. She must therefore
rank among the important initiators of a movement whose end she could not
foresee.

The Queens of Henry VIII

This tradition of Court patronage was continued by the Queens of Henry VIII.
The influence of Katherine of Aragon and her advancement of scholars has
been described as possibly her most important constructive contribution as
Queen.[4] Her Chamberlain was Lord Mountjoy, who provided a direct link with
Erasmus. She was almost certainly behind the appointment of Thomas Linacre
as Royal Physician, and thus contributed indirectly to the foundation of the Royal
College of Physicians. Linacre, in turn, widened her circle to include Colet,
More, and Richard Pace. The Queen's support for scholarship included payment
for poor students at the universities (in whose careers she took a personal

[1]Now available in translation in Penguin.
[2]For details of this see J. K. McConica, *English Humanists*, pp76-9.
[3]For a discussion of Urswyke see J. K. McConica, *English Humanists*, pp70-2.
[4]G. Mattingly, *Catherine of Aragon*, Jonathan Cape 1963, pp136-43.

interest), and contributions to lectureships. She never opposed Wolsey in his educational ventures, and made a tour of Oxford colleges in 1518. She encouraged the future antiquarian John Leland, and allowed him access to her books. But her most important single contribution was her employment of the Spanish humanist Juan Luis Vives in the education of her daughter. Vives' stay in England had two results – his learning broadened and enriched the stream of the English renaissance, and his views on education had permanent importance. The Queen's specific concern for the education of women was natural, since the Princess Mary was her only living child. She established a small school at Court, and encouraged Thomas More in his own similar experiment. Vives wrote specifically on the education of girls. It is therefore partly due to Katherine's interest and influence that a whole generation of highly educated women permeated the upper ranks of English society by the middle of the sixteenth century.

Katherine's successor Anne Boleyn is equally interesting, although the absence of any recent biography makes detailed assessment difficult. Anne herself received part of her education in the service of Marguerite of Navarre, and therefore had direct access to humanistic thought on the continent. It seems clear that Anne and her family were consistent patrons of the new learning. Matthew Parker, the future Archbishop of Canterbury, was singled out for promotion by Anne, and became one of her chaplains. She secured his early preferment, when through her influence he was appointed Dean of the College of Stoke-by-Clare.[1] Her other chaplains were Shaxton and Latimer. The future Secretary of State Sir William Petre also owed his first advancement to the Boleyn family, and was tutor to the Queen's brother. Anne's father the Earl of Wiltshire commissioned a work from Erasmus and, at the King's request, was the early protector of Cranmer; and in the thirties her brother then Viscount Rochford formed part of a reforming Erasmian circle of influence.[2] Fuller's description of Anne confirms this impression:

She had her birth in England, blood by her grandmother from Ireland; and breeding in France under Mary the French Queen: so that so many relations meeting in her, accomplished her with an acceptable behaviour to all qualities and conditions of people. Of an handsome person, and beautiful face; and therefore that pen that reports her lean-visaged, long-sided, gobber toothed, yellow complexioned, with an wen in her neck, both manifests his malice, and disparageth King Henry, whom all knew well read in books, and better in beauties, who would never have been drawn to so passionate a love, without stronger lodestones to attract it . . . In a word, She was a great Patroness of the Protestants, protector of the persecuted, Preferrer of men of

[1] For a biography of Parker see V. J. K. Brook, *Archbishop Parker*, Clarendon Press 1962.
[2] J. K. McConica, *English Humanists*, p 108.

merit (among whom Hugh Latimer) a bountiful Reliever of the poor, and the happy mother of Queen Elizabeth.[1]

Even more interesting, since it is reported in a somewhat hagiographic account of Anne written under Queen Elizabeth, are the stories of her reading Tyndale's *Obedience of the Christian man* and giving it to the King, who must have been encouraged by its magnification of royal power; she also gave her ladies a small book of devotion consisting of a metrical version of thirteen psalms written on vellum and bound in gold 'with a ring on each cover to hang on their girdles for their constant use and meditation'[2]. There is a tradition that she once attended Vespers with the nuns at Syon, and urged them to replace the Latin service with the vernacular. Strype confirms the picture of Anne as a genuine patroness of scholars:

> She was very nobly charitable, and expended largely in all manner of acts of liberality, according to her high quality. And among the rest of her ways of shewing Christian virtue, she was a great favourer of learning together with her father the Earl of Wiltshire, and the Lord Rochford her brother, maintained divers ingenious men at the University. Among the rest were these men of note; Dr. Hethe afterward Archbishop of York and Lord Chancellor; Dr. Thirlby, afterward Bishop of Ely; and Mr. Paget afterward Lord Paget and Secretary of State: all of which in her time were great favourers of the Gospel, though afterwards they relapsed.[3]
> For it was well known in the University how extraordinarily munificent she was towards poor scholars that were studious and virtuous and how liberal in her exhibitions towards them. She only required some good character from Dr. Skip or Parker or some other of her chaplains, of any scholar that expected or sued her charity.[4]

It seems clear that had she lived, the Queen would have promoted and encouraged men of reforming views. Her patronage, though brief, illustrates clearly a continuity of interest as well as of power.

Henry's last Queen, Catherine Parr, was even more influential than her predecessors. Her circle was one of the most important focal points of patronage in the century.

The Queen succeeded Cromwell as the main avenue of promotion for humanist scholars.[5] She reunited under one roof, all the children of the King, and appointed John Cheke of St. John's College Cambridge as the tutor to the young Prince Edward. Like Katherine of Aragon before her, she included a

[1] Thomas Fuller, *The Church History of Great Britain*, London 1655, p206.
[2] *Extracts from The Life of the Virtuous, Christian, and Renowned Queen Anne Boleigne,* by George Wyat, Esq. Written at the close of the XVIth Century and now first printed 1817.
[3] John Strype, *Ecclesiastical Memorials*, Clarendon Press 1822, Vol. I, Part I, Ch. 36, p430.
[4] J. Strype, *Archbishop Parker*, Clarendon Press 1821, Ch. 2, p14-5.
[5] J. K. McConica, *English Humanists*, Ch. 7: 'The role of Catherine Parr'.

number of other children from noble families in what virtually amounted to a royal school. Another notable humanist, Roger Ascham, obviously hovered on the edge of this circle, but failed to penetrate the inner ring, but Sir Thomas Smith became Clerk of her Council. Catherine's close connections with Cambridge, and particularly with St. John's, are important, because Cambridge became at this time the centre of the humanist movement in England. In spite of the fact that Coverdale and Latimer found refuge in her household, Catherine herself seems to have been a moderate Protestant. The whole bias of her influence was more pietistic and less radical, and possibly more Erasmian.[1] The story of the plot to discredit the Queen on the grounds of religion is important, in that its failure indicates the extent of her influence and the success of her methods.

Linked to the Court and next in importance, a number of episcopal households also deserve attention at this time. Bishop Fisher's work with Lady Margaret has already been noted, but he was one of a larger group. Thomas More was educated in the household of Bishop Morton and gives a lively and affectionate description of him in *Utopia*:

> He was a man . . . who deserved respect as much for his prudence and virtue as for his authority. He was of middle stature and showed no sign of his advanced age. His countenance inspired respect rather than fear. In conversation he was agreeable, though serious and dignified. Of those who made suit to him he enjoyed making trial by rough address, but in a harmless way, to see what mettle and presence of mind a person would manifest . . . His speech was polished and pointed. His knowledge of law was profound, his ability incomparable, and his memory astonishingly retentive, for he had improved his extraordinary natural qualities by learning and practice . . .[2]

Bishop Alcock of Worcester (and Ely) founded Jesus Cambridge in 1496, Brasenose was founded in 1508 by Bishop Smith of Lincoln and a layman Sir Richard Sutton, Corpus Christi at Oxford was founded jointly in 1517 by Bishop Fox of Winchester and Bishop Oldham of Exeter. Cardinal Wolsey began Cardinal College in 1525. Bishop Foxe is supposed to have intended his college for the education of young monks as a preliminary to monastic reform, but according to tradition, Bishop Oldham exclaimed:

> What, my lord, shall we build houses and provide livelihoods for a company of buzzing monks, whose end and fall we ourselves may live to see; no, no, it is more meet . . . that we should have a care to provide for the increase of learning, and for such as by their learning shall do good in church and commonwealth.[3]

[1] J. K. McConica, *English Humanists*, p215.
[2] From *Utopia*, Bk. I, ed. E. Surtz S. J., and J. H. Hexter, *The Complete Works of Sir Thomas More*, Vol. 4, Yale University Press 1965, pp59-61.
[3] Quoted in J. Simon, *Education and Society*, p82.

The foundations of Corpus was a turning point. The library was tri-lingual in Latin, Greek and Hebrew, and there was a lectureship in Greek, the first in either university. The scholar Thomas Lupset, and after him the Spanish educationalist Vives, were both lecturers in humanity at the College. It was the hostility aroused by the 'Grecians' of Corpus among the conservative elements within the University that drew from More his famous letter to the 'Trojans' in 1518. Corpus has been described as the first permanent home of the new learning in Oxford, and the first example of true 'Renaissance' education in this country. As such, it is directly comparable with the foundation of Cardinal Ximenes at Alcala and the other trilingual colleges in Europe, at Paris and Louvain. Professor Hexter considers that the widening of academic terms of reference to include Greek and Hebrew was part of a movement spanning the whole of Europe in the early sixteenth century which he describes as one of 'Christian Revival', containing such diverse elements as Savonarola and Erasmus, but with a common aim, the revitalising of the religious structure of Christendom. If this thesis is accepted then it provides yet more evidence of the connection between England and the general evolution of continental thought.[1] This is corroborated by an interesting and complicated cross link between two Oxford colleges, Corpus and Brasenose, and the foundations of Christ's and St. John's at Cambridge in that they were all connected either directly or indirectly with both Lady Margaret Beaufort and the Carthusian monastery at Syon. Bishop Smith, Bishop Oldham, and Bishop Fisher had all risen through the household of Lady Margaret, and Sir Richard Sutton was Steward of Syon, in turn one of the monasteries favoured by the Countess. The aims of all four university foundations were inspired by the desire for liberal and enlightened church reform and taken together they suggest the existence of a close knit group at the influential centre of power. Another connection is added through the Syon foundation, between Sir Richard Sutton and Sir John Hussey, and Hussey was linked by marriage to the influential Mountjoy family. This again widens the circle of influence to include the continent, for William Blount Lord Mountjoy had studied under Erasmus in Paris, and issued the initial invitation which brought Erasmus to England at the accession of Henry VIII. Mountjoy was thus indirectly responsible for the trilingual nature of the Corpus foundation which was almost certainly due to the influence of Erasmus. Mountjoy was in fact a key figure in more ways than one, not only was he a patron of European scholars, in addition to Erasmus he helped the Italian Andrew Ammonius and the Spanish humanist Vives, but he became a member of Katherine of Aragon's household and there continued the Court-humanist link begun by Lady Margaret Beaufort. A study of the Mountjoy family during the sixteenth century would provide a miniature history of Renaissance culture in England. In the

[1] J. H. Hexter, Introduction to More's *Utopia*, Yale edition *The Complete Works of Sir Thomas More*, Vol. 4, ppxcii-xcvii.

troubled middle years of Henry's reign, they remained loyal to Katherine of Aragon without forfeiting the King's favour, and were powerful enough to keep under their protection survivors from Syon such as Richard Whitford.[1] They continued influential patrons of learning without interruption until the nineteenth century. Charles Blount 5th Lord Mountjoy invited the scholar Roger Ascham to be tutor to his son. Ascham was reluctant to leave Cambridge and refused, but he described the Mountjoy circle as having a reputation for learning unrivalled in Europe 'except by that of the Medici in Italy.'[2] Early in the reign of James I the household of Charles Blount 8th Lord Mountjoy and Earl of Devonshire was still regarded as a centre of learning and culture.[3]

It is only when these cross currents of influence and inter-connections of patronage are worked out that the strength and cohesion of the movement for intellectual and educational reform can be seen, and its gathering momentum understood. The Court, the strict Carthusian houses, the powerful administrative bishops and individual laymen were all promoting and encouraging a new and powerful movement, which as it gathered strength, escaped their control.

Wolsey and secular education

Although Archbishop Warham, that neglected and shadowy figure, was a man of considerable learning and a patron of scholars (he gave Erasmus a benefice, and protected Colet when he was charged with heresy) the greatest and most significant of the early ecclesiastical patrons was Wolsey. Dr. McConica suggests that he had little reputation among the humanist élite, and his fall was seen as the removal of an impressive obstacle to reform.[4] To a certain extent this is true, but there was another side to Wolsey. His household was in itself the training ground for most of the leading administrators of the next generation, and in the opinion of Strype resembled a miniature university. In addition to Thomas Cromwell, it contained for varying periods able diplomatists and officials such as Richard Sampson and Richard Pace, and future liberal bishops such as Cuthbert Tunstall. It is also vital to remember that Wolsey was first and foremost an administrator. He may have done little to reform the church from within, but he began to reform the State from without. His 'Ordinances of Eltham' anticipate the reforms of 1540; and his legal decisions did much to clarify and strengthen the law, and provided a body of case law that has permanent importance in the legal system of England. It is also difficult to ignore the significance of the initial foundation of Cardinal College at Oxford. Wolsey endowed six professorships, in medicine, philosophy, canon law, humanity,

[1]J. K. McConica, *English Humanists*, p60.
[2]L. V. Ryan, *Roger Ascham*, Stanford University Press 1963, p39.
[3]J. Simon, *Education and Society*, p348.
[4]J. K. McConica, *English Humanists*, p58.

theology and civil law. The chair of civil law was of crucial importance since it was the first to be established in England, and it must be included in any consideration of the idea that Wolsey might (had he lived) have initiated a 'reception' of civil law into the common law courts.[1] It is also interesting to note that it was held in 1525 by Vives thus linking Wolsey as a patron with Katherine of Aragon.[2] The founding of Cardinal College represents the apogee of the early phase of humanism in England, when for a brief moment all the threads of the new learning were gathered together. Some of the most brilliant minds of the younger generation formed the nucleus of the original foundation. They included a group of about seventeen from Cambridge including Richard Cox, John Frith, Henry Sumner and John Clerk. (Two future archbishops, Thomas Cranmer and Matthew Parker, were invited but declined). From Wolsey's own service came Thomas Lupset, the brilliant but short-lived friend of Reginald Pole, and the future Henrician propagandists Thomas Starkey and Richard Morison. It proved an explosive mixture. By 1528 the whole of the younger members were under suspicion of heresy and the Warden of New College was complaining of the scandal to the Bishop of Lincoln. The immediate result was the imprisonment of most of the group together with the alleged ringleader Thomas Garrett, Curate of All Souls.[3] At least twelve of the original Cambridge nucleus were implicated. The significance of the affair lies in the fact that Wolsey refused to pursue the charges. By the end of the year all had been released.[4] 'As one looks back at the episode of the Cambridge scholars, a patron of learning emerges genuinely interested in its advancement . . . Wolsey's fundamental broadmindedness as illustrated in this affair must remain on record as a factor of importance in the history of learning in Renaissance England'.[5] The Cardinal's other foundation, the school at Ipswich was obviously on a smaller scale, but it led to one important development for which the credit must again be given to Wolsey. The curriculum of the new school was modelled on that of Colet at St. Paul's, and in teaching Latin, the text book used was a combined edition of Colet's *Aeditio* and Lily's *Rudimenta Grammatices*. In 1529, under Wolsey's influence, convocation decreed that to avoid confusion in teaching methods only one grammar was to be used throughout the country, and decided on that used at Ipswich and St. Pauls. Even though Wolsey fell from power, the movement towards a standardised method of

[1]For this see F. W. Maitland, *English Law and the Renaissance*, CUP 1901.
[2]For the details of the Constitution of Cardinal College see J. Simon, *Education and Society*, p137.
[3]For the dramatic account of Garrett's escape and recapture, see edited A. G. Dickens and D. Carr, *The Reformation in England to the accession of Elizabeth I*, in the series *Documents of Modern History*, E. J. Arnold 1967, pp39-42.
[4]Except three who had died while in prison. See A. G. Dickens and D. Carr, *The Reformation in England*, p39.
[5]W. G. Zeeveld, *Foundations of Tudor Policy*, pp35-36.

teaching Latin gained ground. The rival grammars of Stanbridge and Whittington ceased to be printed after this date, and in 1542, following the revision of
Lily's *Grammar* by a royal commission, Henry himself ordered that it should
be the only text book used in schools throughout the realm.[1] There was no
attempt to standardise the teaching of Greek in the same way, and it was
normally learnt from Latin. Dr. Simon has pointed out that in spite of his use
of Colet's methods, Wolsey's aims in education were profoundly different.
'He was not concerned to further learning among laymen so much as to counter-
act the effect of growing literacy.' His argument was that 'as printing could
not be put down, it were best to set up learning against learning and, by
introducing able persons to dispute, suspend the laity between fear and controversy, as this, at the worst, would yet make them attentive to their superiors
and teachers.'[2] Yet whatever his ultimate motives, Wolsey's conception of
learning was fundamentally constructive and fundamentally humanist. It was
a training for future service to the State as well as the Church. He founded his
Colleges for the instruction of boys 'knowing full well that hope for the
commonwealth must rest upon that age, even as corn from seed'. For this reason
he was prepared to ignore, if not to condone, mild deviations in theological
speculation. It was the beginning of a new age.

Wolsey's foundations at Oxford and Ipswich were the only things he really
cared about at his fall.[3] The school at Ipswich did not survive in its original
form, but Cardinal College, after temporary eclipse, was re-established as
Christ Church in 1532. Wolsey's Cardinal's hat still embellishes the outer
walls.

Erasmus and education

Although the great prelates exercised power as patrons and administrators,
when the first years of the sixteenth century are studied in depth, individuals
are also important and it becomes abundantly clear that the underlying influence throughout was that of Erasmus. Erasmus' visit to England was of
decisive importance in the history of English humanism. He held a unique
position in European letters which has been compared to that of Voltaire three
centuries later.[4] Although by writing in Latin Erasmus confined his influence
to the educated classes, for the same reason his influence was international.
'Erasmus is the only name in the whole list of humanists which has remained
a household word all over the globe.'[5] He also had great personal influence
through his numerous contacts:

[1]H. S. Bennett, *English Books and Readers,* pp88-89
[2]J. Simon, *Education and Society,* pp144-45.
[3]See his letter to Stephen Gardiner quoted in W. G. Zeeveld, *Foundations of Tudor Policy,* p38.
[4]J. H. Hexter, Introduction to Volume 4 of *The Complete Works of Sir Thomas More,* plviii.
[5]J. Huizinga, *Erasmus of Rotterdam,* Phaidon Press 1952, p40.

His greatest pleasure was to praise absent friends to friends present. Since he is greatly loved by so many men, and that too in different parts of the world, because of his learning and most charming character, he tries earnestly to bind all men together with the same affection which all have for him alone.[1]

His stay in England affected the whole evolution of English thought. Yet it was a two-way process and Erasmus in turn was influenced by England. From 1509 until his departure in 1514 he was in close contact with the leading members of the 'Hellenistic' circle especially Colet and More, and this period in Erasmus' life was one of great mental stimulation. He stayed for long periods in More's house and wrote the *Moriae Encomium* (*The Praise of Folly*) as a compliment to his host. Colet may well have redirected his thought towards a deeper study of the Scriptures and Fathers and certainly caused Erasmus to rethink and amplify his views on education.[2] The interaction of the ideas of the three men is undeniable and of the greatest interest. All European humanists had a common interest in the improvement of education, derived from the fundamental conception of man as a rational being, and in his writing on this subject Erasmus adapted and extended the ideas of Colet. Like Colet he saw the need for educating laymen to serve the community as a means of serving God:

> It is a duty incumbent upon churchmen and Statesmen alike to educate the youth of the nation. It is a public obligation in no way inferior to the ordering of an army [for] no man is born to himself, no man is born in idleness. Your children are not born to yourself alone but to your country, and not to your country alone but to God.[3]

His originality was not in this conception of the purpose of education which was widely held, but in his methods. In the field of educational theory Erasmus' importance is twofold. He popularised the idea of secular education for secular ends on a wider basis than ever before and as a result 'Humanism ceased to be the exclusive privilege of the few.'[4] He also influenced its content. Because Erasmus like other humanists saw education as a means of forming character for a specific end (the public good) it became something more than a mere acquisition of knowledge. Facts are sterile, but the meaning of facts once correctly understood, can permanently alter a man's life: 'men are shaped by education rather than by birth . . . It is possible for man to follow reason, after the right kind of education has enabled him to recognise it.'[5] Free will in man

[1]More's letter to Dorp, quoted J. H. Hexter, *The Complete Works of Sir Thomas More*, Vol. 4, introduction plxiii. See also E. F. Rogers, *Sir Thomas More Selected Letters*, New Haven 1961.
[2]See above, chapter 2, p38.
[3]Quoted in Joan Simon, *Education and Society*, p104.
  J. Huizinga, *Erasmus*, p39.
  F. Caspari, *Humanism and the Social Order*, p35.

gives him infinite choice, education gives him informed choice. This lies behind Erasmus' emphasis on the importance of classical studies in training the young. Latin and Greek were necessary not only as a mental discipline and a means of international communication but because they offered a philosophical and ethical background in addition to the Bible and the Fathers. Erasmus is quite explicit on this point:

> I must add that a sensible reading of the pagan poets and philosophers is a good preparation for the Christian Life ... So pick out from the pagan books whatever is best. In studying the ancients, follow the example of the bee flying about the garden. Like the bee, suck out only what is sweet, reject what is useless. Follow this rule and your mind will be better clothed.[1]

The whole content of education was broadened as a result, for Erasmus ensured that future generations would be educated along these lines by providing the necessary text books. This was undoubtedly his greatest contribution to the spread of humanism and to education. His famous collection of extracts from classical authors and anecdotes from ancient history, *The Adagia*, the *Colloquia, Notes on Letter Writing, De rationii Studii* ('A Study in Method') and the encyclopaedic *De Copia verborum et rerum* ('On the abundance of words and things') were all extensively used in schools from the sixteenth century onwards throughout Europe. In *De Copia* Erasmus suggests rules for note-taking with indexing and cross-reference, which many students today could read with profit. The *Enchiridion* ('The Handbook of the Christian Soldier') sums up his whole philosophy and explains how any man can achieve a Christian and perfect life in this world by the use of his reason, self-discipline, and correct education.[2] The enormous popularity of Erasmus's works in England is shown by the stock list of the Oxford bookseller John Dorne for 1520. Although the greatest number of items were technical books, such as the grammars of Whittington and Stanbridge, Erasmus' books number 150 out of a total of about 2,000, exceeding those of Aristotle and providing striking proof of the spread of the new learning.[3] The work of Erasmus was aptly summed up by John Aubrey a century later: 'As Fuller sayeth, he was like a Badger, that never bitt but he made his teeth meet. He was the πρόδρομος (forerunner) of our knowledge, and the man that made the rough and untrodden wayes smooth and passable.'[4]

---

[1]Erasmus, *Enchiridion Militis Christiani,* translated by J. P. Dolan, *The Essential Erasmus,* Mentor Omega Books, New American Library 1964.
[2]*The Enchiridion* together with *The Praise of Folly* and a number of other important works by Erasmus are now available in translation in a paperback edited by J. P. Dolan, *The Essential Erasmus.*
[3]J. K. McConica, *English Humanists,* p89; see also H. S. Bennett, *English Books and Readers,* p231.
[4]John Aubrey, *Brief Lives,* edited by Oliver Lawson Dick, Penguin 1962, p192.

Vives

The Spaniard Vives, who lived in England from 1522–1528 in the household
of Katherine of Aragon and at Cardinal College Oxford, was less influential
than Erasmus, and never had the same international reputation – but as an
educationalist he was far more original and went deeper into the whole question,
relating the process of education directly to the mind of man. In this respect
he is far more modern than Erasmus and in many ways in advance of his age.[1]
Vives accepted the current view of man as essentially a rational and inquisitive
being. 'Man has received from God a great gift, viz. a mind, and the power of
inquiring into things'. Knowledge is received through the senses, and retained
by the memory. It can be either factual, that is, scientific; or problematical,
a matter of opinion; but in each case it can only be understood through deduction and reasoning. Man is both a social and rational being:

> I call that knowledge which we receive when the senses are properly brought
> to observe things . . . in a methodical way to which clear reason leads us on,
> reason so closely connected with the nature of our mind that there is no one
> who does not accept its lead; or our reasoning is 'probable' when it is based
> on our own experiences or those of others, and confirmed by judgement resting
> upon probable conjecture. The knowledge in the former case is called science,
> firm and indubitable, and in the latter case, belief or opinion.

Education is a dynamic and not a static process, and each generation can
learn from and surpass the one before it:

> If we only apply our minds sufficiently, we can judge better over the whole
> round of life and nature than could Aristotle, Plato, or any of the ancients . . .
> Is it, then forbidden to us to . . . investigate, and to form our own opinions?
> . . . Truth stands open to all. It is not yet taken possession of. Much of truth
> has been left for a future generation to discover.[2]

Knowledge can only be communicated between men by means of language
either spoken or written. Vives lays great emphasis on the importance of
mastering the basic skills in order to be able to make the maximum use of this
medium. Handwriting, speaking, and facility in reading and the use of words,
are all of vital importance. Like Erasmus he advocated systematic note taking
grouped under subjects, indexed, and with cross-references. But he was more
aware than Erasmus of the need for co-ordinating education and the later
development of the child. History should be studied not only for edification
but as a preparation for active life. The lessons learnt from the past were only
useful if applied to the present. A century before Francis Bacon, Vives was

[1]Dr. Joan Simon gives the clearest and most up-to-date account of his thought and method,
Education and Society, Ch. 3.
[2]Vives, *On Education*, quoted by J. Simon, *Education and Society*, pp116–18.

advocating the study of practical technology. Students 'should not be ashamed to enter shops and factories, and to ask questions from craftsmen, and to get to know the details of their work.' Like Bacon he saw the end of knowledge as the advancement of man: 'this is the goal. Having acquired our knowledge we must turn it to usefulness, and employ it to the common good.'[1] The poor and destitute, especially abandoned children, should be educated in useful crafts for the same reason.[2]

While Vives saw that a complete mastery of a man's native tongue was an essential initial step to the development of his power of rational and coherent thought, he felt also that the study of the classics was vital in order that a means of communication should be kept open across national frontiers. The danger inherent in the rapid development of vernacular language had not escaped him. If the use of Latin was abandoned among educated men, 'there would result a great confusion of all kinds of knowledge and a great separation and estrangement of man'. Vives like many thinkers in the transitional period of the early sixteenth century would have liked to preserve the medieval unity of Christendom while radically changing its ways of thought. Dr. Simon, who considers his educational theories to be of great importance, and who has a whole section on Vives and Erasmus in her book, makes the point that within the apparent contradiction of Vives' thought there lies in fact a synthesis. 'In his questioning of authority, use of the inductive method, insistence on the relation of knowledge to human welfare, support for the vernacular tongues, Vives points the way to the empirical materialist philosophy of the seventeenth century . . . His arguments show that there was a closer relation than is often recognised between the promotion of scholarly study on humanist lines and the beginning of scientific inquiry, just as, paradoxical though it may appear on the surface, concentration on the Latin language and literature did not hinder, but provided a direct lead towards the enrichment and study of English.'[3]

Vives was also far-sighted in his approach to the basic assumptions which lay behind the acceptance of the social order of his time. In a line of thought which goes back in England at least as far as Tiptofts' *Declaration of Noblesse* in the fifteenth century, he argued that true nobility was a matter of character not of birth:

What other thing is nobility now, but a chance to be born of this or that gentle blood . . . which often is got by robbery and like ways. True and perfect nobility springs from virtue, wherefore it is great madness for any man to crake [boast] of his parents, being naught himself . . . Truly we be all made of like elements, and have all one God, father of us all, yet to condemn the birth

[1] Vives, *On Education*, quoted J. Simon, *Education and Society*, p120.
[2] J. Simon, *Education and Society*, p161.
[3] J. Simon, *Education and Society*, p12.

or stock of any man is . . . to reprove God who is the author of every man's birth.[1]

Utopian communism and the State

The ideas behind this passage provide a direct link between Vives and Erasmus' closest friend in England Sir Thomas More, for the same conception of nobility and natural equality is the central theme of More's masterpiece the *Utopia*.

Sir Thomas More, like Vives, combined practical experience of education, with a theoretical conception of methods and aims. He established a school in his own household which became one of the centres of learning in Tudor England. It was justly famed both for the width of the curriculum (Nicolas Kratzer the astronomer and mathematician was a tutor there) but also for the fact that More's daughters and foster-daughters were included. In *Utopia* the same ideas are seen in an idealised form. The educational system envisaged by More was both democratic and selective. All children received a basic education that was partly practical and partly intellectual. The more intelligent were chosen for further education, but dropped out if they failed to maintain the standard required. All adults however could continue their education in their own time if they wished since the hours of work were regulated in order to give everyone leisure. Further education for everyone was therefore perfectly feasible. More envisaged a flexible egalitarian system which nevertheless provided for the more intelligent. He also broke away along humanist lines from the traditional subjects of his own day. Mathematics and medicine were included, as well as a knowledge of law, and a study of mankind through history and philosophy. The whole system was designed to train children to serve the community within their own natural capacity, for although More himself naturally set a high value upon learning, he was fully aware that children's intelligence varies, and that any viable educational system must take account of this.

But *Utopia* is more than an idealised state with an ideal educational system – a sort of mythological *jeu d'esprit* tossed off by More in his spare time on a diplomatic mission to the Netherlands in 1515. It has recently been given a new and critical assessment by Professor J. H. Hexter.[2] His main conclusion is that the attack on private wealth represents the core of More's teaching in *Utopia*. Utopia was not contrasted with Christian Europe in a pejorative sense – the heights to which pagan man can rise by reason alone with the

[1]Vives, *Introduction to Wisdom,* quoted by W. G. Zeeveld, *Foundations of Tudor Policy,* p209, spelling modernised.
[2]J. H. Hexter, *More's Utopia, The Biography of an Idea,* Princeton 1952; and *The Complete Works of Sir Thomas More,* Vol. 4. 'The Loom of Language and the Fabric of Imperatives. The Case of *Il Principe* and *Utopia*', *American Historical Review,* 1964.

implication that the revelation of Christianity will supplement the deficiencies of the system. It was contrasted with Europe to reveal the total bankruptcy of a Christian morality based on privilege. Professor Hexter therefore fundamentally disagrees with the generally accepted view put forward by Dr. Chambers in his standard biography of More[1], and by Dr. Caspari. Dr. Caspari analyses More's purpose in *Utopia* in the following passage: 'In order to carry out the experiment in which he was interested – to see how a society could be organised on the basis of reason alone, and ruled by those who possessed it in the highest degree – he eliminated such factors as property, inherited social position, and, within limits, revealed religion. Thus he was able to isolate reason, and to investigate how it could serve as the only basis for society.'[2] Professor Hexter suggests from internal textual evidence and from references in More's letters and those of his friends Peter Giles and Erasmus that *Utopia* was composed in two parts. While in the Netherlands in 1515, More wrote the opening section in Book I introducing the narrator Hythlodaeus to the point where he says he will describe the customs of the Utopians.[3] He also wrote the bulk of Book II which contains the actual description of Utopian institutions and customs. When he returned to England these parts stood as a unity. Some time during the early part of 1516 More added two important sections. To the end of Book I he appended the whole of the Dialogue of Counsel (the arguments for and against taking service in the government) and the final Exordium before Book II. Then at the end of Book II he added a concluding section pulling the whole work together and completing it. What makes this analysis interesting and supports Hexter's basic theory, is that it is in these later sections, which were written after deliberation and therefore represent More's considered rather than his emotive opinion, that we find the most penetrating criticism of the state of European and English society and the greatest emphasis on the excellence of Utopian institutions. 'Exordium, Conclusion, Peroration hammer away at the same point. What is important, what is absolutely crucial is Utopian communism.'[4]

Utopia therefore represents a scathing and savage attack on the ethos and basic assumptions of the semi-military ruling class of More's day. More genuinely felt that the governments of sixteenth century Europe, if viewed dispassionately, were nothing more than 'a conspiracy of the rich, who are aiming at their own interests under the name and title of a commonwealth', and that their legal systems were travesties of justice condoning laws such as hanging for theft which he knew to be evil. Poverty bred crime, and the cause of poverty was the exploitation of the poor, for:

---

[1] R. W. Chambers, *Thomas More,* Penguin 1963.
[2] F. Caspari, *Humanism and the Social Order,* p50.
[3] J. H. Hexter, *The Complete Works of Sir Thomas More,* Vol. 4, p55.
[4] J. H. Hexter, *The Complete Works of Sir Thomas More,* Vol. 4, pxxi.

In order that one insatiable glutton . . . may join field to field and surround many thousand acres with one fence, tenants are evicted . . . Away they must go . . . from the only homes familiar and known to them . . . what remains for them but to steal and be hanged – justly you say! – or to wander and beg [for] although they most eagerly offer their labour, there is no one to hire them . . . Assuredly unless you remedy these evils it is useless for you to boast of justice when you execute in the punishment for theft . . . what else, I ask, do you do but first create thieves and then punish them . . . I think it is altogether unjust that a man should suffer the loss of his life, for the loss of someone's money. In my opinion, not all the goods that fortune can bestow on us can be set in the scale against a man's life.[1]

Professor Hexter concludes that Utopian communism has one purpose only, to prevent injustice. It is not medieval, *Utopia* looks forward to the seventeenth century 'Diggers' not backward to the communal village. Nor, although the influence of Plato is considerable, does Utopian communism compare with that of the *Republic*. It is far more democratic. 'Plato's communism is . . . the communism of the "Janissaries" a means of singling out the élite, in *Utopia* it is the whole of society. The modernity of Utopia lies in the institutions of the Utopian commonwealth; it is there that More clearly transcends his historical milieu, there that he stands on the margins of modernity. The conditions for righteous living in Utopia were achieved by means of its institutions, and its central institution is Utopian communism.'[2] More in fact emphatically rejected the traditional view of 'order' or 'degree' as the basis of stable government. It is this which makes him unique. The real originality of More's thought helps to explain why More himself made no attempt to realise any of its fundamental precepts in practice. As a seminal book in the history of political thought, *Utopia*'s influence was controversial and its impact delayed, partly by More's own actions, and partly by the 'hedging' in the additional section to Book I. It was also initially restricted in its direct influence by the fact that it was written in Latin and not available in English until the reign of Elizabeth. *Utopia* was created in a moment of intense perception at a turning point in More's own life. It is a comprehensive attack on all privilege: the marxist theory that More attacked the feudal aristocracy as a representative of the 'rising' bourgeoisie, will not stand up to an examination of the text. The military élite, the rack-renting gentry, the professional classes, especially the lawyers, and the merchant entrepreneurs, are all equally condemned as exploiters. In the sections written last, and therefore representing a deliberate statement, More, through the mouth of Hythlodaeus makes the same point

---

[1]Hythlodaeus' speech to Cardinal Morton in *Utopia*, Book 1, pp67-73. For an interesting comparison describing an eviction in modern times see Mary of Unnimore's account in *Morvern Transformed*, P. Gaskell, CUP 1968, pp33-34. Appendix.
[2]J. H. Hexter, *The Complete Works of Sir Thomas More*, Introduction cx and cviii.

again and again, 'Community of property and the abolition of money are the only means of achieving true equality. They are also only the means: the end is equality. For the final equations are simple and radical: the equitable is the good, equality is justice.'[1]

More's rejection of the hierarchical structure of society implied a similar rejection of its values, particularly military values. More was against war as barbarous, against blood sports as corrupting – in fact against the whole code of chivalry as accepted in his day. When he uses the terms 'nobilis' and 'generosus' in *Utopia* he tends to use them in a derogatory sense.[2] It is here that Professor Hexter compares him directly with Machiavelli. Both men were alienated from the world they lived in and profoundly critical of it. To Machiavelli politics were a gigantic swindle with no overall morality. To More in the same way, the whole social structure was a confidence trick based on a wrong premise, that of hierarchical power and pride of possession: 'And at the top of the chivalric heap, at the peak of the predatory pyramid, stood the Princes, the Kings of Christendom at one another's throats in a chronic state of war.'[3] The question of how far More and Machiavelli believed what they wrote is difficult. Machiavelli followed *Il Principe* with the very different *Discourses on Livy*. More followed *Utopia* by a successful career at Court. Both More and Machiavelli reached a moment of heightened perception from which they ultimately retreated.

At the moment of writing *Utopia* possibly the strongest influence on More's thought was that of his friend Erasmus. *Utopia* owes much to Erasmus, more than can ever be known with certainty, since More's early biographers tended to play down the close connection of the two men for hagiographic reasons. But Erasmus lived in More's house in the years immediately preceding its composition, and the whole conception and content come within the framework of the Erasmian 'Christian Revival' once the theory that the Utopians and not the Europeans were the real Christians is accepted. To Erasmus and his circle, Europe of the sixteenth century had absorbed the standards and practices of a pre-Christian age, the social theories of Aristotle with their emphasis on degree and status, and the political and miliary structure of the Roman Empire and its successor feudal Europe. As a result Christian values and ethics were perverted or ignored.[4]

The problem of the nature of true Christianity leads More to raise yet another problem by implication, that of colonialism. For when the Utopians meet actual Christians, they are not converted, they voluntarily absorb the

[1] J. H. Hexter, *The Complete Works of Sir Thomas More*, Vol. 4, Introduction cxxiii.
[2] J. H. Hexter, *The Complete Works of Sir Thomas More*, Vol. 4, Introduction liii; and 'The Loom of Language', *American History Review* 1964, p963.
[3] J. H. Hexter, *The Complete Works of Sir Thomas More*, Vol. 4, Introduction lii.
[4] J. H. Hexter, *The Complete Works of Sir Thomas More*, Vol. 4, Introduction lxix.

teachings of Christ because they recognise them as implicit in their own system. More is aware of the distinction between the anti-Christian such as the Muslim, and the non-Christian or pagan and suggests a new approach to the problem – that of amalgamation rather than conversion.

But having written *Utopia* and seen his vision, More faced another and more practical issue, the question of his future employment. The position of the intellectual reformers was precarious – in the new age of the printing press their support was vital to those in power. If they gave it, they risked losing their independence, if they did not give it, they remained peripheral and ineffectual. More realised this perfectly clearly. In order to get anything done, he must enter the administration; but he realised equally well that in order to enter the administration he must abandon his vision, lower his standards and compromise with the world as it was – for 'the prophet who serves the power of this world, may live on as a man but ceases to be a prophet.'[1] He gives the reasons for his decision quite clearly in the Dialogue on Counsel:

> So the case standeth in a commonwealth, and so it is in the consultations of Kings and Princes. If evil opinions and naughty persuasions cannot be utterly and quite plucked out of their hearts, if you cannot even as you would remedy vices which use and custom hath confirmed, yet for this cause you must not leave and forsake the commonwealth; you must not forsake the ship in a tempest because you cannot rule and keep down the winds. No, nor you must not labour to drive into their heads new and strange informations, which you know well shall be nothing regarded with them that be of clear contrary minds. But you must with crafty wile and subtle train study and endeavour yourself as much as you lieth to handle the matter wittily and handsomely for the purpose, and that which you cannot turn to good, so order it that it be not very bad.[2]

That such a course could prove dangerous More knew very well, for although a Councillor could try to mitigate evil advice, the Court was

> no place to dissemble in, nor to wincke in. Noughtye counselles must be openlye allowed and very pestilent decrees must be approved. He shall be counted worse than a spye, yea almost as evel as a traytour that with a faint harte doth praise evel and noyesome decrees.[3]

More's premonition was right. 'In a fashion almost too pat, his experience vindicated Hythlodaeus' wisdom: his hopes were quite baseless. Under a rather heavy veneer of humane learning and geniality Henry VIII was the very model of the predatory leader of a predatory semi-military ruling class; he was magnificent, splendid, stupefyingly vain-glorious.'[4] *Utopia* therefore remains

[1] J. H. Hexter, *The Complete Works of Sir Thomas More,* Introduction xci.
[2] More, *Utopia,* Everyman edition, J. M. Dent 1916, pp41-42.
[3] *Utopia,* Everyman edition, p43.
[4] J. H. Hexter, *The Complete Works of Sir Thomas More,* Introduction civ.

an isolated masterpiece – isolated not only in More's own life, but in the whole tradition of sixteenth century thought. For this reason it may seem more modern than it is. Hexter's penetrating phrase 'on the margins of modernity' means exactly what it says. It would be a mistake to read too much into More's momentary insight, but it will never again be possible to read too little. *Utopia* stands as the antithesis to the famous speech in *Troilus and Cressida*. It questioned the whole basis of the new society, where education fused with nationalism and grafted the code of chivalry onto the humanism of Erasmus. Hythlodaeus is the anti-hero to Philip Sidney.

Sir Thomas Elyot's 'Governour'

Sir Thomas Elyot, whose treatise *The Boke named the Governour* can be directly compared and contrasted with *Utopia*, was in fact closely linked personally with More. His wife had been educated partly in More's household, and Elyot's friendship was sufficiently close for him to write and excuse it to Cromwell at the time of More's fall. Like *Utopia*, *The Governour* was a composite book probably written in three parts. The first and third sections deal primarily with the education of the sons of the gentry and the virtues necessary to the governing class, the middle section consists of a study of monarchy, linked to the first section by a chapter on magistrates.[1] The important sections are those on education. In sharp contrast to More, Elyot accepted as axiomatic the philosophy that 'degree' and 'order' are the only safeguards of social stability, to such an extent that he almost seems to anticipate Hobbes.

> Take away ordre from all thinges, what shulde then remayne? Certes nothynge finally, except . . . chaos . . . Also where there is any lacke of ordre nedes must be perpetuall conflicte: and in thynges subjecte to Nature nothynge of him selfe onely may be norrisshed; but whan he hath destroyed that where with he doth participate by the order of his creation, be hym selfe of necessitie must than perisshe, whereof ensueth universall dissolution.[2]

Throughout the book Elyot adapted the theories of the humanists to English conditions. He saw clearly that in England the practical application of learning was largely centred on administration. This was an immensely important observation and had far-reaching consequences, for Elyot's treatise published in 1531 broke entirely new ground in that it was written in English specifically for the enlightenment and education of the landed classes. Elyot was trained in common law, and familiar with the conditions prevailing in England. His book was in a sense designed as a practical training manual not a hypothetical

[1] Stanford E. Lehmberg, *Sir Thomas Elyot, Tudor Humanist*, University of Texas Press 1960, p39.
[2] Sir Thomas Elyot, *The Governour*, Everyman 1907, p3.

system, and while it clearly owes much in conception to Castiglione's *The Courtier*, written to instruct Italian nobility in correct and cultivated behaviour, Elyot was more concerned with preparing the children of the English upper classes for their obligations in central and local government. His purpose in his own words was to describe 'the best form of education or bringing up of noble children from their nativity, in such a manner that they may be found worthy, and also able to be governors of the public weal'. There is no suggestion in Elyot of More or Cranmer's advanced democratic principles of equal or universal education. Elyot believed firmly in social privilege, and his advanced training is specifically designed to produce a 'governor' at either local or national level. Yet in his actual methods Elyot is equally humane. Children were to be left in the care of women till the age of seven, and educated at home by a tutor. The importance of education on the formation of character was the basis of Elyot's system. Education was not only book learning but the development of the whole personality. Music and even painting were part of it, and physical exercise. He advocated a wide general education until at least fourteen, and only in the later stages should a young man study philosophy and law. Elyot constantly emphasised the practical use of education and its application to real conditions. History, for example, he considers to be of great importance because from it could be learnt the causes of wars, the reasons for the decline or prosperity of states. He recommended Caesar particularly because of his knowledge of tactics against barbarous tribes, and suggests that his books should be read by 'the princes of this realm of Englande and their councillors, considering that thereof may be taken necessary instructions concernynge the warres agayne Irisshe men or Scottes, who be of the same rudeness and wilde disposition that the Suises and Britons were in the time of Caesar.'[1] Livy was recommended because he showed how Rome out of a small and poor beginning, by prowess and virtue little by little came to the empire and dominion of all the world. Elyot's conception of England's future as a maritime power may have had an effect on the next generation. Whether or not it can be directly attributed to Elyot, in the reign of Elizabeth men like John Dee and Walter Raleigh were specifically advocating colonial expansion in these terms. Elyot's 'Governor' was educated with one end in view – to accept responsibility, to be 'worthy to be in authority' so that 'all under their governaunce shall prosper and come to perfection'. Elyot himself had a career of moderate but adequate distinction. He was Sheriff for Cambridge (an office he sought to avoid) and sat for Cambridge in the Parliaments of 1539 and 1542. He served as a Justice of the Peace, and on legal commissions such as Gaol Delivery and Oyer and Terminer. He was used by Cromwell to survey monastic lands, and acquired some himself in the process. He was clearly a reliable (if conservative) and influential man in his locality. He wrote two other books: one, *The Castel of Health* is of interest

[1] Sir Thomas Elyot, *The Governour*, p46.

rather than of importance, derived from Galen and containing herbal remedies; but the other, his *Latin-English Dictionary* published in 1538, has been described as the only really major work of scholarship to appear in the 1530s.[1]

Political commitment – Pole and Starkey

Elyot wrote *The Governour* when the fate of the early phase of humanism in England hung in the balance. Wolsey's fall in 1529 marked the end of his great educational experiment at Oxford and dispersed the talented group of young men he had so carefully collected to launch it. The fate of the original group is interesting, and illustrates both the continuity and diversity of the English humanist tradition. After the Cardinal's fall, the central core of his young graduates went either to the continent, or like Cromwell moved directly to the Court. Those who went abroad sooner or later gravitated to the household of the King's cousin Reginald Pole at Padua. The circle round Pole therefore becomes at this point one of great interest. The Pole family, with the Blounts and the Boleyns, were the three great examples of aristocratic patronage in the early period of the English Renaissance. Pole is unique within these as being the only one centred abroad rather than in England, and was a cleric not a layman. He went to Padua in 1519 and by 1521 had re-established the ties between England and Italy which had grown tenuous since the return of Colet and Linacre at the beginning of the century. Pole thus provides another cross link this time between English and continental thought. He was supported by a pension of £100 a year from Henry, a stipend regarded by Zeeveld 'as the most significant in the history of Tudor humanism', for Pole's close connection with the King gave him added prestige, and his household became one of the important intellectual centres of Europe.[2]

Pole provided the members of a group of young scholars with a unique experience of Italian culture and learning. Padua was within the Venetian Republic and its tolerant and stimulating atmosphere enabled those studying there to have access to a wide range of learning and enlarged their mental terms of reference. Pole himself during 1525 paid for the production of a complete edition of Galen, edited by Sir Thomas More's son-in-law John Clements, and published by Aldus. More important for the future, in the same city Vesalius was already doing his revolutionary work on anatomy, and the works of Machiavelli were beginning to appear in print.

When Wolsey's able protegés from England such as Thomas Starkey, Richard Morison, John Friar, George Lily and Henry Cole began to appear for varying periods under Pole's roof, this concentration of talent did not escape the notice of the English administration. The setting of 'learning against learning' is

[1] J. K. McConica, *English Humanists*, p196.
[2] W. G. Zeeveld, *The Foundations of Tudor Policy*, p41.

a game more than one can play. Possibly as the result of the extension of Cromwell's influence, the government realised the advantages to be gained by harnessing the brains and knowledge of such scholars in the King's interest, particularly over the technical justification of the divorce which involved intricate questions of canon and civil law. Henry was particularly anxious to get Pole himself on his side. Pole was in Paris in 1529 and Henry immediately ordered him to help obtain an opinion from the Sorbonne as to the validity of his marriage. Pole was later to say that the blow of this commission 'robbed me not only of speech, but of the power of thinking', but at the time he helped obtain the verdict required by the King. In 1530 Henry summoned him to England, and offered him the Archbishopric of York. Pole had been accompanied by Thomas Starkey, and at this point retired with him to the Carthusian monastery at Shene – the Carthusian houses were clearly a favourite retreat for humanists in moments of crisis for after a period of reflection Pole declined the King's offer and returned with Starkey to the continent. It was a momentous decision, not only for Pole himself but for the unity of the humanist circle centred round him. It was also a considered one. Pole had probably made up his mind on the whole issue of supremacy when in England, although he was to maintain a discreet and equivocal silence for another three years. The turning point may well have come from his contact with Cromwell, and the future Cardinal's 'dismay at the discovery that hence forth the guide to English policy would not be Plato but Machiavelli'.[1] The real causes of Pole's final attitude were certainly more complex and possibly took some time to crystallize. Whatever his exact state of mind, Pole returned in slow stages to the tranquillity of Venice and Padua. His friend Starkey, with more acumen, remained at Avignon studying civil law under Giovanni Francesco Ripa.

Political events in England were moving so fast that it was becoming impossible for scholars to avoid commitment. Starkey, the protegé of Wolsey and intimate friend of Pole, wrote direct to the King offering a legal opinion and suggesting a General Council as a possible solution to his matrimonial problem. As a result, he returned to England, initially as Chaplain to the Countess of Salisbury, Pole's mother, but was rapidly promoted to a post as Chaplain to the King and became one of Cromwell's most able propagandists. Starkey's position in the political and religious thought of the 1530s is of great interest. He was the author of one of the most far-reaching (and therefore unpublished) political treatises of the century, the *Dialogue between Reginald Pole and Thomas Lupset* which included the argument that in the ideal state the laws should be supreme even over the Prince, the monarchy elective, and tyrants deposed: '. . . this is in man's power, to elect and chose him that is both wise and just, and make him a Prince, and him that is a tyrant so to depose'. His advanced political views, and his friendship with Pole, proved ultimately fatal to

[1] W. G. Zeeveld, *The Foundations of Tudor Policy*, pp76-77.

his personal career, and he died in relative obscurity. His life illustrates the dichotomy of this transitional period, and with friends on both sides he ended as a sad and perhaps a disappointed man. Starkey's thought has only recently been given adequate emphasis.[1] This is partly because it is only during the last century that Starkey's writings have been available in print. His most important work *The Dialogue* was not published until 1871 and not available in an intelligible modern edition until 1948.[2] Only a few political tracts were printed in his lifetime. Nevertheless these tracts and the evidence provided by the letters show that Starkey has real importance in the history of English political thought. As a propagandist for the government he formed part of the 'reforming' political group which included Cromwell, Cranmer, Marshall and Morison. These men all saw clearly the connection between poverty and social unrest, and attempted in varying degrees to suggest and implement solutions to the problem. Among their writings can be found ideas of equality, at least of opportunity – although the Pilgrimage of Grace led to a stiffening of attitude and a reaffirmation of 'degree' and the duty of obedience. Some at least of these theories can be found in the writings of Starkey, particularly the consciousness that poverty bred sedition. Although *The Dialogue* was in effect still-born, it remains Starkey's most ambitious and longest work. It has been described as 'a comprehensive review of English government and society.' and it contains a detailed section on education, which follows on from the ideas of Elyot.[3]

Like all the humanists, Starkey saw men as innately rational. The education of children, especially of the ruling classes, was therefore of the utmost importance to the state. Starkey raised in this connection a new and interesting point. He attacked the feudal right of Wardship, which had already degenerated from protection to exploitation. In Starkey's opinion the right of Wardship was a responsibility, and it was the duty of the government to see it was exercised as such. Starkey was also unusual for his time in that he thought that communal education for the rich was better than private tuition, and advocated the creation of special schools for the nobility in order to train them for public service. Starkey believed that correct education was essential for the proper exercise of government, and that to neglect the education of the ruling class was to invite political unrest. Starkey went even further than this, and like other members of the Cromwellian circle thought that education should be extended downwards

---

[1] He rates a whole chapter in Dr. Caspari's account of *Humanism and the Social Order*, and Dr. Zeeveld and Dr. Baumer give him considerable prominence in their accounts of the thought of this period. Professor Dickens also deals fully with his contribution to Anglican theory. W. G. Zeeveld, *The Foundations of Tudor Policy;* F. le van Baumer, *Early Tudor Theory of Kingship,* Yale 1940; A. G. Dickens, *The English Reformation.*

[2] T. Starkey, *Dialogue between Reginald Pole and Thomas Lupset,* Chatto and Windus 1948; *His Life and Letters,* edited by S. J. Herrtage, appeared in the Early English Text Society Series in 1878.

[3] J. Simon, *Education and Society,* p156.

in the social scale as a means of securing political stability. The type of education should vary with the social status and ability of the child, but none should be left in idleness. 'Every man, under a certain pain, after he had brought his children to seven years of age, should set them forth either to letters or a craft, according as their nature requireth, after the judgement and power of their friends'.[1]

Starkey's hope that Pole would follow his example and join the King was abruptly shattered when in 1536 Pole wrote his total repudiation of Henry's policy in his *Pro ecclesiastica unitatis defensione*. From this moment Pole was cut off from England until his return under Mary as Cardinal and Archbishop of Canterbury. The fortunes and lives of his family in England were forfeit, his brothers and even his mother the seventy-year old Countess of Salisbury were executed in the 'cleansing of the Tower' in 1540. Pole remained unmolested on the continent (although it is interesting to note that his intellectual Platonism led to an accusation of heresy in 1557 while actually Archbishop); but the Paduan circle was irretrievably broken, Pole's friends had to choose between Catholicism and exile, and supremacy and return.

These two events, the fall of Wolsey and the disruption of the Pole circle following the break with Rome, bring to an end a phase in the intellectual growth of England. It was not an abrupt end: Wolsey fell in 1529, Pole did not write until 1536. Pole's *Pro ecclesia* was a crucial turning point and irrevocably altered the future development of English thought; 'it would be hard to overestimate the importance of the intellectual crisis precipitated by Pole's decision to break with Henry. Up to that time, the community of scholars was unbroken; after that time the Schism among men of learning was as inevitable as it was irreparable'.[2] During these years all the great figures of the early period made their decisions. Vives left England for good in 1528, More resigned form the government in 1533 and was executed with Bishop Fisher in 1535. The pietistic influence which had characterised the patronage of LadyMargaret Beaufort and Katherine of Aragon was replaced by a new attitude towards reform, more aggressive, more secular and more practical. It is possible that this intervening period saw an intensely 'Erasmian' attempt to reform both Church and State within the framework of the Catholic Church, made feasible by Wolsey's fall, and led by the middle group of More, Norfolk, Rochford, Suffolk and Gardiner. If so, it was short-lived and fractured and fell apart when the King opted for supremacy and schism, leaving the way clear for the more effective and possibly more ruthless combination of Cromwell and Cranmer.[3] The theory that the break with Rome profoundly altered English humanism

[1]Starkey, *Dialogue*, pp142-48.
[2]W. G. Zeeveld, *Foundations of Tudor Policy*, p264.
[3]For this theory of the Erasmian undertones of this period, see J. K. McConica, *English Humanists*, p108.

cannot be contested, but it must be remembered that it applies to the decisions made by individual men, not to their ideas. It is true that 'English humanists were faced at once with the choice of a rapprochement with Rome, or of a plunge into the arena of active policy-making . . . which was no longer an academic ideal but a royal command'.[1] But the transition was possibly a less dramatic one than Dr. Zeeveld suggests. More, for example, had been concerned with administration and power as Chancellor, and there is a marked continuity in the thought and ideas of the writers which transcends political decisions and gives an intellectual unity to this period of change.

This underlying similarity of basic ideas is seen most clearly in the various theories on education already discussed, which on examination reveal a common point of view among those in power which transcends their final alignment on the major issues of politics. Cromwell himself points out in the Injunctions of 1536 that idleness led to poverty, and poverty to crime. A sentiment which echoes that of More in *Utopia*:

> [The clergy should] by all ways and means they may . . . persuading the said fathers, mothers, masters and other governors . . . diligently to provide aid and forsee that the said youth be in no manner wise kept or brought up in idleness, lest at any time afterward they be driven, for lack of . . . some occupation to live by, to fall to begging, stealing or some other unthriftiness; forasmuch as we may daily see through sloth and idleness divers valiant men fall some to begging some to theft and murder . . . where, if they had been well educated and brought up in some good literature, occupation or mystery, they should, being rulers of their own family, have profited as well themselves, as divers other persons, to the great commodity and ornament of the common weal.[2]

The general continuity of ideas in this period could not find a more fitting illustration.

The five year interval between the executions of More and Cromwell saw the final definition of the Henrician Commonwealth. Cromwell and Cranmer were the two major figures, but under their control they employed with considerable skill a small group of able men all from the same intellectual background, Starkey, Richard Taverner, Richard Morison, and William Marshall. These men differed in details and emphasis, but they were all to a greater or lesser extent influenced by Erasmus, and except for Starkey (removed by death) they continued to write, translate and publish uninterrupted by Cromwell's sudden demise, and thus provide the essential links with the final period of the reign. For this reason, the work of Cromwell in the sphere of intellectual thought, as in every other, survived his death.

[1] W. G. Zeeveld, *Foundations of Tudor Policy*, p264.
[2] Injunctions of 1536, see *The Reformation in England to the accession of Elizabeth I*, eds. A. G. Dickens and D. Carr.

Dr Elton has suggested that this group of intellectuals may have formed a sort of Cromwellian planning team, and that much of the social and economic legislation of the thirties had its origin in their ideas.[1] Both Cromwell and Cranmer must be regarded as important and consistent patrons of learning and reform within the administration of church and state. The printing of the Bible in English was the greatest intellectual event of the time. Cromwell's Injunctions, which stressed the importance of education at parish level and which placed the Bible in English in every local church to be read by anyone, marked the begining of a new age, and his ideas were implemented by Cranmer under Edward VI. Cranmer's love of learning and profound scholarship were well known in his life time and his reputation as a patron of scholars was widespread. According to Strype, Roger Ascham said of him:

> That he was a Man who was accustomed to express great joy at the good Progress of Learning, such was his singular good-will towards it; and when it went otherwise than well with it, he alone could apply a Remedy; such was his Sway and Authority. And so much was he the known Mecaenas of Learning, that according to the publick Encouragement or Prejudice it received, so the Vulgar accounted the Praise or Dispraise thereof to redound upon Cranmer. So that if Learning were Discountenanced, it was esteemed to cast some Disparagement upon him; if it flourished, it was a sign that Cranmer prevailed at Court.[2]

The blanket argument for Erasmianism in spite of its convenience and intellectual appeal has come under some criticism. Professor Dickens in reviewing Dr. McConica's book, has suggested that whole thesis is too vague. 'If we search for Erasmian humanists and are prepared to define them in the broadest possible terms, we shall naturally find them everywhere . . . The club is the reverse of exclusive. It seems open to any man who was well educated according to the almost universally accepted standards of the period 1509–1553, and who entertained a mildly reforming attitute toward religious and social problems. It includes the Catholic martyrs Fisher and More, the Cromwellians William Marshall and Thomas Starkey, fierce evangelicals like Tyndale and Taverner, successors of the *devotio moderna* like William Bonde and Richard Whitford . . .'.[3] Thomas Cromwell and his associates are thought to represent 'official Erasmianism' despite the fact that they worked for an Erastian nationalism rejected by Erasmus. Professor Dickens makes the cogent point that no literate man or woman living in the 1530s could avoid being influenced by Erasmus. He was the most widely read author of his day and his ideas perma-

---

[1]G. R. Elton, 'State planning in Early Tudor England', *Economic History Review*, 2nd series, Vol. 13, 1960–61.
[2]John Strype, *Memorials of Thomas Cranmer*, Book 2, Ch. 4.
[3]*History*, Vol. LII, No. 174, February 1967.

nently altered the outlook of an age, in the same way as Darwin, Freud, and Marx have affected the early twentieth century. But like his successors he could divide as well as unite, and what appears on the surface as 'Erasmian' continuity may mask fundamental change underneath. 'The plain truth is that the all-pervasive ideas of the great trend-setter proved soft and ineffectual when people came to doing something more than set a trend; when they came to defying the Papacy, founding new churches or religious orders, winning populations for causes, and making deeper marks upon history . . . one can hardly help becoming more than ever suspicious of blanket-words like "humanist" and "Erasmian"; one must appeal for closer definitions . . .'.[1]

Nevertheless it was during this period that the English protestant ethic was being formulated. That this was secular, moderate, with a strong bias towards lay educational reform can be traced directly back to the early humanists in England, Colet, Erasmus, More, and Vives, and to the close knit circle of lay and ecclesiastical patrons who financed them. The political twist of the 1530s dominated by Cromwell was the product of circumstances; but by the inescapable logic of cause and effect, it was a development which in turn affected the succeeding age.

[1] A. G. Dickens, *History*, February 1967, pp77-78.

4. Changes in education under Edward and Mary

The reigns of Edward and Mary are often treated as if they were an interruption in the evolutionary process of Tudor rule. In fact the reverse is true. The decade is a period of unusual importance: the pivot in development as well as in time of the sixteenth century. At the death of Henry VIII the options remained open. At the death of Mary this was no longer true: decisions had been taken in every aspect of life and government which proved permanent. The disturbances on the surface, the contradictory religious policies, the rivalries of those in power, mask but do not obliterate the signs of profound change underneath. Negative forces were in every case balanced by positive; rebellion by unexpected internal stability; corruption by far-reaching administrative reform; iconoclasm by a new intellectual expansion. It is this paradox which makes the period of such interest.

Once a judgement on an age has passed into text books it has a dangerously wide circulation. The reigns of Edward and Mary have been misjudged by historians and are only now being re-examined. Northumberland in particular has had extremely bad press, and his constructive work ignored or underestimated. Yet he alone had the vision to see correctly that England's future lay in a re-orientation of her trade and a development of her maritime opportunities. He was by far the most intelligent even if the most unscrupulous statesman of the age, and under different circumstances might have achieved real greatness. The same is true of Edward. It now seems clear that the King took an informed and intelligent interest in government. In association with Petre, he may well have been planning far-reaching administrative reforms.[1]

It can be argued that in the purely administrative departments the absence of a strong monarchy may have had real advantages in that it enabled officials to rationalise parts of the system without interference from above. The fact that so many of the key men remain in office shows the underlying flexibility and strength of the system.

The weakness of the monarchy undoubtedly laid bare the deficiencies within the government as well as revealing its resilience. But in every case these deficiencies can be shown to be inherent in the system and not peculiar to the decade. The major problem of corruption permeated the whole structure–but

[1]W. K. Jordan, *The Chronicle and Political Papers of Edward VI*, Allen and Unwin 1966; F. G. Emmison, *Tudor Secretary: Sir William Petre at Court and Home*, Longmans 1961; 'A Plan of Edward VI and Secretary Petre for Re-organising the Council 1552-3', BIHR 1958.

it was not new, nor did it end with the accession of Elizabeth. It was the inevitable concomitant of the poverty of the crown. It was the Achilles heel of the whole Tudor system.

In education the period was decisive. The expansion of the school system, combined with the use of English in the Bible and the Prayer Books created a machinery for religious change which was the more effective because it influenced directly the future rulers and administrators as well as those in power. The reorientation of thought had therefore a depth and profundity which ensured its permanence. The reign of Mary could not reverse the trend because it was too short to indoctrinate a whole generation. The age was also decisive because the brilliance of the intellectual ideas found under Edward anticipates the later achievements under Elizabeth and in part caused them. In this, much is owed to the patronage of both Somerset and Northumberland. Somerset used economists like Hales, Sir Thomas Smith, and the intellectual group known as the 'Commonwealth Party', he employed Cecil, and encouraged the great herbalist William Turner, who was his personal physician and for whom he secured the Deanery of Wells. Northumberland promoted and used William Thomas, who was one of the most versatile and brilliant men of the time. Thomas' knowledge of European affairs and economic and political ideas were influential among the inner circle of the Council. The fact that Northumberland immediately grasped the importance of the new scientific discoveries of his time and sought to use them is a further indication of his ability. John Dee, the mathematician and alchemist, began a lifelong connection with the Dudley family when he dedicated two works to the Duchess of Northumberland, one on the causes of the tides, and another on the movement of heavenly bodies. Dedications have to be accepted with reservations, since authors often solicited patrons simply in hope of reward. But it seems clear in the case of John Dee that the Duchess encouraged his research and that he wrote at her request.[1] What is certain is that under Northumberland's administration a movement started, centred round Cabot, Dee, and Robert Recorde, and financed by the Muscovy Company, which applied mathematics and the new principles of projection in maritime charts to practical problems of navigation, and which gave instruction to seamen in English. It was this growing interest in the basic technology of exploration which was ultimately to make Northumberland's dream of maritime expansion a reality.

On a different level, Cranmer was creating in the Anglican liturgy a masterpiece of English prose, not by accident but by design reinforced by penetrating and wide research. Matthew Parker, Roger Ascham, and John Cheke were setting new standards of scholarship, and putting into practice the conceptions of education advocated earlier in the century. William Morison, now Ambassador to Charles V enlivened his diplomatic reports with a sense of humour and

[1] R. Deacon, *John Dee*, Frederick Muller 1968, p27.

turn of phrase reminiscent of his days as a propagandist for the government under Thomas Cromwell and discussed the theories of Machiavelli in the evenings. It was a stimulating and formative period.

If it was a false dawn, the decade was certainly more than 'an interlude during which little emerged but a prayer book', followed by a reign when England was a pawn in the Habsburg-Valois rivalry; it was 'a definitive period, more so perhaps than a later one that has earned a title in history'.[1]

It was a dynamic not a static era. For this reason it was a period of contradictions. While Paulet and Mildmay locked the administrative structure into place; the forces which were to destroy it were already gaining strength in Parliament and the schools. If censorship placed restrictions on the use of print, the spread of ideas through books linked men together beneath the surface by the growth of literacy and a common language. The Spanish marriage which might have taken England into Europe, in effect isolated her from it. Mary's rule (in spite of its appearance of an interruption in effective conciliar government) did not halt, and may even have accelerated the evolution of the 'Tudor Nation-State'.

These inner contradictions persisted until the end of the century. The Elizabethans produced the cult of the protestant military hero like Sidney; yet Sidney himself was a humanist and a poet. There is more than a trace of humanism in Burghley's dictum that a soldier could hardly be an honest man and a good Christian; yet his advice to his son could hardly have been more secular:

> Towards thy superiors be humble yet generous. With thine equals, familiar, yet receptive. Towards thine inferiors show much humanity and some familiarity... The first prepares the way for advancement. The second makes thee known for a man well-bred. The third gains a good report; which once got, is easily kept.[2]

The educational system produced a generation of puritans; yet it also produced Hooker and Whitgift: and corruption grew at the centre of power.

Growth and change are the keys to the age. The fact that the Elizabethans were educated and formed under Edward and Mary must never be forgotton, for the period had sown dragon's teeth. It had started a transformation of society which was to culminate in the Civil War.

The intellectual legacy inherited by the Edwardian age was considerable. The spread of humanism had continued and, through the agency of the printed book, was no longer confined to academic and literary circles. The 'Erasmian' group round Queen Catherine Parr was an important formative influence in the circles of the Court. To this was added a second and newer factor, the strengthening of

[1]J. Simon, *Education and Society*, p268.
[2]Quoted in J. Simon, *Education and Society*, p345.

the social conscience by what may with some justification be called the puritanical views of men like Latimer and Hooper. Latimer in particular as a 'Court' preacher exercised considerable influence especially on the younger generation at the centre of power. The views of Edward himself, of Henry Hastings third Earl of Huntingdon, of Lady Jane Grey, and Catherine, Duchess of Suffolk, were permanently altered by Latimer's opinions and sermons. Their effect can be seen in Edward's notes on the commonwealth and his desire for social justice, in Lady Jane Grey's surviving letters and her steadfastness in death; in Catherine of Suffolk's militant protestantism and choice of exile under Mary; and in Huntingdon's strong puritanism in Elizabeth's reign.[1]

Changes in education

The educational changes of the mid-Tudor period were both extensive and permanent, and persisted until the present re-organisation of school and university education in the twentieth century. They were the most important legacy of the age.

The reign of Edward VI was definitive. Under Mary there were changes in academic personnel on religious grounds, but no changes in the system itself. Under Elizabeth the work begun by Edward was extended, consolidated, and in some sections at least permeated by 'puritanism'. But Dr. Simon's recent research has shown that if 'the reign of Edward is given due weight as a period of educational advance, that of Elizabeth falls into place as a predominantly conservative age.' Dr. Simon points out that under Elizabeth 'the term "puritanism" is a category as difficult to disentangle as "humanism" at an earlier stage; it extends to cover a whole set of attitudes, a way of thought and approach to learning, not merely advocacy of the Genevan form of church government.' As a result the theology of the Elizabethan church was calvinistic, and puritanism was therefore 'in the mainstream of development' not on the periphery.[2] The fact that it was absorbed into the educational system was important for the future.

Edward is associated with three important developments: the Act dissolving the Chantries of 1547, which directly affected education at local level; the Commission on the Universities of 1549; and the Act against Superstitious Books of 1550. Taken together these form the blue-print of the educational changes under the King.

The Chantries Act took over for the crown the lands of all chantries (lands given in perpetuity to support a priest part of whose duties was to pray for the donor), colleges, free chapels, fraternities, and guilds (except those of Oxford

[1]W. Hester Chapman, *Lady Jane Grey*, Jonathan Cape 1962; Evelyn Read, *Catherine Duchess of Suffolk*, Jonathan Cape 1962; Claire Cross, *The Puritan Earl*, Macmillan 1966.
[2]J. Simon, *Education and Society*, pp291-2.

and Cambridge) and certain powerful mysteries and crafts (such as the powerful city guilds).[1] Commissioners were appointed to survey the chantry lands with instructions to keep in being all existing schools attached to chantries, and to grant pensions where applicable to displaced priests. In contrast with the commissions under Henry VIII, these were not headed by Bishops and were composed of local gentry reinforced by lay officials from the Court of Augmentations. This Court was set up by Thomas Cromwell specifically to deal with monastic land and revenues. Its competence was extended to cover chantries. The exact number of chantries, colleges and hospitals affected by the act and the total value of their property is not known with certainty, but Camden puts the number at 2,374 chantries and chapels, 90 colleges and 110 hospitals.[2] The amount of property affected was therefore considerable, and it is important to remember that, unlike the monasteries which were virtually self-sufficient estates, the chantries and endowed hospitals were in direct contact with the laity, and their dissolution, although smaller in scale was therefore greater in impact.[3] Nevertheless the reports of the Commissioners show that viewed as a whole, the chantry system, like the monastic, was in a state of decline. 'However brutal its intrusion, the State discovered here a world already in decay, a world sadly in need of control, reform and revitalising influences'.[4] In many areas the endowments were no longer being used for their original purpose and had either been taken back by the family of the donor, or converted by the local inhabitants to more practical and secular uses. At Henbury in Gloucestershire for example, the rents from chantry lands were being used to repair the river banks against floods.[5] From evidence provided by ten areas selected for exhaustive examination (Bristol, London, Norfolk, Somerset, Worcestershire, Yorkshire, Buckinghamshire, Hampshire, Kent and Lancashire) Professor Jordan has found that 'there were relatively few functioning chantry schools in 1480, fewer still at the time of the expropriation'.[6]

The exact effect of the Chantries Act is still a matter of controversy. Professor Dickens indicates that whatever its intentions, the 'stupid drafting of the Chantries Act, imperilled all endowed chapels' even those serving isolated parishes and that while the government 'spoke of converting the endowments to the needs of education and the poor, yet they failed to found genuinely new grammar schools and almshouses'.[7] Furthermore it is clear that under the pressure of the financial crisis, initially much endowed land was sold or leased

[1]J. Simon, *Education and Society*, p224.
[2]Quoted by A. G. Dickens, *The English Reformation*, p207. Professor Dickens considers these figures are approximately correct.
[3]For the importance of this see A. G. Dickens, *The English Reformation*, p215.
[4]A. G. Dickens, *The English Reformation*, p208.
[5]A. G. Dickens, *The English Reformation*, pp208-9.
[6]W. K. Jordan, *Philanthropy in England 1480-1660*, p286.
[7]A. G. Dickens, *The English Reformation*, pp212 and 210.

to private individuals. In certain areas the effects of the act were nearly disastrous. From a petition in Mary's reign it is claimed that the town of Pontefract which before the Dissolutions had 'one abbey, two colleges, a house of friars preachers, one ancress, one hermit, four chantry priests, one guild priest', was now reduced to 'an unlearned vicar, which hireth two priests'.[1]

The school of Sedburgh very nearly disappeared, and was only saved by the efforts of St. John's College Cambridge, after the lands of its endowment had in fact been sold. In the same way a Court action was necessary to protect Berkhamstead School against attempts by the founders' heirs to regain their endowments.[2]

The final picture however is totally different. Once the immediate sales of chantry lands were over, a process of consolidation and reconstruction began. Nearly all the essential chapels in isolated areas were eventually retained, all the ninety-four chapels in Lancashire for example were kept, and of the chantry schools still remaining in 1547, none was permanently suppressed. The existing records show that with a few isolated exceptions (such as John Maynard the deputy surveyor for Oxfordshire), 'the chantry commissioners took the most elaborate pains to protect existing schools, or more usually the part-time services of a stipendary priest, often searching valiantly and unsuccessfully for a school which a deed of gift suggested should exist, but which had in fact long since lapsed.'[3] A careful distinction was made between the educational and religious functions of chantries. The former were preserved, and the latter, except in special areas, suppressed. In 1548 six months after the initial passing of the Act, Sir Walter Mildmay from the Court of Augmentations, and Robert Keilway from the Court of Wards, were appointed to supervise its working, with the express intention of ensuring that the educational endowments should not be diverted to other uses, and that chantry priests should either be given pensions or continued as schoolmasters.[4] In 1550 a commission was issued to the Chancellor of Augmentations giving him powers to erect grammar schools, and refoundation and extension of educational facilities became national policy. 'It is after this date that the evidence of refoundations accumulates. Some of the towns petitioning for lands had lacked a settled foundation since the dissolution of the monasteries, but others took the opportunity to request lands to endow a school where there had been none.'[5] The control of these schools was placed either directly in the hands of

[1] Quoted by A. G. Dickens, *The English Reformation*, p217.
[2] For these examples see J. Simon, *Education and Society*, Ch. 8. The case of Sedburgh is interesting since the school was situated in an area where the Receiver of the Court of Augmentations (the government department concerned) was later proven guilty of corruption.
[3] A. G. Dickens, *The English Reformation*, pp212-3; see also W. K. Jordan, *Philanthropy in England*, p286.
[4] For the details of the actual Augmentations control of chantry lands see J. Simon, *Education and Society*, pp225-7. [5] J. Simon, *Education and Society*, p231.

the borough concerned, or in those of a governing body composed of leading inhabitants of the town. In some cases, notably more important local schools, or schools directly connected with powerful courtiers such as Stamford (William Cecil), Saffron Walden (Sir Thomas Smith), and Chelmsford (Sir Walter and Sir Thomas Mildmay, Sir William Petre and Sir Henry Tirrel), or Abingdon (Sir John Mason), refoundation was ensured by specific Acts of Parliament. In Yorkshire alone, which had about forty-six schools in 1547, scarcely any were suppressed by the Chantries Act, and sixty-eight new schools had been founded by 1603, giving a total of over a hundred schools in the county at the opening of the seventeenth century. In all there was 'a refoundation or foundation by letters patent in twenty-three English counties (six having more than one newly appointed school). In six other counties schools were augmented or re-endowed by other means.' In Sussex and Gloucestershire, the four main schools fell outside the Act, as did Eton and Winchester. In Oxford, Magdalen College School was retained, although with slightly altered status. In Durham and Cumberland, cathedral schools already existed and were undisturbed. In Derbyshire, a grammar school was set up in Mary's reign from plans drawn up under Edward. The only counties unaffected at Edward's death were Huntingdonshire, Leicestershire, Rutland and Westmorland.[1]

The salient fact about these decisions was the overall control of the state in promoting what in effect was an extensive reorganisation of education on a national scale. The schools were conceived as units of an educational system under secular control serving a protestant nation, and as such played a decisive part in confirming and strengthening the religious changes in the country. Prayers and Bible reading were in English, and the text books used confirmed the spread of Erasmian and humanist ideas. Unfortunately the more humane methods of teaching advocated by Erasmus, Cheke and Ascham (whose treatise *The Schoolmaster* appeared posthumously in 1570) were not assimilated, and apart from exceptional instances only rarely applied, until reinforced in the present century by the theories of modern psychology.

State policy and private charity

It has been argued with some justice that after the initial re-organisation and expansion of the Edwardian period, the impetus towards educational reform died, and a great opportunity was lost. 'Renaissance England had within it the seeds of a truly explosive expansion of grammar school education both in provision and in content and method. Instead the sovereigns of the period faced with religious atomism, political danger and economic dislocation saw the schools as an important instrument with which to maintain public order and achieve political and religious conformity. Instead of acting as breeding

[1] J. Simon, *Education and Society,* p239.

grounds of humanist ideas, a distinct possibility at the beginning of the period, the grammar schools became instruments of national policy, a means of strengthening the state against religious innovation.'[1]

The difficulty lies in the interpretation of the word 'State'. Initially this was the Tudor conciliar administration, supervising refoundations and endowments in the counties through the Court of Augmentations, controlling the content of education by decree, and licensing schoolmasters through the bishops. But in the sixteenth century the government and the landed classes were in broad agreement over the ultimate end of education. The contrast lies in methods of control rather than in objectives. Before the state-controlled system could become effective (if indeed it could have done without extensive financial resources), it was permeated by the local interests and reinforced by the wealth of the laity. Country gentlemen sat on the commissions dissolving the chantries, they acted as school governors and they donated money for the foundation or extension of schools. To a certain extent this was the result of the Reformation itself. It produced a marked change in the pattern of giving. Before 1540 most of the really significant donations for education came from powerful clerics and were mainly for the foundation of colleges at the universities: after 1540 the money came from the laity and was mostly for the foundation of schools.[2] The actual amounts donated in terms of figures for ten representative counties are given by Professor Jordan in his *Philanthropy in England 1480–1660*, but the conclusions he draws from them are invalidated since he failed to adjust the value of the donations to the rapid inflation of the sixteenth century. When Jordan's figures are adjusted to the Phelps-Brown cost of living index and considered in terms of real value, the total amount donated to all charities in the sixteenth century is seen to have fallen steadily in comparison with the preceding period, and while the seventeenth century undoubtedly saw an increase in private charity under the stimulus of the puritan ethic, it was less marked than he assumed. What is clear is that there was a swing away from purely religious donations to those with secular but more useful ends: church building and masses for the dead gave way to education and poor relief. The other interesting development arising directly out of the diversion of bequests from the permanent institution of the Church to secular and possibly transient charitable objectives was the evolution of the legal device of the charitable trust. This was so successful that of the money donated to secular charity in the areas examined by Professor Jordan, 92 per cent is still being used for its original purpose.[3]

[1] K. Charlton, *Education in Renaissance England, Studies in Social History,* ed. Harold Perkin, Routledge and Kegan Paul 1965, p130.
[2] The direct influence of industrial magnates like Lord Nuffield on modern educational systems and in creating opportunities forms an interesting modern parallel.
[3] W. K. Jordan, *Philanthropy in England,* pp124–6.

The motives of the merchant and landed classes whose wealth helped to transform society, were in many ways similar to those of the government: the indoctrination of the protestant ethic, and the alleviation of poverty and idleness with its threat of social disorder by providing education and training for the young and almshouses for the old. In addition lack of adequate educational facilities for their own class, once the need for education became accepted, made an expansion of the whole educational system necessary. It was self-interested altruism, and as the century progressed the control and direction of the system was dominated by the landed classes to an increasing extent and at no time became a state monopoly. Yet the means of royal control over higher education were extensive and were used consistently throughout the sixteenth century. Direct control was exercised periodically by commissioners and the practice of visitation. In 1549, new statutes which had been drawn up by the Privy Council, were presented to both Universities and radical changes in the curriculum, which even listed the texts to be studied, were introduced at the same time. The colleges themselves provided a means of greater supervision. They were 'the educational equivalent of the centralising institutions which formed the basis of Tudor monarchy.'[1] It is significant that the Tudor period saw the evolution of the college and the decline of the hall of residence. Once the importance of royal control over education was realised, interference in college appointments became commonplace.[2] The fact that it was difficult to dislodge a deviant fellow or head of college merely served to intensify the government's determination to control appointments. The spread of puritanism and Ramism in the early years of Elizabeth's reign led to intervention in her later years to check it. The chancellors of both universities were always directly connected with the court. Finally in its control of the printing press the government had a weapon for supervising both the content of education and the formation of opinions.

In contrast to the development of local grammar schools where the greatest beneficiaries were the sons of the local gentry and tradesmen, London provides a clear example of the diffuse and comprehensive purpose of lay charity at this period, and Edward's reign saw an interesting experiment in a complete scheme of poor relief, which included as an integral part the foundation of a school. The plan was initiated in 1550 by a group of men in the Common Council (who significantly enough had been associated with Thomas Cromwell's reforming policies of the 1530s). The leading figures were Thomas Offley who had been one of Lily's original pupils at St. Pauls and who was now Master of the Merchant Taylors Company, William Laxton, Master of the Grocers, Rowland Hill from the Mercers, John Gresham and William

[1]H. Kearney, *Scholars and Gentlemen*, p22.
[2]For Elizabeth's direct interference in college appointments see H. Kearney, *Scholars and Gentlemen*, p79.

Harper, treasurers of St. Bartholomew's Hospital, and Richard Grafton, who had been the King's printer. A census was carried out in the city, and the population divided into categories which included a division of the poor into sick, vagabonds, and children. The sick were taken into St. Thomas' and St. Bartholomew's Hospitals. Vagabonds were to be rehabilitated and trained in the old palace of Bridewell. After 1556 this included several workshops for teaching apprentices, and after 1563 these were opened to the children of poor freemen as well as the destitute. The children were provided for by a school at Greyfriars which became known as Christ's Hospital. In 1552 it took in 350 poor children from the streets and city parishes. They were supplied with 500 feather beds and 500 pads of straw to lay under the feather beds and as many blankets and 1000 pairs of sheets. Tuition was provided by writing and music masters and two petty teachers. The money for the foundation was collected from charitable donations within the city.[1] This comprehensive scheme in London became a model for similar schemes elsewhere, and is an early instance of the whole problem of poverty tackled at ground level; Dr. Simon has similar examples of the foundation of schools in response to the demand for schooling to at least elementary level from the poorer sections of the community particularly in urban areas such as Southwark where both St. Saviour's and St. Olave's were founded in 1562 with this end in view.[2]

The process continued: Elizabeth's reign saw some important individual foundations. Sir Walter Mildmay's puritan college of Emmanuel at Cambridge for example, or Richard Rich's establishment of a school at Felsted, characteristically endowed from lands given to found a chantry in an excess of piety under Mary. Although Professor Jordan's estimate of one school for every 4,400 inhabitants has rightly been queried by Dr. Simon, who cannot accept that by 1660 there was a school 'within the reach of any poor and able boy who thirsted for knowledge and aspired to escape the grip of poverty', the undoubted expansion of education by local and private enterprise in the mid-Tudor period acted as a template for future generations who extended the method but did not alter it.[3]

Education for administration

State policy and the private charity of the wealthy classes were important factors in this marked increase in educational facilities, but equally significant was the complete reversal of the attitude of the gentry towards learning as the ideas and values of the humanists took hold. Once it became obvious that

[1] J. Simon, *Education and Society*, p240 and pp283-4.
[2] J. Simon, *Education and Society*, p313.
[3] J. Simon, *Education and Society*, p398; W. K. Jordan, *The Charities of Rural England*, p165.

learning and education was a necessary qualification for high office in the administration and at Court, and the landowning classes realised that 'they could not hope to maintain their position by adhering stubbornly to a social code that no longer met the needs of the state, with some exceptions they adapted themselves to the requirements of the age shedding antiquated notions and accepting humanistic ideas.'[1] The ensuing increase in the number of gentry entering the grammar schools, Inns of Court, and Universities, would in itself have forced an expansion irrespective of the Chantries Act or the re-orientation of lay charity, in the same way as similar pressure on places in the House of Commons resulted in the enfranchisement of boroughs. There was to a certain extent a virtual 'take over' of the 'public' and grammar school system by the landed classes, so that the gentry could qualify for inclusion in central and local government. Charitable foundations, which in the middle ages had been specifically endowed in order to train younger sons and poor children for the church, found themselves re-orientated towards the production of gentle-men trained for the service of their own class and the state.

The process had begun before the death of Henry VIII and is clearly illustrated in the well-known incident involving Cranmer and the new school at Canterbury. The local commissioners at the time of the Dissolution wanted the school to be restricted to the sons of gentlemen for 'It is meet for the ploughman's son to go to the plough and the artificer's son to apply the trade of his parents' vocation, and gentlemen's children are meet to have knowledge of government and rule in the commonwealth.' Cranmer had to fight for a compromise on this issue, but in the end it was agreed that 'if the gentleman's son be apt let him be admitted, if not apt, let the poor man's child being apt enter his room'. It is clear that by the middle of the century the social back-ground of the leading schools was undergoing a marked change, and that by the end of the century this had spread to the Universities.

Eton and Winchester both illustrate the process. They were exempted from the Chantries Act and received special treatment. They were visited by special commissioners and were permitted to retain their endowed lands, but freed from the religious obligations which went with them. The curriculum was 'reformed', the works of Erasmus and the New Testament in English and Latin were to be studied and copies of the Bible made available to scholars. The Bible in English was to be read 'distinctly and apertly at dinner and supper' and all graces and prayers to be said in English. The end result was both the indoctrination of the protestant ethic and the rise of the vernacular.[2] The Eton College registers are incomplete for the sixteenth century, but even from fragmentary evidence it is clear that the period saw a change both in the class of origin of the boys at the school, and the careers they eventually followed.

[1]F. Caspari, *Humanism and the Social Order*, p138.
[2]J. Simon, *Education and Society*, p265.

In his examination of the registers, Professor Hexter has illustrated the process by an investigation of boys whose name began with C. Between 1444 and 1500 about three-quarters of these boys followed the accepted formula of a career in the church – but from 1520 onwards the pattern began to change, and out of a total of twenty-eight C's who followed secular careers, twenty-six are found after 1520. 'A dozen go on to the Inns of Court, five are Members of Parliament, two are Soldiers, three become Knights and one a peer. The social complexion of Eton had begun to change.'[1] If the register is examined to see how many boys became Members of Parliament the picture is confirmed. There is only one Etonian in the House of Commons between 1444 and 1500, and less than ten between 1444 and 1540, but during Elizabeth's reign there were forty future M.P.'s at the school, and their family backgrounds are entirely from the upper social classes. 'Eighteen are sons of Knights or of peers, six sons of Knights' or peers' daughters. Twenty become Knights themselves, six become peers, and a considerable number marry daughters of Knights or peers.' Only six of the forty had no obvious connection with the landed gentry and these included a Temple, a Hampden and the son of the Archbishop of York.[2] At Winchester a similar process was taking place, and had the amusing result of a sharp increase in the number of applications for free admissions by gentlemen's sons as 'Kin of the Founder.' In his original endowment William of Wykeham had made provision that his relations should be admitted without hindrance; what he did not foresee was that his aunt would have 'thirteen extremely philoprogenitive daughters, whose sequelae two centuries later knew a good thing when they saw one . . . Only the judgement of a commission headed by the Lord Chancellor, recommending that but ten of the founders' kin be allowed at one time . . . prevented Wykeham's gentleborn descendants from taking over the school altogether.'[3] The increase in fee-paying pupils which was a corollary of this new demand began a period of prosperity for both schools. At Eton this was increased even further by the appointment of Sir Thomas Smith as Provost in 1548. His intelligent and conscientious control of the college finances, particularly his introduction of a new form of leasehold of college property, proved invaluable in a period of rising prices.[4] Smith later applied the same principles at Cambridge with equally beneficial results.

There were therefore three parallel streams in school education in the sixteenth century, running at different rates and with different volumes. At the top, with a few notable exceptions such as Fulke Greville and Philip Sidney (who were both educated at Shrewsbury), the aristocracy were either

[1]J. H. Hexter, 'Education of the Aristocracy in the Renaissance', *Reappraisals in History*, Longmans 1961, p51.
[2]J. H. Hexter, *Reappraisals in History*, p52.
[3]J. H. Hexter, *Reappraisals in History*, p53.
[4]M. Dewar, *Sir Thomas Smith: an Intellectual in Office*, Athlone Press 1964, pp69-70.

educated at home or at the house of some important man by private tutors. The Mountjoys belong to this group, so do Burghley's aristocratic wards, and the small group of specially selected well-born companions educated with Edward VI. For women, this was virtually the only form of academic education possible, and a surprisingly large number of women were literate, and a few were learned. The daughters and women in the household of Sir Thomas More, Lady Jane Grey, Catherine of Suffolk, and the four formidable daughters of Sir Antony Cooke, were all highly accomplished by any intellectual standards. The second stream which grew steadily in volume until it began to siphon off water from the first, was the increasing number of gentlemen's sons who sought education at one of the school foundations. Strictly speaking a school was only a 'grammar' school if it taught Latin and Greek and prepared pupils for admission to the University. These schools educated the bulk of the Tudor 'official' class, men like Burghley, Sir Thomas Smith, Sir William Petre and Sir Walter Mildmay, and to them as the century progressed the gentry flocked in increasing numbers, so much so that to meet the demand the private school began to appear by the seventeenth century.[1] The third stream was the village school, teaching basic literacy to the poor. These schools taught the rudiments of learning but did not attempt to go beyond them. Exact estimates of literacy are difficult to come by, and certainly varied from area to area and with the capacity and energy of the local incumbent or hired schoolmaster. Sir Thomas More, familiar with the urban area of London, estimated that nearly half the population was literate in the early sixteenth century. The spread of the Bible in the vernacular gave an added incentive to read throughout all sections of society. But in many instances particularly in rural areas and the North it can only have been very rudimentary.[2] A certain amount of evidence for the early seventeenth century is given by Mr. Stone from the proceedings of the Middlesex justices in 1612-1614. Of 204 men sentenced to death during this period, 95 or 47 per cent successfully pleaded literacy and were thus able to secure 'benefit of clergy', 'to a petty thief the capacity to read made all the difference between death by slow strangulation and a scarred thumb. "The said Paul reads, to be branded; the said William does not read, to be hanged".' What is self evident is that literacy increased with social status. At Limpsfield in 1642 20 per cent of the servants, but 62 per cent of the Householders were able to sign their names to the Protestation of loyalty ordered by Parliament.[3] It is therefore necessary to remember the limitations of the third and lowest stream when considering the educational achievements of the sixteenth century. For

[1] L. Stone, 'The Educational Revolution in England, 1540-1640', *Past and Present*, No. 28, 1964, p46.
[2] For examples see L. Stone, *Past and Present*, No. 28, p47; for an interesting case of rural literacy see A. G. Dickens, *The English Reformation*, p191.
[3] L. Stone, *Past and Present*, No. 28, pp43-4.

a large section of the population, although technically a school was available, it only offered a rudimentary education, and although opportunities still existed for able children of humble origins to reach the grammar schools and even the Universities, the flood of the gentry seeking enlightenment threatened to engulf even these.

In the two Universities the effect of the Chantries Act and the visitations which followed it, was to accelerate both the evolution of the modern college system, and the adoption of an improved and more modern curriculum. But the catalyst was still the increase in the pressure for places from the gentry. It was as great on the Universities as it was on the grammar schools. The Reformation may have closed many opportunities for advancement within the church, but it expanded them within the state. The 1540s saw the education at Cambridge of a remarkable number of Elizabethan statesmen. The influx of nobility and gentry, many of them very young and accompanied by tutors and servants (the register of Caius in 1564 recorded the admission of one under-graduate aged 9) created new problems which demanded new solutions. The result was the steady decline in the 'halls' of residence. There were only eight in Oxford in 1550 and by 1600 there were none; and the development of the college as a self-sufficient teaching institution with a system of resident Fellows whose main duty was to teach. The heads of colleges became more powerful both within their own foundations, and also within the University. The Universities became in effect federations of autonomous colleges each with its own internal government and teaching facilities and represented at University level by the Master and Senior Fellows. At Cambridge the statutes of 1549 laid down that the officials of the University, the Vice-Chancellor, the Proctors and Taxors, were to be elected by the regents (the resident teaching fellows), and the Chancellor (theoretically) by the whole body of graduates. The Marian visitation of 1557 further strengthened the power of the Senior Fellows. The doctors of all faculties and the bachelors of divinity, now chose two names for the position of Vice-Chancellor, and the regents then elected one. Finally under Elizabeth, the choice of candidates was limited to the heads of colleges, although the regents could still choose one of the two. In 1571, an Act was passed 'incorporating' both Universities, and thus securing them what was virtual independent status.[1]

Although the medieval system of teaching and disputations was still retained, with the increase in book learning, and the growing strength of the college system, the tutorial within the college became part of the accepted method of instruction. Even the establishment of Regius Professorships failed to reverse the trend. The whole development is seen most clearly in the statutes of Trinity College Cambridge which were drawn up in 1549. They were modelled on those of St. John's but in the Trinity Statutes the duty of teaching was

[1] J. Simon, *Education and Society*, p318.

placed on college fellows, who were required not only to lecture in hall, but also to tutor the students.

The visitation of the Universities in the same year reinforced the new movement. The curriculum was to be revised and the elementary teaching of grammar abolished. All new entrants were therefore required to have a basic knowledge of Latin. The Arts course now included the study of some science (based on classical texts) so that an undergraduate acquired some knowledge of cosmography, astronomy, and mathematics. But except for Tunstall's new arithmetic, the majority of the books studied were medieval and to a large degree 'scholastic'. Aristotle rather than Plato was the dominant philosophical influence, and both Universities were slow to absorb new ideas. As late as the second decade of the seventeenth century when the Savile chair of astronomy was set up at Oxford, Ptolemy was taught alongside Copernicus as a viable alternative. The attempts of the great Parisian teacher, Peter Ramus, to modify the rigid outlook of the philosophers had relatively little success in this country although his ideas made some headway at Cambridge in the later years of the century particularly through the teaching of Lawrence Chaderton and Gabriel Harvey (at Christ's, and later at Emmanuel and Pembroke). The advanced theories of a new type of education, put forward by Francis Bacon and Humphrey Gilbert, had a theoretical but not a practical influence. The real 'Renaissance' at Oxford was under the Commonwealth when Wilkins was at Wadham and Wren and Hooke in residence. It was a brief one, and was followed by a slow ossification until modern times.

One project of Edwardian reform failed at Cambridge. The suggestion that Trinity Hall and Clare Hall should be dissolved and their endowments used for a new college devoted to the study of civil law, foundered on the combined objections of the common lawyers and the clergy. The visitors' attempts at rationalisation were more successful at Oxford: New College was ordered to concentrate on divinity and All Souls on law, but there is little evidence that any real attempt was made to implement these decisions.

The change in social background of those attending the Universities was a gradual but steady process. Already by the end of the reign of Henry VIII some of the sons of the nobility were going to the University for at least part of their education. In the late 1540s Cambridge had studying at St. John's, the son and heir of Lord Wentworth, Henry and Charles Brandon – the two sons of the Duke of Suffolk, John Manners second son of the Earl of Rutland and his brother, and Thomas Sackville the only son of Sir Richard; Queens had Henry Hastings son of the Earl of Huntingdon, Henry Fitzalan son of the Earl of Arundel, John Lord Lumley, and Thomas Howard son of the Earl of Surrey; the heir of Lord Sheffield, and Lord Willoughby were also at the University. The general trend is clear although the statistics for Oxford and Cambridge are particularly hard to interpret. There is no Oxford matriculation register before the 1550s and no complete one until the end of the seventeenth century, and a factor which must be allowed for in any evaluation of the evidence is that many of the undergraduates from the higher social groups attended the University for a comparatively short time, and did not take a degree having no financial incentive to do so. Mr. Stone suggests a figure of between 20 per cent and 30 per cent as a minimum for the number of undergraduates who failed to take degrees during the period.[1] Nevertheless such registers as do exist show a steady increase in the numbers of gentry and above attending Oxford and Cambridge for varying periods of time. During the reigns of Edward and Mary, although the process had begun, it had not yet reached flood proportions. The register of Gonville and Caius which starts in 1560, reveals that out of the first hundred names, fifty-nine were described as 'mediocris fortunae', twelve as 'esquire', seventeen as 'gentlemen', eight as the 'sons of merchants', and there was one son of a peer, one of a knight, and two from the professional classes.[2] The figures at Oxford are similar. 'By the third quarter of the century, the squirearchy has elbowed its way into Oxford in force. For every five men matriculating there as "filii plebei", three describe themselves as "gentlemen's sons". At the beginning of the seventeenth century the proportion is six gentlemen to five plebeians.'[3] Corroborative evidence is provided by Sir John Neale's analysis of the social background of the Elizabethan House of Commons, which shows a decisive increase in the members with higher education in the last quarter of the century amounting to 'an invasion of the Universities and the Inns of Court on a large scale'. By 1593 nearly a quarter of the House, 106 members, had both legal and University training, and 252 members (nearly half the house) had some form of higher education.[4] The problem lies in the depth of the education so acquired. In the 1584 Parliament only 12 per cent had actually taken degrees, in 1593 only 13 per cent of the total. Professor Hexter is probably nearer the truth when he suggests that the members of Parliament in the Elizabethan period had been exposed to some sort of higher education without specifying to what extent. Dr. Charlton suggests that there is little real evidence that 'while they were up at the University the sons of gentlemen who were later to serve the State displayed any great seriousness of purpose. Indeed there is evidence to show that the University authorities were on occasion in doubt as to whether they should be treated as bona fide students or not'.[5] By Elizabeth's reign it was said that:

most of them study little other than histories, tables, dice and trifles. . . Besides this, being for the most part either gentlemen or rich men's sons they

[1]L. Stone, *Past and Present*, No. 28, p47.
[2]K. Charlton, *Education in Renaissance England*, p136.
[3]J. H. Hexter, *Reappraisals in History*, p54.
[4]J. Neale, *The Elizabethan House of Commons*, London 1949, p302.
[5]K. Charlton, *Education in Renaissance England*, p139.

oft bring the university into much slander. For standing upon their reput-tion and liberty, they ruffle and roist it out, exceeding in apparel and hunting riotous company . . . and for excuse when they are charged with breach of one good order think it sufficient to say they be gentlemen which grieveth many not a little.[1]

He also points out that even had students wished to learn, the authors studied and the methods of teaching used were still so medieval that they were more likely to confirm out of date ideas and methods than to expand or enliven the minds of students. Aristotle and Cicero were still the foundations of the system, and the middle of the sixteenth century saw a decline in the study of Greek and Hebrew, which was tantamount to a drying up of the 'humanist' impulse at its source and a slow return to conservatism of outlook: 'despite Erasmus' efforts, despite Fox's foundation of what was to be England's *collegium trilingue*, despite the endowment of a Regius Professorship in Greek, no important school of Greek studies developed in the Universities, the seeds of a possible revolution . . . in learning . . . were sown in the early years of the century but very few of them germinated. Most lay dormant in an inhospitable soil.'[2]

If the Universities left something to be desired as advanced centres of cultivated learning for the wealthy laity, they still continued their purpose of educating the next generation of clerics. Here the Edwardian period is again of some interest, for not only were the important divines of the next generation such as Parker, Whitgift, Grindal, and Cartwright, either Fellows or under-graduates, but they were influenced by the influx of distinguished theologians from abroad whom Cranmer encouraged to come to England as part of govern-ment policy. Peter Martyr became Regius Professor of Divinity at Oxford, Martin Bucer at Cambridge, where he was joined by the Hebrew scholar Paul Fagius. In spite of the fact that both Fagius and Bucer died soon after their appointments, Cambridge at this time became a centre of protestant theology and anticipated in this field its later pre-eminence under Elizabeth.

If, in conclusion, the evidence provided by the Edwardian reforms and their aftermath is combined with the available statistics for University intake and the known pattern of charitable bequests, two major facts become apparent. There was a virtual takeover of the higher system of education by the wealthier classes, so that 'public' schools originally founded to train poor scholars for the church were transformed into institutions for training the sons of gentry to take their place in a secular society. But the extension of educational facilities by charitable bequests also opened up new opportunities for the less wealthy, who through local schools and scholarships could still obtain places at the Universities.

[1]William Harrison's *Descriptions of England*. ed F. J. Furnival, New Shakespeare Society Series VI, pt. 1, 1877, quoted K. Charlton, *Education in Renaissance England*, p144.
[2]K. Charlton, *Education in Renaissance England*, p159-160.

Mr. Stone provides a clear and useful summary of one aspect of the situation: 'in the middle years of the sixteenth century the propertied classes began demanding University education for their children, and seized upon the college system as convenient for their purpose . . . The result was a flow of charitable gifts to increase the capital assets and buildings of the colleges and a sharp rise in the emoluments of dons, who now made a comfortable living by the supervision of these well-heeled pupils.' But this is not the whole picture, although it is true that the sons of the rich were taking over places at schools and scholarships at the Universities designed originally for the poor (figures for the early seventeenth century show that nearly half the scholarships at Wadham Oxford and Caius Cambridge were held by sons of gentry and above), men of humble social origins were able to retain a proportion of the available places. On the eve of the Civil War at St. John's Cambridge, while one third of the intake were gentlemen, one sixth were sons of citizens and shop keepers. Charitable bequests had created 500 new scholarships and as a result, 'the poor were now enjoying a substantially smaller share of a very much larger cake and were better off in consequence'. Once at the University students from poorer families could earn their way by acting as sizars or servants to the Fellows or their wealthier colleagues. 'It was the influx of the sons of wealthy landowners which made possible the parallel increase in the number of poor students . . . The argument about what class was profiting from the growth in higher education is thus largely a meaningless one. So great was the boom – much greater than has hitherto been recognised – that all classes above a certain level took part.' The only section excluded was the very poor where economic and social factors militated too strongly against their being able to profit from the increased opportunities.[1]

In Dr. Charlton's view, although the social spectrum in higher education continued to be fairly broad, the sixteenth century was the period when 'the Universities ceased to be the true *community* of scholars which had been their chief characteristic in the middle ages, and it is naive to claim that "Yeoman's sons and earl's sons, merchant's sons and the heirs of the landed gentry were all bred together in learning".' The different social strata may have lived together within a college, but there is little evidence that they mixed, and much that they did not. Nor did education itself lead to social mobility. In the sixteenth century, social status was founded primarily on landed wealth. Acquired education had become by the end of the century a necessary adjunct, but education alone was not sufficient. The only function of the Universities here to anyone wishing to rise in the social scale was to further connection and patronage.[2] When Sir Thomas Smith in the famous passage in *De Republica*

[1]For this argument see L. Stone, 'The Educational Revolution in England, 1540-1640', *Past and Present,* No. 28, pp65-8.
[2]K. Charlton, *Education in Renaissance England,* p149.

Anglorum described the expanding conception of the gentry, he is careful to add the essential factor of economic wealth to the necessary qualifications of learning. 'As for gentlemen', he wrote, 'they be made good cheape in England. For whosoever studieth the lawes of the realme, who studieth in the Universities, who professeth the liberal sciences, and to be shorte, who can live idly and without manual labour, and will bear the port and charge and countenaunce of a gentleman . . . a King of Heralds shall give him for money, armes newly made and invented, the title whereof shall pretende to be found by the sayd Herald in perusing and viewing olde registers . . .'. Smith knew what he was talking about, for the pedigrees of a large number of highly placed Tudor officials including Cecil and Mildmay are now known to be entirely fictitious. After Paget's temporary fall from grace in 1550, one could not be too careful.

The real gain from the Edwardian expansion in the schools and Universities was the fact that within the oligarchical structure of society there was at least a modicum of learning and culture. Professor Hexter has noted that: 'Even in remote and backward Cornwall at least four of the eight gentlemen in the commission [Justices of the Peace] during Sir Walter Ralegh's lieutenancy were university educated . . . Bookish learning had gone with them into the shires and was widely scattered among the men who ruled the countryside.'[1]

Reformation and the destruction of books

In contrast with the Edwardian Acts concerning the Chantries and Universities, the Act of 1550 against Superstitious Books is usually regarded as largely destructive. In Fuller's words, it was 'the last dish of the last course, after Chantries, as after cheese, nothing to be expected'. It was the period when according to Aubrey, 'manuscripts flew about like butterflies', and Fuller mourned their loss in a famous passage in his *Church History*:

> What beautiful Bibles, rare Fathers, subtle Schoolmen, useful Historians – ancient, middle, modern; what painful comments were here among them! What monuments of mathematics all massacred together; seeing every book with a cross was condemned for Popish; with circles; for conjuring. Yea, I may say that the holy divinity was profaned, Physic hurt and a trespass, yea a riot, committed in Law itself.[2]

Stow in his *Survey* recounts how the Duke of Somerset sent for the whole of the great library of the Guildhall, collected since the bequests of Richard Whittington and William Burie: the books filled three barrow loads but only

[1] J. H. Hexter, *Reappraisals in History*, p56.
[2] Quoted Hope Mirrlees, *A Fly in Amber, a Biography of Sir Robert Cotton*, Faber and Faber, 1962, p57.

nineteen volumes have yet been traced.[1] Out of the Eton College library, which in 1535 contained 500 books, only 62 are now extant. Duke Humphrey's Library at Oxford was so depleted that the empty shelves were ultimately sold for firewood. It cannot therefore be denied that there is considerable contemporary evidence for the dislocation if not the destruction of books and records in sixteenth century England. The traditional view is that of the Cambridge scholar M. R. James: 'What does it all mean? Who is responsible for the wholesale destruction which the facts imply? I am afraid the answer is all too clear. We have to thank the commissioners appointed under Edward VI to reform the Universities.'[2] Raymond Irwin, in his study of *The English Library*, adds the forces of change to religious iconoclasm: 'The impact of humanism on English thought, together with the coming of the printed book meant inevitably that the old libraries seemed useless and out-of-date'. It was this fatal alliance of contempt of the old learning and religious prejudice that caused such apparently wholesale destruction, hence he concludes, 'the enemies of scholasticism combining with the enemies of the old faith were too powerful and the end was violent and indiscriminate'[3] It was no accident that the bonfire of books in Oxford was called 'Scotus' Funeral'.

There are however indications that this cataclysmic view must be revised. It has now been established that the effects of the Reformation on institutional libraries varied both with the locality and the type of book; and that it was supplemented and in the end counteracted by other factors. At the time of the Dissolution there were three main types of monastic records: the muniments and legal documents, (cartularies, rentals, inventories, mortuary rolls, and letterbooks), which passed initially to the Court of Augmentations, and then to the purchasers of the lands; the service books such as missals, libraries, and choral books; and finally the library proper. The books obviously most at risk during the period of religious change were the service books. It is probable that about a quarter of a million of these were destroyed and replaced by Edwardian or Elizabethan Prayer Books. The process began even earlier: when Anne Boleyn lectured the nuns of Syon on their superstitious practices, she presented them with a set of English Primers to replace their existing Latin ones, 'to exercise themselves withal, that they might both understand what they do pray for, and thereby be stirred to more devotion'.[4] Very little

---

[1]N. R. Ker, *Medieval Libraries of Great Britain. A List of Surviving Books*, Royal Historical Society, 2nd edition 1964, p126. In 1968 the Guildhall received five lorry loads of documents weighing several tons, which comprise the entire records of Christ's Hospital. They form a partial and appropriate recompense.
[2]Quoted by R. W. Hunt, 'Medieval inventories of Clare College Library', *Cambridge Bibliographical Journal*, 1950.
[3]Raymond Irwin, *The English Library*, Allen and Unwin 1961, p127.
[4]Quoted by C. C. Butterworth, *The English Primers, 1529-1545*, University of Pennsylvania Press 1953, p55.

medieval church music now exists for similar reasons.[1] The libraries themselves are an entirely different matter. There is no proof that the state was
directly responsible for the loss or destruction of books on a large scale. The
monastic libraries were dispersed through government indifference rather than
by deliberate intention. Henry VIII had three libraries at Westminster,
Greenwich and Hampton Court, and just before the Dissolution in 1535 the
King sent the antiquarian John Leland to examine and report on the monastic
libraries. The royal libraries increased from 910 books in 1542 to 1,450 by the
end of the reign: but it has been noted that the Visitation Articles contain no
mention of books and that no definite action to preserve them was taken by the
government.[2] Leland found that some of the libraries were already being
plundered. He wrote to Cromwell:

> it would be a great profit to students and honour to this realm; [if an attempt
> could be made to save the books, for] now the Germans perceiving . . . our
> neglegience, do send young scholars hither, that spoileth them, and cutteth
> them out of the libraries returning home and putting them abroad as monu-
> ments to their own country.[3]

The situation was much worse when the libraries had fallen into private hands;
when John Bale described Leland's *Labouryouse Journey* in 1549 he recounted
how:

> A great nombre of them whych purchased also those superstycyouse man-
> syons, reserved of those librarye bokes some to serve theyr iakes, some to
> scour theyr cantlestykes, and some to rubbe theyr bootes. Some they solde
> to the grossers and sope sellers, and some they sent over see to . . . boke-
> binders, not in small nombre, but in whole shyppes full, to the wonderynge
> of foren nacyones . . . yea what maye brynge our realm to more shame and
> rebuke than to have it noysed abroade that we are despysers of lernynge?[4]

A number of fragments of known manuscripts have in fact turned up in the
bindings and end papers of later works.

Bale's lamentations were not entirely justified, and Leland's lists must be used
with caution. Dr. Wright has shown that manuscripts were undoubtedly hidden
by their owners in the 1530s; Leland records only 6 Anglo-Saxon books, a small
proportion of those now known to have existed in the monastic libraries of the
time. He missed, for example, the *Exeter Book*, several manuscripts of the *Anglo-
Saxon Chronicle*, An Anglo-Saxon manuscript of Bede at Worcester, Alfred's

[1]For this analysis of monastic records, see C. E. Wright, 'The dispersal of the monastic
libraries and the beginnings of Anglo-Saxon studies. Matthew Parker and his circle. A
preliminary survey', *Cambridge Bibliographical Journal*, Vol, I, Part III, 1951.
[2]May McKisack, *Medieval History in the Tudor Age*, Clarendon Press 1971, p3.
[3]Quoted by C. E. Wright, 'The dispersal of the monastic libraries', p210.
[4]C. E. Wright, 'The dispersal of the monastic libraries', p210.

translation of *Gregory's Pastoral Care,* the *Abingdon Chronicle* and some early books of Homilies and a Prayer Book[1]. The detailed research of Dr. N. R. Ker and his colleagues at the Bodleian Library has identified the whereabouts of approximately 6000 books from the monasteries of England and Scotland, and there are probably more extant. How great a proportion of the total numbers this represents it is difficult to say. Professor Sears Jayne suggests a possible figure of at least 6000 books dislocated, most of them manuscripts, from the 800 English houses dissolved by Henry, but this (even though it does not include the Scottish houses and the chantries) would seem to be on the low side. Dr. Simon estimates that the libraries of Christ Church Canterbury, and of Bury, each had about 2,000 volumes at the beginning of the sixteenth century,[2] nevertheless Dr. Ker's figures are impressive enough.[3] Dr. Ker has pointed out that the survival of libraries or of individual books is largely a matter of chance: 'By the fallacious test of surviving books fourteen libraries appear vastly more important than all the others. They are the libraries of the great Benedictine houses at Bury, Christ Church and St. Augustine's Canterbury, Durham, Norwich, Reading, Rochester, St Alban's, and Worcester, of the secular cathedrals of Exeter, Hereford, Lincoln and Salisbury, and of the comparatively unimportant Augustinian priory of Lanthony in the suburbs of Gloucester.' Dr. Ker lists over 550 surviving books from Durham, over 350 from Worcester, nearly 300 from Christ Church Canterbury, 250 from Bury and St. Augustine's, and over 200 from Salisbury, and over 100 each from the other seven libraries. In contrast there are only 92 surviving manuscripts from the entire monastic libraries of Scotland, although there are some early printed books; and there are over four hundred houses in England which have only between 1 and 10 identifiable books each. These 'include all the nunneries, all the Cluniac, Premonstratensian, and Gilbertine houses and all the convents of the Trinitarian and Austin friars which occur in the list at all.' Syon, which in 1526 had 1,421 books, is only represented by 90.[4] For some reason, only a small proportion of the great libraries in the West Country, such as that at Wells, has survived. Of the educational institutions, Eton with 62, and Winchester with 76, were relatively fortunate, as were some of the libraries at Oxford and Cambridge. But the overall picture is more gloomy. Dr. R. Hunt has given the numbers of the known manuscripts still surviving in their original libraries at Cambridge: the University Library has only 22 out of a medieval library of 330 volumes, Corpus 3 out of 75, Queen's only 1, King's College 3 out of 176, Trinity Hall

[1] C. E. Wright, 'The dispersal of the monastic libraries', p217.
[2] J. Simon, *Education and Society,* p56.
[3] For the Sears Jayne estimate see Sears Jayne, *Library Catalogues of the English Renaissance,* University of California Press 1956, p41. Professor Jayne only had access to the first edition of N. R. Ker's book. For more recent figures see N. R. Ker. ed. *Medieval Libraries of Great Britain. List of surviving Books,* Royal Historical Society, 1964.
[4] Sears Jayne, *Library Catalogues,* p83; N. R. Ker, *Medieval Libraries,* pxi.

2, while St. Catharine's and Clare College (the last of which is known to have had an extensive library in the early sixteenth century) have not a single volume of their original books.[1]

The real cause of the loss of medieval books was not so much deliberate policy as simple neglect. Dr. Birley has drawn attention to this in the case of Eton College books; and the same conditions prevailed elsewhere. 'The visitors appointed by King Edward VI are blamed, commonly, for the spoliation of these libraries, but it is better to suppose that there are various reasons why, for example, very many of the books noticed in the college libraries by Bale in his collections compiled between 1547 and 1557 are not there now. Shelves became overcrowded and new printed books pushed out old manuscripts. Over a dozen Oxford college books found their way to Antwerp some time during the sixteenth century and are now in the Plantin-Moretus Museum there. The Exeter College copy of the *Life and Miracles of St. Thomas,* now Douai MS. 860, was rescued from "amonge a caos of caste books and waste papers" in the same century.'[2] In 1528 the University Library at Cambridge had between 500 and 600 volumes, yet in 1547 it was so depleted and so little used that the remaining books were moved to the 'Little Library' so that the 'Great Library' should be turned into a theological school; by 1556 the number of books was listed as 175.[3] The depletion of Duke Humphrey's Library at Oxford was probably due to similar causes. Another factor was the lack of official librarians early in the century, and the indisputable fact that scholars tended to borrow books and not return them. Roger Ascham for example is known to have taken a Greek manuscript given by Cuthbert Tunstall to the University Library, Cambridge, and not returned it. It is now in the Library of Trinity College. Ascham may have hidden it for safe keeping, but even so it strayed from its original home.[4] The problem seems to have continued into modern times, and it is possible to argue that at least as much has been lost since the sixteenth century as was destroyed during it. The book thief is no new phenomenon. Dr. Philip Gaskell has an amusing story of one Henry Justice, who was transported for seven years in 1736 for stealing books from the library of Trinity College, Cambridge, and the University Library. Yet he died a rich man in Rotterdam, leaving a collection of 7798 books and manuscripts to be sold by auction.[5] A similar case from the same period involved a Fellow of Trinity Hall who forged the keys of

[1]R. W. Hunt, 'Medieval Inventories of Clare College Library', *Cambridge Bibliographical Journal,* Vol. I, 1950, p105.
[2]N. R. Ker, *Medieval Libraries,* p xv.
[3]J. C. T. Oates, and H. L. Pink, 'Three sixteenth century catalogues of the University Library', *Cambridge Bibliographical Journal,* Vol. I, Part IV, 1952.
[4]J. C. T. Oates, and H. L. Pink, 'Three Catalogues', *Cambridge Bibliographical Journal,* Vol. I 1952.
[5]P. Gaskell, 'C. Henry Justice, a Cambridge Book Thief', *Cambridge Bibliographical Journal,* Vol. I, 1952.

the Librarians of St. John's, Trinity College, Trinity Hall, and the University Library, and removed books from all of them for a considerable period before he was discovered.[1] Thieves were not the only hazard. Libraries were moved, and books lost in the process: the Royal Library was moved seven times between 1707 and 1759. Until the importance was understood of keeping individual collections intact, duplicates were often sold as a matter of routine. The Lumley collection, which numbered 3000 volumes when it became part of the Royal Library in 1609, now only numbers 1350. Lumley himself gave 89 duplicates to the University Library Cambridge in 1598, of which only 34 now remain. He gave a similar bequest of 34 books to the Bodleian, but it now posseses only 6 identified as belonging to the Lumley collection. Fire has always been a serious danger. The Royal Library, easily the most important single collection in England, was twice damaged by fire, once in 1697, and more disastrously in 1731. The recent flood damage to books and manuscripts in Florence and Lisbon is a reminder that even today much can be lost from accidental or natural causes. In modern times the Sale Room is probably the greatest single agent in the dispersal or collection of sixteenth century books. Books sold at auction usually find their way into institutional libraries throughout the world, but some fall into private hands, in which case they may temporarily disappear, like those collected in the nineteenth century by Sir Thomas Phillipps: the Phillipps collection is only now coming again onto the market, and has already been found to contain some books, such as the part of the Caxton Ovid, previously considered lost.[2] Dr. Ker gives a list in an appendix of medieval books which have disappeared in recent times.[3]

In the sixteenth century the fate of the monastic libraries which passed into lay hands clearly varied with the ownership. Some suffered the fate described by Bale, others were dispersed at a later date, like that of Monks Bretton, which is known to have been in the possession of the last Prior in 1558, but which then simply disappeared, with the exception of two volumes traced by Dr. Ker, one in the British Museum, and the other in University College Oxford.[4]

Tudor collections

The situation was saved by the fact that at the same time that neglect and change were endangering the existence of the medieval libraries, the counter process of collection by private individuals had begun. Dr. Ker has shown that among Cromwell's visitors, Sir John Prise was collecting manuscripts where he could.

[1] Owen Chadwick, 'The Case of Philip Nicols', *Cambridge Bibliographical Journal*, 1953, p422.
[2] For information on the vicissitudes of the Royal Library and Lumley Collection see *The Lumley Library, The catalogue of 1609*, edited Sears Jayne and F. R. Johnson, Trustees of the British Museum 1956. For the Phillipps Collection, see A. N. L. Munby, *Phillipps Studies*, CUP 1951-1956, 6 vols.
[3] N. R. Ker, *Medieval Libraries*, pp403-404.
[4] N. R. Ker, *Medieval Libraries*, p131.

H.—4*

His library contained some important historical manuscripts from Bury, and he was one of the few people who saved books from the West of England. Sir John White, who purchased Southwick Priory in Hampshire, gave 8 books from the library to St. John's College Oxford. The Southwick Library was interesting in that it contained a 'legendary', a copy of a translation of Bede, a west Saxon genealogy and an illustrated life of St. Cuthbert, all in English. The first is now in Corpus Christi Cambridge, the others in the British Museum.

The great opportunity to form a royal library out of the displaced monastic books was lost by Henry VIII, but the idea was revived in the reign of Mary by the scholar and scientist Dr. John Dee. In 1556, Dee presented Mary with a treatise entitled *A Supplication to Queen Mary for the Recovery and Preservation of Ancient Writers and Monuments.* Dee produced detailed plans for the founding of a 'Library Royall' and urged the Queen to appoint a commission to examine the project. What Dee proposed in 1556 might well have revolutionised England's heritage. The plan came to nothing, partly from lack of perception on the part of the Queen, partly from lack of the requisite finance, and from the opposition of vested interests at Court. Sir Robert Cotton proposed a similar scheme to Queen Elizabeth with equal lack of success.

Collecting was therefore left to private individuals, and collections, like their owners, differ in character. Some are simply blocks of books and manuscripts from a single source gathered together by one man living in the vicinity. Books from the Yorkshire monasteries were common in the library of Sir Henry Savile (1568–1617) who lived near Halifax. William Smart of Ipswich bequeathed 100 manuscripts from Bury to Pembroke College Cambridge in 1599.[1]

Other collections were working libraries and are of specialist interest. They were often annotated by their owners, and therefore have a double value in showing the books actually available and used on a particular subject in the period during which they were collected, and the uses made of them by their owner. John Stow for example covered his copy of *The Great Chronicle of London* with marginalia. Men with antiquarian interests collected what they could from monastic records and books. In fact a whole intellectual movement was started by the dispersal of so much first hand material, a movement which culminated in the work of Stow, Camden and Agarde, and which led to the formation of the Society of Antiquaries in the 1580s.[2]

Four libraries collected at least in part from the books of the dissolved monasteries can be used to illustrate this point. Those of Dr. John Dee, John Lord Lumley, Matthew Parker, and Sir Robert Cotton.

The books and manuscripts of the mathematician and scientist Dr. John Dee have been scattered, but two catalogues exist, one of 1556, and another of 1583.

---

[1] N. R. Ker, *Medieval Libraries*, pxiii.
[2] For a detailed account of the stimulus given to medieval studies, see May McKisack, *Medieval History in the Tudor Age*, Clarendon Press 1971.

The last one shows that at that date Dee possessed 170 manuscripts and 2,500 printed books, a considerable collection for a man who lived in chronic poverty. Dee's catalogues are invaluable for a knowledge of the scientific books available in England in the later sixteenth century, and the 1556 catalogue alone has been described as 'the best source of primary information about books on astrology' in the period.[1] Dee's private diary was written in the margins of old almanacs. It has been printed, together with his list of his manuscripts written in 1583, by the Camden Society.[2]

The collection of John Lord Lumley which passed into the Royal Library in 1609, when it was aquired by Henry Prince of Wales the eldest son of James I, is in fact three distinct libraries joined in one. The earliest is the library of Archbishop Cranmer. This was forfeited to the crown under Mary, and given by her to Henry Fitzalan Earl of Arundel, who was a Catholic, added his own books, and then in his lifetime passed the library on to his son-in-law, John Lord Lumley. The collection is interesting in itself, but it is Cranmer's books which give it its unique importance. Cranmer left no catalogue, but his books can be identified by his name. Even a cursory glance through the Lumley Catalogue is enough to show the depth of Cranmer's erudition, his interest in the liturgy and his debt to the early Christian writers and in particular the Greek Church. Cranmer probably possessed about 100 manuscripts and 500 printed books. Like Dee's it was essentially a working library, 'a theological arsenal which he used himself and made available to scholars; he bought books because he needed them, not because he had room to fill.'[3] Cranmer based his Prayer Book on the York and Sarum Missals, but from his library it can be seen that he had access to diverse and widely ranging authorities. In addition to the works of the German and Swiss reformers and those of Erasmus, he had some knowledge of Mozarabic liturgies and of the Greek Church. The Lumley Catalogue shows that Cranmer possessed several copies of the works that went under the name of St. Athanasius, including *De Trinitate et Spiritu Sancto,* and a commentary on Athanasius by the English mystic Richard Rolle bound up with an interesting collection of commentaries on the Bible (Lumley Catalogue Nos. 42, 531, and 338). There is another interesting collection, significantly grouped together, of tracts on Free Will, two of which are by Erasmus (No. 327); a group of works by St. John Chrysostom (Nos. 198, 199, 211), and by St. Basil (Nos. 133, 135, 136, 169, 170, 635); works by St. Gregory of Nyssa and St. Gregory of Nazianzus, bound together with a tract by Bishop John Fisher against Luther and two commentaries on the psalms, one by Erasmus (No. 473). Other working copies of the early Fathers and Greek writers possessed by Cranmer included those of St. Cyprian (No. 194), St. John of Damascus

[1]Sears Jayne, *Library Catalogues of the English Renaissance,* pp6, 108, 125.
[2]Camden Society, Vol. XIX, 1842.
[3]Sears Jayne and F. R. Johnson, *The Lumley Library,* p2.

(No. 266), and Dionysius the Areopagite (No. 266 and 268). Cranmer's library contained all the traditional theological authors, but included general philosophical works such as those of William of Occam, whose views on the papacy he must have found encouraging, and those of the encyclopaedic and enlightened Nicolas of Cusa. The Cranmer books in the Lumley Catalogue are the perfect example of the information which can be provided by a study of such lists. Cranmer's books explain his work, and why for example the Anglican Prayer Book not only contains the Athanasian Creed ('Quicunque vult' placed just before the Litany), but also the moving prayer of St. John Chrysostom, 'When two or three are gathered together . . .' in Matins and Evensong. 'The library catalogue preserves for us associations which would otherwise be lost, and we see in it the central documents of the English Reformation in the intellectual atmosphere in which they were produced: the growing concern with the text of the Bible, the burgeoning importance of Greek and Hebrew, . . . the immense (now almost forgotten) popularity of the psalm paraphrase, the persistence of the Sentences of Peter Lombard and the works of Duns Scotus, and most intriguing of all the revived interest in the Greek church . . . The arrangement of Lumley's catalogue also reminds us that the Reformation was not merely a return to the Bible – that the handmaiden of Puritanism was Platonism.'[1]

The other three contemporary libraries which are of particular interest, those of Archbishop Matthew Parker, Sir Robert Cotton, and Sir Thomas Bodley, fall outside the mid-Tudor period proper, but the first at least was begun during it, and all contained a large amount of material from the monastic houses.

Matthew Parker was Master of Corpus Christi College under Edward. He was deprived under Mary, but lived unmolested in retirement until the accession of Elizabeth. He had been one of the highly intelligent young men of the Boleyn circle, and he was already noted for his learning before the death of Henry VIII. His main interest was in the collection of Anglo-Saxon and early English manuscripts in order to prove the antiquity of the Anglican Church. Parker not only collected books, he published them, reprinting medieval chronicles such as Matthew Paris and Thomas of Walsingham, and ancient manuscripts such as Gildas' account of the conquest of Britain by the Saxons, and Asser's *Life of Alfred*. Parker marked manuscripts if they seemed to confirm the Anglican rite, for instance his copy of Gervase of Canterbury has a sentence underlined which describes the position of the altar in the body of the church, and the margin is marked 'altare in nave', and the description of episcopal elections is noted 'cum consensu Regis' (with the King's consent). Parker, with Elizabeth's support, tried to trace the whereabouts of the monastic books and records, and among his papers there are some interesting lists of those who were thought to possess collections from the monasteries; they include such men as Paget, Sir John Mason, Henry Fitzalan Earl of Arundel, the executors of Robert Recorde the

[1] Sears Jayne and F. R. Johnson, *The Lumley Library*, p29.

mathematician, and of Sir John Cheke the humanist scholar, Dr. Nicolas Wotton, John Stow, the Earl of Huntingdon, the Earl of Sussex, and William Bowyer the Keeper of the Tower, who at one time possessed the *Lindisfarne Gospels*. Parker's library was divided at his death and by bequest during his life into three lots, one going to his old college, Corpus Christi, one to the University Library Cambridge, and the third group to Trinity Cambridge.[1]

The life of Sir Robert Cotton falls partly outside the scope of this study. He belongs to the late Elizabethan period and died in the reign of Charles I. He was part of the antiquarian movement of the late sixteenth century, which itself was partly legal, partly parliamentarian, and partly an aspect of the English Renaissance, and which deserves more careful study. He was a pupil of Camden at Westminster, and entered Jesus College Cambridge at the age of ten. Cotton was an omnivorous collector, and amassed other things besides books. In 1599, for example, he went with Camden to the Roman Wall and brought back inscribed stones, and he possessed a fossilised skeleton over twenty feet long which he had found on his own estate while making a pond.[2] But his library is his enduring monument. Cotton began to collect books, manuscripts and documents of all sorts when still under twenty. He was still adding to his library in 1629, two years before his death. He collected partly for pleasure, and partly for information. His library finally included 958 volumes of manuscripts, many of which consisted of a number of separate items bound together. It included the *Lindisfarne Gospels*, a Greek *Genesis* said to have once belonged to Origen (it had been presented to Henry VIII and given by Queen Elizabeth to Sir John Fortescue, who gave it to Cotton), the only known manuscripts of *Beowulf*, the *Pearl* (an important 14th century mystical poem), and the romance of *Sir Gawain and the Green Knight*.[3] His historical manuscripts included a Matthew Paris, two copies of Magna Carta, the story that he bought one of them from his tailor for fourpence in order to prevent it being cut up as a pattern, is unfortunately apocryphal.[4] Cotton searched systematically for charters, legal documents and state papers such as copies of Acts of Parliament and treaties. His library became of vital importance to other historians like Raleigh, Bacon, Camden, and Selden, (who dedicated his *History of Tithes* to Cotton); to purchasers or owners of monastic property in search of title deeds; and above all to the legists and

[1]C. E. Wright, 'The Dispersal of the monastic libraries and the beginnings of Anglo-Saxon studies Matthew Parker and his circle', *Cambridge Bibliographical Journal*, Vol. I, Part III, 1951.
[2]Hope Mirrlees, *A Fly in Amber*, Faber and Faber 1962, pp76, 83. Miss Mirrlees quotes a delightful story from Selden's *Table Talk*; 'It was an excellent question of my Lady Cotton when Sir Robert Cotton was magnifying of a shoe, which was Moses's or Noah's, and wondering the strange shape and fashion of it. But, Mr. Cotton, says she, are you sure it is a shoe?', p89.
[3]M. McKisack, *The Fourteenth Century*, p525.
[4]Hope Mirrlees, *A Fly in Amber*, p59.

members of both sides in the constitutional disputes of the seventeenth century in search of precedents. His collection was considered so dangerous by Charles I that he seized it. The library was however restored to Cotton's son, but ultimately became part of the Royal Collection in the early eighteenth century.[1]

Sir Thomas Bodley, who like Cotton began his collection under Elizabeth, gave it during his lifetime to the University of Oxford. Bodley's library never therefore remained static, but has continually expanded ever since. It was opened to students in 1602, and was catalogued by its first librarian, Thomas James, in 1600. By 1605 it had 400 manuscripts and 5000 printed books, by 1620 it had grown to 1,026 manuscripts and about 15,000 printed books, and was the largest library in the country. It has always been regularly catalogued.

In the Universities the strengthening of the collegiate system during the mid-sixteenth century had the effect of enlarging the individual college libraries as well as the expansion on a university basis. Colleges still relied mainly on gifts and bequests for their books, and expansion was therefore spasmodic rather than regular. Dr. Ker suggests that during the sixteenth century as a whole most colleges at Oxford only spent about two pounds a year on books, and the poorer colleges even less.[2] The richer colleges like Magdalen and New College were able to finance their purchases out of corporate revenue, but others like Oriel and Merton sold ecclesiastical plate (unnecessary under the new regulations) to buy books. The rate of increase varied with the college, Magdalen for instance spent £73 on books between 1530 and 1550, purchasing possibly 150 volumes, and was the first college to appoint a salaried librarian in that year. Merton, on the other hand, spent very little after the late 1540s until the end of the century, and Christ Church library was not even begun until 1561.

The Marian visitation of 1556 should be a valuable source of information on the contents of the college libraries of both Universities at that date, since the commissioners demanded lists of all books remaining in the libraries for their inspection. Those extant are extremely interesting but only six have actually been found, those of King's College, Trinity Hall and University College at Cambridge; and Merton, All Souls, and Brasenose at Oxford. From their contents at Oxford, in the three colleges concerned, there seem to have been no incunabula – books printed before 1500 – at all remaining, and comparatively few books printed between 1500 and 1530. There was also an almost complete absence of any books printed in English. English bibles had been bought for the chapels during the reigns of Henry VIII and Edward, but the only others apart from these were a copy of the Statutes in English printed by Thomas Berthelet in 1543 in the law library at All Souls, a copy of Elyot's English-Latin dictionary

[1]It was badly damaged by the fire of 1731. It is now in the British Museum, and is still catalogued under the names of the classical busts which stood on the top of Cotton's shelves.
[2]N. R. Ker, 'Oxford College Libraries in the Sixteenth Century', *Bodleian Library Record*, Vol. VI 1957-1961, p468.

of 1538, and the first volume of a translation of Erasmus' paraphrases printed by Edward Whitchurch in 1548, both owned by Magdalen. In the main the contents of the Oxford college libraries as listed in 1556 were conventional enough, the Church fathers and theology were strongly represented, and a selection of commentaries and law books. The accepted classical authors were possessed but there were relatively few examples of Latin poets or of the fifteenth century humanist writers. Merton for example had no Latin poets at all and the only humanistic work was a copy of the 'Opera' of Lorenzo Valla in the 1540 edition. But although at least one cartload of books had been taken away to be burnt in 1550 Merton still possessed 300 manuscripts and 200 printed books mostly less than twenty years old, indicating perhaps that after the Cromwellian visitations and those of 1549–1550, some attempt seems to have been made to bring college libraries up to date. Dr. Ker even suggests that Merton may have bought the printed books en bloc, probably in 1549.[1] The individual libraries differ however in content, partly as the accidental result of individual bequests, and partly because of the attempt to rationalise the subjects studied at the various colleges by the visitation of 1549. All Souls was naturally strong on law, but had benefited from Archbishop Warham's bequest of ninety-one books in 1532 (which included a copy of Bucer). The college also possessed a small section of scientific and philosophical works.[2] The Oxford lists for 1556 and surviving books in other colleges show that many of the colleges had made some attempt to keep abreast of current thought. Vesalius' great study of anatomy *De Humani Corporis Fabrica,* was possessed by All Souls, Merton and Magdalen. Merton also had a copy of Charles Estienne's book on dissection *De dissectione partium Corporis humani,* Giovanni Arcoli's pioneering work on dentistry in the 1540 edition (which contained a description of filling cavities with gold leaf), and two important works on botany – Leonard Fuchs' Latin Herbal of 1542, and Jean Ruel's treatise on plants *De natura Stirpium* of 1538. Ruel's book was also possessed by All Souls. Mathematical books were represented by Regiomontanus' *De Triangulis,* in both Magdalen and Merton, and Merton had in addition Albert Dürer's treatise *De Symmetria.* Three colleges had a copy of Euclid, Corpus and Magdalen in Simon Grynaeus the elder's Greek edition dedicated to Cuthbert Tunstall, and All Souls had one in Latin. In astronomy most of the books were conventional, Magdalen and Merton both had Venetus' *De harmonia mundi,* but Merton (perhaps because the college bought late) had an

---

[1]N. R. Ker, 'Oxford College Libraries', p483.

[2]Lists available for the All Souls library early in the sixteenth century include the actual arrangement of the books on the desks. Thus in 1502 the Library had 250 manuscripts and 100 printed books. There were 10½ desks of theology, 5½ desks of philosophy, science and the classics, on the East side; and 14½ desks of legal books with 2½ desks of medicine and classics on the West side. The desks were rearranged in 1512-1513. Dr. Ker points out that until modern shelving was introduced 500 folio size books was probably the maximum convenient size for any library. N. R. Ker, 'Oxford College Libraries', p477.

interesting collection of essays by Calcagni of Ferrara, one of which put forward the Copernican theory. Copernicus' own book *De Revolutionibus orbis coelestium* was not in any college library in 1556 although published in 1543, but at least two copies were in the hands of private individuals, and later found their way into the college libraries of Merton and Christ Church. Geographical exploration and the new discoveries were represented by two works, an edition of Ptolemy's *Geography* of 1522 belonging to Corpus which included a map showing part of the North Coast of America with a reference to Columbus, and a preface describing the voyages of Amerigo Vespucci, and a collection of 1537 by Simon Grynaeus which included detailed accounts of both Vespucci and Columbus possessed by Merton.[1] There is no equivalent account of the contents of the three known Cambridge Lists, but a brief introduction to the present contents of the college libraries is available.[2]

The 1556 inventories are not the only means of obtaining information as to the contents of libraries and the books possessed and read by scholars at the Universities during the Tudor period. In some colleges parts of the medieval libraries survived in their original settings with a substantial proportion of their original books. These include All Souls, Oriel, New College, Lincoln, and Balliol at Oxford; and Pembroke (150 manuscripts), Peterhouse (200 manuscripts), and St. John's (270 manuscripts) at Cambridge. As libraries expanded records of bequests and purchases were kept by the colleges themselves, and in addition some of the colleges at both Universities and the University Library at Cambridge made periodic catalogues of their books. Cambridge University Library has catalogues for 1424, 1473, 1556, 1573, 1574 ,and 1582. All Souls Oxford produced seven sixteenth century catalogues, Merton eleven, and Christ Church five. In all, forty-three catalogues survive from Oxford and Cambridge for the sixteenth century.[3] These catalogues often have their original press marks – the distinguishing code marks indicating the position of a book on the shelves – and these can provide valuable clues in tracing the provenance of a book.

Booksellers' and printers' lists have long been known as an important source as to the number, price, and type of books required and available in any century. For the Tudor period one of the most often quoted is that of the Oxford bookseller John Dorne, who in 1520 had a stock of 1,952 titles. These ranged from ABCs and ballads to more serious academic works such as Whittington's Grammar, Latin authors, and above all Erasmus. Dorne sold 150 copies of Erasmus' works in one year, more than any other author. Dorne's prices ranged

[1]N. R. Ker, 'Introduction to Oxford College Libraries in 1556', *Bodleian Library Catalogue of the Exhibition of 1956.*
[2]A. N. L. Munby, *Cambridge College Libraries,* Heffer and Sons, Cambridge 1962.
[3]Sears Jayne, *Library Catalogues of the English Renaissance,* University of California Press 1956, pp40-42.

1. Medieval scientists with a sighting tube. (*Bodleian Library*, *MSS Ashmole 304*)

2. Portrait of Dr. John Dee. *(Ashmolean Museum)*

3. Portrait head on the last page of Billingsley's *Euclide*, said by Aubrey to be of John Dee. John Daye, London, 1570.

The fyrſt Booke

of the perpendiculare intercepted with the Scale in the cliffes altituꝛe
before meaſured, and diuide by the partes of the ſcale cutte, the quotient
will ſhew the lyne Hypochenuſal, oꝛ diſtance of that parte of the ſhippe
which your lyne viſuall touched from your eye, oꝛ adioyning the ſquare
of the longitude firſte founde to the ſquare of the altitude, the roote qua-
dꝛat of the pꝛoduct is alſo the true length of the line viſuall.

Example.

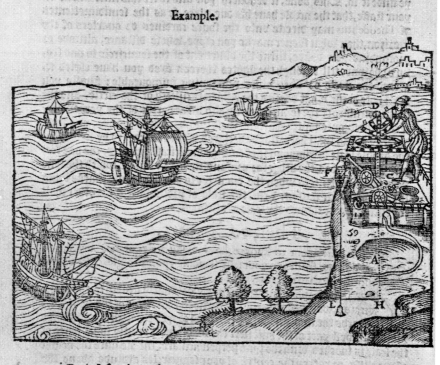

*A*Dmit I ſtande on the cliffe *A*, and ſee the ſhippe *B* lying at rode in the
ſea, I deſire to know how farre offſhe is from me, mine inſtrument conue-
niently placed at *C* (as is tofore declared) J turne my dimetient of my ſemicir-
cle towarde the ſhippe, mouing it vp and downe till J eſpye through the ſightes

the

4. Illustration from Leonard and Thomas Digges' *Pantometria*, London, 1571.
   (British Museum)

To the Reader.

Auing of late (gentle Reader) correctted and
reformed sondry faultes that by negligence in
printing haue crept into my fathers Generall
Prognostication: Amonge other thinges I
founde a description or Modill of the world, and
situation of Spheres Cælestiall & Eleméetare according to the doctrine of Ptolomy, whereunto
all vniuersities (led thereto chiefly by the aucto-
rity of Aristotle) sithens haue consented. But in this our age, one rare
wit (seeing the côtinuall errors that frô time to tíme more & more haue
bin discouered, besides the infinit absurdites in their Theorickes, which
they haue bin forced to admit that would not confesse any mobilitie in
the ball of the earth) hath by long study, painefull practise, and rare in-
uention deliuered a new Theorick, or Modill of the world, shewing, that
the Earth resteth not in the Center of the whole world, but onely in the
Center of this our mortall world or Globe of Elements, which enuiro-
ned & inclosed in the Moones Orb, and together with the whole Globe
of mortality is caried yearely rounde about the Sunne, which like a
king in the middest of all raigneth and geeueth lawes of motion to the
rest, sphearically dispersing his glorious beames of light through all
this sacred Cælestiall Téple. And the earth it selfe to be one of the Pla
nets, hauing his peculiar & straynge courses, tourning euery 24 hours
rounde vpon his owne Centre: whereby the ☉ and great Globe of fixed
starres seeme to sway about and tourne, albeit in deede they remaine
fixed. So, many wayes is the sense of mortall men abused. But reason
and deepe discourse of witte hauing opened these things to Coperni-
nicus, & the same being with demonstrations Mathematicall, most ap-
parantly by him to the world deliuered: I thought it conuenient together with the olde Theorick also to publish this, to the ende such noble
English mindes (as delight to reache aboue the baser sort of mé) might
not bee altogether defrauded of so noble a part of Philosophy. And
to the ende it might manifestly appeare that Copernicus meant not
as some haue fondly excused him, to deliuer these grounds of the Earthes mobility only as Mathematicall principles fayned, & not as Philo-
sophicall truly auerred: I haue also from him deliuered both the Philo-
sophicall reasons by Aristotle and others, produced to maintaine the

M.   Earthes

5. The opening page of Thomas Digges' addition to his father's work, *A Perfit
Description of the Caelestiall Orbes . . .*, showing references to Copernicus. From
A Prognostication Everlasting . . ., Thomas Marshe, London, 1585. *(British
Museum)*

The manner of their fishing.

6. Indians fishing, from John White's *A Briefe and True Report of the New Found Land of Virginia*. *(British Museum)*

7. Drawings of butterflies by John White and given to Thomas Penny in 1587. (*British Museum, Sloane 4014*)

8. Portrait of William Clowes. *(By courtesy of the Wellcome Trustees)*

from a halfpenny or a penny to six shillings and eightpence for a leather bound copy of Lyndewood's *Constitutions*.[1]

Inventories made for probate and wills provide another important source of information as to the number of books owned by individuals, and their type. Unfortunately as the quantity increased with the spread of printing, the energy and industry of the probate officials diminished, and instead of the detailed lists of titles common in the early part of the sixteenth century, all that is recorded at the end is a brief summary '18 small books', 'books parchment and the like', (this for a bookseller!), or finally the tantalising phrase 'all his books'. This does not apply, fortunately, to specific bequests, and here the growing practice of cataloguing gifts provides invaluable information as to the contents of important libraries.

These various sources of evidence dealing with the cultural background of the sixteenth century – the catalogues, inventories, and wills which include books – have yet to be fully explored. When this has been done, they may (in the opinion of Professor Sears Jayne) 'alter the general outline of our picture of the intellectual life of the period'.

Professor Sears Jayne has studied the Renaissance catalogues between 1500 and 1640. He includes institutions such as the University and college libraries, the Cathedral libraries, those of the major schools, a few monastic libraries, and finally those of some private individuals, in all a total of 848 catalogues; 244 from 1500 to 1550; 314 between 1550 and 1600: and 290 from 1600 to 1640. He does not however, except in four sample wills, list the names of any of the books, although he gives a valuable summary of those commonly possessed. Nevertheless his lists show certain clear developments. In particular, the records of both Universities are of unique value in that they 'provide a rich, finite, and representative sampling, uncoloured by the prejudices which affect a single man's collection.'

As might be expected the number of books owned by both institutions and individuals increased. In the early years of the century, the average university scholar had ten to twenty books, but by 1600 it had risen to seventy with a few individuals owning considerably more than two hundred.[2] The steady increase in numbers continued inexorably and in the next century collections of private men often amounted to over 1,000 printed books, while those of institutional libraries numbered considerably more.

[1] H. S. Bennett, *English Books and Readers*, Vol. I, 1475-1557, pp22, 231-4; also Sears Jayne, *Catalogues*, p175. Booksellers' lists continue throughout the century and are given by Professor Sears Jayne in an appendix to his book. Printers Lists are obviously more complicated and are discussed fully in the two volumes of H. S. Bennett's work. As the century progressed printers tended to specialise in various fields such as grammars, law books, ABCs, and most important of all financially the Bible and Church Primers.

[2] The 1583 shelf list of Dr. Dee's Library which lists 170 manuscripts and 2,500 printed books is a good example, Camden Society 1842.

Certain books appear in all the individual collections. All scholars, as one would expect, had a Bible (probably the Geneva version unless otherwise stated). Nearly all had in addition a Gospel, a Testament or a missal, and most possessed Calvin's *Institutes*. Among secular authors the classics found are Cicero, usually *De Officiis*, Aristotle, the *Organon* with commentaries, Ovid, Horace and Virgil. Erasmus is represented by the *Adagia* and *Colloquies*. Letter books in Latin for copying, and handwriting books are also numerous and almost all the inventories include a Cooper dictionary and a *Catholicon*. Professor Sears Jayne draws two interesting conclusions from his examination of individual book lists at both Universities. His first is that there is a marked contrast between conservative scholastic Oxford, and reforming humanist Cambridge '. . . In contrast with the Oxford catalogues there are almost no scholastic writers in the Cambridge catalogues, and most of the Cambridge catalogues already reflect the specialisation of the scholar in foreign literature, law, theology, medicine, classics, or some other field.'[1] In support of this theory Sears Jayne includes in an appendix four examples of Cambridge book lists, two of which show definite specialisation. George Arundél's books catalogued in 1554 show a marked interest in law, though Ovid's *de Arte amandi et epistolii* and a collection of the works of Cicero found a place. The other, that of Abraham Tilman made in 1589, is considerably longer and includes works in Hebrew, Greek, French, Spanish (a Bible), and Italian. The Italian works include two Grammars, two dictionaries and a copy of Petrarch. This Library represents a wide range of interests since it includes a copy of 'Plato in Latin', Calvin's *Institutes*, Aristotle, 'Smale poets in greek', Valerius *Ethicks and Phisicks, Piscator upon Ramus Logicke*, and Regiomontanus' *De Nativitatibus*. This is clearly a collection revealing a wide range of knowledge and of outlook.

Professor Sears Jayne's second and pertinent observation is that very few books in any of the sixteenth century inventories are in English except the Bible. 'The Cambridge lists are a forceful reminder that Hebrew and Greek were common scholarly equipment in the Renaissance, and that the language of learning and culture in Elizabethan England was still Latin . . . The tendency of modern scholars to believe that they can understand Elizabethan England adequately in terms of its English works alone is one reason why so much remains to be learned about that period.'[2]

This study and analysis of library lists is of more than antiquarian interest. It provides tangible proof of the revolution brought about by the printed book. 'Under the combined influence of the invention of printing, and the intellectual pressure of the Renaissance and Reformation, English Libraries of the period underwent at least three radical changes. First, books in general began to shift from institutional collections into private hands; secondly, books changed from

[1]Sears Jayne, *Catalogues*, pp51, 53.
[2]Sears Jayne, *Catalogues*, pp52-53.

a few expensive manuscripts to relatively cheap printed books in great numbers, many sizes and formats; and third, the library ceased to be regarded as a static collection of standard authorities within four fixed fields of revealed truth and came to be thought of as a dynamic, ever-growing collection of miscellaneous works, and on subjects which changed constantly with the ever-shifting frontiers of limitless human knowledge.'[1] This revolution was common to the rest of the Western World, but in one respect the emphasis was stronger than in many European countries. 'In 1500 the principal owners of books in England were ecclesiastical institutions; there were few important libraries at Oxford or Cambridge, and fewer still important private collectors. By 1640 the situation had been reversed: both Universities boasted libraries of thousands of volumes each, and there were several private collections of more than a thousand volumes, and there was not a single important ecclesiastical library in the country'.[2] Just as Baskerville found that the place to look for the dispersed monks was the rural parishes of England, the place to look for monastic manuscripts is in the private collections and institutional libraries after 1558.[3]

Law and foreign travel in education

While education in schools and Universities retained a religious content, there were two areas in the educational pattern, training in the law, and foreign travel, which were by contrast predominantly secular in influence.

The Inns of Court had in earlier centuries provided a strict and formal training for those intending to practise and study the law. The junior members of the Inns had to dispute hypothetical legal cases regularly with their elders by means of formal but unrehearsed discussions known as 'moots,', and twice a year there were 'Readings' or lectures by an experienced lawyer on statutes and common law. In the sixteenth century there was a marked decline in both these activities. Fines for non-attendence at 'moots' increase in frequency, and in spite of a sharp rise in the amount levied, it proved impossible to reverse the trend. At the same time the Inns of Court admitted an ever expanding number of members who had no intention of pursuing a legal career, and who entered purely for general educational reasons. If the Inns of Court became in the sixteenth century (in the words of Sir Edward Coke) the third university of England, then like Oxford and Cambridge they exposed many of their students to a legal training rather than educated them in the law. The professional lawyers were so busy with litigation that they were reluctant to undertake formal teaching duties at the 'Readings' and the 'moots'. 'Sixteenth century England was by comparison with previous centuries a fluid society, with a tremendous amount of land changing hands. It is not surprising, therefore, that it was a

[1]Sears Jayne, *Catalogues*, p29.   [2]Sears Jayne, *Catalogues*, p39.
[3]G. Baskerville, *English Monks and the Supression of the Monasteries*, Jonathan Cape 1958.

litigious age and that the profession of the law, i.e. the common law flourished.'[1] Fines on senior members of the Bar were as frequent as those on students, and only those ambitious for high legal office found it necessary to undertake duties that were both unprofitable and onerous. As for the students, Dr. Charlton cites two facts that were incontrovertible: 'their increased numbers, and their unsatisfactory behaviour'.[2] It was this alteration in the conditions of legal education that stimulated an important change of emphasis in legal studies. By the end of the sixteenth century the essentials of law were initially mastered from books by serious and dilettante students alike. This in turn led to the production of legal text books, such as the *Year Books,* the various *Abridgements,* Littleton's *Tenures,* Plowden and Dyer's *Reports,* Lambarde's *Eirenarcha* (a guide to the knowledge required by a Justice of the Peace) and in the seventeenth century to the publication of Coke's *Institutes.*

After the middle of the century, travel abroad became an essential part of the education of a nobleman, it also became a useful preparation to a career at Court. There was nothing particularly new in this, but like all other forms of cultural activity it increased in extent and in social range. It was necessary to avoid some areas – strongly Catholic countries like Spain were obviously suspect, but less obvious was the distrust of Italy, which Burghley clearly regarded as the sink of iniquity, where the pernicious doctrines of Machiavelli would inevitably corrupt impressionable young men, and the Papal States were too near for safety. The marked increase in the awareness and knowledge of foreign and European conditions which marked Elizabeth's Parliaments, was not primarily due to this, since foreign travel for education or pleasure alone was still beyond the means of the average Member of Parliament. The cause was more probably the influence of the returned Marian exiles, whose experience of continental conditions was deeper and not always happy;[3] the trading links with France and the Low Countries; and the heightened sense of the dangers inherent in the religious divisions. Even though the average Englishman did not travel widely himself, he could and did read popular books on foreign countries, merchants at least had a direct need of a working knowledge of both Dutch or Low German, and French. From Caxton onwards books in French were available in print, Palsgrave's monumental work on the French language appeared in 1530, and a small introduction intended for the teaching of French in schools appeared in about 1553, William Thomas followed his *History of Italy* by an Italian grammar in 1550.[4]

Easily the most interesting and informative book on foreign travel appeared

[1]K. Charlton, *Education in Renaissance England,* p184.
[2]K. Charlton, *Education in Renaissance England,* p185.
[3]For an unusual and informative description see E. Read, *Catherine Duchess of Suffolk,* Jonathan Cape 1962.
[4]H. S. Bennett, *English Books and Readers,* Vol. I, pp93-97.

in the early years of Edward's reign (although it was written in 1542), Andrew Boorde's *Fyrst Boke of the Introduction of Knowledge*, dedicated to Princess Mary. His work is the earliest example of the complete tourist's handbook written in English. It is partly in verse, and partly in prose, and gives an account of Ireland, Scotland, Wales, all the main European countries, including Poland, Hungary, and Greece, and the Moslem areas of North Africa and the Levant. Many of Boorde's description of foreign conditions were first-hand, since he had travelled widely, and they are always practical. Here for example is his description of how to start for Jerusalem:

> Who so ever thet dothe pretende to go to Jerusalem, let him prepare himselfe to set forth of England after Ester vii or viii dayes, and let him take his waye to London, to make his banke, or exhaunge of his mony, with some merchant to be payed at Venis, and then let him go or ride to Dover or Sandwich.[1]

His description of the great organ at St. Andrew's cathedral at Bordeaux is clearly first hand, 'in which organ be many instruments and vyces, as giants' heads and stars, the which do move and wag with their jaws and eyes as fast as the player plays.'[2] The real interest of the book lies in the fact that Boorde included at the end of each section a glossary of words and phrases in each language, where necessary giving the foreign words spelt phonetically. This basic information included numbers, and phrases of greeting and farewell. The languages covered included those of the Moslem countries, Hebrew and Yiddish, those of east Europe, and the celtic tongues of Britain – Gaelic Welsh, Irish and Cornish. Boorde incidentally asserts that many Cornishmen could speak no English. Boorde, who was noted for his sense of humour, clearly envisaged his Englishman as intending to learn, if not actually doing so:

> I wyl go to learnyng a hoole somers day;
> I wyll learne Latyne, Hebrew, Greeke and Frenche,
> And I wyl learne Douche, sittyng on my benche.[3]

Boorde's book and its method of compilation was indicative of a new attitude of mind. It is not without interest that Boorde himself was a protegé of Cromwell, a practising physician and a scientist.

Conclusion

The continuing power of the State to oversee education, particularly as to the content of religious teaching, is illustrated by the steps taken under Elizabeth to undo the Marian changes and re-introduce the protestant doctrine. The

[1]Andrew Boorde, *The fyrst Boke of the Introduction of Knowledge*, ed. F. J. Furnivall, EETS 1870, p219.
[2]Andrew Boorde, *The fyrst Boke of the Introduction of Knowledge*, p207.
[3]Andrew Boorde, *The fyrst Boke of the Introduction of Knowledge*, p117.

Court of High Commission established by the Act of Supremacy and including laymen as well as ecclesiastics, was given the power to amend statutes as necessary, both in existing schools and in new foundations. In this way the State retained overall control even when the money came from private sources.[1] The State through the Church retained control over individual teachers by continuing the Marian licensing system, and by examining teachers as to their beliefs and qualifications during episcopal visitations. In spite of the incorporation of the two Universities with independent status in 1571, the government still interfered, acting to reduce both puritan and catholic influence as it thought necessary, for instance the action against Cartwright, and Dr. Caius.

If the decade 1548–1558 is examined in its setting as a link period between Henry VIII and Elizabeth, at first sight it corroborates the general impression given by the administrative system that the age was one of evolution. The profound changes which took place throughout education were the logical conclusion of the humanist theories of the preceding years. Yet, far more than in the administration, the changes in education were revolutionary. For the general ideas of the great educationalists of the first half of the century were extended and transformed by the force of protestantism. As the use of the vernacular spread, and text books and communal activities became imbued with protestant ethics, the seeds of 'puritanism' in its most general sense were spread throughout the younger generation. Professor Sears Jayne has noted the widespread possession of the Geneva Bible and of Calvin's *Institutes* in the book inventories at the end of the sixteenth century; and Dr. Simon ends her study of the effect of education on social change with a quotation from an Elizabethan schoolmaster which is a perfect expression of the forces at work. Teachers, wrote John Brinsley,

> are they to whose charge that rich treasure, both of church and commonwealth is committed in trust . . . We are they who help either to make or to mar all; for that all the flower of our nation, and those who will become leaders of all the rest, are committed to our education and instruction; that if we bring them up aright, there is great hope, that they shall prove godly lights, and marks to all the land, especially to the towns and countries where they are; and clean contrarily, most woeful examples . . . if they be spoiled through us, or for lack of our better care. . . We are therefore the men upon whom the flourishing of this our Canaan doth very much depend.[2]

The greatness of the Elizabethan age had its origin in the extension of education under Edward. In that simple fact lies the foundation for the outburst of creative achievement in every sphere of intellectual activity – from music and literature to antiquarian studies and scientific discovery – which marks the last years of the century.

[1]See the detailed list of instructions for Tonbridge school in 1664. J. Simon, *Education and Society*, p308.   [2]J. Simon, *Education and Society*, p403.

5. Pre-Tudor mathematical sciences

The remarkable acceleration of thought and technical invention between 1500 and 1600 was part of the change in mental outlook produced by humanism, and humanism since it had many facets produced remarkably diverse results. The initial momentum for all the intellectual upheavals of the sixteenth century came from two sources, the invention of printing, and the re-examination of classical texts. The effect of printing, though complex, was straightforward: the re-examination of classical texts was not. It is part of the great interest of the sixteenth century that it was precisely during this period that the split between scientific truth, that is truth which can be proved by empirical observation and mathematical calculation, and moral or aesthetic truth which cannot, became apparent. For most men of the sixteenth century the distinction between scientific methods derived from mathematical and experimental calculations and a more subjective and philosophical approach to the same problems was not clearly understood, and the phenomena of the natural world were examined in both ways. Even in a single individual the two methods could exist side by side. Dr. Dee was probably the most influential mathematician of his day in England, yet he saw number as part of a vast metaphysical structure with a mystic power in its own right which could be used in conjunction with Cabalistic magic to penetrate the unknown regions of angelic powers and attain knowledge directly communicated by God and beyond the comprehension of the unaided human mind.[1] This dichotomy in sixteenth century science persisted even after its existence had been realised.

Classical origins

The scientific thought inherited by the sixteenth century from the middle ages was in the main theoretical and derived from the teachings of the Greeks. In cosmology the most generally accepted version consisted of 'a combination of the physical theories of Aristotle with the mathematical constructions of Ptolemy.'[2] The universe was regarded as finite; the earth as a stationary sphere round which revolved the moon, sun, and planets, in a series of complicated

---

[1]For these two contrasting aspects of Dee, see E. G. R. Taylor, *Tudor Geography*, CUP 1930; and I. R. F. Calder, 'John Dee studied as a Neoplatonist', unpublished thesis, London University 1954.
[2]F. R. Johnson, *Astronomical Thought in Renaissance England*, John Hopkins Press 1937, p16.

movements calculated by Ptolemy in the second century AD in an attempt to make the geocentric theory fit observed phenomena such as the retrograde motion of the planets. The whole system was enclosed by the sphere of the fixed stars which revolved round the earth once every twenty-four hours and beyond which nothing existed. Matter consisted of four elements: earth, water, air and fire; and could exist in four conditions; hot, cold, moist, and dry. There were only two kinds of pure motion: linear, or straight line, and circular. Each element had its own appropriate motion, and deviations from it were the result of mixtures of elements. Everything below the circle of the moon was imperfect and subject to change: everything above it was eternal and perfect. Ptolemy's *Almagest*, which contained mathematical calculations for the movements of the heavenly bodies, added a ninth sphere beyond that of the fixed stars in order to account for the precession of the equinox (the slow circular movement of the celestial poles). This outermost sphere was known as the 'primum mobile'. The Arab philosophers modified Ptolemy by adding one further sphere, so that in its final form the 'primum mobile' became the tenth sphere. The Ptolemaic system, though complicated, largely accounted for the apparent motions of all the heavenly bodies within the limits of observed accuracy. It also had the merit of being visually satisfactory: the heavens *appear* to revolve, and the earth *appears* to be still. It was therefore easy to accept in principle by those who had no understanding of the complex and unsatisfactory nature of the mathematics involved. It is this apparent correctness of the system which explains why it dominated cosmological thinking for over fourteen centuries and was only replaced by the alternative heliocentric theory after prolonged resistance. Ptolemy was one of the great thinkers of antiquity and his 'mathematical system of the universe, deserves our whole-hearted respect. He . . . sought only to devise a method whereby all the complexities of the planetary motions might be portrayed and calculated. He did not allow himself to be diverted by any preconceived metaphysical notions as to first causes, nor seek to simplify his task by ignoring any of the observed facts.'[1] Ptolemy himself thought of his spheres as mathematical areas of motion, but many of his successors, following Aristotle, believed them to be solid and crystalline, holding the appropriate heavenly body in its place and moving it according to the complicated Ptolemaic mechanics. In this form the system proved capable of absorbing a certain amount of Platonic thought. Plato's view of the universe was animistic and hierarchical and he accepted the Pythagorean view that number lay at the root of all things, and that a natural harmony in perfect mathematical relationships was the key to the construction of the heavens. The 'singing spheres' of late medieval and Renaissance thought ultimately derive from the Platonic idea of essential harmony. Both Aristotle and Plato were influenced by the Pythagorean emphasis on number and proportion, and both knew of the theory put forward

[1] F. R. Johnson, *Astronomical Thought*, p52.

by Philolaus in the fifth century BC that the earth, together with the sun, moon and planets revolved round a central fire hidden in the depths of space. The views of Aristarchus of Samos (310–230 BC) that the earth turned on its own axis and travelled annually round the sun, made little impact until they were revived in support of the Copernican theory. Unlike Ptolemy, Aristarchus did not work out his theory mathematically. It therefore lacked proof and remained a clever conjecture. One other curious anticipation of modern thought which became known in the middle ages simply because Aristotle spent a considerable amount of time refuting it, was the theory of Democritus (5th century BC) that matter was composed of infinitely small atomic particles. In this theory everything had its cause in the movements, combinations, and separation of these atoms. In infinite space, this infinite number of atoms produced an infinite number of worlds which were subject to continual change. When two worlds collided, they perished.[1] Democritus also held a vortex theory to account for the solidification of atoms into the earth, and correctly interpreted the Milky Way as a band of very faint stars. Since Aristotle also refuted the Philolaic theory of the central fire in *De Caelo* it is clear that a critical study of the text would introduce a number of new and potentially revolutionary ideas into European thought.

The ideas of Aristotle, Plato, and the other Greek philosophers never entirely disappeared in the West. The early church fathers such as Clement of Alexandria, Origen, Basil, and St. Augustine were familiar with Platonic thought in particular, and did much to preserve it in Europe, if only in an indirect form. A much more important link between the thought of the ancient world and the revival of scientific learning in Europe was the survival of Greek thought in the Arab world and its gradual translation into Latin. Among astronomical and mathematical texts, Euclid was translated from Arabic into Latin in the twelfth century by Adelard of Bath and Gerard of Cremona. It was first printed by Radholt in Venice in 1482. The first Greek edition appeared at Basle in 1533, and was dedicated to the English mathematician Cuthbert Tunstall. Euclid had direct practical importance since a basic knowledge of geometry was essential for a number of professions and trades, although the extent to which mathematics was studied by artisans is a matter for conjecture. Euclid's *Elements* were translated into French, Italian, German, Spanish and English before the end of the sixteenth century. The English edition was in 1570, translated by Henry Billingsley, and with a mathematical preface and textual notes by John Dee. Archimedes was not available so early, but a part of his work was translated by Gerard of Cremona. The first printed text of a portion of his work was produced in Venice in 1503, and this was followed in 1543 by another incomplete edition edited by Nicolas Tartaglia. The Greek princeps appeared at Basle in the following year. Another mathematical writer of considerable importance was

[1] F. R. Johnson, *Astronomical Thought*, pp27–8.

Apollonios of Perga, whose work on conics extended Euclid and was essential to the development of astronomical thought. Books 1–7 of Apollonios were preserved by the Arab school at Baghdad but only Books 1–4 were available in the West during the Renaissance. Ptolemy's *Almagest* was translated from the arabic in Spain and Sicily in the twelfth century, and direct from Greek in Sicily at the same time. Ptolemy's cosmology was also available through the works of the Arabic scientist Alfraganus. Alfraganus was printed at Ferrara in 1493 whereas the first printed edition of the *Almagest* was not until 1515, and the Greek princeps was not until 1538 at Basle.[1]

The combined fruits of Greek and Arab cosmological thought were available in manuscript by the end of the twelfth century and from that date European astronomy developed along Aristotelian and Ptolemaic lines through the influence of Albertus Magnus (1193–1280) and Thomas Aquinas (1227–1274). Between them they incorporated the earlier cosmological theories into Christian theology. Reinforced by the Catholic church, the Ptolemaic cosmology took on a new lease of life and was elevated to the status of accepted dogma. It also became widely known. Simplified versions of which the Englishman Sacrobosco's *Sphaera Mundi,* written in the thirteenth century, was the most popular, had wide circulation as textbooks and for private reading. Thirty editions of Sacrobosco were printed before 1501, and at least seventy by the middle of the seventeenth century. A similar work was Proclus' *De Sphaera* printed among *Scriptores astronomici veteres* by Aldus in 1499, translated by Linacre.

Baconian tradition in England

The monopoly of the Aristotelian Ptolemaic system was never absolute. In particular, England developed her own tradition in scientific and mathematical thought, and this divergence from the mainstream of continental thought placed her in a peculiar position to take advantage of the flood of new ideas released by the invention of printing and the revival of classical studies. The work of Roger Bacon in the thirteenth century is of special interest because copies of his writings were possessed by the small group of mathematicians and astronomers round John Dee in the reign of Elizabeth. Bacon has been described as 'the first great physicist in the modern sense of the word'.[2] His *Opus Majus* has a long and important section on optics beginning with a discussion of the physiology of the eye, but ending with a series of practical experiments with lenses. These experiments have a direct bearing on those done in the sixteenth century. In the *Opus Majus* Bacon describes the focusing of the rays of the sun

[1]G. L. Sarton, *The Appreciation of Ancient and Medieval Science during the Renaissance,* University of Pennsylvania Press 1955, Lecture 3.
[2]R. T. Gunther, *Early Science in Oxford,* OUP 1923, p29.

through a hemisphere of crystal half filled with water so that materials placed below the sphere were set alight, and continued.

> If therefore a concave spherical mirror is exposed to the sun, an infinite number of rays will converge to one point by means of reflection. And therefore of necessity fire is kindled when a concave mirror is exposed to the sun.

Bacon used a glass to magnify letters and seems to have constructed some instrument with lenses.

> The wonders of refracted vision are still greater: for it is easily shown that very large objects can be made to appear very small, and the reverse, and very distant objects will seem close at hand and conversely. For we can so shape transparent bodies and arrange them in such a way with respect to our sight, that the rays will be bent in any direction we desire, and under any angle we wish we shall see the object near or at a distance. Thus from an incredible distance we might read the smallest letters and number grains of dust and sand owing to the magnitude of the angle under which we viewed them . . . So also we might cause the sun, moon and stars in appearance to descend here below . . .[1]

Bacon was aware of the possible military use of lenses both for spying on the enemy and for starting fire. His idea that they could be used to send 'poisonous infectious influences' seems a little credulous, but cannot detract from the genuine experiments he seems to have carried out.[2]

Bacon was followed by the mathematicians of the Merton school, and their achievements are significant. Richard of Wallingford constructed an astronomical clock at St Albans, and made a Rectangulus with an adjustable rule carrying sight vanes and three other hinged rules for measuring altitudes. He left a complete description of the method of construction, and an identical instrument can be made from his writings. Together with another Merton mathematician John Maudit he anticipated trigonometry. He wrote a number of advanced mathematical works: *De sinibus demonstrativis, De sinibus et arcubus, De chorda et arcu recto et verso et umbris, Tabulae chordarum,* and *Calculationes chordarum.* Another member of this group, Simon Bredon, wrote a commentary on the *Almagest,* a book on Boethius' arithmetic, and a work on the theory of the planets which was entirely derived from an earlier work by Gerard de Sabionetta. Bredon was a physician and his works included a monumental summary of

[1]Roger Bacon, *Opus Majus,* trans. R. B. Burke, University of Pennsylvania Press and OUP 1928, Vol. I, pp132-134, Vol II pp574, 582.
[2]For the uses of perspective glasses envisaged by Bacon see *Frier Bacon His Discoverie of the miracles of Art Nature and Magick faithfully translated out of Dr. Dee's own copy by T. M.* Printed for Simon Miller at the Starre in St Pauls' Churchyard 1659. Bacon also thought that Julius Caesar had used such glasses to watch the Britons across the Channel.

medical theory only part of which has survived. Bredon tried to fix the position of Oxford, and calculated a table of sines. He had at least two astrolabes. A copy of his explanation of Boethius is known to have been in the library of John Dee, and was later acquired by Kenelm Digby and is now in the Bodleian Library, Oxford.[1]

Two contemporaries of Bredon, John Asheden and William Rede, combined to write a treatise on the lunar eclipse of 1345. William Rede fixed the position of Oxford at 51° 50′N and 15°W (the correct position is 51° 46′N and 1° 16′W), and calculated a set of tables from 1340 to 1600 for the meridian of Oxford. A manuscript belonging to Dee, now MS Digby 176, contains a large number of observations by Rede and other members of the Merton School. Rede became Bishop of Chichester and left over 300 books in his will. William Merle another fellow of Merton kept the first meteorological record in Europe, finally Thomas Bradwardine perhaps the ablest pure mathematician of the group wrote a series of works on abstract mathematics which were published among the early printed mathematical texts. His *Tractatus de Proportionibus* was printed in 1495, the *Arithmetica Speculativa* in 1502, the *Geometria Speculativa* in 1511 and 1530, and the *De Quadratura Circuli* in 1495. Two of Bradwardine's works are found among the Dee manuscripts.[2] Much of what was accomplished by the Merton School in the fourteenth and fifteenth centuries has been lost since the mathematical manuscripts were destroyed at the time of the Edwardian visitations in 1550, but enough has survived to show that during this period Oxford became one of the scientific centres of Europe. But it was a centre somewhat apart from the rest of continental thought because in England the Aristotelianism of Thomas Aquinas never completely displaced the earlier Platonism, and the attitude towards mathematical and experimental science that was implicit in Plato's philosophy made possible a full utilisation of the scientific knowledge of the ancients. 'The truly scientific spirit of Grosseteste and Bacon, and of their contemporaries at Oxford, was of tremendous significance coming just at a time when the University of Paris was abandoning the mathematical sciences and turning its back on experimental methods.[3]

The Platonic revival

Nevertheless it was not in England that the first attempts at breaking away from the Aristotelian-Aquinas world system took place. The first important speculative thinker in the new world of humanist revival was Nicolas of Cusa,

[1]No. 142, Boetti Musica, 'Exposito Simonis de Bredon super duos libros arithmeticae Boetii'. List of manuscripts given in *The Private Diary of Dr. John Dee*, ed. J. O. Halliwell, Camden Society 1842. It is now MS Digby 178. For a discussion of Simon Bredon, see C. H. Talbot, 'Simon Bredon 1300-1372: Physician, Mathematician, Astronomer', *British Journal for the History of Science*, 1962-3.
[2]Nos. 37 and 181 in the list of Dee's manuscripts in *The Private Diary of Dr. John Dee*.
[3]F. R. Johnson, *Astronomical Thought*, p78.

and although his thought was entirely theoretical and incapable of proof, it was revolutionary in concept and daring in its implications. Nicolas of Cusa wrote his *Learned Ignorance* (*De Docta Ignorantia*) in 1440. He began with the assertion that man, imprisoned within his own sensory perception, can never know the full truth of the universe. He cannot therefore define it except in reference to himself, nor can he regard it as finite or infinite because both ideas limit the omnipotence of God. The universe therefore is 'indeterminate' in the sense that it cannot be the subject of precise knowledge. By purely intellectual methods, Cusa reached the conclusion that when dealing with general conceptions taken through to their logical maximum, the accepted laws of matter do not hold. In infinitely small or infinitely large circles, the circumference and the centre, or the circumference and the tangent, coincide: and a body moving infinitely fast in a circle will always be at rest. In considering the universe, Cusa reached the conclusion that it was impossible for the world to have a motionless fixed centre and that it had relative motion within the universe. For 'if we consider the diverse motions of the (celestial) orbs, it is impossible for the machine of the world to have any fixed or motionless centre . . . For there can be found no absolute minimum in motion, that is no fixed centre, because the minimum must necessarily coincide with the maximum.'[1] In fact, in Cusa's metaphysical reasoning, we find that it is impossible to consider objectively the world or the universe, because it is impossible for man to see either in relation to anything outside the visible world. 'Since therefore, it is impossible to enclose the world between a corporeal centrum and a circumference, it is [impossible for] our reason to have full understanding of the world, as it implies the comprehension of God who is the centre and circumference of it.'[2] Nicolas of Cusa cannot rank as a scientist for although his thought is astonishingly perceptive, he lacked the mathematical knowledge to provide adequate proof for his theories. But he is important as a thinker, for the startling nature of the ideas he put forward, and his implicit rejection of Aristotelian metaphysics had a broadening and unsettling effect on subsequent thought, and opened the way for a new interpretation of observed cosmology. He is like a man loosening a door but failing to open it completely.[3]

The second formative influence on sixteenth century philosophical thought, and one far more important than Nicolas of Cusa, was the rediscovery in 1460 of the *Corpus Hermeticum*. The writings of Hermes Trismegisthus are vital to a correct understanding of the scientific ideas of the Renaissance: they deflected astronomical thought throughout the period and their influence continued well beyond it. The *Corpus* consisted of fifteen books concerned with the occult and

[1]Quoted by A. Koyré, *From the Closed World to the Infinite Universe,* John Hopkins Press 1957, p11.
[2]Quoted by A. Koyré, *From the Closed World,* p11.
[3]There is an English translation of *De Docta Ignorantia* by Fr. Germain Heron, London 1954.

the practice of talismanic magic for drawing down the influences of the stars and making contact with daemonic and angelic powers outside the earth. They included an elaborate description of the sympathetic virtues of colours and of certain flowers, plants, and stones. (Relics of Hermetic lore persist today in astrological practice, and in lucky birth stones). These writings had been known by repute from references in the early church fathers, St. Augustine, Clement of Alexandria and Lactantius, who all accepted the legend that Hermes or Mercurius Trismegisthus was a priest – law giver of the ancient Egyptians – far older than Plato or any of the Greek philosophers. He is sometimes described as earlier than Moses, sometimes as a contemporary. Lactantius regarded him as divinely inspired with a fore-knowledge of the coming of Christ, Augustine condemned his magical practices but acknowledges his existence and his antiquity. This placing of Trismegisthus at the very beginning of revealed religion gave to his writings a quasi-divine authority and elevated him above other pagan philosophers. He was regarded as the source from which Plato obtained his gnostic ideas, and the forerunner of the truths revealed by Christianity. The phrase 'Son of God' in association with a 'Created Word' actually occurs in the two major treatises of the *Hermetic Corpus*, the *Pimander* and the *Asclepius*.

The supposed antiquity and even the actual existence of Hermes Trismegisthus was a myth due to a mistaken dating and uncritical acceptance of the *Corpus*. In 1614 Isaac Casaubon proved that the *Corpus Hermeticum* was written by various authors between the second and fourth centuries AD. The Egyptian provenance was probably spurious, and the main influence seems to have been the Greek philosophic thought of the period combined with Jewish, Egyptian and Persian writings. Far from being one of the original sources of revealed religion, the writings of Hermes postdated Christ. Yet the importance attached to the *Corpus* in the fifteenth and sixteenth centuries was enormous. The manuscript was brought to Cosimo de Medici from Macedonia in 1460, at the time Marsilio Ficino was translating the newly discovered Platonic dialogues. At the express orders of Cosimo he was compelled to put these aside and translate the *Corpus Hermeticum*, in order that Cosimo should know the revealed wisdom of original truth before his death.[1]

The translation of Hermes Trismegisthus had an immense effect. There are more manuscripts of it in existence than of any other work by Ficino. It was printed for the first time in 1471 and went through sixteen editions before the end of the sixteenth century. In the *Corpus* lie the clues and the explanation of the Renaissance revival of magic. It dominated to an extraordinary extent the whole of later scientific thought. Its strength lay in the fact that it seemed to offer a short cut to truth and to knowledge of the universe. It offered a pathway

[1]F. A. Yates, *Giordano Bruno and the Hermetic Tradition*, Routledge and Kegan Paul 1964, pp13-14.

to a union with God through nature by the practice of sympathetic magic designed to draw down supernatural powers to the earth; and with proper safeguards a man could protect himself against the powers of darkness. All life, all nature, was interconnected. The situation has been well described by Dr Yates: 'It was believed that continual effluvia of influences were pouring down on to the earth from the stars, and that these influences could be canalised and used by an operator with the requisite knowledge. Every object in the material world was full of occult sympathies from the star on which it depended. The operator who wished to capture . . . the power of the planet Venus, must know what plants belonged to Venus, what stones and metals, what animals, and use these only when addressing Venus. He must know the images of Venus and know how to inscribe them on talismans made of the right Venus materials and at the right astrological moment. Such images were held to capture the spirit or power of the star, and to hold it or store it for use.' The same applied to the constellations and to all spheres of heaven, all of which were controlled by the various orders of angelic powers. 'The magician was one who knew how to enter into this system and use it, by knowing the links of the chains of influences descending vertically from above, and establishing for himself a chain of ascending links by the correct use of occult sympathies in terrestial things, of celestial images and names.'[1] Since in actual fact the composite authors of the *Corpus Hermeticum* were strongly influenced by Greek thought and by Plato in particular, and were yet at the same time post-Christian they offered (provided the spurious date was accepted) the ideal link for which the Florentine humanists had been seeking between pagan and Christian metaphysics. The ideas in the *Corpus* were rapidly assimilated by the Neo-platonic school and through them became a permanent influence on Renaissance thought. The danger lay in the fact that the Christian and Platonic sources had been mixed with a third Egyptian or Persian element which led directly to astrological daemonic magic. The *Corpus* contained descriptions of the thirty-six decans who ruled over the 360 degrees of the Zodiac, each had particular images, and each had astrological power over those born under their rule. They were in fact Egyptian sidereal gods of time which had been grafted on to a complex system of gnostic thought. The works of Hermes Trismegisthus were deeply influenced by decan worship and were certainly partially known in fragmentary form in the middle ages: there are references to Trismegisthus in Albertus Magnus and Roger Bacon, and in a number of astrological and alchemical works, in all of which his great authority and even greater antiquity are stressed. The same information on sympathetic and talismanic magic, together with a list and description of the decans occurs in another work called the *Picatrix* which also influenced the Florentine School, and through them a whole generation. The *Picatrix*, which was not written by Trismegisthus, although strongly influenced by Hermetic thought, came to

[1]F. A. Yates, *Giordano Bruno and the Hermetic Tradition*, p45.

Europe via Arab culture and dates from about the twelth century.[1] The *Picatrix* if properly used was virtually a complete guide to astrological magic.

The extent to which this magical thought lay behind that of the Renaissance Neo-platonists can be seen in Ficino's work *De vita coelitus comparanda* (On Capturing the Life of the Stars) which is the third book of his *Libri de Vita*. Ficino's own astral magic was harmless enough, he sang Orphic hymns on a specially constructed Orphic lute in an attempt to awake the natural harmony of the universe, but the fact that the Neo-platonic school in Florence which took such extreme care to present the revival of Plato and Neo-platonism as a movement which could be accorded with Christianity, allowed a fringe of magic to penetrate this movement was of profound importance. For 'this comparatively harmless attempt at astral magical therapy was to open a flood-gate through which an astonishing revival of magic poured into Europe.'[2] Ficino's younger contemporary Pico della Mirandola went further and definitely linked Hermetical talismanic magic with true cabalistic magic developed from Jewish mystical teaching in medieval Spain, and embodied in the *Zohar* which was written in the thirteenth century. This was based on the permutations of the ten Sepiroth or Names of God which taken together formed the one 'Name', and the twenty-two letters of the Hebrew alphabet. It was linked with the hierarchial structure of the universe, since the ten Sepiroth are equated with the ten spheres of the cosmos. It thus entered the sphere of astrology and astronomy. It was also partly Pythagorean, for one of the paths to the 'Name' was that of Gametria, which used the numerical values of the Hebrew letters, by which when words were calculated into numbers, and numbers into words, the entire organisation of the world could be read off in terms of word numbers. This raised mystical thought to a level of considerable mental agility, and it is not surprising that Pico della Mirandola asserted that pure cabala could only be done by the 'intellectual' part of the soul, whereas other forms of natural magic could be done by the 'spiritual'.

Although in itself a dead end which distracted the abilities of scientists throughout Europe, the Hermetic cabalistic movement cannot be dismissed as purely negative. It differed fundamentally from the superstitions of astrology of the uninitiated and had a more creative and constructive approach. The belief that man was under the control of astrological influences was replaced by the attempt to learn to control these influences by intellectual methods. The most extreme example of this type of number magic occurs outside Italy and is

[1]The *Picatrix* contains a full list of the thirty six decans, and is quoted by F. A. Yates in *Giordano Bruno*, pp51-3. She gives as examples the three decans of Aries. First decan 'A huge dark man with red eyes holding a sword and clad in a white garment.' Second decan 'A woman clad in green and lacking one leg.' Third decan 'A man holding a golden sphere and dressed in red.'

[2]F. A. Yates, *Giordano Bruno*, pp58-61.

found in the *Steganographia* of Johannes Trithemius. Trithemius, who is connected directly with the German philosopher Cornelius Agrippa and indirectly with Reuchlin, came from an entirely different background from the Florentine Neo-platonists. In the *Steganographia* he combined a complicated system of writing in numerical ciphers (later considered and possibly used by Burghley) which can claim to be in some ways the ancestor of the numerical cipher codes still in use, with the practical but useless idea of using angels to transmit messages by telepathy. His activities together with those of Lefèvre d'Etaples and Reuchlin are dismissed somewhat critically by Professor Lynn Thorndike who remarks that their works, (together with the whole Hermetic corpus) 'are so mystical and cloudy that a definite exposition of their contents is difficult, and one does not care to stand for long on the quicksands of their reveries.'[1] But it is important to remember that whereas cabala was in itself a sterile type of intellectual gymnastics, the belief in the importance of number as the basis of scientific knowledge was correct, 'the subsequent history of man's achievements in applied science has shown that number is indeed a master-key, or one of the master-keys, to operations by which the forces of the cosmos are made to work in man's service.'[2] Pico's cabalistic theories were more advanced than the rather innocent naturalistic activities of Ficino. Natural magic led upward to God through the various degrees of angels, while cabalistic magic could approach God directly through the ten Sepiroth. Both aspects had a direct affinity to the mystical teachings of the pseudo-Dionysius and both have had a fluctuating but constant influence on religious thought ever since. Pico's theories were sufficiently unorthodox to attract the attention of the church, and a commission sat to inquire into his beliefs and he was forced to withdraw a number of his theses. After a short imprisonment in France, he returned to Florence and lived under the powerful protection of the Medici. The respectability of the Hermetic writings were not however in question and not only does a portrait of Hermes Trismegisthus holding a quotation from the Asclepius figure in the floor of Siena cathedral, but Alexander VI placed the thirty-six decans and Hermes in the form of Mercury round the frieze of the Borgia apartments in the Vatican. There is even a theory that Botticelli's 'Birth of Venus' and 'Primavera' are in fact talismanic pictures designed to evoke beneficial astral influences.[3]

Scientific thought in England was directly and continuously affected during the sixteenth century by this development of the occult on the continent. The

[1] L. Thorndike, *A History of Magic and Experimental Science,* Columbia University Press 1948, Vol. VI, p437.
[2] F. A. Yates, *Giordano Bruno,* p146.
[3] F. A. Yates, *Giordano Bruno,* pp42-3, 76, quoting an article by E. H. Gombrich, 'Botticelli's Mythologies: a study in the Neoplatonic symbolism of his circle', *Journal of the Warburg and Courtauld Institutes* VIII 1945.

links between Colet and Marsilio Ficino were direct and have been examined in Chapter two. Colet himself wrote a Dionysian treatise on the celestial hierarchies, while Thomas More translated the *Life of Pico della Mirandola* in which he refers to 'ye olde obscure philosphye of Pythagoras Trismegisthus and Orpheus'. The influence of Nicolas of Cusa and of Hermetic thought can also be seen in More's description of the religion of the Utopians:

> some worship for God the sonne: some the mone: some, some other planettes
> . . . But the most and wysest part [rejecting all these] believe that there is a
> certyn Godlie power unknown, everlastinge, incomprehensible, inexplicable,
> farre above the capacitie and retche of mans witte, dispersed throughout all
> the worlde, not in bignes, but in vertue and power. Him they call the father
> of al. To him alone they attribute the beginninges, the encreasinges, the
> procedinges, the chaunges and the endes of al thinges.

A further indication of the knowledge and influence of this branch of quasi-scientific thought in England can be obtained from the Lumley Library catalogue. There are seven copies of Cornelius Agrippa's *De occulta Philosophia*, which although not a profound work, gave a wide survey of the existing magical practices, and these included a copy of the first edition published in 1533 which belonged to Cranmer. There are six copies of the works of Ramon Lull on alchemy and natural magic, one of which is the commentary on Lull by Cornelius Agrippa,[1] and one is bound together with Albertus Magnus on stones and minerals.[2] Since the majority of the scientific works in the Library were collected by Lumley rather than Cranmer or Arundel, the inclusion of so many copies of these works together with a number of Arabic and other alchemical and occult treatises is interesting.[3] Particularly so, since the English scientists of his own day are poorly represented: Robert Recorde has only three works, John Dee only two – he possessed William Turner's *Herbal* in two volumes[4] – and there are four editions of Leonard Digges' *Prognostication* with the additions of Thomas Digges.[5] But the important works of William Bourne on navigation and gunnery are not represented at all, nor are works by William Borough, Robert Norman or William Gilbert's epoch making *De Magnete*. The catalogue is interesting for what it omits, as well as what it contains. It is worth noting that it does contain a single copy of Copernicus in the 1566 edition.[6] The conservative nature of Lumley's outlook is confirmed by the section on medicine where there are a large number of editions of Galen and Avicenna and the comparatively few sixteenth century medical works.

There were thus two forces behind English scientific development in the early sixteenth century, the Platonic revival of the humanists, and the continuing

[1]No. 1879, p219.   [2]No. 2409, p271.
[3]See Sears Jayne, *Catalogue of the Library of John Lord Lumley*, p9.
[4]No. 2426.   [5]No. 2030.   [6]No. 2087.

influence of Roger Bacon and the Merton school: but whereas the Platonic revival contained elements which proved unscientific, the Baconian tradition of technical and practical inquiry, did not. In the library of Dr. John Dee, which until its dispersal at the end of the sixteenth century was the largest and most comprehensive scientific library in England, the works of Roger Bacon out-number those by any other author. Manuscripts of Grosseteste are numerous and the various fourteenth century English mathematicians and astronomers are well represented. William Batcumbe's writings on astronomy (he was a fifteenth century Fellow of Merton) are found also among the manuscripts of Robert Recorde. In England therefore there was a scientific tradition still available in surviving manuscripts which was of definite importance. The scientists of sixteenth century England were indeed fortunate in the tradition of learning and the spirit of independent research that they inherited from their compatriots of an earlier era. They were likewise favoured by the sympathetic attitude toward the mathematical sciences that was characteristic of most of the leading humanists of the late fifteenth and early sixteenth centuries. The scholars who played the leading part in the revival of Greek learning in England did not confine their interest solely to literary works, but lent their support to the promotion of scientific knowledge.

It was of great importance for the later flexibility of English scientific thought that the tradition which it inherited from Roger Bacon and his successors, and the impetus from the early humanists, were both free of Aristotelian dogmatism, so that Bacon's emphasis on experimental proof, and the Platonic revival which was a characteristic of the English humanists were both absorbed into the English scientific tradition. But it was fortunate that the two aspects of science, the theoretical and the practical and technical, developed parallel to each other rather than in a single stream; for whereas the scholars who could read Latin were inevitably affected by Hermetic thought, and on occasion deflected by it, the technicians and craftsmen, and those who in the later years of the century began the real popularisation of science, were not.

Navigation, exploration, and astronomy

In exploration and navigation an important catalyst was Ptolemy's *Geographia* which became available in Europe for the first time in the fifteenth century. It was printed early, there are seven incunabula and one German abstract.[1] Ptolemy discussed a number of methods of map projection and the *Geographia* immediately became a book of vital importance as the basis for advance in cartography and navigation.

In both these fields the initial leap forward took place on the continent,

G. Sarton, *The Appreciation of Science*, p147.

particularly in Spain and Portugal. England's share in the fifteenth century was confined to the spasmodic attempts of merchants, particularly from Bristol, to open up new trading areas in the Mediterranean and the North Atlantic.[1]

England's late start both in scientific thought and its practical implications was a positive advantage; for once started she advanced with a rapidity which soon placed her in the forefront of Europe. The clearest and most dramatic example of this is the speed with which England mastered the intricate mathematical background necessary before successful oceanic voyages could be undertaken. Portugal and Spain had begun their theoretical training in the fifteenth century and had built up a formidable expertise, and a large amount of practical knowledge which they kept secret, and which for a century gave them a virtual monopoly of the new discoveries. England had nothing to compare with the Casa de Contrataçion at Seville, and was fighting the Wars of the Roses when Henry the Navigator was training the pilots of Portugal. As Commander Waters points out, 'What is remarkable is not that the English took no part in and no interest in the great discoveries of the fifteenth and early sixteenth centuries, but that, awakening in the latter half of the sixteenth century to the reality of the discoveries, they mastered the art of oceanic navigation that made them possible so rapidly and so effectively that within thirty years they had defeated the leading maritime state in a battle at sea, and within half a century had planted colonies of their own overseas, and were trading regularly round the Cape to India and the Far East, and making original contributions of their own of fundamental importance to the art of navigation.'[2]

The fact that England made such a slow start in maritime exploration is interesting, but not in itself surprising. Henry VII's concern with trade formed a vital part of his policy, but he made no attempt to follow up the successful oceanic voyages of the Cabots from Bristol for the simple reason that transatlantic trade was neither practically possible nor politically desirable. Henry was too wise and too insecure to challenge the combined interests of Spain and Portugal; and even more important, he had no reserve of native trained pilots capable of making oceanic voyages. As late as the death of Henry VIII most of the pilots employed by the King were foreign. The early sailing directions for English waters were also foreign. The only exception was a fifteenth century manuscript covering the circumnavigation of Britain and a voyage to Gibralter which was copied in manuscript in the reign of Edward IV. The first printed 'rutter', or manual of sailing directions, in the sixteenth century to cover English waters was French. The oldest known printed book of sailing directions

[1]See E. Carus Wilson, *Medieval Merchant Venturers*, Methuen 1954; J. A. Williamson, *The Voyages of the Cabots and the English Discovery of North America under Henry VII and Henry VIII*, London 1929.
[2]D. W. Waters, *The Art of Navigation in England in Elizabethan and Early Stuart Times*, Hollis and Carter 1958, p80.

is an anonymous Italian 'portolare' published in Venice in 1490. The rutter of Pierre Garcie was written 1483–1484, and covered the coasts of England, Wales, France, Spain, and Portugal to the Strait of Gibraltar. A version probably by Garcie called *Le Routier de la Mer* was printed between 1502 and 1510. It was followed by the larger *Le Grant Routier* in 1520 with a second edition in 1521. The first English version, a translation of *Le Routier de la Mer* was published by Robert Copland in 1528. It was reprinted throughout the middle of the century and in 1541 a *Rutter of the Northe* was added, compiled by Richard Proude from the fifteenth century English manuscript.[1] The *Rutter of the Northe* did not include Scottish waters. These were covered by Alexander Lindsey's *The Rutter of the Sea, with havens, roades, sounds etc from Humber northward, round about Scotland, 1540*. This existed only in manuscript until late in the century. These rutters were all that was needed, for 'few Englishmen could navigate a merchant or a royal ship across the great ocean to a known landfall. None could navigate to the East and none had seen the Pacific.'[2] Few ships existed of over 250 tons displacement, and their equipment, a lead and line, and a crude compass consisting of a magnetised needle gummed onto a paper card rotating on a pin (with no allowance for variation and needing frequent remagnetisation with a lodestone), was totally inadequate except for coastal navigation.

The sixteenth century saw a great expansion of English maritime activity. Henry VII built the first dry dock in Europe. Henry VIII did more. He recognised the increasing importance of coastal trade by legalising the existing seamen's guilds at the important coastal ports, Bristol, Lynn, York, Hull, Newcastle-on-Tyne and London. The reorganisation of Trinity House at Deptford Strand, which was granted its first Charter in 1514, had far-reaching effects. By training pilots, it made possible the safe negotiation of the dangerous estuary of the Thames, and so was one of the chief factors making possible the phenomenal growth of the port of London and the diversion of trade away from south coast ports, such as Southampton, direct to the capital.[3] In 1562 and 1565 Acts enlarging its powers gave it overall responsibility for the maintenance of lights and buoys for the safety 'of mariners haunting the sea'. It was also given the right to grant certificates of competance to trained seamen, who were then exempt from military service; and a register of qualified seamen was to be kept, and a list of merchant shipping. In this way, the government by the end of the century could see the position of the merchant marine and its reserve of competent sailors in time of war. The muster of 1582, for example, showed 1,600 merchant vessels, of which only 250 were over 80 tons, and a total of 16,500

[1] All these rutters are reproduced in facsimile with an introduction by D. W. Waters in *The Rutters of the Sea. The Sailing Directions of Pierre Garcie*, Yale 1967.
[2] D. W. Waters, *The Art of Navigation*, p79.
[3] A. Ruddock, 'Trinity House at Deptford', *English Historical Review* 1950, p458.

registered seamen, of which 6,500 were fishermen.[1] Henry VIII also went further than his father in creating a Royal Navy designed for war. The Navy Office was in existence by 1545, and Henry clearly attached importance to seapower. The reign saw the evolution of permanent administrative institutions in the Navy Board and Trinity House. Under the guidance of foreign experts, Italian shipwrights and German gunfounders, English naval technology steadily advanced. Cannon were mounted on board ship, and the design of the ships themselves modified in consequence. A French pilot, Jean Rotz, served the King, and French charts were in use for the coasts; and, stimulated by foreign workmen, the art of instrument making developed in London.[2] The existence of this permanently armed force though commanded by the gentry and nobility, should not be forgotten when assessing the power of the monarchy under Henry. This accession of strength was, however, lost through neglect under Edward and Mary. Henry left 53 royal ships with a total tonnage of 11,268, the greater part built since the Dissolution. Mary, on her accession, found most of them so rotten that she had to sell them for timber, and at the time of the fall of Calais she had only 5 ships available in the Channel. She left at her death a total of 26 ships, with a tonnage of 7,110, but many were unserviceable. Elizabeth faced a formidable task in restoring England's naval as distinct from her mercantile power.

The decision of Henry VII to confine his expansion of trade to Europe, the Baltic and the Levant, was politically expedient, but was also dictated by practical considerations. Expansion of trade to the New World was in fact unnecessary. Recent examinations of the Spanish archives have shown that until Henry VIII's break with Rome raised acute difficulties over religion and political obedience, English merchants under certain conditions were perfectly free to trade across the Atlantic, and that the story of their total exclusion from the Spanish discoveries in the New World is a myth. In 1505 Ferdinand of Aragon instructed the Casa de Contrataçion (which controlled all trade with the Americas on behalf of the government) that foreigners resident in Seville, Cadiz or Jerez, who possessed real estate and a family, and who lived in Spain for over fifteen years, were to be considered as naturalised Spaniards for the purpose of trade with the Americas. This decree was later extended to all foreigners resident in Castille, provided they did not act as principals but in partnership with other Spanish merchants. The Treaty of Medina del Campo also gave English merchants special privileges, and while they were not free from restrictions, they could trade, subject to the same controls as Spanish merchants. In fact no merchant, Spanish or English, could trade freely with the New World. All trade was strictly regulated in the interests of the Spanish Monarchy, and all merchants had to handle their business through the Casa de Contrataçion, which acted as a central clearing house.

[1] D. W. Waters, *The Art of Navigation*, pp106-112.   [2] D. W. Waters, *The Art of Navigation*, p82.

These favourable conditions for English merchants continued throughout the first thirty years of the century. Surviving documents in the Spanish State Archives at Seville and the Notorial registers for the Andalusian ports show 'that the Spaniards did not, in effect, ignore or refuse to apply the terms of the treaties between England and Spain to their New World colonies, but that in the reign of Henry VIII an open and flourishing trade to the Indies was carried on by a considerable number of English merchants.'[1] The most important group was centred at Seville and had direct connections with Bristol and London. The chief figures were Robert Thorne, Roger Barlow and Thomas Bridges, who were all resident in Spain, and Thomas Malliard of London who carried on an extensive exporting business via Southampton and Bristol to Seville. Malliard made Thorne, Barlow and Bridges his executors with powers of attorney for his property in Spain, and the winding up of his estate by Barlow in 1523 shows the extent and variety of this overseas trade. Malliard's son was given authority to claim 'six hundred and seventy-four pesos of gold ... registered from the Indies in the King's register', which was the return on a cargo of wine sent out by Barlow on Malliard's behalf.

Besides the principal merchants like Thorne and Barlow there were a number of lesser figures, but of importance because of their opportunities of acquiring knowledge of Spanish trade and methods, like the professional pilot Henry Latimer, or Thomas Tison, the factor for English merchants resident at San Domingo, or Thomas Howell, who was at one time Malliard's factor, and who built up a considerable business on his own account before his death. Howell was a London Draper and his ledgers, now preserved in the Drapers Hall in London, give a detailed account of his activities in the Spanish-American trade between 1518 and 1528; while records of the cargoes handled by Thorne show that he dealt in 'flour, foodstuffs, candles, white soap, wrought tin, iron goods, esparto, and wine', and that he employed agents in Spain to buy on his behalf, besides taking goods from England.[2] What is of great interest is that Robert Thorne had three brothers, all in the church (one became Bishop of St Davids after the Dissolution), and all agents of Cromwell.[3] Thorne himself was convinced of the value of the Atlantic trade routes to England, and coming from Bristol he had inherited the knowledge of the earlier attempts by Bristol merchants to exploit Western sea routes in the late fifteenth century. Together with Barlow, Thorne made determined efforts to interest the English government in trade with the Americas. In 1526 he deliberately invested money in the La Plata voyage, in order to secure places on the ship for Henry Latimer and

[1]G. Connel-Smith, 'English merchants trading to the New World in the early sixteenth century', *Bulletin of the Institute of Historical Research*, Vol. XXIII, 1950.
[2]G. Connel-Smith, *Bulletin of the Institute of Historical Research*, Vol. XXIII, 1950.
[3]E. G. R. Taylor, 'Roger Barlow, A New Chapter in Early Tudor Geography', *Geographical Journal* 1926, p157.

Roger Barlow, with the sole object of finding out as much as possible of the route and pilotage in order to open up an English route to the Spice Islands.

On his return, Roger Barlow wrote *A briefe Somme of Geographia,* based on the Spanish work of Ferdinand of Enciso, but with an introductory section on the sphere and art of navigation, with a plan for a voyage to Cathay and the Spice Islands by a trans-polar route, and containing the first nautical tables in English. It also included an account of the 1526 voyage which incorporated in it a description of the Canaries and Azores. The manuscript, however, was not presented to Henry VIII until 1541, when it was too late to be of practical use, and for diplomatic reasons Henry did not allow it to be published.[1] It is not generally known that from 1525–7 England had the chance of legitimately acquiring the right to trade to the Spice Islands. During this period the Archbishop of York, Edward Lee, was in Spain on behalf of Henry VIII, where he naturally met Robert Thorne, who interested him in the possibility of purchasing on England's behalf the Spanish share in the Spice trade which Charles V was planning to sell to Portugal. Lee wrote to Wolsey, suggesting that Henry VIII should buy the Spanish trading rights, but his proposals were not followed up and the chance was lost.

This apparent lack of interest by the government was mirrored by a similar lack of interest among London merchants. In 1517 there was little support for the abortive voyage of Sir Thomas More's son-in-law, John Rastell, to cross the Atlantic, and Rastell was again ahead of his time in putting on the stage in London in 1519 *A new interlude and a mery of the nature of the iiii elements,* in which the characters displayed maps and nautical instruments to the audience, and urged the translation of navigational and scientific works into English. It is significant that there were no general books on geography in English at the time of Henry VIII's death. Wolsey, who tried to get Sebastian Cabot back to England in the 1520s, and who showed a personal, if indirect, interest in mathematical science, might have had the vision and initiative to support Thorne's plan at an earlier stage, but in 1527 his fall was imminent, and neither the King nor the London trading community was ready to act.

The Reformation and the deterioration of Anglo-Spanish relations inevitably affected the position of English merchants in Spain. It was this factor rather than any deliberate 'closed shop' policy which excluded English merchants from the New World. With the increasing power of the Inquisition the position of many, such as the Thorne brothers, became impossible and they returned to England.[2] Anglo-Spanish trade to the New World declined with Anglo-Spanish

---

[1]Now MS Royal 18 B xxviii; see E. G. R. Taylor, *The Mathematical Practitioners of Tudor and Stuart England,* CUP 1954, pp166, 313.

[2]The Thorne brothers left an important collection of nautical books, charts, and instruments, to found a sailors' library at Bristol; see E. G. R. Taylor, *The Mathematical Practitioners,* p166.

goodwill. The only English merchants to survive were those who remained Catholic and virtually became Spanish, often marrying and settling in Spain, such as the Sweeting family group in Andalusia, and Thomas Harrison, another leading member of the Andalusian Company who stayed and acted as agent for the other English merchants who had sold up and fled. The reign of Mary produced a short-lived improvement in the position during which Stephen Borough, later chief pilot of the Muscovy Company and a Master of Trinity House, visited the Casa de Contrataçion and brought back a copy of the Spanish manual of navigation, the *Arte de Navegar* of Martin Cortes. But the reign of Elizabeth forced the issue and from then on the mercantile co-operation between the two countries ceased to exist and was replaced by competition and war.

It is clear that the most closely guarded secrets of this newly opened trade were navigational. The methods used, the routes taken, the hazards of tides, currents, shoals and reefs were all filed at the Casa de Contrataçion and inaccessible to those outside the Iberian Peninsula. It is this which made the knowledge acquired by Barlow and Latimer in 1526 so important; it is this which made the eventual return of Sebastian Cabot, who had been Spain's Pilot General, a turning point in the middle years of the century: it made Stephen Borough's short stay in Spain of real significance, and Richard Eden's translation of Cortes's *Arte de Navegar* so influential. Through the knowledge and information thus gained England was able by using her own trained mathematicians to improve upon Spanish methods, and by adding experience to theoretical knowledge she eventually took the lead in maritime exploration. But it is salutary to remember that the first thing Drake did on his voyage round the world, when he captured any Spanish or Portuguese vessel, was to seize the charts and sailing directions and co-opt the pilots.[1] The enormous debt owed by England to Spain cannot be over-emphasised for it was the greatest single influence on English expansion of trade in the sixteenth century. Commander Waters makes it clear that the English 'turned to Spain for expert tuition in the art of navigation and the economics of ocean trading. At first by bribery and then by virtue of the fact that the King of Spain was Consort of their Queen, they learned all the Spaniards could teach them of the art of navigation. While French, Italian and Portuguese pilots also assisted them, their mainstay was the knowledge of the Spaniards, with their highly organised system of navigational instruction and examination, their remarkable hydrographic office and its products. It was the Spanish system as interpreted for them by Sebastian Cabot in the 1550s and by Stephen Borough in the opening years of Elizabeth's reign, and as modified by the Privy Council to suit the English temperament and institutions, that lay behind the chartered trading companies, of which the Muscovy Company was the first to foster navigation,

[1] See D. W. Waters, *The Art of Navigation*, Appendix 12, pp535-6.

and behind the legislation of the 1560s which ensured sufficiency of seamen, and through Trinity House of licensed masters, to serve the country in peace and war. It was the Spanish system which provided the English with their first manual of navigation, which was also their standard one throughout Elizabeth's reign, and indeed up to the Civil War in the seventeenth century. It was the Spanish system which inspired the lectureships on navigation which were eventually established.'[1]

The geographical discoveries were tangible proof of new ideas and technologies, but they did not themselves produce any immediate change in scientific thought. The theoretical framework of the universe, the cosmological 'terms of reference', were not altered. They remained those of the medieval church. The reality of God, the essential cosmic order, the 'chain of being', the hierarchical structure of the natural world with man as the only rational creature standing midway heaven and earth; these ideas were accepted as axiomatic throughout Europe. The danger lay in the fact that as soon as the framework began to be investigated empirically, it was seen to be incapable of proof. Yet even when no proof could be found and man's view of nature changed in response to the discoveries of the scientists, the framework persisted. This created a dangerously unstable situation, a perpetual conflict which is still unresolved. But in the sixteenth century the links in the cosmic chain were only loosened, they were not broken. Shakespeare could talk about the singing spheres with perfect sincerity, and what is more, was believed by his audience. It is against the theological and cosmographical background of the middle ages (which it should be remembered included such advanced thinkers as Nicolas of Cusa), and the resurgence of the Hermetic tradition, that the achievements of English scientists should be seen.

The heliocentric theories of Nicolas Copernicus which initiated the reassessment of the old cosmology were themselves less revolutionary than is often thought. Copernicus had studied in Italy and was deeply influenced by Neo-platonism and included a reference to Hermes Trismegisthus in support of his theories.

> But in the center of all resides the Sun . . . Therefore it is not improperly that some people call it the lamp of the world, others its mind, others its ruler. Trismegistus [calls it] the visible God, Sophocles' Electra, the All Seeing. Thus, assuredly, as residing in the royal see the Sun governs the surrounding family of stars.[2]

It was largely in pursuit of a more harmonious and therefore more Platonic mathematical system that Copernicus worked out his ideas. He did not

[1]D. W. Waters, *The Art of Navigation*, p496.
[2]Quoted in A. Koyré, *From the Closed World to the Infinite Universe*, p33.

overthrow the Ptolemaic system, he tried to modify and amend it.[1] He thought of celestial movement in terms of perfect circular orbits, and as a result although he regarded the sun as static, it was not in point of fact the exact centre of the Copernican system. The observed orbits of the planets still possessed a marked eccentricity and it was necessary to use the Ptolemaic solution of deferrents and epicycles to overcome the difficulty. Copernicus achieved two things in *De Revolutionibus Orbium Coelestium,* he reduced the eccentric and epicyclic circles of the *Almagest* from 80 to 34 and thus produced a simpler solution; and he introduced the idea of movement into the behaviour of the earth, which revolved on its own axis every 24 hours, and traced a circular path round the sun each year, and wobbled slightly on its axis round the poles. It is this attribution of movement to the earth which is the most important and significant part of *De Revolutionibus.* Between Copernicus and his Aristotelian predecessors, the chief difference was that the earth was thought of as being in motion in the Copernican, indeed as having three different motions. The Ptolemaic system was devised to represent things as they appear to an observer on the earth who supposes himself to be at rest. It might be more appropriate to designate the Ptolemaic system as geostatic and the Copernican as geo-dynamic.[2] It was not until Kepler broke away from the idea of perfect circular motion and crystalline spheres and substituted elliptical orbits along which the planets moved round the sun at varying speeds, that the need for eccentric orbits disappeared and a truly heliocentric system was evolved.

Copernicus' *De Revolutionibus* was published as a mathematical alternative to Ptolemy's *Almagest* in 1543, but it was only gradually that the full implications of the theory were understood. Many educated men were aware that the theory existed, it was used as a simpler and more accurate version, but it was not accepted as being true. This applies at all levels. For while the leaders of scientific thought were affected directly by Copernican and Neo-platonic ideas and gradually accepted them, literate society as a whole was more influenced by the popularisation of the medieval conception of the universe through the medium of the printing press.

In England during the opening years of the sixteenth century Caxton's translation of a thirteenth century French poem issued as *The Mirrour of the Worlde* in 1481, was the most comprehensive account of astronomy available in English, and remained so for over fifty years. It was naturally entirely Ptolemaic in outlook. *The Kalendar of Shepherdes* translated from the French in three different versions in 1503, 1506 and 1508 and printed by both Pynson and Wynkyn de Worde also gave a simple account of the universe along Ptolemaic lines, and as an almanac represented a slightly different but even more widespread printed source of astronomical information. The popular almanacs

[1]L. Thorndike, *A History of Magic and Experimental Science,* Vol V, p422.
[2]L. Thorndike, *A History of Magic,* Vol V, p423.

which sold for a few pence are of the greatest importance in the spread of scientific ideas connected with astrology and cosmology. They acted as diaries, but also contained much miscellaneous information. *The Shepherdes' Kalendar* which continued in print until the middle of the seventeenth century, gave the movable feasts of the Church, and tables for finding the Sunday letter. It also contained a calendar showing the entry of the sun into the zodiac, information about astrology, a method of establishing the meridian line, and how to read the hour from the stars. It was in fact a calendar, encyclopaedia and picture book all in one. Since they had a wide circulation, these almanacs can be used to establish what astronomical ideas were available to ordinary readers at any one time, and at the same time they reflect the changes in outlook which took place. By the early seventeenth century publishers were including the Copernican and Tychonic systems as viable alternatives to Ptolemy. The earliest almanacs which openly supported the Copernican theory were those of Edward Gresham and Thomas Bretnor in the early years of James I.

The importance of almanacs and their increasing accuracy is illustrated by the career of John Tapp. Tapp became interested in navigation as a young man after reading Richard Eden's translation of Cortes' *Arte de Navegar*. In 1600 he transferred from the Drapers Company to the Stationers in order to concentrate on the publication of books 'of nautical and kindred interest'. Such was the demand that Tapp was filling a real need when he decided upon the regular publication of an almanac containing all those tables which he had collected as being most useful and necessary to seamen. Tapp's *Seamans Kalendar* contained daily tables of the sun's ascension and declination, the phases of the moon with an explanation of how to 'shift the tides'; and a catalogue of fixed stars and a table of longitudes. The *Kalendar* also included a certain amount of astrological information, for example the name of the planet governing each hour, but its main emphasis was nautical and scientific. By 1615 Tapp added a table of sines to his mathematical information and urged his readers to make use of Handson's *Trigonometrie* published the previous year. The real importance of these almanacs can be gauged from the fact that, according to Professor Taylor, they were 'often the only book to be found in farm or cottage apart from the Bible', and if a widespread growth of literacy is assumed following Dr. Simon's figures for the numbers of local schools, a certain amount of the information must have been read, even if not fully understood. At the other end of the intellectual scale, the actual diary of Dr. John Dee was written in the margins of an almanac. The inclusion of astronomical and cosmological *theory* in these books which were used by everybody, directly formed public opinions and ultimately paved the way for the acceptance of the heliocentric theory in the seventeenth century.[1]

[1] For information on the effects and contents of almanacs, see E. G. R. Taylor, *The Mathematical Practitioners,* pp55–8; and F. R. Johnson, *Astronomical Thought,* pp249–50.

The only other source to rival the almanac in popular influence was the school text book, and here the use of Marcellus Palingenius' *Zodiacus Vitae* is probably the most important. An English translation appeared in 1560, and during the reign of Elizabeth it was a prescribed text book in many grammar schools. The *Zodiacus* played a significant part in preparing the way for the rejection of the authority of Aristotle and ultimately of the whole Ptolemaic system, simply because though conventional in content and in his description of the universe, Palingenius is strongly influenced by Neo-platonic ideas, and did query the universal validity of Aristotelian thought in particular and all rigid theories in general.

> Whatsoever *Aristotle* sayeth, or any of them all,
> I passe not for: since from the truth they many times do fall.
> Oft prudent, grave, and famousmen, in errours chance to slide,
> And many wittes with them deceive when they themselves go wide.

And continues:

> Let no man judge me arrogant, for reason ruleth me
> She faithful guide of wiseman is: let him that seekes to finde
> The truth, love hir, and follow his with all his might and minde.[1]

It was a portent for the future.

---

[1] F. R. Johnson, *Astronomical Thought*, p147.

6. Tudor mathematical scientists

The inner confusion of scientific thought throughout the sixteenth century was reflected in its practical advance, but did little to stop it. The pressures forcing technological change were too strong to be resisted and with new technologies came new discoveries, and ultimately a new theoretical framework to support them, which owed nothing to the Hermetic tradition. In England the factors which produced this stimulus were the use of artillery which demanded mathematical calculation, the demand for accurate land surveying following the Dissolution, and the need for new trade routes as a result of the increasing difficulty in marketing cloth in Northern Europe. Except for the use of artillery, these factors only became operative after 1540: the real advance in scientific thought therefore took place after that date.

Humanist impetus

Earlier in the century, the main impetus came from humanism. Humanistic thought, with its more flexible approach to education, provided the intellectual background against which science was to develop. Two of the early English humanists made direct contributions to scientific knowledge. Linacre translated Proclus' *Sphaera* into Latin and it was published by Richard Pynson in 1510, and Cuthbert Tunstall, Bishop of Durham, produced a text book which contained examples of the various methods of computation. Known as *De arte supputandi libri quattuor* it was printed three times during the century, by Pynson in 1522, and in Paris in 1529 and 1538. The new approach to learning can be seen in Sir Thomas More's employment of the Bavarian mathematician Nicolas Kratzer, who was later astronomer and horologer to Henry VIII, as tutor in his household. Wolsey founded a lectureship in mathematics as part of his scheme for Cardinal College, and at Cambridge John Cheke and Sir Thomas Smith promoted the study of mathematics with considerable success. Smith founded two readerships at Queen's College in arithmetic and geometry with instructions that they were to include demonstration as well as theory. Many of the mathematical practitioners were graduates of Cambridge, although it is doubtful if practical instruction at either university was ever more than rudimentary, and the cause was more likely to be actual personal contact and patronage. Among those known to have been directly influenced by Cheke and

Smith were the following: Robert Recorde, John Dee, Richard Mulcaster, William Cecil, Richard Eden, John Ponet, William Bill, Roger and Antony Ascham and Gabriel Harvey. Roger Ascham is the only one who later in life turned away from mathematics and reproached Leicester for his interest in the 'prickes and pointes' of geometry. As tutor to Edward VI, Cheke designed an astronomical quadrant for the king. A beautiful astrolabe engraved with Cheke's arms and with those of the Duke of Northumberland is still extant. Sir Thomas Smith's library contained a large number of scientific books including Ptolemy's *Almagest* in Greek and a copy of Copernicus.[1]

Robert Recorde

The first really original mathematician, the product of the new interest in calculation for technological purposes was Robert Recorde. Recorde's influence is still underestimated and his early death prevented him from completing his work. His importance lies in the fact that he broke with tradition and taught mathematics in English. He did so deliberately as part of a movement aimed at making England more competitive in mathematical theory and practice. His chief aim was the intensely practical one of arousing interest in the many useful applications of mathematical knowledge, and so training his pupils that they would at the earliest possible moment be able to employ their new learning in solving specific problems. Recorde planned a series of text books in English, written in dialogue form, which aimed at providing a comprehensive groundwork in mathematics, each book following the other in increasing complexity. Recorde was insistent that the student must grasp the basic essential concepts of mathematics before learning the proof or application. His books were intended to be studied in the order in which they were published or projected. *The Grounde of Artes*, printed in 1542, was the first English text book on arithmetic and continued printing till 1699. *The Pathway to Knowledge* followed in 1551, and was the first book in English on geometry. It was followed by a book extending geometry to mensuration and which dealt with the construction and use of the necessary instruments: this work, *The Gate of Knowledge,* is no longer extant. His next important work, *The Castle of Knowledge,* appeared in 1556 (dedicated hopefully to Queen Mary and Cardinal Pole), and was a text book on astronomy which dealt with the use of the globe and sphere. It was a more ambitious and a more difficult work than Recorde's previous publications, and he was insistent that it should not be studied unless the student was fully familiar with both arithmetic and geometry. Professor Johnson has pointed out that *The Castle* contains a reference to, but not a discussion of, the Copernican theory. Recorde projected one more work – the *Treasure of Knowledge* – in

[1] F. R. Johnson, *Astronomical Thought,* pp87–92. For Smith's influence and his lifelong interest in science, see Mary Dewar, *Sir Thomas Smith,* Athlone Press 1964.

which he probably intended to fill this gap and discuss the rival merits of the various cosmological systems, and possibly to apply the general principles of astronomical observation to navigation, but it was never finished. His final work, *The Whetstone of Witte,* was on algebra, the first book to appear in English on this subject. It was published in 1557 within a year of Recorde's death. Recorde is reported to have been a brilliant teacher:

> he publically taught arithmetic and the groundes of mathematics and the art of accompting. All of which he rendered so clear and obvious to all capacities that none ever did before him in the history of man.[1]

His other claim is that he invented the = sign for 'equal'. Recorde himself illustrates the width of learning and diversity of interests which were characteristic of this period. He was born in 1510, and educated at Oxford, becoming a Fellow of All Souls in 1531. He then migrated to Cambridge and became a doctor of medicine in 1545. He published one medical work, a book on urines which contained nothing original. He taught publicly both in London and Oxford, and until his death in 1558 was General Surveyor of Mines. He knew Greek and was interested in antiquarian studies and learnt Anglo-Saxon. His library was dispersed at his death, and is known to have contained some important monastic books.[2]

Recorde held the view that it was by knowledge that the human race had advanced: 'informed reason', he wrote, 'was the only instrument, or at least the chiefest means to bring men into civil regiment from barbarous manners and beastily conditions.'[3] He believed that the way to national greatness lay through technical knowledge, and he wrote to educate his countrymen. Recorde could on occasions become lyrical over the complexity and order of the natural world, and the Preface to the *Castle of Knowledge* describing the heavens is an extraordinary piece of rhythmic prose.

> Oh woorthy temple of Goddes magnificence: O throne of glorye and seat of the lorde: thy substance most pure what tongue can describe? thy beuty with starres so garnished and glyttering: thy motions so mervailous, thine influence strange, thy tokens to terrible, to stonish mennes hartes: thy signes are so wondrous surmounting mannes witte, the effects of thy motions so divers in kinde: so harde for to searche and worse for to finde. Thy greatness so huge, thy compasse so large, thy rolling so swifte, and yet seemeth slowe: thy staye so unknowen, thy place without name: thy spheres are mere wonders

---

[1]Antony à Wood quoting Bale's account in 1557, given by F. R. Johnson and S. V. Larkey in 'Robert Recorde's Mathematical Teaching and the Anti-Aristotelian Movement', *Huntington Library Bulletin,* No. 7, April 1935.

[2]A list of Recorde's manuscripts is given by R. T. Gunther, *Early Science in Oxford,* Vol I p107.

[3]R. Recorde, *The Grounde of Artes,* 1542, preface.

and so is thy frame . . . O marvailous maker, oh God of good gouvernaunce: thy workes are all wonderous, thy cunning unknowen, yet seedes of all knowledge in that book are sowen.[1]

Recorde was a pioneer, and his importance is twofold. He made mathematical theory to a high level available in English, and by his public lectures in London (sponsored by the Muscovy Company) he helped to train the first generation of English navigators.

John Dee

He was succeeded by a much more complex figure, John Dee. Dee, like Recorde, had been educated at Cambridge when the influence of Cheke and Sir Thomas Smith had stimulated interest in mathematics, but unlike Recorde he had travelled abroad, studied at Louvain and lectured on Euclid at Paris. Dee, far more than Recorde, had an international reputation and an international circle of friends. His influence was wider and more varied and more personal, for unlike Recorde he published little in English. If one puts together Dee's patrons in this country, his circle of friends on the Continent and his pupils in England, the extraordinary nature of his influence becomes apparent. Dee's patrons included the Dudley and Sidney families, the Earls of Arundel, Lincoln and Bedford, Sir Thomas Smith, Sir William Pickering, Sir James Crofts, Sir Christopher Hatton, Sir Francis and Lady Walsingham, Sir Walter Ralegh, and finally the Queen herself. His personal friends on the Continent included all the important geographical mathematicians of his day, Pedro Nuñez, Gemma Frisius, Gerard Mercator, Abraham Ortelius, Orontius Finaeus; he corresponded with the Danish astronomer Tycho Brahe, and from his time in Paris he knew Peter Ramus. He spent part of his life in the service of the Emperor Rudolf II. The list of Dee's pupils includes all the first generation of English explorers – Richard Chancellor, Stephen and William Borough, Martin Frobisher and Christopher Hall, Antony Jenkinson, Charles Jackman and Arthur Pet, Humphrey and Adrian Gilbert, and possibly even Drake; he also taught Edward Dyer and Philip Sidney, all the sons of the Duke of Northumberland, and the most brilliant of the next generation of mathematicians, Thomas Digges and Thomas Harriot. Among his literary friends were the antiquarians William Lambarde, John Stow and William Camden, and (naturally enough) both the Hakluyts.

Dee's enormous network of inter-relationships is part of the background to the development of scientific thought of the Elizabethan period. It reinforced the already existing personal relationships of the Continental geographers Ortelius and Mercator with England, and created a flexible and international

[1] R. Recorde, *The Castle of Knowledge,* 1556, preface.

framework for the interchange of information and ideas.[1]

Dee's house at Mortlake, where he had three laboratories, a quantity of astronomical instruments, and above all his library of books and manuscripts, became the focal point of all scientific advance in mathematical and allied subjects in the first half of the reign of Elizabeth. 'It was undoubtedly the greatest scientific library in England, and probably not surpassed in Europe, for Dee not only collected a vast store of important medieval manuscripts on science . . . but he had also seen to it that all the latest printed works on the mathematical sciences should be found on his shelves . . . If one believes that the first essential and true centre of any university is its library, Dee's circle might be termed the scientific university of England during the period 1560 to 1583'.[2] In a certain sense it was even more important than either university, for Dee placed his library and his knowledge at the disposal of all who came to seek it, and included among his pupils ordinary seafaring men and technicians as well as the aristocratic Dudleys and Philip Sidney. Discussion and speculation were far freer than would have been possible at Oxford or Cambridge.

Dee on navigation

Dee was vitally important in three spheres of scientific and mathematical development. As technical adviser to the Muscovy Company he was responsible for training their pilots in navigation; and at the same time as a geographer he had a significant influence on the direction and aims of the English voyages of discovery; finally as an original mathematical thinker he not only influenced the next generation but himself contributed towards a new conception of the universe.

Dee was most influential from 1550 to 1583. He brought back with him from the Continent a collection of navigational and mathematical instruments designed by Frisius and made by Mercator; and with the help of Richard Chancellor he made new instruments of his own for astronomical work. His main work in these years was to teach the captains of the Muscovy Company the difficult art of 'oceanic' as opposed to 'coastal' navigation. The 'rutter' which was little more than a coastal guide book was now replaced by the oceanic chart. But the normal oceanic projection made no allowance for the curvature of the earth's surface, and showed both latitude and longitude as

[1]Ortelius's cousin married John Rogers, the first protestant martyr, thus linking him with part of the radical protestant element in England. The connection was carried on into the next generation by the son, Daniel Rogers. Mercator's connections with England were initially directly through his friendship with Dee and Ortelius, but his son, Rumbold Mercator, travelled regularly to London as representative of the Cologne publisher Arnold Birckmann; see E. G. R. Taylor, *Tudor Geography*, pp87–8.

[2]F. R. Johnson, *Astronomical Thought*, pp138–9.

straight lines. This meant that there was an increasing error in scale near the poles. This point was at once appreciated by Dee, who claimed to have solved it by his 'paradoxall compass' and 'paradoxall chart'. The exact nature of these is not known, since Dee's own description has been lost.[1] But through the work of Dee and the Continental mathematicians the use of a true scale on charts and maps was being introduced and navigation was slowly becoming more accurate.

Mathematicians like Dee were able to teach sea captains how to find their latitude by the ascension of the sun and stars with reasonable precision. Longitude was a more difficult problem and various methods were put forward for its solution. It was known that it was dependent on time and this lay behind the increased emphasis put on accurate calculations of the course run in any period by dead reckoning, that is by timing with a sand glass or clock and noting any changes of direction on a wooden traverse board.

From a recently discovered manuscript by Thomas Bavin on Humphrey Gilbert's projected voyage of 1582, it is clear that an attempt was to be made to fix the longitude of the expedition by watching an eclipse predicted for 4.5 a.m. in London. Bavin was to take as equipment parchment, paper royal, pencils, gum, compasses, ephemerides, a flat watch clock showing minutes as well as hours, and a universal dial to tell the time from the sun. This is the earliest reference to a chronometer as part of a navigator's equipment – but the experiment in this case would have failed, even if it had been tried, since the eclipse would have been before sunrise on the eastern shore of the Atlantic. The idea, however, was perfectly correct.[2]

Apart from the paradoxall chart Dee did not publish any new method of projection, although he knew the general principles of the solution of the nautical triangle and influenced Thomas Harriot, John Davis and Edward Wright who solved the problem at the end of the century.[3] During the period of Dee's active influence captains took to sea a plane chart (one with the latitude shown as straight lines), and actual globes on which they plotted their course. The list of instruments for Frobisher's voyages of 1576 includes three spheres,

[1]Commander Waters suggests that it was in fact a type of projection for use in polar waters with a table of mathematical adjustments necessary to lay off a course. E. G. R. Taylor reproduces Dee's tables from the surviving manuscript Ashmolean 242 in her edition of William Bourne, *A Regiment for the Sea*, CUP for the Hakluyt Society 1963. They are headed 'Canon Gubernauticus. An Arithmetical Resolution of the Paradoxall Compass' and she defines Paradoxall Compass as 'the curving line (not a great circle) which a wind rhumb or fixed compass direction followed when traced on a globe or projection of a globe.' The mathematical tables given by Dee were the list of points fixed by latitudes and longitudes by which the paradoxall line could be plotted.

[2]D. W. Waters, *The Art of Navigation*, p164.

[3]J. V. Pepper, 'Harriot's unpublished papers', *British Journal for the History of Science*. 1967, p37.

a blank metal sphere for working out navigational problems, an armillary sphere for astronomical calculations, and a brass nautical sphere.[1]

Dee on geography

As a geographer Dee is mainly interesting because of his influence on the search for a route to China. Dee, supported by Mercator, was convinced that navigable passages existed both to the North East and the North West. He thought that the Russian coast turned sharply south from Cape Chelyvskin (called Cape Tabin and placed at approximately 70°N) and that conditions would therefore improve rapidly once the Cape had been rounded. He also thought that a large river, the 'Orchades', gave access into the interior of China. Dee's route to the North West hinged on the theory that a large strait (called either the Strait of Anian or the Strait of the Three Brothers) connected the Atlantic and the Pacific and offered (once discovered) an equally simple route to the Far East. Dee may have had confirmation of this from Sebastian Cabot, who is thought to have known of the entrance to Hudson's Bay. It is possible that Pet and Jackman's voyage of 1580 was intended as a rescue operation to find Drake, who was known to have reached the Pacific, and who had instructions to coast north looking for the western outlet of the Straits of Anian. If the two expeditions met, Pet and Jackman were to lead Drake home through the North East passage if it seemed the more feasible.[2]

Both Dee and Mercator were wrong and the idea of a northern passage to the East was to prove sterile. But it was a constructive error, and contributed directly to England's development as a maritime power. The extreme difficulty inherent in navigating in high latitudes acted as a stimulant. The proximity of the magnetic pole encouraged a deeper study of magnetism itself and improvement in compass manufacture, the convergence of the meridians led to the paradoxall chart, whatever this was, and in turn to new methods of chart projection; finally the difficulty of obtaining sights in periods of perpetual daylight and with the sun at a low altitude led directly to the practical invention of the backstaff, by which the navigator did not need to look directly at the sun and the horizon but could measure the sun's altitude by a shadow cast by a vane.

By the end of the century English navigators and seamen were contributing to, rather than learning from, the navigational methods of Western Europe, 'in the space of seventy years, the English from being ignorant of the art of navigation had, almost by their own efforts, largely transformed it into a science. Only the solutions to the mechanical problems of measuring time and

[1]D. W. Waters, *The Art of Navigation*, Appendix 10, p530. Commander Waters also lists Frobisher's books, which included Recorde's *Castle of Knowledge*, Cunningham's *Cosmographical Glasse, Sir John Manderville's Travels*, a Bible, and foreign navigational works.
[2]E. G. R. Taylor, *Tudor Geography*, Ch V.

longitude still eluded them.'[1] The credit for this transformation largely belongs to Dee, both on account of his own original contributions to the mathematical problems involved and because his teaching (which he twice put into manuscript with a view to publication, but could not find a sponsor) illuminated the path for the new generation that came to the fore in the 1580s, 1590s and 1600s – Hood, Hues, Harriot, Wright, Briggs, Gunter and Handson – who were to solve mathematically many of the outstanding problems of navigation.[2]

What Dee did publish is important enough. His *General and Rare Memorials pertaining to the Perfect Arte of Navigation*, which was printed in 1577, was originally planned in four volumes, of which one (vol. 3) is totally lost, one (vol. 4) is partially destroyed, and the volume dealing with navigation and the paradoxall compass existed only in manuscript.[3] In it Dee put forward all his ideas on national maritime policy and explained how they should be achieved. The first volume is dedicated to Hatton and suggests the establishment of a permanent fleet, a 'Pety Navy Royal' to consist of sixty ships between 160 and 200 tons, twenty small barques, and 6,600 men well paid. Dee estimated the cost at £200,000 yearly and suggested that it should be raised by taxing foreign fishing vessels in British waters, a poll tax on all resident foreigners and a 'perpetual benevolence for sea security'. Dee also urged the expansion of an organised fishing fleet. If both were to be accomplished he foresaw almost as 'a Mathematicall demonstration', a victorious British monarchy existing in marvellous security. Dee's vision of a British Empire (the phrase is Dee's) led him to claim on Elizabeth's behalf sovereign rights over large tracts of land in North America by virtue of their prior discovery by Owen Medoc in the twelfth century. (Dee was a Welshman.) The manuscript of this tract *Brytanni Imperii Limites*, like so much of Dee's written work, has disappeared, but his views on this question, which were repeated in other works, may well have influenced Ralegh. Burghley and Elizabeth were more discreet but possibly more effective in their claims. Elizabeth began her reign with a firm statement of her position as regards the New World, which she put into effect before its close. She calmly denied the validity of the Treaty of Tordesillas: 'Cecil simply said that the Pope had no authority to divide up the world' wrote the Spanish Ambassador in his report to Philip in November 1561.

Dee on theoretical mathematics

By far the most important as well as the most interesting of Dee's surviving works is his *Preface* to Billingsley's English translation of Euclid published in 1570. It reveals most clearly his theoretical and Neo-platonic views on mathe-

[1] D. W. Waters, *The Art of Navigation*, p500.
[2] D. W. Waters, *The Art of Navigation*, Appendix No 8, p525.
[3] E. G. R. Taylor, *The Mathematical Practitioners*, p322.

matics as a whole, and for this reason, as well as the fact that it placed the groundwork of geometry in the hands of anyone who could read English, it remains one of the most important books to appear in the Tudor period. Dee's own feelings on the value of the book to the ordinary mechanic or craftsman are summed up in the last paragraph of his *Preface*:

> Besides this, how many a Common Artificer is there in these realms of England and Ireland that dealeth with Numbers, Rule and Compass, who with their own skill and experience already had, will be hably . . . to find out and devise new workes, straunge Engines and Instruments for sundry purposes in the Commonwealth, or for private pleasure, – and for the better maintaining of their own estate? For no man (I am sure) will open his mouth against this enterprise. No man (I say) who has Charitie towards his brother (and would be glad of his furtherence in vertuous knowledge), nor any that hath care and zeal for the bettering of the commonwealth of this realme.

The *Preface* is among the most complete and the most interesting of the Renaissance summaries of knowledge. It remains one of the most comprehensive and important statements on learning ever written by an Englishman. For in deriving everything from number and proportion, Dee includes artistic as well as scientific knowledge. Architecture, for example, is partly mechanical and partly visual.[1] Music is included through harmony; and painting, which Dee calls Zographie, because it is by applying mathematical principles even without knowing it, that the painter gets his effects.

> Great skil of Geometrie, Arithmetick, Perspective and Anthropographie with many other particular Arts hath the Zographer need of for his perfection . . . This mechanical Zographer (commonly called the Painter) is marvellous in his skil, and seemeth to have a certain divine power: as of friends absent to make a friendly comfort, yea and of friends dead, to give a constant silent presence: not only with us but with our posterity for many ages.

Even medicine is brought in, for the humoral theory with its four qualities is capable of being reduced to mathematical proportion and a diagramatic scale.

Dee begins by dividing all things into three general categories: *supernatural* which are 'immaterial, simple, indivisible, incorruptible, and unchangeable'; things *natural* which are compounded, divisible, corruptable and changeable; and things *neutral* 'or of a third being'.

Things supernatural can only be understood through the mind, things natural only through the senses – the third category, things mathematical, can be studied by both the intellect and the perception of man, and stand midway between the other two categories. 'A mervaylouse newtralitie have these

---

[1] For a full discussion of this and reprint of the whole of Dee's section on architecture, see Frances M. Yates, *The Theatre of the World*, Routledge and Kegan Paul 1968.

The eleuenth Booke

The line which produceth the base of the Cone, is the line of the triangle which together with the axe of the Cone contayneth the right angle. The other side also of the triangle, namely, the line *A C*, is moued about also with the motion of the triangle, which with his reuolution describeth also a super-

A conicall superficies.

ficies, which is a round superficies, & is erected vpon the base of the Cone, & endeth in a point, namely, in the higher part or toppe of the Cone. And it is commonly called a Conicall superficies.

Eightenth definition.

18 A cylinder is a solide or bodely figure which is made, when one of the sides of a rectangle parallelogramme, abiding fixed, the parallelogramme is moued about, vntill it returne to the selfe same place from whence it began to be moued.

This definition also is of the same sort and condition, that the two definitions before geue were, namely, the definition of a Sphere and the definition of a Cone. For all are geuen by mouing of a superficies about a right line fixed, the one of a semicircle about his diameter, the other of a rectangle triangle about one of his sides. And this solide or body here defined is caused of the motion of a rectangle

parallelograme hauing one of his sides contayning the right angle fixed from some one poynt till it returne to the same agayne where it began. As suppose A B C D to be a rectangle parallelogramme, hauing his side A B fastned, about which imagine the whole parallelogramme to be turned, till it returne to the poynt where it began, then is that solide or body, by this motion described, a Cylinder: which because of his roundnes can not at full be described in a playne superficies, yet haue you for an example thereof a sufficient designation therof in the margent such as in a plaine may be. If you wil perfectly behold the forme of a cilinder. Consider a round piller that is perfectly round.

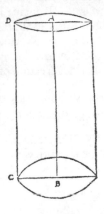

Ninetenth diffinition.

19 The axe of a cilinder is that right line which abydeth fixed, about which the parallelogramme is moued. And the bases of the cilinder are the circles described of the two opposite sides which are moued about.

Euen as in the description of a Sphere the line fastened was the axe of the Sphere produced: and in the description of a cone, the line fastened was the axe of the cone brought forth: so in this description of a cilinder the line abiding, which was fixed, about which the rectangle parallelogramme was moued is the axe of that cilinder. As in this example is the line *A B. The bases of the cilinder &c.* In the reuolution of a parallelogramme onely one side is fixed, therefore the three other sides are moued about: of which the two sides which with the axe make right angles, and which also are opposite sides, in their motion describe eche of them a circle, which two circles are called the bases of the cilinder. As ye see in the figure before put two circles described of the motio of the two opposit lines A D and B C, which are the bases of the Cilinder.

7. Page from Billingsley's *Euclide* showing the use of different typefaces.

things Mathematical, and also a straunge participation betwene things Supernatural . . . and thyngs naturall . . .'

In the same way Dee's *Preface* stands midway between the two aspects of his work, between the scientist and the metaphysical speculator. In it are found some of the clues to the mystical and speculative side of his character which in the end absorbed all his creative energy. He begins by defining number as a unit or sum of units. Mathematics as a whole, he divides into number and magnitude:

Neither number nor magnitude have any materialitie. How Immateriall and free from all matter, *Number* is, who doth not perceave, yea who doth not wonderfully wonder at it.

Dee following Boethius thinks that:

All thinges (which from the very first originall being of thinges, have been framed and made) do appeare to be formed by reason of Numbers, For this was the Principall example and patterne in the mind of the Creator . . . O comfortable allurement, O ravishing persuasion to deal with a Science, whose Subject, is so Auncient, so pure, so excellent, so surmounting all creatures, so used by the Almighty and incomprehensible Wisdom of the Creator, in the distinct creation of all creatures . . .

Dee even suggests that by the contemplation of number a man may rise to a state of revelation and view God himself.

By Numbers . . . we may both winde and draw ourselves into the deep search and view, of all creatures distinct virtues, natures, properties, and Formes: And, also, farder, arise, clime, ascend and mount up (with Speculative Winges) in spirit, to behold in the Glas of Creation, the *Forme* of *Formes*.

Dee's almost mystic views of number did not prevent him from being in practice one of the ablest mathematicians of his age. The clues to this ability in the *Preface* are not to be found in his speculations on number as an essential ingredient of all matter, but in his consideration of the actual properties of number itself. He writes:

Both Number and Magnitude have a certain originall sede (as it were) of an incredible property: and of man, never hable, Fully to be declared. Of Number, an unit, and of Magnitude a poynte doo seem to be much like Original causes. But the diversitie is great. We defined a unit, to be a thing mathematicall Indivisible, A Point, like wise we sayed to be a Mathematicall Thing indivisible. [But a point can have motion from place to place, a unit cannot.] A point by his motion produceth Mathematically a line . . . a unit cannot produce any number. A Line though it be produced by a Point that moved, yet it doth not consist of points. Number though it be not produced of units, yet it doth consists of units, as a material cause. But formally, Number is the union and unitie of units. Which unity and knotting, is the workmanship of our mindes.

Dee is also extremely interesting when dealing with perspective, which he defines as

the Art Mathematical, which demonstrateth the maner, and properties, of all Radiations Direct, Broken, and Reflected . . . It concerneth all Creatures, all Actions, and passions, by Emanations of beames performed.

Dee is aware of the unreliability of the human eye and considers this a pertinent part of the study of apparent phenomena:

We may be ashamed to be ignorant of the cause why [in] so sundry wayes our eye is deceived and abused: as while the eye weeneth a round Globe or Sphere (being farre of) to be a flat and Plaine Circle: and so likewise judgeth a plaine Square, to be round: supposeth walles parallels, to approche, a farre of: . . . Againe, of thinges in like swifnes of moving to think the nerer, to move faster, and the farder, much slower . . . what an errour is this of our eye? Of the Raynbow, both of his Colours, of the order of the colours, of the bignes of it, the place and heith of it (etc) to know the causes demonstrative is it not pleasant, is it not necessary? of two or three Sonnes appearing: of Blasing Starres: and such likethinges: by natural causes brought to passe . . . is it not commodius for man to know every true cause, and occasion Naturall? Yea, rather, is it not greatly, against the Soverainty of Man's nature, to be so overshot and abused, with thinges (at hand) before his eyes? as with a Pecockes tayle and a Doves necke: or a whole ore, in water holden, to seme broken. Thynges farre of, to seme nere: and nere, to seme farre of. Small things, to seme great: and great, to seme small.

Dee is in advance of his time too in his description of 'Pneumatithmie', which

demonstratheth by close hollow Geomatricall Figures, (regular and irregular) the straunge properties (as in motion or stay) of the Water, Ayre, Smoke, and Fire . . . This Arte, to the Natural philosopher, is very profitable: to prove that vacuum or emptiness is not in this World. And that, all Nature abhorreth it so much, that, contrary to ordinary law, the Elementes will move or stand. As Water to ascend: rather than betwene him and the Ayre, Space or place should be left, more than (naturally) that quantity of Ayre requireth or can fill. Againe, water to hang, and not to descend: rather than thereby descending to leave emptiness at his back . . . Hereupon two or three men together, keeping Ayre under a great Cauldron, and forcing the same down orderly, may without harm descend to the sea bottome: and continue there a tyme . . .

The section on architecture has recently been studied by Dr. Yates of the Warburg Institute.[1] Dr. Yates has concentrated on the relevance of the *Preface* to the assimilation of Vitruvius in England. Dee's section on architecture is

[1] Frances A. Yates, *The Theatre of the World*, p21.

one of the longest and most interesting parts of the *Preface*, although it is not, as Dr. Yates suggests, the underlying theme. It contains long quotations from Vitruvius, Alberti and from Dürer on the idea of the perfection of the proportions of man as the Imago Mundi, the microcosm or reflection of eternal proportion. Architecture, by expressing mathematically and artistically perfect proportion, also reflects man himself. In practical terms this is expressed in the geometry of the square in the circle. As applied to cosmology this is Aristotelian, but as applied to art it becomes the reflection of perfect proportion and therefore of eternal truth.[1] John Dee, through his *Preface*, was teaching the middle-class Elizabethan public the basic principles of proportion and design. What makes this interesting is the fact that England lagged behind the rest of Europe in applying the revival of classical proportions to buildings. In 1570, when Palladio published his book on the principles of design, as Dr. Yates remarks, 'Elizabethan London still presented a medieval aspect: Queen Elizabeth was not building a Louvre: no neo-classical churches were being built or planned.'

Although it is not possible to see the *Preface* as simply a comment on Vitruvian influences, the width and importance given to the theory of architecture based on harmony and proportion is important, and was to have important results. Dee's *Preface*, written in English, was specifically intended, as Dee himself tells us, to help ordinary men understand the true meaning and significance of the mathematical sciences. His influence therefore was not so much on the Court as on the growing class of technologists and artizans. There is a tenable theory that Burbage's design for the Globe Theatre was in fact strongly influenced by Dee's *Preface* and followed the classical Vitruvian proportions. There is evidence that the Globe was hexagonal without and circular within, the Swan was a duodecagonal, again with a circular interior. The stage would provide the square within a semi-circle and the whole design could be broken down into the elements of 'equilateral triangles within the circle of the Zodiac'. If this is accepted, then the symbolism of the design, its relation to the microcosm-macrocosm theory of man's necessity for harmony with the universe of which he is a part and a representation, bears a direct and important relation to the *Preface*, simply because it puts the theories contained in the section on architecture into practice. The Globe therefore becomes the first example of a *classical* Renaissance building in London.[2]

The sources for the ideas in Dee's *Preface* exist in the unpublished catalogue of his library.[3] As might be expected, Dee's library contained all the important works of the Florentine Neo-platonic school: there was a special section on

---

[1]The inconsistency in Dee's ideas here is not commented on by Dr. Yates and it is of course a subject for discussion how far Dee actually accepted the Copernican theory.

[2]This is the main thesis of Dr. Yates's book, but her evidence is concentrated into Chapter VII. She also examines the influence of Dee upon Robert Fludd.

[3]This has been examined from this point of view by Dr. Yates in *The Theatre of the World*.

cabalistic books, and a section on Raymond Lull and his followers. Dee also possessed some of the French Neo-platonists, the works of Trithemius and Cornelius Agrippa's *De occulta philosophia*. He had the *Pimander* and *Asclepius* of Hermes Trismegisthus, together with the *Commentary* of Lactantius, the works of the pseudo-Dionysius and Augustine's *Civitas Dei*. Taken as a group all these books indicate a strong influence of talismanic and hierarchical thought. Even so, they do not represent the whole of Dee's interest in this field. He had the most important Renaissance text book on 'Cosmic Harmony', the *Harmonia Mundi* of Francesco Giorgi. He had five books on the art of memory, derived from the classical idea that memory can be trained by associating ideas with actual places along a road or rooms in a house, so that they could be recalled by direct association with known but unrelated objects. There was a large scientific and mathematical section which contained the works of the fourteenth century English scientific school of Roger Bacon and his followers, and the main works of Dee's own contemporaries, including a copy of the first edition of Copernicus's *De Revolutionibus*. A section on Paracelsian medicine indicates that Dee continued to keep abreast of current medical ideas. Yet the library is the more interesting because it is not entirely scientific. Dee was deeply interested in history and contemporary literature. He had a large collection of historical works which he used when defending Elizabeth's claim to overseas territories, and copies of the major playwrights and poets. He also had a section on art and architecture which in some ways Dee regarded as an extension and application of mathematical principles. He possessed a copy of Vitruvius and his Renaissance commentators; Dürer and Pacioli on proportion; books on perspective and Vasari's *Lives of the Painters*. It was an extraordinary collection. 'The whole Renaissance is in this Library. Or rather it is the Renaissance as interpreted by Ficino and Pico della Mirandola, with its slant towards philosophy, science and magic, rather than towards purely grammarian humanistic studies.'[1] Yet in the final analysis the influence of Roger Bacon was decisive. The whole section on perspective is heavily indebted to the *Opus Majus*. Details like the examples of the peacock's tail and the dove's neck are taken directly from Bacon's section on Optics.[2] Bacon's works outnumber those of any other author in the library.

Dee as a Neo-platonist

The *Preface* reveals Dee at his best. His experimental mind (his own, and not an imitation of Roger Bacon, although like all great men he stood on the

[1] F. A. Yates, *The Theatre of the World*, p12.
[2] Bacon wrote: 'Thus light falling in different ways can either make clear or hide, or soften the intensity of colour, or augment it in various ways, as is evident in the pigeon's neck and the peacock's tail, and in many other things.' Roger Bacon, *Opus Majus*, trans R. B. Burke, Vol 2, pp557-8 and 570.

shoulders of the past) sparked off inquiry and observation in his readers, and so laid the foundation of thought for the great experimental scientists of the seventeenth century. It also reveals Dee at his most mystical and so provides the bridge which leads to an understanding of Dee as a Platonist, who valued numerical abstractions as a way to God (God himself being 'that true fountain of perfect number, which wrought the whole world by number and measure') so much that in the last resort he abandoned objective science as illusory and concentrated on Hermetic and Cabalistic lore in an attempt to by-pass the senses and achieve a universal knowledge by what seemed, at the time, a more direct and well tried way. For it is against the background of the enormous error of dating Hermes Trismegisthus that Dee's later years must be judged. The long periods of crystal gazing with a Welshman called Kelley as his medium (for Dee was too honest a scientific observer to claim to see phenomena which for him did not exist); his supposed contact with angels, and long and patient compilations of angelic (and totally indecipherable) language; his attempts to reach God, and through God total knowledge by cabalistic and mathematical means (foreshadowed in an early work, the *Monas Hieroglyphica*, published in Antwerp in 1564 and continued in his researches by 'scrying' after 1580); are all derivations from the philosophy of the Neo-platonic school.[1] They ended for Dee in disillusion and defeat: for Edward Kelley, the medium, they ended in death. At their worst they were a waste of a brilliant man's time; at their best they represent something unique which occurs in every age, a genuine desire to reach Truth.[2]

What is interesting is that although the title page of Billingsley's *Euclide* shows the figures of the scientists which sit in honour with the allegorical figures of Music, Arithmetic, Geometry and Astronomy, and includes Ptolemy, it does not include Copernicus. Dee's position on the Copernican theory is obscure. In 1557 in a preface to the English *Ephemerides* published by John Feild, he states that the new tables are based on the Copernican theory as being more accurate, and in 1573 he wrote an account and explanation of the nova in Cassiopeia, and another short treatise of trigonometrical theorems for calculating the stellar parallax. No astronomer was able with the instruments then in use to observe a stellar parallax (the slight movement in a star's position

[1]Dee's scrying glass, a flat black obsidian mirror, probably of Aztec origin, is now exhibited in the British Museum. There are references to the seances with Kelley in Dr. Dee's *Diary,* published by the Camden Society 1841, and also in the *A True and faithful relation of what passed for many years between Dr John Dee . . . and some Spirits,* published by Meric Cassaubon in 1659.

[2]Dee and Kelley went to Cracow in 1583 and made several attempts to transmute copper into gold for the Emperor Rudolf II. Dee returned to England in 1589 after quarrelling with Kelley, who had actually informed Dee that the angels were commanding the sharing of their wives. Kelley was finally imprisoned by the Emperor and was either murdered or died trying to escape.

which should be observed if the earth in fact circled the sun), but that Dee should have written on the question is suggestive that he took the Copernican theory seriously. His work on the nova is also interesting since he put forward the theory that its gradually diminishing brightness meant that it was receding away from the earth. Like the other major astronomers, Dee firmly placed the nova among the fixed stars. The idea of its recession therefore raises the possibility that Dee may have considered the realm of fixed stars as having no definite boundary. In view of his close connection with Thomas Digges, this is very probable. In any case the theory that a celestial body could move in a straight line was in itself revolutionary since it was directly against the Aristotelian theory of motion.[1]

Dee is only now being given serious consideration as one of the great formative influences of the English Renaissance. His misadventures with Kelley, the neglect and poverty of his last years when his daughter sold his books one by one to buy food, the fact that he never in his lifetime held any official position from which he could teach, the fact that so little of what he actually wrote was printed, meant that his influence was more indirect and more obscure than it might have been. His relations with Ralegh, for example, are still not clear. Did Dee influence Ralegh towards the occult and the hypothetical School of Night? There is little evidence to prove it, but a connection exists. The suggestion that Dee was one of Walsingham's secret agents is plausibly argued by Richard Deacon.[2] His knowledge of ciphers and rather obscure references in his diary partially substantiate, but do not prove that he was. He remains a giant, the formative figure in the history of Elizabethan science, but in many respects still an enigma.[3]

[1]The significance of the nova was not lost on ordinary observers, the following description appeared in Holinshed for the year 1570:

The eighteenth of November in the morning was seene a star northward verie bright and cleere, in the constellation of Cassiopeia, at the backe of hir chaire . . . This starre in bignes at the first appearing seemed much larger than Iupeter and not much lesse than Venus when she seemeth greatest. Also the said starre never changing his place was carried about by the dailie motion of heaven, as all fixed starres commonlie are, and so continued (by little and little to the eie appearing lesse) for the space of almost sixteene months: at what time it was so small, that rather thought by exercises of oft viewing might imagine the place, than anie eie could judge the presence of the same. And one thing is herein cheeflie to be noted, that (by the skill and consent of the best and most expert mathematicians, which observed the state, propertie, and other circumstances belonging to the same starre) it was found to have beene in place celestiall far above the moone, otherwise than ever anie comet hath been seene, or naturally can appeare.

R. Holinshed, *Chronicles of England, Scotland and Ireland*, London 1808, in six vols.
[2]R. Deacon, *John Dee, Scientist, Geographer, Astrologer, and Secret Agent to Elizabeth I*, Frederick Muller 1968.
[3]The spiritual phenomena described in *The Diary* and *True Relation* bear a striking similarity to comparable experiences in modern seances.

Thomas Digges and modern astronomy

Dee's most able pupil was Thomas Digges, the son of Leonard Digges. Leonard Digges was himself a mathematician and published Almanacs to which he added astronomical tables and notes on navigational problems for use at sea. The first, printed in 1553, has been lost, but the second, *A Prognostication of right good effect*, originally issued in 1555, has survived. He also wrote an important book on surveying called *Tectonicon*, in which he described the instruments necessary for an accurate land survey, and the methods of calculation. He invented a form of theodolite, which is described in *A geographical Practice named Pantometria* published in 1571, and is known to have used some kind of telescope. Leonard Digges took part in Wyatt's rebellion, and was attainted. It was at this time he sent his son, then aged eleven, to be brought up and educated by Dee. He died in 1571.

Thomas Digges achieved international fame as a mathematician before he was thirty, by a work on the new star of 1572 (the nova in Cassiopeia) called *Alae seu Scalae Mathematicae*. In it Digges suggests that the appearance of the star offered an opportunity to support the Copernican theory for if its brightness fluctuated in a regular fashion this could be attributed to the movement of the earth. Although the gradual disappearance of the star prevented Digges from proving his theory, the 'research on the new star marked a turning point in the history of astronomy in England. The severe blow it dealt to the Aristotelian physical theories helped to remove one of the chief obstacles to the progress of the Copernican hypothesis'.[1] A further blow was dealt by the appearance of the comet in 1577 which not only cut across the crystalline spheres, but clearly went into orbit round the sun. Digges established his international standing by the *Alae*, which was used by Tycho Brahe in his own work on the nova. His real reputation as an original thinker rests on a small but vitally important treatise which he added onto a re-issue of his father's ephemerides, *The Prognostication Everlasting* in 1576. Digges revived his father's work and brought it up to date, but he added a supplement in which he described fully the Copernican system, included a diagram, and gave an English translation of large sections of Book One of *De Revolutionibus*. The importance of this supplement, which was known as *A perfit Description of the Caelestiall Orbes according to the most aunciente doctrine of the Pythagoreans, lately revived by Copernicus and by Geometrical demonstrations approved*, is that instead of enclosing the universe in the diagram with an outer circle of fixed stars, Digges represented it as being infinite by scattering stars to the edge of the page. By doing this, as Professor Johnson remarks, 'Digges had the courage to break completely with the older cosmologies by shattering the finite outer wall of the universe. He was the first modern astronomer of note to portray an

[1] F. R. Johnson, *Astronomical Thought*, p160.

infinite, heliocentric universe with stars scattered at varying distances through-out infinite space'.[1] Digges described

> This orbe of starres fixed infinitely up extendeth itself in altitude sphericallye, and therefore immovable: the pallace of felicitye farre excelling our sonne both in quantitye and qualitye the very court of coelestiall angelles devoyd of greefe and replenished with perfit endlesse joye the habitacle for the elect.

Digges *Perfit Description* was reprinted seven times before 1605. After its publication references to the Copernican system become much more frequent; it became in fact part of the accepted scientific background of educated men, whether they actually believed it or not. Digges' claim to priority in the vitally important conception of the infinity of the universe has been challenged by Professor Koyré, who considers the Digges' conception is limited in scope. From the wording round the sphere of fixed stars it can be seen that 'Thomas Digges puts his stars into a theological heaven: not into an astronomical sky.' Professor Koyré considers that Giordano Bruno, who was far more explicit on the subject than Digges, should be given credit for really conceiving infinity and void in astronomical space.

> There is a single general space, a single vast immensity which we may freely call Void: in it are innumerable globes like this on which we live and grow: this space we declare to be infinite, since neither reason, convenience, sense – perception nor nature assign to it a limit.[2]

Bruno's deep familiarity with Hermetic thought must, however, be remembered when interpreting his writings which are based on imaginative intuition rather than objective science. 'The truth is that for Bruno the Copernican diagram is a hieroglyph, a Hermetic seal hiding potent divine mysteries of which he has penetrated the secret.'[3] Bruno, no more than Digges, could not conceive of a universe outside some sort of theological cosmological framework. Digges' *Perfit Description* antedates Bruno's *Cena de le Ceneri* by eight years, and Bruno's cosmology is 'vitalistic, magical; his planets are animated beings that move freely through space of their own accord' – not so very different from the theological setting of Digges' celestial orbes.[4] Yet in the same Preface to the *Prognostication* Digges was capable of a completely traditional description of the earth:

> The Globe of Elements enclosed in the Orbe of the Moone I call the Globe of Mortalitie because it is the peculiare Empire of death. For above the moon they feare not his force . . In the midst of this Globe of Mortalitie hangeth this darke starre or ball of earth and water balenced and sustained in the midst

[1]F. R. Johnson, *Astronomical Thought*, pp164–5.
[2]Giordano Bruno, quoted by A. Koyré in *From the Closed World*, p40.
[3]F. A. Yates, *Giordano Bruno and the Hermetic Tradition*, p241.
[4]For this discussion of Bruno, see A. Koyré, *From the Closed World*, pp53–4.

of thin ayer onely with that propriety which the wonderful workman hath given at the Creation to the Center of this Globe with his magnetical force vehemently to draw and hale into itself al such other Elementall things as retaine the like nature.

The modern and the old cosmology could still exist side by side even in the same author.

The optical experiments of Dee and Digges

The experiments in optics conducted by Leonard and Thomas Digges and John Dee, are well documented by references in the *Pantometria* and the *Stratioticos,* and are referred to by William Bourne in his treatise on optical glasses presented to Burghley. It is therefore quite clear that such experiments took place. These investigations with an early form of telescope constitute one of the most interesting incidents in the history of science in England. It is also one of the most tantalising since no detailed report of the experiments was ever published, and their exact nature is obscure. They antedated the development of the telescope in Holland, but there is no proof that the instrument used was a true telescope, although in view of Harriot's later work it is not improbable. In any event it was left to others to exploit the full potentialities of the instrument. It seems clear that it was an entirely English development with connections back to Roger Bacon rather than to the Continent. The proof of this lies on Thomas Digges' account of his father's experiments with lenses, 'which partly grew by the aid he had by one old written book of the same *Bakon's Experiments,* that by strange adventure, or rather Destinie, came into his hands, . .'[1] This book was probably the *Opus Majus* with its section on optics and experiments. That Leonard Digges repeated and improved on Bacon's experiments is confirmed by Thomas Digges' references in *Pantometria :*

My father by his continuall paynfull practises assisted by demonstrations *Mathematicall,* was able and at sundrie times hath by proportionall glasses duely situate in convenient Angles, not only discovered thinges farre off, read letters, numbered peeces of money with the very coyns and superscription thereof, cast by some of his freends of purpose uppon Downes in open Fieldes but also seven Myles off declared what had been done at that instante in private places: Hee hath also sundrie times by the Sunnes beames fixed Powder, and discharged Ordinance halfe a mile and more distante . . .[2]

Digges expands this description in chapter twenty one:

[1]Thomas Digges, *An Arithmetical Warlike Treatise named Stratioticos.* London 1579, 2nd edition 1590, p359.
[2]Leonard and Thomas Digges, *A Geometrical Practical Treatize named Pantometria*, London 1571, preface.

But marveilous are the conclusions that may be performed by glasses concave and convex of Circulare and parabolicall formes using for multiplication of beames sometime the aid of Glasses transparent, which by fraction should unite or dissipate the images or figures presented by the reflection of the other. By these kinde of glasses or rather frames of them, placed in due Angles yee may not onely set out the proportion of a whole region, year represent before your eye the lively image of every Towne, Village . . . but also augment and dilate any parcell therof, so that whereas at the first appearance an whole towne shall present it selfe so small and compact together that yee shall not discerne any difference of streates, yee may by application of Glasses in due proportion cause any particular house or roume thereof dilate and shew itself in as ample forme as the whole towne first appeared, so that ye shall discerne any trifle, or read any letter lying there open, especially if the sunne beames may come unto it, as plainely as if you were corporally present, although it be as distante from you as eye can descrie.[1]

That Dee was included in these experiments is clear from William Bourne's treatise presented to Lord Burghley. Bourne states that he has not done experiments himself but that others have, 'and specially Mr Dee and Mr Digges . . .'. In his memorandum Bourne describes the making of two sorts of glasses:

The one concave with a foyle uppon the hylly syde. the other grounde and polished smoothe, the thickest in the myddle, and thynnest towardes ye edges or sydes.[2]

Bourne informs Burghley that he is assured that

the glasse that ys grounde, beynge of very cleare stuffe, and of a good largnes, and placed so, that the beame dothe come thorowe, and so receaved into a very large concave looking glasse, That yt will show the things of a marvellous largeness in a manner incredible to bee beleeved of the common people.[3]

Bourne correctly saw that one glass augmented the other, and told Burghley that 'those things that Mr Thomas Digges hathe written that his father hathe done, may be accomplisshed very well, withowte any dowte of the matter. . . .' Besides his copies of the *Opus Majus* of Roger Bacon, Dee possessed an interesting manuscript *Rogerii Bachonis epistolae ad John Parisiensem, in quibus latet sapienta mundi,* which contained a section on the uses of perspective glasses. It was printed in the seventeenth century from Dee's actual copy.[4] There is no direct evidence that Dee and Digges used their perspective glasses

[1] Leonard and Thomas Digges, *Pantometria,* 1571, Ch 21.
[2] William Bourne, *Treatise on the Properties and Qualities of Glasses for Optical Purposes,* Lansdowne Mss. 121.13. No. 13 Ch. 9 A.6v.
[3] William Bourne, *Treatise,* A.7r.
[4] *Frier Bacon, His Discovery of the miracles of art nature and magick faithfully translated out of Dr Dee's own copy by T. M. and never before in English,* printed for Simon Miller at the Starre in St Paul's Churchyard 1659.

astronomically in a systematic way, but Digges conviction of the infinity of 'stars innumerable' indicates some kind of optical penetration of space. Digges actually refers to having written a book on perspective glasses, but it has disappeared.

Thomas Harriot – experimental scientist

England produced two more scientists of European calibre before the end of the century. The first was the controversial and shadowy figure of Thomas Harriot. The Harriot papers in the British Museum and Petworth House are only now being examined, but already it is clear that Harriot was an outstanding mathematician and experimental scientist whose work anticipated many of the advances made in the seventeenth century, and whose astronomical observations stand comparision with those of Galileo.[1] Harriot was born in 1560. He was educated at Oxford and on leaving the University he became the friend and scientific adviser of Sir Walter Ralegh. In Ralegh's service he sailed on the 1585 expedition to Virginia, and his account was the first scientific description in English of the flora, fauna, mineral resources, and inhabitants of the New World. He was fortunate in having as an illustrator the artist John White, and the result is a minor masterpiece. It was twice printed by Hakluyt and a European edition was published by Theodor de Bry at Frankfurt in 1590. It is from *A Briefe and True Report of the New Found Land of Virginia*' that we know that Harriot took a perspective glass with him on the voyage.

> Most thinges they the [Indians] saw with us, as Mathematicall instruments, sea compasses, the vertue of the loadstone in drawing yron, a perspective glasse whereby was shewd manie strange sightes, burning glasses, wilde-fire woorkes, gunnes, books, writing and reading, spring clocks that seem to goe of themselves, and manie other thinges that we had, were so straunge unto them, and so far exceeded their capacities to comprehend . . . that they thought they were rather the works of Gods rather than of men . . .[2]

Sometime in the 1590s when Ralegh was in eclipse at Court, Harriot entered the service of Henry Percy, 9th Earl of Northumberland, without forfeiting Ralegh's friendship. From 1598 he had an annual pension from the Earl. Northumberland's patronage enabled Harriot to concentrate on scientific research until his death in 1621. He was able to employ a technical assistant Christopher Tooke, and had properly equipped laboratories. He became one of an important group of scientists and writers surrounding Northumberland. It included Robert Hues, Walter Warner, Nathaniel Torporley, Nicolas Hill

[1] Add Mss 6782–6789; Harley Mss 6001–2, 6083; Leconfield Mss 240–241.
[2] Thomas Hariot, *A Briefe and True Report of the New Found Land of Virginia*, ed. Henry Stevens, London 1900, p57.

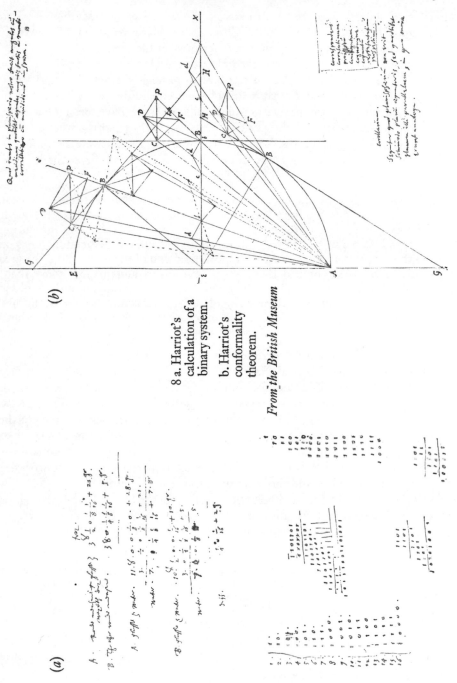

8 a. Harriot's
calculation of a
binary system.

b. Harriot's
conformality
theorem.

From the British Museum

and possibly Giacopo Castelvetro among the scientists, and Mathew Royden, George Chapman, and probably Christopher Marlowe among the writers. Harriot was easily the most important scientist in the group.

A Briefe and True Report was the only work of Harriot's to be printed in his lifetime. The reasons for Harriot's failure to publish are not clear. A letter to Kepler from 1608 indicates that he may have been afraid to do so.[1] Some of his mathematical work on navigation and ballistics may have been of a secret nature; or the security of the pension from the Earl of Northumberland may have removed any incentive. That he was aware of the possible consequences is clear from an interesting letter from his friend and pupil Sir William Lower warning him of the consequences of failing to publish:

> Do you not here startle to see every day some of your inventions taken from you: for I remember long since you told me as much [as Kepler], that the motions of planets were not perfect circles. So you taught me the curious way to observe weight in water, and within a while after Ghetaldi comes out with it in print a little before Vieta prevented you of the gharland of the great Invention of Algebra. al these were your duees and manie others that I could mention; and yet too great reservednesse had robd you of these glories . . . Let your countrie and your friends injoye the comforts they would have in time and great honour you would purchase yourself in publishing some of your choice workes.[2]

Harriot may finally have regretted his decision for he bequeathed his mathematical papers to his friend Nathanial Torporley for publication. Torporley was unable to complete the task but in 1631 the *Artis analyticae praxis, ad aequationes algebraicas nova expedita, et generali methodo, resolvendas* was published. This work, which was the first to contain the signs for inequality $>$ $<$, lies at the basis of modern algebra. The notation of inequality was itself of fundamental importance, 'For inequality is not merely the foundation of mathematics . . . it is probably by far the most important tool in the workshop of the mathematician, and the most responsible for shaping mathematics as we know it.'[3] A study of the mathematical sections of the Harriot papers has shown that he conceived of negative numbers and worked out a binary system.[4] Harriot also left an interesting manuscript consisting of 21 folio sheets, stitched and paginated, now among the Leconfield manuscripts, in which he calculated

[1]'Things with us are in such a condition that I still cannot philosophize freely. We are still struck in the mud. I hope Almighty God will soon put an end to it.' Quoted C. Hill, *Intellectual Origins of the English Revolution*, Clarendon Press 1965, p32–3.
[2]Letter from Sir William Lower, February 1610. Add Mss 6789, quoted by Henry Stevens, *Thomas Hariot, The Mathematician, The Philosopher, and the Scholar*, London 1900.
[3]R. C. H. Tanner, 'On the role of equality and inequality in the history of mathematics', *British Journal for the History of Science*, Vol 1 No 2, 1962–3.
[4]Add Mss 6786 Folio 347; and J. W. Shirley, 'Binary numberation before Leibnitz', *American Journal of Physics*, Vol 19, 1951, pp452–4.

meridional parts by a method far in advance of his time, and which was 'tantalizingly close to calculus'.[1] Later research among the Harriot papers has shown that his navigational manuscripts contain much important and original work on the conformity of stereoscopic projection, the rectification and quadrature of the logarithmic spiral, the exponential series and interpolation formulas, and that he applied this theory in his logarithmic table of meridional parts in 1614. He calculated tables of dip, analysed the corrections to be made to Pole Star observations in order to estimate latitude, and prepared a table of amplitudes of the sun or a star to be used in comparison with observed directions from a compass card to determine magnetic variation. He solved mathematically the problem of the nautical triangle thus making possible the construction of an accurate Mercator chart. He anticipated Davis in the invention of the backstaff for nautical observations, indeed Davis may well have got the idea from Harriot and acknowledged his debt in his writings. It is also possible that Harriot was responsible for the world chart on Mercator's projection which was added to the 1600 edition of Hakluyt.[2]

His work on optics is equally interesting. Harriot experimented on the refraction of light for over twenty years. His papers contain tables showing angles of refraction through glass.[3] Harriot used a solid glass prism placed on a table which was ruled with lines, to calculate the angles of incidence and refraction, and using this method he discovered Snell's Law about 1601, which states that the ratio of the sines of the two angles is a constant, more than twenty years before Snell and thirty-six years before it was published by Descartes.[4] Harriot also used a hollow glass prism filled with different liquids to investigate variations in the refractive index – there are tables for salt water, turpentine, spirits of wine, and water.[5] From his calculations on the scattering of light, Harriot was the first to solve the radius of the rainbow mathematically, again anticipating Descartes. Other topics covered in the manuscripts include work on ballistics, specific gravities, chronology, and shipbuilding.[6]

[1]E. G. R. Taylor and D. H. Sadler, 'The doctrine of nautical triangles compendius', *Journal of the Institute of Navigation*, Vol 6 1953, and R. C. H. Tanner, 'Thomas Harriot as a Mathematician', *Physis Revista Internazionale di Storia della Scienza*, vol 9 1967; and British Museum Pamphlet 1857.

[2]A. C. Crombie, J. V. Pepper, D. B. Quinn, J. W. Shirley, and R. C. H. Tanner, 'Thomas Harriot (1560–1621): an original practitioner in the scientific art', *Times Literary Supplement*, 23 October 1969; J. V. Pepper, 'Harriot's unpublished papers'. *British Journal for the History of Science*, Vol 6 1967; and J. V. Pepper, 'Harriot's calculation of the meridional parts as logarithmic tangents', *Archive for History of the Exact Sciences*, IV, 1967–8.

[3]Add Mss 6789 Folios 88–89.

[4]J. W. Shirley, 'An early experimental determination of Snell's Law', *American Journal of Physics*, Vol 19, 1951.

[5]Add Mss 6789 Folio 198, and J. Lohne, 'Thomas Harriot 1560–1621: The Tycho Brahe of Optics', *Centaurus* Vol 6 No 2 1959.

[6]Add Mss 6788.

Finally from at least 1609, Harriot was using a telescope for astronomical observations. His papers contain detailed and accurate records giving particulars of the place, viewing conditions, instrument and the names of other viewers.[1] He compiled the first known map of the moon.[2]

He also saw the satellites of Jupiter and the crescent of Venus. He made a number of observations of sunspots, and from calculations in the manuscripts, it has been said that he may have attempted to solve the duration of the sun's rotation from the movement of the spots. The origin of Harriot's original telescope is obscure. It may have come from the Low Countries, but it is at least possible that it evolved from the 'perspective glasse' and the experiments of Dee and Digges. Harriot knew both men, and it is significant that he took a 'perspective glass' to Virginia in 1585. Harriot's assistant Christopher Tooke soon became an expert in the making of telescopes and produced a number of increasing power for Harriot and his circle, so that it became possible for simultaneous observations to be made in different parts of the country. During the winter of 1609–1610 Harriot seems to have organised such a series of observations in various parts of England, a fact which indicates that he probably possessed telescopes before that date. Harriot's will shows that at the time of his death he possessed a number of telescopes of various powers which he divided between the Earl of Northumberland and his friends.

> Item I give to the aforesaid Earl of Northumberland my two perspective trunks wherewith I use to see Venus horned like the Moone and spotts on the Sonne. The glasses of which trunkes I desire to have removed into two other of the fairest trunkes by my said servant Christopher Tooke. Item I bequeath unto everyone of my executors hereafter to be named, One perspective trunke a piece of the best glasses, and the fairest trunkes, as my said servant can fit to their liking. Item I give unto my said servant Christopher Tooke the residue of my cases of perspective trunkes (excepting the two great long trunkes consisting of many parts which I give to the said Earl of Northumberland to remain in his library for such uses as they may put unto).

Harriot's failure to publish his research has led to difficulties over the exact priority of some of his work, and his exact relationship with other European scientists. He corresponded with Kepler in rather general terms. He had very probably a more direct relationship with the French mathematician Viète, since Nathaniel Torporley may have been assistant to Viète. The Harriot manuscripts contain a number of references to Viète's work, and Harriot's debt is acknowledged in the *Artis analyticae Praxis*. His work on logarithms was done at the same time as that of Napier, and there is no known connection between them. Once again Harriot's reluctance to publish prevented his work from being

[1] A. C. Crombie et al, *Times Literary Supplement*, 23 October 1969.
[2] Leconfield Ms 241 Vol ix Folio 30.

acknowledged. His law of sines is a particularly interesting problem. It was the common property of his circle, and may have reached Snell and subsequently Descartes through indirect channels.[1] Another relevant factor is that although Harriot's work was not available in print, his reputation as a mathematician and therefore some knowledge of his methods, was widely known in Northern Europe. It is posterity rather than his contemporaries who were left in ignorance of his full achievements.

Harriot refused to be diverted by Hermetic influence: there is no sign whatever in his work of Neo-platonic thought. His reputation of atheism arose, like Ralegh's, largely from hearsay, although his intellectual approach and his advanced views on cosmology may have given some foundation to rumour. Harriot was an atomist and believed in the plurality of worlds and in the infinity of matter. He was clearly sensitive to the accusations and noted down contemporary references to himself possibly in case he needed to make a defence.[2] Harriot was the most versatile and original mathematician in the late sixteenth and early seventeenth century, and only his failure to publish prevented him from being so acknowledged by posterity.[3]

Harriot's patron, the Earl of Northumberland, was born in 1564. His main interest as an experimental scientist was in chemistry and medicine. His importance to science is indirect: he acted as a focus for a number of able and creative men, and he collected an important library. It has been estimated from the press marks on the surviving volumes that it probably contained at least 1,250 books: 826 of these have been traced into the twentieth century and 552 actually located. Northumberland regularly spent at least £50 a year on books, and possessed a number of scientific works by his most important contemporaries, including Paracelsus, Napier, Kepler, Brahe, and Gilbert. 'Science is naturally to the fore, and within science medicine, alchemy and mathematics'.[4] But the Library also included literary and philosophical works as well as travel, geography, history, and the art of war.

William Gilbert

The second scientist of international importance was William Gilbert. Gilbert was more fortunate than Harriot in that he published his results, and was

[1] Possibly through Walter Warner, Thomas Hobbes, or Sir Charles Cavendish.
[2] D. B. Quinn and J. W. Shirley, 'A contemporary list of Hariot references', *Renaissance Quarterly*, No. 1 1969.
[3] The Harriot manuscripts are almost entirely composed of mathematical calculations with no written explanation. This in itself would make subsequent publication difficult and still stands in the way of reproduction of his work.
[4] G. R. Batho, 'The Library of the "Wizard" Earl: Henry Percy Ninth Earl of Northumberland 1564–1632', *The Library* 5th Series, No 4 December 1960.

recognised during his lifetime. His discovery was of immense importance and superficial simplicity. By careful experiments he found that the earth itself is a magnet, and that all the phenomena of terrestial magnetism can be explained by this fact. Gilbert was born about 1540 in Colchester. He migrated to London and became a doctor of medicine, rising ultimately to the position of President of the Royal College of Physicians. He was therefore one of the group of scientific theoreticians based on the Court, but Gilbert differed from the others in that he watched and learnt from craftsmen, particularly from metalworkers. He illustrates the productive fusion of craft lore and science. His great book *De Magnete* was published in 1600 and has been described as 'the first physical treatise to be based on experiment'. It took twenty years to write. In his Preface he states his methods:

> Clearer proofs, in the discovery of secrets and in the investigations of the hidden causes of things being afforded by trustworthy experiment and by demonstrated arguments than by the probable guesses and opinions of the ordinary professors of philosophy ... Nor have we found this our labour idle and unfruitful since daily during our experiments, new and unexpected properties came to light; and our philosophy has grown so much from things diligently observed.

He dedicated the book:

> To you alone, true philosophizers, honest men, who seek knowledge not from books only, but from things in themselves, have I addressed these magnetical principles of this sort of philosophizing.[1]

Gilbert himself drew on the ideas and observations of a wide circle which ranged from pure theoretical mathematicians like Henry Briggs, who was later to hold both the Gresham and Savilian professorships of Geometry, to the brilliant instrument maker and theoretician Edward Wright, and the compass maker Robert Norman, whose book *The New Attractive* first described the phenomenon of the 'dip' of the compass needle towards the Pole.[2]

In *De Magnete* Gilbert describes his careful experiments with small spherical lodestones or 'terrella' with which he had been able to reproduce all the phenomena of terrestial magnetism including magnetic variation and dip. He then made the logical but startling deduction that the earth itself was a giant magnet with lines of force running towards the poles. The terrella had

> poles, not mathematical points, but natural termini of force ... and there are poles in like manner upon the earth which our forefathers sought even in the sky: it has an aequator, a natural dividing line between two poles, just as

[1]W. Gilbert, *On the Magnet*, Gilbert Club translation, ed. Sylvanus P. Thomson, London 1900, introduction.
[2]E. G. R. Taylor, *The Mathematical Practitioners*, p49.

the earth has: for of all lines drawn by mathematicians on the terrestial globe, the aequator is a natural boundery, and is not . . . merely a mathematical circle.[1]

Gilbert again showed by experiment that whereas 'attraction' was greatest at the poles, 'direction' was strongest at the equator. If the 'terrella' was divided, a change in the terminal poles was inevitable 'for the verticity always changes in consequence of any change in the mass.' Lodestones derived their magnetic properties from the magnetic field of the earth. These observations so delighted London, that the smiths and cutlers made a great lodestone which lifted an anchor weighing 24 lbs, and which was subsequently bought by Lord Arundel.[2] Gilbert was, however, not correct in all his deductions. He thought that both dip and variation were constant in any one place, and could therefore be used in combination to determine a position on the earth's surface. The angle of dip was calculated from a ring dial, an instrument with a graduated edge, in which when suspended a magnetised needle moved, the variation could be observed from the compass itself. He considered that the variation of the compass was due to the 'pull' of land masses and that the easterly variation of $11\frac{1}{4}°$E observed in London indicated a large continent to the East, and was therefore an argument for a North East passage. If Gilbert's theories had been correct the whole question of latitude and longitude could have been determined from the compass needle; but in the early years of the seventeenth century between 1622 and 1626, a series of experiments by Edmund Gunter, John Marr and Henry Gellibrand proved that the variation at Deptford London had decreased by nearly 50 percent and read only 6°E. and that it therefore varied with time. But Gilbert correctly argued that the core of the earth differed from the exterior and was probably of iron. He also used the diversity of surface rocks to demolish the over-simplified four categories of Aristotle. The outer crust of the Earth was

loamy or clayer or sandy, or full of various soils and marls: or lots of stones and gravel meet us, or beds of salt or a metallick lode, and metals in abundance . . . No where does the Aristotelian element of earth come to light: and the Peripateticks are the sport of their own vain dream about the elements.[3]

Gilbert in fact condemned the whole Aristotelian conception of the universe in a passage which is worth quoting in full, since it illustrates clearly that in spite of his experimental objectivity Gilbert was strongly affected by Hermetic mysticism. He begins Chapter 12 in Book V by declaring

Magneticke force is animate or imitates life; and in many things surpasses human life . . . A lodestone is a wonderful thing in very many experiments,

[1] W. Gilbert, *On the Magnet*, Bk I Ch 17.
[2] E. G. R. Taylor, *The Mathematical Practitioners*, p174.
[3] W. Gilbert, *On the Magnet*, Bk I Ch 17, p41.
        H.—6*

and like a living creature. [But Aristotle gave life and movement to the planets but not to the earth.] Wherefore Aristotle concedes life to the sphaeres themselves, and to the orbes of the heavens (which he feigns), because they are suitable and fitted for a circular motion and are carried along in fixed and definite courses. It is surely wonderful, why the globe of the earth alone with its emanations is condemned by him, and cast into exile (as senseless and lifeless) and driven out of all the perfection of the excellent Universe. It is treated as a small corpuscle in comparison with the whole . . . it is obscure, disregarded, and unhonoured . . . Let this therefore be looked upon as a monstrosity in the Aristotelian Universe, in which everything is perfect, vigorous, animated; whilst the earth alone, an unhappy portion, is paltry, imperfect, dead inanimate and decadent. But on the other hand Hermes, Zoroaster, Orpheus, recognise a universal life. We, however, consider that the whole universe is animated, and that all the globes, all the stars, and also the noble earth, have been governed since the beginning by their own appointed souls and have motives of self-conservation.

Gilbert then goes on to put forward his own version of the hierarchical structure of life.

But in the several bodies of the stars, the implanted force acts otherwise than in those divine existences which are supernaturally ordained; and in the stars, the sources of things, otherwise than in animals; in animals again otherwise than in plants. Miserable were the condition of the stars, abject the lot of the earth, if the wonderful dignity of life be denied to them, which is conceded to worms, ants, moths, plants, and toadstools . . .[1]

The type of life which in Gilbert's view resided in all heavenly bodies was therefore utterly unlike the evanescent life of the animal world. Animals only live by a constant effort which is soon spent:

bodies are not moved by them without labour and waste. They are brought and carried away by a breath, and when this has . . . been supressed by some untoward influence, their bodies lie like the dregs of the Universe and the refuse of the globes. But the globes themselves remain and continue from year to year, move and advance, and complete their courses. The human soul uses reason, sees many things and inquires about many more; but even the best instructed receives by his external senses (as through a lattice) light and the beginings of knowledge. Hence come so many errors and follies, by which our judgement and the actions of our lives are perverted; so that few or none order their actions rightly or justly. But the magnetick force of the earth, and the formate life or living form of the globes, without perception, without error, without injury from ills or diseases . . . has an implanted activity, vigorous through the whole material mass, fixed, constant, directive, executive, governing and consistent.

[1] W. Gilbert, *On the Magnet,* Bk V Ch 12, p209.

Gilbert reinforced his theory of a 'living earth' by the idea of spontaneous generation of life from the soil, which if exposed on a tower soon produced plant life from nothing.

Gilbert dismissed Ptolemy's suggestion of the rotating sphere of fixed stars as ridiculous, and thought the stars were at varying distances from the earth and implies but did not state that space is infinite. The outermost stars

> are very remote, being located in the heaven at varying distances, either in the thinnest aether or in that most subtle quintessence, or in the void; How immeasureable then must be the space which stretches to those remotest of fixed stars. How vast and immense the depth of the imaginary sphere.[1]

Gilbert is therefore committed to a rotating earth, but he did not accept the Copernican theory in its entirety, and possibly hesitated between it and some of the alternative ideas of Tycho Brahe.[2]

Gilbert's ideas had a strong influence on Kepler, and magnetic force provided a possible means of holding the planets in orbit until the discovery of gravity.[3]

Other practical scientists

By the time *De Magnete* was published in 1600, London had become a centre for an increasing number of mathematical practitioners. A new generation of educated mathematicians had grown up, men like Thomas Hood, Robert Hues, Nicolas Hill, Mark Ridley, and Thomas Blundeville. Thomas Hood gave the mathematical lectures instituted by the Lord Mayor and the City of London in 1588 in order to give instruction in elementary mathematics to the captains of the trained bands. They were given in the Staplers Hall and were open to the public. Hood proved a teacher of exceptional ability. To help his pupils he issued cheap simplified texts in dialogue form which sold for 1d or 2d, and which he elaborated in his lectures. He wrote on the use of the globes in order to explain the two globes designed by the instrument maker Emery Molyneux, and in his treatise on *The use of the Celestial Globe in plano* he gave a long and detailed account in English of the nova of 1572.

> That starre appeared of so great a bignesse and light at the first that it seemed to exceed the Evening starre: but within certaine moneths it did so diminish

[1] W. Gilbert, *On the Magnet*, pp215–16.
[2] Tycho suggested an immovable earth and finite circle of fixed stars. The sun revolved round the earth, as did the moon, but all the other planets revolved round the sun. The fact that under this system the orbit of Mars has to intersect the sun's orbit round the earth meant that Tycho definitely abandoned any ideas of crystalline spheres. See F. R. Johnson, *Astronomical Thought*, pp222–3.
[3] Gilbert also correctly defined 'electricity' using the word for the attractive force in amber.

that it was judged to be but equal to the Pole starre: in that quantity it continued to the ende. It was a thing most strange and wonderfull, whereby the wittes of many men were set on worke. Some thought it a new star, some a comet, some an existing star previously obscured or made greater by exhalations.

Robert Hues was one of the group of scientists supported by the Earl of Northumberland. In 1586 he sailed round the world with Thomas Cavendish, and in 1594 he published in Latin a book on the globes of Emery Molyneux. Nicolas Hill was also a pensioner of Northumberland, and his thought was profoundly influenced by the work of Gilbert. He was convinced of the rotation of the earth, the Copernican system, and put forward an atomic theory of matter, which links his thought with that of Harriot. Mark Ridley was a doctor of medicine and spent sometime as physician to the Czar. His main scientific work was a series of experiments continuing the work of Gilbert. His *Short Treatise of Magnetical Bodies and Motions* was published in 1613. Ridley, like Hill, was convinced by Gilbert's experiments of the rotation of the earth and the truth of the Copernican system. Thomas Blundeville was a teacher and populariser of scientific theory. He wrote a number of works including important manuals on horsemanship, and *Six Treatises* explaining the work and instruments of other scientists for students. He published a work for seamen based on Gilbert's experiments in which it was suggested that latitude could be found by observing the magnetic dip.

An increasing characteristic of this phase of English scientific development was the close connection between these educated theoreticians and the practical scientists, particularly those connected with the sea; and between both these groups and the instrument makers. The money for the patronage of science came from merchant companies, individual merchants and from courtiers like Leicester, Ralegh, Arundel, or Northumberland, who were either pursuing a definite policy, or who were themselves directly interested. Since in every case part of the interest was financial, it is not surprising that those aspects of science that had a technological bias, for example navigation, mining, and fortification, were those which received most of the direct patronage.

The development of practical seamanship revived with the return of Sebastian Cabot under Somerset in 1548 and with Northumberland's support the barque *Aucher* was sent (on what was in effect a training cruise for future captains) to Chios and the Levant. The captain, Roger Bodenham, in later years told the younger Hakluyt, 'All the Mariners that were in my sayle which were besides boyes, three score and tenne, for the most part were within five years or six years after, able to take charge and did.'

It was for these men that Recorde and Leonard Digges wrote in English, and their example was followed by an increasing number of authors. William Cunningham's *Cosmographical Glasse*, one of the first books published in Elizabeth's reign and dedicated to Leicester, 'did for cosmography and to some extent for navigation what Robert Recorde's books had done for mathematics; it brought the subject from the recesses of the scholar's closet to the shelves of the gentry and the desks of the merchants.'[1] Cunningham was an educated man, but he was followed by a large number of authors who were largely self-taught, and who wrote simply and directly about the practical aspects of their craft. One of the earliest of these was William Bourne, who had no formal education, but was inn keeper and port reeve at Gravesend. His most important book *A Regiment for the Sea* was published in 1574 and reprinted five times before the end of the century. It was based on Eden's translation of the *Arte de Navegar* but was easier to understand and brought up-to-date. It included the first description of the use of the log-line to calculate distance run. In the final edition Bourne added a section on 'Five Ways to Cathay' which discussed the problems of navigation in high latitudes, but also suggested a trans-Polar route.[2] Bourne also wrote a technical work on gunnery *The Arte of Shooting in Great Ordnaunce* based on the Italian treatise by Tartaglia, and two other works, *A Treasure for Travellers*, dealing with map making, and *Inventions and Devises*, which included a description of a 'trailing log' invented by the great Elizabethan instrument maker Humfrey Cole. Some books were actually the direct result of experience. William Borough, the younger brother of Stephen, served before the mast in the Chancellor Expedition of 1553, and sailed as mate with his brother in 1556 making a series of observations on the variation of the compass. He later became one of the chief pilots of the Muscovy Company, served as a captain with Drake, and ended his career as Comptroller of the Navy. His *Discourse of the Variation of the Cumpas*, published in 1581, was based directly on his own experiments and experience. He also gave all the necessary equipment for a shipmaster or pilot, and suggested the use of spring driven watches for finding the longitude. His work was often bound together with Robert Norman's *The New Attractive*, published in the same year, which described the discovery of the magnetic 'dip'. Norman was primarily an instrument and chart maker. William Barlow described him as 'not learned, but a very expert mechanician'. In later editions when Norman's book was bound up with that of Borough, Norman added a table of the sun's daily declination to last 30 years, and a table of conjunctions of the sun and moon, while in the 1596 edition Borough added the longitude and declination of 32 fixed stars, and a table of the sun's position in the Zodiac.

At the same time two translations from the Dutch greatly improved the expertise of coastal navigation. In 1584 Norman translated *The Safeguard of*

---

[1]D. W. Waters, *The Art of Navigation*, p99.
[2]William Bourne, *A Regiment for the Sea*, ed. E. G. R. Taylor, CUP for the Hakluyt Society 1963. Bourne included some meteorological information in his books. See D. W. Waters, *The Rutters of the Sea*, p7.

Saylers or Great Rutter in direct response to the increasing demands of the North Sea trade. This extremely useful book gave the marks, soundings, and general navigational directions for the coasts and principal harbours of England, France, Spain, Ireland, Flanders and the Sounds of Denmark. It was followed by an even more important work which was to revolutionise the charts and navigation of the waters of North West Europe. This was Antony Ashley's translation of the *Spiegel de Zeeraert* by L. J. Waghanaer, published in 1588. Although the title was correctly *The Mariners Mirror,* it was always known as 'the Waggoner', and became a standard part of every captain's equipment. It consisted of a series of maps, charts and sailing directions for European waters, but it also contained nautical tables, a star list and instructions how to make a cross-staff incorporating a zenith distance scale. 'The Waggoner's' descriptions for coastal sailing were accurate, simple and clearly expressed, and read like a modern pilot. It even printed examples of coastal craft in different areas as a help in finding position.[1]

In 1594 Captain John Davis, who had made three voyages in search of the North West passage, wrote a book with the title *The Seaman's Secrets,* published in 1595, which was as important for oceanic navigation as 'the Waggoner' had been for European waters. Davis had a great advantage over the previous writers on oceanic navigation. He was a trained mathematician, an original instrument maker, and an actual seaman. Davis insisted on accurate observations and accurate log keeping as the basis for successful oceanic navigation. He constructed the earliest backstaff and describes its use, his specimen 'layout' of a ship's log helped to standardise the practice of log keeping. His book contains a clear section on the different methods of navigation, 'horizontal', 'great circle', and 'paradoxall', which here is clearly rhumb line sailing, that is a course cutting the meridional lines at a fixed angle and therefore tracing a spiral course on the earth's surface. His description of plane chart sailing and the use of the globe by seamen is brilliant; far clearer than those of the purely theoretical mathematicians. 'Despite Hood's and Hues's treatises on the use of celestial and terrestrial globes, John Davis' brief sketch of the use of the terrestial globe by seamen was outstanding, probably because he was the only one of the three to be a professional navigator. Davis was indeed the first professional navigator to write on navigation at all.'[2] It is because of Davis' description of paradoxall sailing that Commander Waters holds the view that Dee's paradoxall compass was in fact a polar chart with the pole at the centre and the meridians straight. It was thus not strictly an 'instrument' at all. In support of this theory it is worth noting that in the list of instruments for Frobisher's expedition of 1576 there is no specific mention of a paradoxall compass. Finally, in the last year of the sixteenth century, there appeared a book that set the seal on the supremacy

[1]D. W. Waters, *The Art of Navigation,* p175.
[2]D. W. Waters, *The Art of Navigation,* p207.

of the English in the theory and practice of the art of navigation. This was Edward Wright's *Certaine Errors in Navigation,* which continued to sell in revised editions until the end of the seventeenth century. Wright had been educated at Cambridge, but he had practical experience of the sea as mathematician and navigator on the Azores expedition of 1589. Wright criticised the common chart projections of his day as being inaccurately drawn; he pointed out that sights taken with a cross-staff could be in error by as much as 1° because of the difficulty of aligning it correctly: he noted that the declination and stellar tables in common use were often wrong. Wright himself pioneered a new chart projection derived from Mercator's but with only two scales – a fixed scale of longitude and a changing scale of latitude. It had the tremendous advantage that the spiral rhumb on Mercator's globe now became a straight line enabling the course to be plotted easily. It could not be used in polar regions because of distortion.

By the end of the sixteenth century therefore most of the outstanding navigational problems were understood if not solved. After Wright's book, improved *Ephemerides* such as those edited by John Tapp began to appear, and whether he liked it or not, the discipline of science, with its precision, was beginning to impose itself and the English sea captain was made to face the intellectual problems of oceanic navigation and taught to solve them. The only really outstanding difficulty was that of determining longitude, which was not overcome until the invention of accurate chronometers in the eighteenth century.

During the same period, surveying, mapmaking, and training in gunnery and the art of war were all moving from an unscientific and pragmatic ignorance, to a precise, informed and above all instrument-using science. Surveying became of great importance once a market in land transfers developed, but even before that, in 1540, there is an interesting group surveying and charting Dover Harbour on the instructions of Henry VIII, consisting of Richard Cavendish, John Bartelot and John à Borough, which illustrates the close connection between surveying and military problems.[1]

Of the mapmakers proper, the most important is Christopher Saxton (1542–1610), who surveyed the whole of England and Wales, county by county between 1573 and 1579. His name also appears on one Irish map. Estate surveying and town plans of London, Oxford and Cambridge were done by Ralph Agas, who also wrote a description of the methods he used. John Norden produced estate and county maps, which were among the first to include roads. Norden planned a *Speculum Britanniae* with a map of every county. In spite of encouragement from Burghley, only five, Middlesex, Essex, Hertfordshire, Cornwall, and Northamptonshire, were completed, and only one, Hertfordshire, appeared in his lifetime. With the invention of the plane table, theodolite

[1] E. G. R. Taylor, *The Mathematical Practitioners,* p167.

and various instruments for calculating heights, the whole practice of cartography became more scientific.

Bourne's treatise on gunnery, and Leonard Digges's *Pantometria* laid the foundations of technical knowledge in military affairs, and in 1588 Cyprian Lucar improved upon Bourne with another translation of Tartaglia supplemented with extracts on gunnery and allied subjects, which included estimating heights and mapmaking. In 1579 Thomas Digges completed and published his father's *An Arithmetical Warlike Treatise named Stratioticos*. This was a popular introduction to the use of mathematics in warfare, especially in gunnery.

It was common for scientists to devise their own instruments. Leonard Digges invented a theodolite; John Davis popularised the backstaff. They also instructed craftsmen to make their instruments for them. Harriot relied on Christopher Tooke for his perspective trunks. Instrument makers were themselves expert craftsmen and were capable of original observation. Robert Norman wrote *The New Attractive* describing the dip of the compass needle as a result of his work on the construction of compasses for use at sea. The craft of instrument making developed alongside mathematical theory. The early instrument makers were considerably more than technicians. Thomas Gemini, who came originally from Liege, was a map engraver and printer. He published the works of Leonard Digges, and made the instruments recommended by Digges in his books. Humphrey Cole, who may have been taught by Gemini, was also an engraver, a metallurgist trained at the Mint, and an expert on mining. Cole was possibly the greatest of the late Tudor instrument makers and a number of his works survive. He equipped Frobisher's expedition of 1576 and made a compendium (or watch dial) for Francis Drake. In 1571 he is noted as being prepared to make all the instruments recommended by Digges. Emery Molyneux was a compass maker, but he is most famous for his celestial and terrestial globes. He was helped by a London merchant William Sanderson. His globes were the first to be made in England.

With the increasing sophistication of instruments, the makers divide into three distinct groups: those who worked in metal, those using wood, and finally those working in glass and specialising in optical instruments. Gemini and Cole worked in metal, but an important instrument maker who worked mainly in wood was the elder John Read. He made plane tables, set squares, and boxed compasses. His successor in the seventeenth century was John Tompson, who made in wood the instruments which Elias Allen made in brass or silver. Instrument makers tended to congregate in certain defined areas. There was one near Temple Bar, another near Lombard Street and a small group near the Navy Office on Tower Hill.[1]

While the specialist groups evolved, a finer precision and greater accuracy

[1]A map showing the location of mathematical practitioners is given by E. G. R. Taylor, *The Mathematical Practitioners,* p163.

was demanded under the stimulus of the scientists, and this practical aspect of much of the pioneering work led to a continued improvement in the techniques used and quality of the instruments themselves. Professor Taylor has shown that there was a close and interesting association between instrument makers, publishers, booksellers, and mathematical teachers by the end of the century: it was usual for a leaflet or pamphlet to be presented with each instrument purchased, explaining its use, but many customers also required personal instruction. She quotes an actual example of such an advertisement which appears on the title page of William Barlow's *Navigators' Supply*, published in 1597.

> If any desire to have instruction concerning the use of these instruments let him repayre unto John Goodwyn dwelling in Bucklersburie teacher of the Groundes of these Artes. The instruments are made by Chas Whitwell over against Essex House, maker of all sorts of mathematical instruments . . .[1]

Founding of Gresham College

Elizabeth's reign closed with an event of great importance in the history of science, the founding of Gresham College under the will of Sir Thomas Gresham. Gresham had been financier to three Tudor monarchs, Edward, Mary, and Elizabeth. He had made a fortune, and following up the idea put forward in Edward's reign founded the Royal Exchange in London. At his death he left a sum of money to the City of London and the Mercer's Company to endow a college in London. Gresham deliberately excluded Oxford and Cambridge as being too reactionary, and gave his college a scientific basis. There were to be seven professorships in law, rhetoric, divinity, music, physic, geometry and astronomy. Each lecturer had a set of rooms, a salary of £50 per year, and was required to deliver lectures with experiments in both Latin and English. The reason was entirely practical, 'for that the greater part of the inhabitants within the city understand not the Latin tongue, whereby the said lectures may become solitary in a short time, if they shall be read in the Latin tongue only . . .' It was added in the case of Dr Bull, the lecturer in music, 'being not able to speak Latin, his lectures are permitted to be altogether in English, so long as he shall continue the place of music lecturer there.'[2] The lectures were to be followed by discussions. By his foundation Gresham provided a free grounding in science, which neither of the two Universities could offer. It is interesting that while this was remedied theoretically at Oxford by the founding of the Savilian professorships early in the seventeenth century, Cambridge has no chair of mathematics until 1663. Gresham College was more than a teaching institution, it was a place where scientists could meet and discuss

[1] E. G. R. Taylor, *The Mathematical Practitioners*, pp58–9.
[2] John Ward, *The Lives of the Professors of Gresham College*, London 1740, ppv and viii.

ideas and do research. It is this practical element, and the fact that many of the Gresham professors were men of ability, that made the College a genuine centre of English scientific advance. For this reason, it is often regarded as the precursor of the Royal Society. Certainly while Henry Briggs was Professor of Geometry, the college was actively linked with important practical research and discussion, in precisely the same way as the later Royal Society. Gilbert's experiments on the magnet, for example, led to further experiments on magnetism in which the College was directly involved. The interesting group round John Wells, Keeper of the Stores at Deptford, which included master shipwrights such as Phineas Pett, was connected directly with Gresham College through Edmund Gunter, the Professor of Astronomy, and it was there that the initial experiments were performed under Gunter's direction which led to the discovery of the change in magnetic variation.

Briggs himself was responsible for introducing Napier's logarithms into standard mathematical practice and started the recalculation to base 10. Briggs also compiled complete tables of magnetic dip for every degree of latitude.

Gresham College had another function. It not only encouraged research, it popularised it. The scientific theories of men like Gilbert meant little or nothing to seamen who could not read Latin, but demonstrations and lectures in English could and did. In this respect Gresham College succeeded the Muscovy Company in promoting the teaching of science in English, and the success of its methods is a standing indictment of Oxford and Cambridge, where mathematics was regarded as a mechanical art, only fit for tradesmen, technicians and artizans. In the 1630s the mathematicians of the next generation, such as Seth Ward and John Wallis, learnt their mathematics from an obscure country parson, William Oughtred. Mathematics was not considered an essential subject in any grammar school. Gresham College, while it existed, thus provided an educational centre which was found nowhere else in England.

It was also puritan in sympathy and democratic in outlook. The growing isolation of the scientists and their interdependance upon one another, mathematicians, craftsmen, and the actual men who applied the knowledge, meant that there was an overriding unity of interest which worked towards the ignoring of social status within the cultural group. This is the theory taken up by Christopher Hill in his *Intellectual Origins,* and it is the point made directly by Gabriel Harvey in 1593.

> He that remembereth Humfrey Cole, a mathematical mechanician, Matthew Baker, a ship-wright, John Shute, an architect, Robert Norman, a navigator, William Bourne, a gunner, John Hester, a chemist, or any like cunning and subtle empiric, is a proud man, if he contemns expert artisans, or any sensible industrous practicioners, howsoever unlectured in schools or unlettered in books.

But it is a theory difficult to sustain fully in the face of more detailed analysis.

In the first place the constitution of Gresham College was not purely scientific. It had professors of divinity, music, civil law and rhetoric, as well as medicine, astronomy and geometry. It had close links with both Universities, and many of its professors combined their posts with fellowships at Oxford and Cambridge. Gresham was an extension of the Universities to London, rather than a rival institution. It differed from the older Universities only in emphasis; in the fact that the most brilliant of its early professors happened to be scientists and mathematicians, and in its more flexible methods of teaching. The connection between science and puritanism may exist in that both involved resistance to accepted dogma, but it cannot be taken beyond that point. A common ground is the rejection of Aristotelianism, but this rejection of scholastic philosophy is a far wider movement and can be seen all over Europe and in many branches of learning. It is an offshoot of early humanism and culminates on the Continent with the teaching of Peter Ramus. This raises another point. What is undeniable is that Ramism was one of the great intellectual influences of the late sixteenth and early seventeenth centuries. Ramus was a humanist but a humanist with a difference. He stressed the importance of those classical authors whose works were useful in practical life, Virgil's *Georgics* for example. From Aristotelian logic, he removed all features which in his eyes were useless, and fashioned an instrument which professional men could use as well as students.[1] Ramism became a force in the intellectual life of England during the latter years of Elizabeth. There was a school of Ramism at Cambridge which had close connections with Cambridge puritanism.[2] Ramus influenced Sidney, and at one remove he influenced the puritans of the mid-seventeenth century. Ramism ran parallel to the thought of Bacon and the one helped the other to weaken the dominance of traditional learning. Ramism was regarded with suspicion by the government, and a state initiated reaction against it in the universities of both England and Scotland took place in the seventeenth century.[3]

The founding of Gresham College made London the cultural centre for all mathematics and science at the end of the sixteenth century, and reinforced the close personal connections among the active leaders of the movement. Whether it anticipated the Royal Society is a more difficult question. On balance, the answer is probably not. It was too traditional and too general a body. The galaxy of scientific talent in its early years was the result of circumstances rather than design.

Yet it is undeniable that London from the mid-Elizabethan period onwards

[1]H. F. Kearney, 'Puritanism, Capitalism and the Scientific Revolution', *Past and Present,* No 28, 1964.
[2]H. Kearney, *Scholars and Gentlemen. Universities and Society in Pre-Industrial Britain,* Faber and Faber 1970. Dr Kearney points out that the names of many prominent Ramists are identical with those of prominent puritans, e.g. Cartwright, Perkins, Travers, Penry.
[3]A full account of Ramism at the Universities is given in H. Kearney, *Scholars and Gentlemen.*

became in a marked degree the focal point of forward-looking ideas. Above all it housed the major printing presses, and it was the function of the press to spread these new ideas throughout the country.

Here the work of the elder and younger Hakluyt in collating and collecting all the evidence and descriptions of voyages of discovery was of vital importance. Since they were acquainted with all the leading scientists and seamen in London, they were able to provide a central fund of information. By editing and printing *The Principal Voyages of the English Nation* they made public the achievements of the Elizabethan age in maritime expansion, and so began the creation of public support for an active policy of overseas expansion. It can be said that the Hakluyts did for the English colonial Empire what Foxe's *Book of Martyrs* did for the Protestant religion. They created a climate of opinion which had permanent results.

7. Pre-Tudor medicine and natural history

The effect of printing on the natural sciences and medicine was complicated by the fact that the evolution of the engraved illustration was of parallel importance. In fact it acted as a catalyst since the development of scientific and observational accuracy meant that by the middle of the century the illustrations of such works as herbals frequently surpassed the text. While printing did not of itself produce any change in the accepted theories, in certain spheres such as anatomy and botany the excellence of the printed illustrations stimulated closer observation and so ultimately led to advance.

Origins

The underlying principles of the related sciences of medicine, botany and zoology were derived originally from the Greeks. All created matter was seen as a whole, formed of the four elements, fire, air, water and earth. Man himself was a reflection of the cosmos and contained the four elements and their related qualities. The art of medicine was based on the theory of the four humours (themselves related to the four elements) hot, cold, moist and dry, which together made up the complexion of man. In normal health the balance of the humours was stable and appropriate to the age and character of the individual. Disease was caused by an imbalance of humours, and diagnosis consisted in interpreting the signs of imbalance, and cure in taking the appropriate counteraction. Health was maintained by correct diet, sleep and exercise; the proper 'regimen' for each individual. Remedies were largely herbal although non-organic substances such as mercury, antimony or the precious metals were used in specific cases. The German *Herbarius* printed by Peter Schoeffer at Mainz in 1485 opens with a summary of the accepted theory held throughout Europe in the early sixteenth century. The interest lies in the emphasis laid on the interconnection and therefore the underlying unity of all matter. It also implies a belief in astrology which was still influential in a large part of medical thought. Schoeffer begins:

> Many a time and oft have I contemplated inwardly the wondrous works of the Creator of the universe: how in the beginning He formed the heavens and adorned them with goodly shining stars, to which he gave power and might to influence everything under heaven. Also how He afterwards formed the four elements: fire, hot and dry – air, hot and moist – water, cold and

moist – earth, dry and cold – and gave to each a nature of its own; [God then] formed herbs of many sorts and animals of all kinds and last of all man, the noblest of all created things . . . I considered further how that in everything which arises, grows, lives or soars in the four elements named, be it metal, stone, herb or animal, the four natures of the elements – heat, cold, moistness and dryness are mingled.

It is also noted that the four natures in question are also mixed and blended in the human body in a measure and temperament suitable to the life and nature of man. While man keeps within this measure, proportion or temperament, he is strong and healthy, but as soon as he steps or falls beyond the temperament or or measure of the four natures,

for example if heat, or cold became dominant and upset the balance of the four elements in his body, man falls of necessity into sickness, and draws nigh to death.

The causes of imbalance in man are numerous.

Of a truth I would as soon count there the leaves on the trees, or the grains of sand in the sea, as the things which are the causes of a relapse from the temperament of the four natures, and a beginning of a man's sickness. [But God who made man liable to disease also provided a cure] that is with all kinds of herbs, animals and other created things to which He has given power and might to restore, produce, give and temper the four natures mentioned above. One herb is heating, another is cooling, each after the degree of its nature and complexion . . . By virtue of these herbs and created things the sick man may recover the temperament of the four elements and the health of his body.[1]

The main exposition of the humoral theory in classical times was the *Corpus Hippocraticum* a collection of seventeen books, not all by the same author, which probably constituted the remains of the medical library of the school under Hippocrates at Cos (5th century BC). Hippocrates seems also to have held the 'pneumatic theory' which believed in a general world 'pneuma' which is common to all living things and is manifested by breathing.[2]

The theories of the Hippocratic school were developed in the second century AD by Galen of Pergamon. Galen lived between 129 AD and 200 AD and studied medicine in the Near East, becoming eventually physician to the Emperor Marcus Aurelius. Galen produced a complete system of medical

[1]*The German Herbarius*, translated by E. G. Tucker, quoted in Agnes Arber, *Herbals: Their Origin and Evolution, 1470–1670*, CUP 1938, pp23–4. A shortened version of this Preface was used in *The Grete Herball*, published by Peter Treveris in 1526 and 1529.
[2]For a description of the main schools of medical thought in the ancient world, see Charles Singer, *Galen on Anatomical Procedures*, OUP for the Wellcome Historical Institute 1956.

teaching round the humoral theory which he enlarged by the argument that there could be more than one variety for each humour. He taught for example that there were seven kinds of yellow bile, and he also argued that the delicate balance of humours in the body altered with age – youth, for example, was hot and moist; manhood, hot and dry; middle age cold and dry; and old age cold and wet.

Galen also wrote on the anatomy of man and certainly did some human dissections:

> As poles to tents and walls to houses, so are bones to living creatures, for other features naturally take form from them and change with them. If an animal has a round skull, the brain must be round; if elongated, so must the brain be . . .[1]

For later anatomists the main stumbling block in the use of Galen as an authority was that the major part of his anatomical work was done not on men, but on apes: his text is 'in general . . . a description of the soft parts of an ape imposed upon the skeleton of a man . . . For the gluteal region and the pelvis the misfit is of a gross order . . . For the hand and arm . . . the difference is less, though there are many divergent details.'[2] What is interesting is that such was the authority given to Galen's work that many Renaissance anatomists, including Vesalius, perpetuate his mistakes – for example, that the right kidney is higher than the left (which is true in apes but not in man) and in stressing the importance of veins rather than arteries.

Other important writers in the early Christian era were Celsus (1st century AD) who was not himself a doctor but who endeavoured to write an encyclopaedia of knowledge. Only the medical section is extant. It was particularly valuable on surgery but was too bulky to be widely read and only four manuscripts have survived from the medieval period. A more influential writer was Soranus of Ephesus (2nd century AD) whose works on acute and chronic illness were translated into Latin by Caelius Aurelianus in the late fourth or early fifth century.[3]

In the Renaissance Caelius Aurelianus' name replaced that of Soranus when the works were printed. Soranus is interesting since he was perhaps the greatest exponent of an alternative school to Hippocrates known as Methodism which was founded by Asclepiades of Bithynia in the first century BC. According to the Methodists, the body consisted of minute atoms or pores and disease resulted from their malfunction. From this was derived the idea of 'general states'. The basic types of disease were an excessively dry state, an excessively

---

[1] Galen, *On Dissection,* Book 1, Ch 2, quoted C. Singer, *Galen,* p2.
[2] Charles Singer, *Galen,* pxix.
[3] C. H. Talbot, *Medicine in Medieval England,* Oldbourne 1967, p13.

fluid state, or a mixture of both. Treatment consisted in counteracting the 'state' with either astringent or relaxing measures.[1]

The sheer bulk of these early medical texts led to a demand for selective compilations and these in their own right became a second group of source material. The most important of these Byzantine writers, who from the fifth to the seventh centuries gathered together and summarised the work of their predecessors were Oribasius of Pergamos in the fourth century, Aetius of Amida and Alexander of Tralles in the sixth century, and Paul of Aegina in the seventh century. The writings of these men were bulky enough. Oribasius wrote an encyclopaedia based largely on Galen of seventy books, he later summarised its contents into nine books, known as the *Synopsis*, and finally wrote an even more simplified version in four books called the *Euporistes*.

The writings of both the classical and Byzantine schools were preserved and enlarged by the great Arab writers of the ninth to the eleventh century. During the period when intellectual contact between East and West was almost non-existent, a vast corpus of literature, including medical and scientific works, was concentrated at Baghdad. All the most important authorities of antiquity became available in Arabic translations, including 129 genuine and spurious works of Galen. In the second half of the ninth century a complete revision of all existing translations was undertaken by Hunain Ibn Ishaq, and Hunain, known to the West as Johnnitus, wrote an introduction to the works of Galen known as the *Isagoge*, which became one of the most influential text books in European medicine. The Arabs did more than codify and summarise earlier authorities, they wrote themselves and thus made their own contribution to the sum of existing knowledge. The most important Arab writer after Hunain, was Rhases in the ninth century whose books, the *Continens* and *Almanson*, were largely derived from Greek and Byzantine sources, but which contained notes from his own experience which indicate that he was both practical and empirical as a doctor. He was followed by Haly Abbas who wrote a text book in twenty volumes, ten dealing with theory and ten with practice, a work without any originality but which was influential in Europe after its translation in the twelfth century. The most famous of all the Arab medical writers was Avicenna who lived in the eleventh century and wrote a summary of medical knowledge known as the *Canon*. Avicenna made Galenism into a philosophical system. 'His book was the final codification of Graeco-Arabic medicine, so closely interwoven that no single item could be subtracted without damaging the whole.'[2] Avicenna had immense influence once his work became available in the West. He was followed by a school of writers from Moorish Spain, Albucasis, Avenzoar and Averroes. Albucasis laid particular emphasis on surgery and this

[1] G. Sarton, *The Appreciation of Ancient and Medieval Science during the Renaissance, 1450–1600*, University of Pennsylvania Press 1955, p15.
[2] C. H. Talbot, *Medicine in Medieval England*, p3.

section of his book *al-Tasrif* was translated and used in the Middle Ages. Avenzoar who wrote in the eleventh century was the most original, and had the practical common sense approach and accurate observation of symptoms which was vital to any medical advance. In contrast Averroes was essentially a theorist and his *Colliget* is simply a detailed analysis of Avicenna.

The study of botany and natural history was closely related to medicine and the sources are similar. The Greek philosophers, particularly Aristotle, were studied in so far as they were relevant, the works of Aristotle in particular were never entirely lost. The *Historia, De partibus, De motu, De incessu, De generatione animalium* and *De anima* were all known, and after the twelfth century the commentaries of Averroes and other writers became available. Aristotle left his library to his pupil Theophrastus who lived in the fourth century BC, and the notes of a pupil of Theophrastus survived as a small treatise *De Plantis*. A more important book which became the foundation for the herbal treatment of disease was the *Materia Medica* of Dioscorides. Dioscorides, who was a contemporary of Galen and served in the armies of Nero, compiled a comprehensive text book listing over six hundred plants found in the mediterranean area, together with the disease each would cure. It is true to say that Dioscorides' *Materia Medica* became the basis for all the sixteenth century herbals of Europe. The delicate water colour drawings which formed the illustrations were unsurpassed until the publication of Otto Brunfels' *Herbarum Vivae Eicones* in the sixteenth century.[1] The final classical authority in this field was the elder Pliny whose *Natural History* was dedicated to the Emperor Titus in 77 AD. The text of the *Natural History* was never lost and Pliny must rank as one of the most formative influences on scientific thought in the West. It was from Pliny that the traditional method of describing diseases or characteristics from head to foot took its origin, and his encyclopaedic book is the source of much medieval animal lore. The *Natural History* was written in Latin, but many of Pliny's ideas and much of his knowledge came from Greece so that Pliny is not himself an original authority but an important link transmitting Greek scientific thought to the West. He was certainly one of the most widely used and widely read classical authors in the sixteenth century.

The fact that certain classical texts and scientific ideas which can be traced back to Greek and Roman thought never disappeared from Western culture can be seen from groups of traditional questions and answers which were preserved and used in centres of learning from the fifth to the ninth centuries. These questions are also found in a number of early texts. The *Quaestiones Naturales* of Seneca, the *Noctes Atticae* of Aulus Gellius, the *Solutiones* of Priscianus Lydus, and the *Homilies* of St Basil, all contain questions on cosmology, the four

[1]Unsurpassed as botanical illustrations, the drawing of flowers in the borders of illuminated manuscripts and in the early Italian paintings of the Renaissance were of course equally accurate and realistic but are not directly comparable.

elements, botany, zoology, and anthropology and form an important source of scientific ideas. St Basil's sources include Theophrastus, the Stoics, Oppian, the works of Aristotle and Plato's *Timaeus*.[1] By drawing attention to the existence of these early questions, Dr Lawn has shown that a great deal of Greek philosophy and scientific theory was available in the West long before the translations from the Arabic and before the twelfth century Renaissance. A total of fiftynine medical codices for the eighth and ninth centuries have been found including Oribasius, Celsus, Soranos, and Caelius Aurelianus. Manuscripts of these authors, found in association with works by Galen and Hippocrates, form what Dr Lawn considers may have been an ancient 'summa' of medicine.[2] There was clearly an important independent tradition coming directly and continuously from classical times in early medieval scientific thought.

Salerno school

The first change and expansion in medical ideas came from the school of Salerno. Southern Italy and Sicily lay on the frontier of the Islamic world. Greek was still spoken and the ties with Byzantium were close. For this reason, the rise of the medical school at Salerno at an early date, and the fact its fame rested on teaching derived from Greek medical texts and subsequently from translations of the Arabic corpus into Latin, is not altogether surprising. Salerno became closely associated with the Benedictine Abbey of Monte Cassino in the eleventh century through the friendship of Abbot Desiderius with Alfanus Bishop of Salerno. Alfanus may himself have established a tradition of Greek learning at the school. His writings have disappeared but he was the author of two tracts, one on the four humours, and another on the pulse. More significant is a reference in the library list of Henry of Eastry at Christ Church Canterbury, dating from the early fourteenth century to a set of questions composed by Alfanus. This manuscript has been lost but it indicates that Alfanus may well have been influenced by the earlier question form.[3] Alfanus' main claim to fame is not his writings but the fact that he taught Constantine the African and was instrumental in introducing him to Abbot Desiderius of Monte Cassino. Constantine entered the monastery and spent the rest of his life from 1077 to 1087 translating from Arabic into Latin. His works include books by Galen and Hippocrates, the writings of Hunain, Haly Abbas, Isaac Judaeus and other Jewish and Arabic writers.. It seems clear that although ultimately Salerno came

[1]Brian Lawn, *The Salernitan Questions,* Clarendon Press 1963, p2.
[2]See table in B. Lawn, *The Salernitan Questions,* p7.
[3]The library list is interesting since it contains fifty nine codices on natural science covering the Graeco-Latin medical classics, the works of Constantine, herbals, bestiaries, works on geology and a large number of Salernitan texts. It indicates that Christ Church Canterbury may well have been a centre of scientific studies at that time. B. Lawn, *The Salernitan Questions,* p19.

to be associated with the work of Constantine and the reception of Arabic medicine, initially his translations made little impact. The writings of Adelard of Bath, although directly associated with Salerno and usually associated with Arab learning, show no debt to Constantine, or directly to Arabic thought in spite of the misleading preface to Adelard stating that he had learnt Arabic.[1] Nevertheless from the early years of the twelfth century Salerno became the centre of advanced medical studies and the studies were based on a new knowledge of Greek medicine and the natural philosophy of Aristotle. It is at this point that the Salernitan questions proper make their appearance. They consisted of a series of queries on natural phenomena with answers which covered the whole philosophy of natural science. Some of the questions antedate Constantine, others show his influence and the final version of the questions may have been the work of Urso of Calabria in the late twelfth century or of a pupil. Salerno also produced a series of commentaries for teaching purposes. A codex has survived which included the *Antidotarium* of Nicolas, the *Isagoge* of Johannitus (Hunain), the *Tegni* of Galen, the *Aphorisms* and *Prognostics* of Hippocrates, and the *De urinis* of Theophilus. Dr. Talbot suggests that this manuscript probably also contained a commentary on a treatise by Philaretes on the pulse, and if so it was a set of commentaries on the texts of the 'summa' of medicine which was later known as the *Articella* and which became the basis of all medical teaching.[2]

It seems clear that the Salernitan teaching and the questions and answers made considerable impact in England. A number of Salernitan manuscripts have survived dating from the early twelfth century: the *Liber Melancholie* of Constantine and the *Experimenta Archiepiscopi Salernitani* at Westminster, his *Pantegni* at Bury St Edmunds, the *Passionibus Galieni* from Norwich Priory, an *Antidotarium Nicholai* at Durham. Copies of works by Constantine are found at Exeter, Battle and Canterbury, and at Lanercost Priory there was an interesting group of Salernitan texts comprising the *Isagoge*, the *Aphorisms of Hippocrates*, a *Liber Galeni*, a *Liber urinarum Theophili*, a *Liber Philareti de negocio pulsuum* and a *Tegni Galieni*. Five English texts of the questions have survived, and one, now in the Bodleian Library in Oxford, has an interesting reference indicating that there was a centre of medical learning at Hereford in addition to the existing school of mathematics and astronomy in the twelfth century.[3] The library list of Henry of Eastry indicates a similar centre at Christ Church Canterbury in the late thirteenth century. England had direct links with Southern Italy and Sicily which have facilitated the spread of Salernitan theory and practice. The Chancellor of Roger II of Sicily was an Englishman, Robert of Selby, and at the end of the twelfth century William II of Sicily married Joanna, daughter of

[1] For an analysis of this question see B. Lawn, *The Salernitan Questions*, pp20–30.
[2] C. H. Talbot, *Medicine in Medieval England*, pp42–3.
[3] Auct.F.3.10.SC 2582.

Henry II, and employed several Englishmen at his Court. Salernitan learning also came through Chartres which was a centre for English students. There, William of Conches helped to promulgate the new ideas derived from the Constantine translations and in addition taught Henry II himself. Dr. Talbot has pointed out that Peter of Blois in giving a diagnosis relied heavily on a Salernitan text.[1] St Albans appears to have been another centre of Salernitan influence, the Abbot and three other monks at the end of the twelfth century had all been trained at Salerno, and Alexander Neckam in the *De Natura Rerum* which became an important source book of natural science relies heavily on Salerno, making use of the Constantine translations, the writings of Urso of Calabria and of the questions themselves.[2] The curious fact that the writings of his close friend Alfred of Sareschal on the heart (*De motu Cordis*) show absolutely no Salernitan influence indicates that the spread of the teachings of the school were not general at this date.

The other aspect of the teachings of Salerno that had lasting influence throughout Europe was the *Regimen Sanitatis*. This was a series of rules for diet and hygiene ostensibly written for Robert of Normandy, the son of William the Conqueror. The rules quote Hippocrates, Galen and Pliny but the principal source was a poem *De Virtutibus Herbarum* composed in the dark ages and itself based on a lost poem of the Roman poet Aemilius Macer. The advice given was full of practical commonsense and based the preservation of health on the proper use of the six non-naturals, air, food, sleep, exercise, excretion and coition.

> Shunne busie cares, rash angers, which displease;
> Light supping, little drinke, doe cause great ease.
> Rise after meate, sleepe not at afternoons
> Urine and nature's neede, expell them soone.
> When physick needs let these thy doctors be
> Good diet, quiet thoughts and heart mirthful, free.
> Sleepe not too long in mornings, early rise
> And with cool water wash both hands and eyes
> Walke gently forth, and stretch out every limbe:
> Combe head, rub teeth, to make them clene and trim.

The *Regimen* circulated widely throughout Europe. There are twenty incunabula. It was translated into German, French, Italian, Dutch, Bohemian, Polish and Gaelic. There are fifteen English editions between 1528 and 1613.[3] There is an Irish version, and a text was known to have been in the hands of the Beatons or MacBeths hereditary physicians to the Scottish kings. There are

[1]Copho's *De Febribus;* C. H. Talbot, *Medicine in Medieval England,* p47.
[2]B. Lawn, *The Salernitan Questions,* p63 et seq.
[3]Shorter Title Catalogue 21596–21610.

thirty Gaelic medical manuscripts preserved in Scotland which include translations of Galen, Avicenna, Lanfranc, Guy de Chauliac and John of Vigo.[1]

The twelfth century saw a new and important series of translations from the Arabic in the work of Gerard of Cremona, Mark of Toledo and other translators in Spain. These included new works of Hippocrates and Galen, Rhases' *Almansor*, Albucasis' *Chirurgia*, Avicenna's *Canon*, the *De elementis and De definitionibus* of Isaac, Serapion's *Breviarium* and Al-Kindi's *De gradibus*. This led to a shift in the gravitational centre of medical teaching, and the northern Italian cities and Montpellier in France came to rival Salerno.

Europe 1100-1500

During the following centuries medical knowledge remained firmly based on the humoral theory, and while there was constant restatement there was little advance. The real development took place in surgery where changing methods of warfare and the need for direct action continually produced new solutions and improved methods. The teaching of Salerno was initially of great importance. Roger of Salerno in the late twelfth century wrote a text book of surgical practice which was widely used throughout Europe reaching even to Iceland. Roger was followed by a series of Italian teachers based on the northern towns, such as Bologna; Roland of Parma, Hugh of Lucca, his son Theodoric, and Bruno of Longoburgo, whose work broke with the Salernitan tradition. Bruno was followed by William of Saliceto in the thirteenth century, and William's methods were taken to France by his able pupil Lanfranc. Lanfranc wrote two important surgical treatises, the *Chirurgia Parva* and the *Chirurgia Magna*. He was followed in France by Henri de Mondeville in the early fourteenth century, and at Montpellier Bernard de Gordon wrote a general medical work of wide diffusion and continuing influence, the *Lilium Medicinae*. The first treatise on anatomy based on the dissection of the human body was written by Mondino di Luzzi who was a contemporary of de Mondeville. It was based on direct experience, but Mondino still followed tradition in his explanations of what he saw and so perpetuated the Galenic errors. But through his pupil Bertuccio he influenced Guy de Chauliac who wrote an influential work on surgery which stressed the value of anatomical dissection, although in other respects it was conservative and without originality.[2]

The position of surgeons in the medieval period has been the subject of much discussion. Certain passages in the Arabic writers, such as Avenzoar, indicate that although the physician must have a knowledge of surgery he did

[1]H. Cameron Gilles, *Regimen Sanitatis. The Rule of Health from the Vade Mecum of the famous MacBethes*, University of Glasgow Press 1911; Winifred Wulff *Rosa Anglica*, Simpkin Marshall 1929, pxiviii; Sir A. Croke, *Regimen Sanitatis Salernitanum*, Oxford Talboys 1830, pp67–94.
[2]C. H. Talbot, *Medicine in Medieval England*, Ch 7 and pp116–8.

not normally carry out the simpler manual operations himself but left them to an assistant. Nevertheless there are numerous examples throughout the middle ages of surgeons who were also highly qualified physicians. The statutes regulating medical practice in Venice in the thirteenth and fourteenth centuries show that a knowledge of medicine was regarded as essential before a licence was given to practise surgery and that the physicians had the right to examine prospective candidates. The practical knowledge of surgery had to be gained from watching an experienced surgeon but there is no evidence that this was the only form of training required or that surgeons lacked academic education or a knowledge of medical theory.

England 1100-1500

England did not at this stage rival the Continent in originality, but in the twelfth century she produced two writers who show knowledge of the teachings of both Salerno and Montpellier and whose writings show an acquaintance with the new translations from the Arabic. Richard Anglicus wrote a summary of medicine known as the *Micrologus,* and Henry of Winchester compiled a set of questions and answers in the Salernitan manner and wrote a treatise on blood letting.[1]

In the thirteenth century the first English writer of importance was Gilbertus Anglicus. His major work was known as the *Compendium Medicinae*. It was a comprehensive work and his authorities include all the great medical writers of antiquity, the major Arabic compilers and the Salernitans. His book combines scholastic reasoning with practical observation and includes sections on leprosy, mental illness, remedies for seasickness, a long section on surgery and gynaecology. But his ideas are entirely derivative, the section on seasickness is written as though from direct experience but it is taken almost verbatim from earlier sources. The section on surgery is interesting since it indicates that a knowledge of surgery was an essential part of medical training.

A more renowned writer of the same century was Bartholomaeus Anglicus, a Franciscan friar who compiled an encyclopaedia of natural history known as the *De proprietatibus Rerum*. This book exercised an immense influence and was read throughout Europe. It was printed in translation by Wynkyn de Worde in 1470 and at the end of the century appeared enlarged and brought up to date by Stephen Batman. It was again largely derivative, mostly from Constantine, and consisted of nineteen books on the following subjects: God, the Angels, the Soul, the four elements and humours, Man, normal life (pregnancy, childhood, maturity, age and death), illness (the various ills are described in the conven-

[1]Henry of Winchester's authorities include Plato, Aristotle, Galen, Gariopontus, Oribasius, Isaac Judaeus, Constantine, Seneca, Remigies, Ovid, Al-Kindi and Alexander of Tralles. C. H. Talbot, *Medicine in Medieval England*, p62.

tional method beginning at the head and ending at the feet, derived from Pliny), cosmology, chronology, the elements and their changes (i.e. chemistry), weather, birds, water, the earth and its parts, geography, stones and metals, trees and herbs, beasts, and colours.

In the fourteenth century the most important medical writer in England was John Gaddesden who was a Fellow of Merton in the early years of the century, and was Rector of Abingdon from 1316. His book, the *Rosa Anglica*, was a compilation drawn from Arabic and European sources and including borrowings from two writers on surgery, Henri de Mondeville and Bernard de Gordon. His work was both comprehensive and scholarly.[1] Although he relied heavily on his predecessors, when Gaddesden did give his own opinion it was moderate and full of commonsense. He disliked too much bleeding and urged doctors to consider the patient's condition before prescribing remedies. His book is well constructed and clearly written giving in each case the description of the disease, its causes, the prognosis, and finally the cure. 'In the *Rosa Anglica* there was something for everyone, for the professional and the amateur, for the academic and the country practitioner, for those who could afford expensive remedies, and those who had to fend for themselves.' The *Rosa Anglica* was a synthesis of all that had appeared on the Continent during the previous two centuries: the translations from Arabic writers, the writings of the Salernitans, the fruit of progressive work in surgery from Italy and from the two most recent products of Montpellier and Paris.[2] In spite of the criticisms of Guy de Chauliac, the work was immensely popular. The measure of its influence can be seen from the fact that Gaelic manuscripts exist both in Ireland and Scotland where a copy was possessed by the Beatons. In this same century, England produced an outstanding surgeon in John Arderne. Arderne seems to have had no formal academic training, although little is known about his early life and his writings show him to have been extremely well read by any standards. He quotes nearly all the previous writers on surgery in the West, as well as the Arabs and the works of Galen and Hippocrates. His experience was gained in the armies of John of Gaunt. His written work, the *Practica*, consists of a collection of treatises on specific subjects – haemorrhage, obstetrics, eye diseases, gastro-intestinal disorders, gout and fistulae. It is illustrated throughout including pictures of the instruments used. An added interest is given by Arderne's own reminiscences where he describes various patients he has treated – when these were noblemen he tactfully identified them by their coats of arms.[3] Arderne was a careful painstaking surgeon who prepared well for his operations and who insisted on cleanliness.

[1] Dr Talbot notes that he gives exact references, e.g. to Avicenna, and even compares different readings of the text in order to elucidate the meaning. C. H. Talbot, *Medicine in Medieval England*, Ch 8.   [2] C. H. Talbot, *Medicine in Medieval England*, p111 and 115.
[3] C. H. Talbot, *Medicine in Medieval England*, p121–2.

In the later years of the fourteenth century a new phenomenon appeared, the writing of medical treatises, books of remedies and medical lore, in English. They were often written in verse to facilitate memorising, although the more scientific works continued to be written in prose. In 1373 a school master, John Love, translated the *Liber Floridus,* attributed to Macer, into English and it is found bound in with other treatises in English and French including Galen's *De Sectis.* During the same period a friar, Henry Daniel, translated a book on the properties of rosemary and a technical work on urinoscopy called *The Dome of Urines.* Books appeared which combined extracts from accepted authorities with standard and local remedies, designed presumably for home preparation. There were also books on regimen or diet and not unnaturally tracts on the plague and possible remedies in order that a man may 'be his own physicien in tyme of nede agenst the venym and the malice of the pestilence'. Another book which appeared in translation was the *Secretum Secretorum* attributed to Aristotle. This was first translated in 1412 by Thomas Occleve as *The Regement of Princes,* Lydgate also did a translation and a number of other versions appeared in the fifteenth century. Vernacular compositions based on the standard authorities and designed for use by physicians and surgeons seem to have been used since surviving examples show annotations in the margins. The ordinary medical practitioner also sometimes carried a sort of shorthand ready reckoner consisting of strips of parchment on which were written the essential knowledge he needed for diagnosing astrological phenomena such as eclipses and tables of planets, the appropriate sites for blood letting, and the rules about urine. Chaucer's well known description of the physician of his day in the Prologue to *The Canterbury Tales* well illustrates this close connection between astrology and medicine:

> He watched the patient's favourable star
> And, by his Natural magic, knew what are
> The lucky hours and planetary degrees
> For making charms and effigies.
> The cause of every malady you'd got
> He knew, and whether dry, cold, moist or hot;
> He knew their seat, their humour and condition.
> He was the perfect practising physician.

Natural science was to a great extent engulfed in the encyclopaedic works, such as the *De Proprietatibus Rerum,* already discussed. There was a school of botanical illustration in England between the tenth and twelfth centuries which produced the Anglo-Saxon translation of the *Herbal* of Apuleius and the illustrated codex of the middle of the eleventh century, the remains of which are now in the British Museum.[1] A more remarkable herbal, now in the Bod-

[1] Cotton Vitellius C.III.

leian, was written at Bury St. Edmunds in the twelfth century. The illustrations have obviously been drawn from life and not copied from other manuscripts. No school of naturalistic botanical illustration followed, and the *Herbal* remains an isolated example.[1] Roger Bacon, far in advance of his time in this as in all his other scientific work, attempted the crucial but difficult problem of the exact identification of plants and animals, but his influence because of his originality was limited. Stray examples of direct observation of natural things can be found among the English medieval chroniclers. Giraldus Cambrensis in the twelfth century describes from actual observation the habits of animals that interested him, both in the *Itinerary of Wales* and in the *Topographia Hiberniae*. There is a useful list of fishes in the *Topographia*. Both he and Matthew Paris, although at differing dates, gave an accurate description of the rare invasions of crossbills. Giraldus' account shows considerable detail.

> At the turn of the same year, at the season of fruits, certain wonderful birds never seen before in England appeared, particularly in orchards. They were little bigger than larks and ate the pips of apples and nothing else from the apples. So they robbed the trees of their fruits very grievously. Moreover, the parts of the beak crossed and with them they split the apples as with pincers or a pocket knife.

Matthew Paris records a similar event in 1251, and drew a picture of a crossbill in the margin of his book.[2] A recent article on Matthew Paris gives some examples of his marginalia and notes that many of them were drawings of animals and birds.[3] Yet Giraldus at the same time as writing an accurate account of a recognisable event, could with all seriousness assert that a soldier called Gilbert Hagernal, after he had experienced the pains 'as of a woman in labour, in the presence of many people, voided a calf.'[4] Giraldus also gives as an example of the theory that all animals including man contract the nature of the female who nurses them, the story of a wild sow suckled by a bitch which 'became, on growing up, so wonderfully active in the pursuit of wild animals, that in the faculty of scent she was greatly superior to dogs.'[5]

St Albans also produced 'the most veracious of all books on nature written in English', the treatise on *Fysshynge with an Angle*, by an anonymous author which was printed by Wynkyn de Worde in 1496. This small book contains a list of fish to be found in English rivers, the earliest of any British fauna, and describes the methods of catching them, the making of rods and lines (plaited horse hair dyed specially for different rivers), the tying of artificial flies and the

[1]W. Blunt, *The Art of Botanical Illustration*, Collins 1950, pp16-7.
[2]Quoted by C. E. Raven, *English Naturalists from Neckham to Ray*, CUP 1947, p25.
[3]W. N. Bryant, 'Matthew Paris Chronicler of St Albans', *History Today*, November 1969.
[4]Giraldus, *Itinerary through Wales*, Everyman edition 1935, p25.
[5]Giraldus, *Itinerary*, p25.

H.—7

making and use of the appropriate lures. *Fysshynge with an Angle* is remarkable for the delightful enthusiasm of the author, which spans the centuries and unites together all who have ever enjoyed the sport of fishing. Angling, he argues, is far superior to the chase: for a huntsman

> bloweth until his lyppes blister; and when he weneth it to be an hare, full oft it is an hegge hogge [but for the angler success is only part of the pleasure] yf there be nought in the water, atte the least he hath his holsom walke, a swete ayre of the swete savoure of the meede floures, that maketh hym hungry. He heareth the melodyous armony of fowles. He seeth the yonge swannes, herons, duckes, cotes, and many other foules wyth theyr brodes whiche me semyth better than alle the noyse of houndys . . . And yf the angler take fysshe, surely thenne is there no man merior than he is in his spryryte.

The author brings his book to a close with some wise advice:

> fyssch not in noo poore mannes severall water, breke noo mannes hegges . . . ne open no mannes gates.[1]

England was fortunate in having so human, so accurate, and so humorous a book as part of her legacy from the Middle Ages.

Printing of medical texts

The transmission of the sum of traditional knowledge in medicine and natural history by means of the printed book was surprisingly complete. There are twenty three Hippocratic or pseudo-Hippocratic works in Latin among the incunabula and the first 'complete' edition in Latin which included eighty genuine and spurious works appeared in Rome in 1525, and in the following year a rival Latin edition was published at Basle and the Greek princeps was printed by Aldus at Venice. A more accurate Greek edition was published by Froben which made use of the Galenic commentaries on the original text. At the end of the century two further editions appeared, the Graeco-Latin version of Geronimo Mercuriali, published in Venice in 1588, and finally the scholarly edition of Anuce Foes printed in Frankfurt in 1595 together with critical notes and accompanied by an encyclopaedia called *Oeconomia Hippocratis*.[2]

Celsus was also printed early. The discovery during the fifteenth century of two unknown manuscripts reawakened interest in his writings and there are four incunabula, the princeps appearing in Florence in 1478. There were at least fifteen editions in the sixteenth century.[3]

Soranus was not printed under his own name until the nineteenth century,

[1]Quoted by C. E. Raven, *English Naturalists*, pp28–9.
[2]G. Sarton, *Science during the Renaissance*, pp7–12.
[3]G. Sarton, *Science during the Renaissance*, pp12–14.

but his work on obstetrics and on acute and chronic disease was published under the name of Caelius Aurelianus in six editions during the century.

Galen was the most widely influential and most sought after of the classical authorities. The majority of the medieval manuscripts were derived from the Arabic but a few existed in translations from the Greek. There are thirteen separate treatises among the incunabula including the important collection edited by Giorgio Valla and published in Venice in 1498. Two of Galen's treatises formed part of the important 'summa' of medieval medicine, the *Articella,* which was first printed in 1476 and went into six incunabula editions. The first Latin edition of the *Opera* was published in Venice in 1490. The Greek princeps also printed by Aldus at Venice appeared in 1525 and a rival edition was produced at Basle in 1538. The words of Galen were constantly printed and translated into Latin throughout the century. The influence of Linacre on the Greek *Princeps* and through his own translations was considerable and did much to enhance the reputation of English scholarship among the humanists. John Caius also translated the works of Galen chiefly into Latin but a few into English.[1] An important contribution to Galenic scholarship of the Renaissance was the compilation of an index by Antonio Brasavola which was added to the Juntine edition of 1550 and remained the best key to Galen until the nineteenth century.

The Byzantine writers were also printed during the sixteenth century. Only a fraction of Oribasius appeared in the original Greek but there was a Latin translation produced at Basel in 1529, another of his commentary on the *Aphorisms* in Paris 1533. A large section of his encyclopaedia was translated by Giovanni Battista Rosario and published as the *Collecta medicinalia* in Paris in 1555 and 1567, in Basel in 1557, and in an undated Aldine edition. The *Synopsis* was printed by Aldus in Venice in 1554 and the *Euporistes* in 1558.

The works of Aetius of Amida were published in part by Aldus in 1534, the whole of his writings were printed by Froben in 1533-35, and a better translation came out in 1542 and was twice reprinted.[2] Sections of the works of Alexander of Tralles may well have been printed before 1500 although the date of *Practica Alexandri yatros greci* is uncertain. An incomplete Latin edition appeared in 1533 (Basel) and twelve books were printed in Latin in 1549, 1560 and 1576. The Greek princeps was published in Saris in 1548 and a Graeco-Latin edition at Basel in 1556. The Greek text of Paul of Aegina was

[1]Linacre translated into Latin the following Galenic texts: *De sanitate tuenda* (Paris 1517), *De medendi methodo* (Paris 1519), *De temperamentis et de inaequali temperie* (Cambridge 1521), *De naturalibus facultatibus* (London 1523?), *De pulsuum usu, De symptomatum differentiis et causis* (London 1524). Caius translated *De medendi methodo* (Basel 1544, reprinted Louvain 1556 and Basel 1558), six treatises in a composite edition dedicated to Henry VIII in 1544, *De anatomicis administrationibus Libri IX, De tuenda valetudine* (Basel 1549). For details, see G. Sarton, *Science during the Renaissance,* Lecture 1, Section 4.

[2]Aetios was particularly useful on eye diseases.

published by Aldus in 1528 and a Basel edition came out ten years later. The first complete Latin edition was printed in Paris in 1532 and was reprinted three times at Strasbourg, Venice and Lyons. There were six other Latin editions during the century. There was a French translation of the section on surgery (Book VI) in 1540.

Sections of both Rhases and Haly Abbas were printed before 1500. There are fourteen incunabula of Avicenna's *Canon*, one of which is in Hebrew. The Latin editions were all based on the text of Gerard of Cremona until the Juntine editions issued at Venice between 1527 and 1597. In these, the translation of Gerard of Cremona was revised by Andreas Alpagus and an Arabic-Latin glossary was added to the text. The first Arabic edition was printed by the Typographia in Rome in 1593.[1] There was still a demand for the *Canon* in the seventeenth century.

The famous collection of medical texts known as the *Articella* and Salernitan in origin, was first printed in 1476, a second and more complete edition appeared in 1483. There were six incunabula editions and it continued reprinting throughout the sixteenth century. A more original collection of texts, the *Fasciculus medicinae* was printed in 1491 and there were eight incunabula, one of which was in Italian and three in Spanish. It was reprinted at least five times in the sixteenth century. It was the first illustrated medical treatise to be printed and the first edition contained six full page woodcuts. A surgical collection, the *Collectio chirurgica veneta* was printed in Venice in 1498 and five other editions appeared before the end of the sixteenth century. It was based on the *Chirurgia* of Guy de Chauliac. Another, based on more ancient texts, Hippocrates, Galen and Oribasius, was published in Paris in 1544. Conrad Gesner edited a more forward-looking collection which was printed at Zurich in 1555 called the *Chirurgia de chirurgia scriptores optimi quique veteres et recentiores*. Three collections of gynaecological tracts were also published in the sixteenth century, and two medical dictionaries.

In natural history, Aristotle's *Works* with and without Averroes' commentary went into eight incunabula editions, and Aldus produced an edition in Greek together with the botanical works of Theophrastus between 1495 and 1498. Erasmus prepared another Greek edition published at Basel in 1531 which was reprinted twice. In all there were five Greek editions of Aristotle's works in the sixteenth century – and there were even more editions in Latin. These editions of Aristotle's *Opera* included the two books on plants now credited to Nicolas of Damascus and the inclusion of the works of Theophrastus in the early Aristotelian editions further complicated the issue. But all the works of Theophrastus were printed in Greek in Basel in 1541. Dioscorides had been widely available in Greek, Latin and Arabic in the Middle Ages, but there were only two incunabula one in Latin printed at Colle in 1478 and the Aldine Greek

[1]For the reasons why no printer existed at this time in Islam see Chapter I.

edition of 1499 but both were reprinted. New versions of the text appeared in the sixteenth century, the most important being by Hermolaus Barbarus and by the French physician and botanist Jean Ruel – a Graeco-Latin edition appeared in 1549. There were no illustrations in the early editions but some of the later ones were illustrated with woodcuts. Dioscorides was translated into Italian, French, German and Spanish, and several commentaries on him appeared during the century. Pliny was also printed before 1500. There are eighteen incunabula, three in Italian, the first edition appearing in 1469. Pliny was translated into other European languages in the second half of the sixteenth century; the English translation by Philemon Holland appeared in 1601. There were four commentaries on the text, one of which by Niccolo Leoniceno had the merit of being based on direct observation rather than purely textual criticism.

What printing did in the fifteenth and sixteenth centuries was to make the texts of earlier authorities available and easily accessible. To a large extent the early interest was philological and an accurate text was of prime importance – yet by the middle of the sixteenth century this was being replaced by a greater and more critical interest in the content. Yet the overall effect of printing, especially in medicine, was to reinforce the authority of the ancient texts. In spite of the great observational advances in anatomy the basis of all medical thought remained the humoral theory often reinforced by astrological lore. Treatment followed well tried and (sometimes successful) traditional remedies. The real benefit of the printed book was not in the spread of new thought, but in the raising of the general standard of learning of the medical profession by the provision of an increased number of accepted texts.

8. Tudor medicine

Linacre

The first great name in Tudor medicine is that of Linacre. Linacre took his degree at Padua in 1496. His importance to science is twofold: he translated into Latin a portion of the works of Galen with critical annotations, and he persuaded Henry VIII to found the College of Physicians. His work for Aldus gave him prestige outside England, and the establishment of the College introduced a new professionalism into medicine, improving the training and therefore the status of physicians throughout the country. Linacre was employed at Court as physician in 1501. From 1511 to 1520 he was drawing a salary of £50 per annum, and in 1521 Erasmus referred to him as the senior physician at Court. During this period he translated into Latin an important and influential section of Galen's works, which influenced the development of medical thought in England for the rest of the century, and above all, freed medical teaching from the useless and confusing medieval commentaries.[1]

Linacre, like all the early humanists, was a paradox. He was not an original thinker; his highest aim in scholarship was to edit and translate the learning of the past, but he used his power at Court to raise the standard of his profession and to provide for the education of a new generation of doctors. He belonged to the Erasmian circle in England: Colet, Lily, Grocyn and More, and above all Erasmus himself, were his friends. He became a priest, although he exercised his functions by deputy and seems to have begun to study the New Testament for the first time when over sixty years of age.[2]

The whole picture of Linacre is conservative, yet he was preparing the way for a revolution in thought and practice which was eventually to destroy the whole Galenic system he revered. His monument was not his literary, but his administrative work. It is as the founder of the College of Physicians, not as the Greek scholar and translator of Galen, that he is now remembered.

[1] The works translated by Linacre were *De Sanitate Tuenda* published 1517, *Methodus Medendi* 1519, *De Temperamentis* and *De Inaequali Temperie*, *De Naturalibus Facultibus* and *De Pulsuum Usu* 1422, *De Symptomatum Differentiis* and *De Symptomatum Causis*. Galen's great work on anatomy *De Anatomicis Administrationibus* was not discovered until after Linacre's death, and was first published in Paris with a commentary by the French physician Guinther in 1531. See Marie Boas, *The Scientific Renaissance*, Collins 1962, pp134–6; Sir George Clark, *A History of the Royal College of Physicians*, Clarendon Press 1964; W. S. C. Copeman, *Doctors and Disease in Tudor Times*, London 1960, p20.
[2] Sir George Clark, *A History of the Royal College of Physicians*, p51.

Foundation of the College of Physicians

The foundation of the College was the first step towards a closer organisation of the profession as a whole. In the sixteenth century, by far the largest part of medicine was home medicine. A physician would only be called in cases of extreme gravity, in cases of highly infectious diseases such as the plague, or for attendance on the wealthy. The importance of books of home remedies, and books by laymen giving the basic outline of medical theory with recognised cures by diet and herbal remedies, is therefore obvious. Sir Thomas Elyot, a courtier, educationalist and layman, wrote his *Castel of Helth* (published in 1534) in English for this reason, and by so doing incurred the wrath and indignation of the medical profession. The lack of qualified doctors per head of population also meant that a large number of unqualified men, who had only the vaguest knowledge of the humoral theory and medical techniques, were practising throughout the country. Known as 'Empirics' or 'Quacks', their skill varied with their commonsense, but in the long run they constituted a danger to the status of the profession, and it is precisely this question of status that lay at the root of the foundation of the College. This need for greater definition also applied to the exact relationship between the physician and the surgeon. The line between the two, while not clearly defined, undoubtedly existed. The Barber Surgeons were of lower social status because of their lower educational qualifications. They were not required to be university graduates, and were therefore not always fluent in Latin. This meant that a proportion of practising surgeons did not study the theory of medicine as a preliminary to their training, and were cut off from all the scholarly work of their time except in translation. Nevertheless during the fifteenth century under the stress of war the importance of surgeons had greatly increased. This had a double effect: physicians began to take an interest in surgery and often possessed surgical text books, and the surgeons themselves increased in status.[1] The distinction between the two branches of medicine persisted, and although a physician could practise surgery, a surgeon could not act as a physician unless qualified as one. Surgeons were subordinate to the physician in the treatment of disease and were only meant to deal with external injuries, perform amputations, set broken bones, lance abesses and apply ointments and plasters. All internal remedies and a large part of diagnosis remained the province of the physician; and it was to preserve this province against the surgeons, and maintain standards against the Empirics, that the College was founded. The Charter of 1518 specifically named six 'elects' who were all leading scholar physicians. These 'elects', (who had the power to co-opt two more) chose the President each year from among their number. By granting the Charter of 1518, Henry VIII had created a corporate body of professional men with legal, administrative, and

[1] C. H. Talbot, *Medicine in Medieval England*, pp206-7.

political powers. Before the existence of the College some control over the medical profession had existed in the powers of Bishops to license physicians and midwives in their diocese. These episcopal powers, which had been defined by an Act of 1511, were not specifically revoked by the Charter, and seem to have co-existed with those of the newly formed body. The Acts of 1533-4 separating England from Rome, for example, gave the Archbishop of Canterbury the right to license physicians, hence the existence of 'Lambeth degrees' in medicine. The College, as it gained in prestige, eventually extended its control beyond London and the suburbs until it virtually became the final licensing authority for all physicians throughout the country with the exception of graduates in medicine of Oxford and Cambridge, and even these could not practise in London without permission from the Fellows; whereas, from the confirmation of the Charter in 1522, the validity of the College licence was extended to the whole country. As the powers of the College grew they became more independent of royal control, and gradually the medical profession built up its own standards and had its own ethics. The College became the embodiment of the social and intellectual status of physicians, and from it 'there branched a perpetually shifting network of clientage, patronage, protection, and mutual support', which still exists in the twentieth century.[1] The College had its own seal; it had the right as a corporate body to own land and wealth; it could sue or be sued in the Courts; and it had the power to examine and discipline its own members.

Linacre clearly modelled his conception of the College on similar bodies on the Continent, but he was also following a general trend, common to the whole of England at this time, towards the incorporation of professional groups.[2] Sir George Clark points out that the College resembled a City Company but was not identical since it did not cover apprenticeship (it differs in this from the College of Surgeons); nor was it a craft guild with an academic veneer. It belonged to a new type of association which was emerging as the professions separated out from the crafts. He compares it with the College of Arms, granted its Charter by Richard III, and reconstituted in 1555, or the association of lawyers known as Doctors Commons. The College was fortunate in that it maintained its independent status in an era which saw a steady increase in royal control elsewhere in Europe. In France, for example, the King controlled the great medical school at Montpellier and nominated the professors, and by the end of the sixteenth century the French medical profession had lost any chance of fully independent development.

In England the College was too small, both in numbers, which were probably never more than eighteen, and in property, to attract state control. In its

---

[1] For an interesting account of the College as a corporation with influence independent of the Crown, see Sir George Clark, *A History of the Royal College of Physicians*, p76.
[2] For this tendency see Jacob, *The Fifteenth Century*, p289.

early years it met in Linacre's own house near St Paul's which also housed its library. The College was also, to a certain extent, protected by the traditional independence of the City and the City Companies. By the end of the sixteenth century in England the reality of power had shifted away from the Crown, and the professional independence of the College was assured. The high proportion of Fellows holding positions at Court meant that the College could in any case exert considerable influence. Here, as in government, the conditions in France did not apply in England.

Initially the College was not envisaged as a teaching body. In 1524 Linacre endowed three lectureships of £30 per annum at Oxford and Cambridge for this purpose, and Henry VIII set up a Regius Professorship in medicine at both Universities at the time of the Dissolution. There was no University in London. But by the middle of the century it had become obvious that more was needed and in 1565 the College was given four bodies to dissect per year (bringing it into line with the College of Surgeons). The teaching of anatomy had then at last a centre among the Physicians. This was of considerable importance since 'the science of physic doth comprehend, include, and contain the science of surgery.'

The teaching powers of the College of Physicians were fully defined before the end of the sixteenth century. Apart from the lectures on dissection, they consisted mainly in the right to examine and license all practising physicians in the London area. Examinations lasted three days and were entirely theoretical and confined to a knowledge of the works of Galen. Nothing comparable with the practical training in diagnosis given in the great French medical school at Montpellier (where students watched the teaching professors during actual examinations of patients) existed in England. Physicians had to pass through the normal university training and then proceed to a doctorate in medicine either in this country or abroad.

Sir George Clark has pointed out that the number of doctors qualifying in England does show a slight increase during the century. In Cambridge only one doctorate was awarded between 1500 and 1541, but there were sixty-three between 1542 and 1589. At Oxford the numbers were less but between 1571 and 1602 there were nineteen doctorates awarded. The numbers of Bachelors of Medicine were of course higher, and Clark estimates a possible three hundred during the reign of Elizabeth.

Rejection of humoral theory

As a teaching body, the College inevitably exercised a strong influence on the evolution of medical theory. Initially this influence was conservative and there was a rigid enforcement of the humoral theory. In 1559, Dr John Geynes was censured by the College for questioning the authority of Galen. All examinations included a knowledge of Galenic texts and the humoral theory lay at the basis of medical thought. By the end of the century this was no longer true. The situation had been saved by two things. Galen's theories were proved inadequate in practice, and at the same time an alternative theory of the nature of disease and its cure was introduced into medical thinking by Paracelsus. The Galenic theory was weakened by the appearance of new diseases, of which Galen had no knowledge and for which therefore he provided no explanation. The worst of these was syphilis. Whatever its origin, syphilis became rapidly, and has remained ever since, a major problem throughout Europe. Although the nature of the disease and its transmission by sexual contact was soon understood, no really effective cure Galenic or otherwise was found. Another new and alarmingly fatal disease was the sweating sickness. This appeared in England in 1485, and although extremely contagious was confined to this country. It continued with periodic outbreaks of extreme severity until 1578, when it abruptly disappeared. Both these diseases forced physicians to think afresh about the nature of disease; and because they were new, forced doctors to work from direct observation. Although neither of these developments necessarily involved the destruction of the humoral theory, they undoubtedly undermined its absolute authority.

The Swiss physician known as Paracelsus (1493-1541) was the first man in Europe to question the validity of the theory as a whole, and by inference, the teaching of Galen. His ideas, therefore, mark a turning point in scientific medicine.[1] Paracelsus, like many scientists, was deeply involved with the occult, and a large part of his thought is directly linked with that of the Hermetic Neo-platonists. 'Magic has power to experience and fathom things which are inaccessible to human reason. For magic is a great secret wisdom, just as reason is a great public folly.' A view which, in isolation, has a strange affinity to the thought of Blake.[2] But Paracelsus in this respect was part of the general pattern of Renaissance thought held by mathematicians like Dee and Copernicus, and experimental scientists like Gilbert. The intrinsic unity of all matter, the reflection of the Whole in the One, the 'macrocosm-microcosm' theory, where man embodies within himself all the powers and influences of the universe, was part of the accepted intellectual background of the age; and like the hierarchical theory of the great chain of being, where all created matter ascends in layers of ever increasing complexity and power to God, the source of all creation, was accepted and partly understood by any literate European.[3]

In its dynamic rather than its contemplative form, the Hermetic influence

---

[1]His real name was Phillipus Aureolus Theophrastus Bombastus von Hohenheim.
[2]For a popular but brief account of Paracelsus, see Marie Boas, *The Scientific Renaissance*, Collins 1962.
[3]For the ubiquity and general acceptance of these concepts in England, see E. M. Tillyard, *Elizabethan World Picture*, CUP.

produced an entirely new outlook on the world of nature and a drive towards direct observation. Paracelsus himself wrote one of the first studies of an occupational disease in describing the sickness he observed among the miners in the Fugger works at Villach. Peter Severinus, the Paracelsian physician to the King of Denmark, urged scholars to:

> sell your lands, your houses, your clothes, your jewelry: burn up your books . . . buy yourselves stout shoes, travel to the mountains, search the valleys, the deserts, the shores of the sea, and the deepest depressions of the earth; note with care the distinctions between animals, the differences of plants, the various kinds of minerals, the properties and mode of origin of everything that exists. Be not ashemed to study diligently the astronomy and terrestial philosophy of the peasantry. Lastly, purchase coal, build furnaces, watch and operate with the fire without wearying. In this way and no other will you arrive at a knowledge of things and their properties.[1]

Paracelsus symbolised his total rejection of all the theories of Galen, as transmitted by Avicenna, by burning the latter's works in public at Basle in 1527. He taught that God created the world from 'prime matter' out of which all other things evolved by a chemical process. He accepted the existence of the four basic Aristotelian elements air, fire, earth and water, all of which derived from the original 'prime matter'; but he added to the four, three 'qualities' which in their chemical form were represented by sulphur, mercury and salt. 'Sulphur is the cause of combustability, structure and substance. Solidity and colour are due to salt, while the vaporous quality is due to mercury.' Paracelsus, therefore, abandoned the accepted association of the four elements with the four corresponding qualities (as illustrated by Dee's *Preface*), which lay at the basis of the Galenic theory, and substituted a system which was based on the chemical reaction of the elements with the principles, and which, once the true nature of matter and its interactions was discovered, proved essentially more correct. Disease for Paracelsus was no longer an imbalance of humours which could be corrected by a remedy of the contrary quality, but a chemical reaction within the body, which could be treated by chemical means. As a result, the only possible method of diagnosis was clinical examination. In place of the traditional physician 'viewing' a sample of urine, Paracelsus advocated a series of chemical tests with a view to a definite analysis. Since he thought

---

[1] Petrus Severinus, *Idea Medicinae Philosophae,* quoted by Allen G. Debus, *The English Paracelsians,* Oldbourne 1965, p20. An interesting example of the learning of natural lore from peasants is given by A. G. Dickens in his account of the 10th Lord Clifford, 'the shepherd Lord', who was hidden at the age of seven by his mother among the shepherds of Cumberland in order to save his life during the Wars of the Roses, and who later in life studied astronomy, the elements of which he had learnt during his childhood. See A. G. Dickens, *The Clifford Letters of the Sixteenth Century,* Surtees Society, Vol CLXXII, 1957.

disease occurred locally in the body, it must be treated locally. This in turn necessitated a proper examination of the patient.

A more controversial contribution of Paracelsus to medical thought was the doctrine of 'similarities', that 'like cures like'. If a man had a fever, he should be kept warm not cold; if he was poisoned, the same poison properly administered in minute doses was the proper cure. Most important of all, Paracelsus investigated and used the earlier techniques of alchemy, which had always been linked with Hermetic magic and were part of the whole corpus of secret and traditional learning known both in Europe and the Arab world: but he used alchemy, which in any case was empirical chemistry, not to search for a mythical Elixir or to compound Mithridate as a universal panacea, but to prepare chemical compounds which used in carefully controlled dosage could safely be administered to patients in the cure of specific illness. For example, in the treatment of syphilis, Paracelsus denied the efficacy of the fashionable and expensive Guaiacum or Squima woods from the New World, and advocated the administration of mercury, but not in its pure form or in enormous doses, but as a compound and in minute amounts. It is in the development of alchemy into chemical medicine that Paracelsus is a real and important innovator in Europe, and in this respect is superior to Dee.

His acceptance of Hermetic magic to a certain extent lessened the impact and affected the ultimate value of his work, but it could not destroy it. Between them, syphilis and Paracelsus together helped to overthrow Galen and produce a more sceptical approach to disease as a whole by an important minority among the leaders of medical thought. By the end of the century there were signs within the profession itself that the ideas of Paracelsus were gaining ground.[1] Nevertheless the importance of the College of Physicians in England was rather that it provided a framework for a common standard of skill within the profession, than for the direct instruction it provided.

Development of medicine in England

Although most physicians wrote in Latin if they wrote at all, there were one or two conspicuous exceptions in the Tudor period, and the number of works in the vernacular steadily increased. The most colourful was Andrew Boorde (1490–1549). Boorde was an original character, who started life as a Carthusian monk, but found conditions too severe and rapidly secured a dispensation from the rule. He studied and took his M.D. at Montpellier and travelled all over Europe and the Near East. It seems virtually certain that Boorde acted as one of Cromwell's agents. Cromwell was instrumental in getting him released from close confinement in 1534 (his Prior, Howghton, was one of the Carthusians executed in 1535), and Boorde then visited Cromwell at his house at Bishops

[1]Sir George Clark, *The History of the Royal College of Physicians,* pp163–5.

Waltham in Hampshire before going overseas, possibly to report on foreign reactions to Henry's policy. This aspect of Boorde's career and the exact nature of his relationship to Cromwell needs further investigation. In 1536 he seems quite clearly to have been acting as an English spy in Scotland, his genuine medical training providing excellent cover. In a letter to Cromwell from Leith dated 1 April 1536, he wrote:

> I resortt to the skotysh Kynges howse, and to the erle of Aryn, namyd Hamylton, and to the lord eryndale, named stuerd, and to many lordes and lardes, [ladies] . . . and truly I know their myndes, for they takyth me for a skotysh manes sone. for I name my selff Karre [Carr or Ker] and so the Karres kallyth mc cosyn, thorow the which I am in the more faver. shortly to conclude, trust yow no skott, for they wyll use flattering wordes and all ys fal[s] holde.

He also reported that as he journeyed through England

> I mett and was in company off, many rural felows, englich men, that nowe nott our gracyose Kyng . . .

After warning Cromwell of the danger from aliens, he continued

> yff I myght do yngland any servyce, specyally to my soveryn lorde the Kyng, and to yow, I wold do ytt, to spend and putt my lyff in danger and Iuberdy as far as any man, god be my Iuge.[1]

Boorde's two medical works, *The Dyetary of Helthe* and *The Breviary of Helthe* are both unoriginal.[2] *The Dyetary* is an expansion in prose of the *Regimen Sanitatis Salernitanum. The Breviary,* published in 1547, is a more technical work and deals in the usual way with the parts of man and their diseases. There is a section on urine and its use in diagnosis. The book itself contains nothing new but the fact that Boorde wrote in English and his direct and practical outlook are both of interest. Boorde lists the qualities he thought essential for the successful practice of medicine. A doctor must be trained in logic to sift the true from the false; he must have rhetoric, to be able to explain his decisions; he must know geometry and arithmetic to weigh and calculate the correct amounts of drugs, astronomy to calculate the most propitious time for their administration; and finally 'to knowe natural philosophy, the which consisteth in a knowledge of natural things.' The quack he regarded as dangerous. 'Such ignorant persons may do great harme, although they think no evil . . .'

Boorde nevertheless was against a rigid reliance on books, and in his advice to

[1]Andrew Boorde's *Introduction and Dyetary,* ed. F. J. Furnivall, E.E.T.S. 1870, pp59–60.
[2]ed E. J. Furnivall, E.E.T.S. 1870.

use observation and reason, and to follow them in preference to any other
authority, he marks the beginning of a new attitude of mind which was eventually to alter the whole of medical theory itself: 'For if doctoures of pisicke
shulde at al tymes folow theyr bokes they shulde do more harm than good. And
some blynde phisians wyl say I was taught of such and such a doctour to
practise this thing and [that] thyng, such practising doth kyll many men.[1]
Boorde defined the soul in conventional terms:

> The soule of man is the lyfe of the bodye, for when the soule is departed from
> the body, the body is but a dead thynge that can not se, heare nor feele. The
> soule can not be felte nor sene, for it is lyke the nature of an Angell, havynge
> wyll, wyt, wysdome, reason, knowledge and understandynge . . . The soule
> also is a creature made with man and connexed to man, for man is of ii
> natures, which is to say, the nature of the soule, and the nature of the body,
> which is fleshe and bloud, the fleshe or body is palpable and may be sene and
> felte. The soule is not palpable nor can not be sene nor felt, but both beyng
> together nore and shal be after the general resurrection in tyme to come, doth,
> and shal do, fele ioy or payne. It is not the soule onely doth make a man, nor
> the body of a man is a man, but soule and bodye connexed or ioyned together
> maketh a man.[2]

Boorde thought that while God had

> put a tyme to every man, over the which tyme no man by art nor science
> cannot prolonge the time . . ., [But God has given man free will,] the
> whyche of his righteousness, as longe as we do lyve, he cannot take it away
> from us. [Man, therefore, can shorten his life by evil living such as drunken-
> ness] taking the pockes with women . . . beside robbying, fyghtyng, kyllyng
> and many other myschaunces. [Once ill, a man should not hope for a miracle
> or a speedy cure], for sycke men and women be lyke a pece of rustye harnys,
> the whiche cannot be made bryght at the fyrst scourynge; but lette a man
> continewe in rubbynge and scourynge and then the harnys wyll by bryghte:
> so in lyke maner a sycke man cannot be made whole of his malady in the fysrt
> day, but he must continue with his medicines.[3]

Boorde died in prison probably of typhus, being incarcerated by Bishop
Ponet for keeping three women in his house while still technically a professed
monk. Boorde's personal influence in his own generation seems to have been
slight, and he never seems to have attained high professional standing. Boorde
also wrote a manual of astronomy, an itinerary of England, another of Europe
which was lost, a guide for travellers, and a treatise on beards.[4]

[1]A. Boorde, *The Breviary of Helthe,* 1547, fol. iii.
[2]A. Boorde, *The Breviary,* fol. xiiii; and *The Dyetary,* ed Furnivall, Introduction p10.
[3]*The Breviary,* quoted in *The Dyetary,* E.E.T.S., p104.
[4]See Ch. 4, pp104-5.

Another physician who wrote entirely in English was Robert Recorde. Recorde's importance as a mathematician eclipses his work as a doctor, but he wrote a short book on urines, *The Urinall of Physick,* and in his mathematical text books he stresses the importance of quantification in medicine in a way which anticipates John Dee:

> And as for Physicke, without knowledge and aide of nomber it is nothinge. Wee see that nature in generation, hathe of manne and beastes, yea and of all thynges els doeth observe nomber exactly as well as in the tyme of formation, as in the moneths of quickenying and of birthe . . . For the use of the pulse, and for critical dayes, besides the proportion of degrees in simple medicines and mixture of compounde medicines and other infinite maters what nomber can doe and what aide it giveth, onely the ignoraunte doe doubt.[1]

Dr John Dee in his famous mathematical *Preface to Billingsley's Euclide* took a strikingly similar attitude to the importance of number in medicine.[2] He included a short and interesting section on the application of mathematical calculation to the humoral theory complete with a diagram showing the divergence away from normal in the four humours dry, heat, moist and cold, marked in degrees so that the physician or any reader could, once he had made a diagnosis, calculate from the diagram the appropriate remedy to counter balance the specific condition. 'And honourable physicans', he writes, 'wil gladly confesse themselves much beholding to the science of *Arithmetick* and that in sundry ways: but chiefly in their Art of Graduation and compound medicines. Also in the calculation of the quantities of the degrees above Temperament'.[3]

Dr William Turner, the naturalist, while not particularly important as a physician, wrote an informative and practical treatise on baths in English. It opens with some commonsense remarks on hygiene in communal bathing. Baths should be scoured every twenty-four hours, if this is not practicable, no-one should bathe at the spring, instead the water should be piped into individual baths which could be drained. In this way the spread of infection could be minimised. Turner describes a number of spas on the Continent and in England, and discusses the regimen to be followed. He finishes with a list of herbal drugs for the poor; the rich, he remarks, can take their doctor's advice:

> If any poore man by the reason of the heate and drynes of the bath cannot slepe inough let him eat Lettuce or Porcellayne or the sedes of poppye called Chesboule in some places of England or let him eat sugar and poppye seed together: let this be done at night . . . These are remedies for poor folke that are not able to have a Physician wyth them to gyve them councell. Let the

---

[1]Robert Recorde, *The Whetstone of Witte,* John Kyngston London 1557, bijr.
[2]Dee shows a number of parallels to the thought of Recorde by whom he seems to have been influenced, although they had a common source in Neoplatonic and Hermetic thought.
[3]John Dee, *Preface* to *Billingsley's Euclide,* London 1570.

ryche use such remedies as theyr Physicians councell them.[1]

Dr Caius, Turner's contemporary and fellow naturalist, has more direct importance to the development of medicine. He was the first man to lecture in public on the new anatomical methods of Vesalius, with whom he had lodged while studying in Italy. He began a series of lectures in the Barber-Surgeons' Hall in 1546 at the personal request of Henry VIII. He continued them for twenty one years. The fact that Caius held the post for so long, and the fact that he was a graduate and President of the College of Physicians for part of the period, meant that the gap which existed between the physicians and surgeons narrowed; and it established that these anatomical lectures should always be given by a graduate. It was Caius who obtained for the College of Physicians the right to dissect, and it can be argued that this aspect his of career provided an example which eventually led to the fusion of the two branches of medicine. In 1581, after Caius' death, the College of Physicians instituted the Lumlean Lectures on anatomy, which are still given. This interest of physicians in anatomy meant that, although the techniques of dissection and the understanding of the structure of the human body advanced more quickly in the sixteenth century than any other branch of medicine, their interpretation remained dominated by Galen. So much so that it is said that at the end of the century when Dr John Bannister was lecturing, if he found anything different during a dissection, he argued that the body of man had changed, rather than that Galen could be wrong.[2]

Caius' career is typical of the position of the scholar physician in the sixteenth century. He was a doctor, a naturalist, and an academic. His work in Cambridge was of great importance and he secured the refounding of Gonville Hall as Gonville and Caius in 1557. He became Master in 1559 and from then on divided his time between Cambridge and the College of Physicians in London, of which he was President from 1555 to 1560, and from 1562 to 1563, and finally in 1571. He remained Catholic and this finally led to his resignation from academic life just before his death in 1573. Caius' influence on medicine was to a large extent conservative. As President of the College he enforced a high standard of qualification for membership, organised the ceremonial still observed, and was in constant warfare with unlicensed practitioners and empirics, both in London and in the provinces.[3] Caius' written work was mainly concerned with natural history.[4] However he did produce an important book on the sweating sickness published both in Latin and English. His *Boke or Counseill*

[1]W. Turner, *A Booke of the bath of Baeth in England and the vertues of the same with divers other baths, most holsom and effectual, both in Germany and in England*, p16V. Turner's treatise was published with the 1st and 2nd parts of the *Herbal* in 1562 and again with the complete *Herbal* in 1568.

[2]W. S. C. Copeman, *Doctors and Disease*, p87.

[3]See Sir G. Clark, *A History of the Royal College of Physicians*, Ch VII.   [4]See p215.

against the disease commonly called the sweate or sweatyng sicknesse was printed in London in 1552. It is interesting as one of the first clinical studies based on direct observation, 'Therefore as I noted, so I wrate'. Caius' remedies for the disease were also practical and direct – rest but not sleep for the first twenty-four hours, and warmth. Almost the most interesting part of Caius' treatise is the Preface, where he excuses himself for writing in English on the grounds that the disease itself was confined to England: in general he is against the practice

> because the commoditie of that which is so written passeth not the compasse of England, but remaineth enclosed within the seas . . . [and also] that the common settyng furthe and printing of every foolish thing in English, both of phisicke unperfectly and other matters indescrettly [leeds to a diminution of] the grace of thynges learned.

Caius was definitely not a populariser of knowledge, in this respect as in others he was a traditionalist.

By Elizabeth's reign there was a steady demand for medical books in English. Books in this category from the earlier part of the century were continually republished. Elyot's *Castel of Helth* finally went into thirteen editions by 1595, and Boorde's *Breviary* was reprinted four times under Elizabeth.[1] Robert Recorde's *The Urinall of Physick* was published in 1547, and a number of comprehensive medical works designed to help ordinary people appeared before 1600. Some, like Humphrey Lloyd's *Treasury of Helth*, were simply translations of earlier works. Others were original, like Thomas Phaer's *Regiment of Lyffe*, William Bullein's *Bulwarke of defence against all sicknesse, sores and woundes*, and Phillip Barrough's *The Method of Physicke*. Bullein and Barrough were writers of considerable importance and Barrough's book went through nine editions before 1639.[2] A similar book of equal popularity was Thomas Cogan's *Haven of Health* which was reprinted six times in the same period.[3] Since the bubonic plague was both endemic and fatal in the sixteenth century, it is not suprising that a number of books appeared on the subject. Some of these were either new editions, or translations into English, of established works such as *A moste profitable treatise against the pestilence* which was simply translated from the Latin original of Bishop Knutsen by Thomas Paynell in 1534. But it was not long before more original works began to appear. One of the most important was William Bullein's *Dialogue against the Fever Pestilence*, which went through three editions in 1564, 1573, and 1578. It contains much interesting material on

[1] H. S. Bennett, *English Books and Readers 1558–1603*, pp179–89.
[2] P. H. Duffy, 'Medicine in Elizabethan England as illustrated by certain dramatic texts,' unpublished thesis, Harvard University 1942.
[3] Cogan noted with considerable shrewdness that 'husbandmen and craftsmen for the most part doe live longer and in better health, than gentlemen and learned men, and such as live in bodily rest', T. Cogan, *The Haven of Health*, Melch Bradwood for John Norton 1612 Aij.

medical ethics and social conditions, and is set in the form of a conversation between a group of people which include a doctor, his patients and Death. It gives a detailed account of the symptoms, with recommendations for prevention and possible cures. The onset, Bullein observes, occurs most frequently in hot and changeable weather when the wind is in the south or east, and when

> flies or thinges bredyng under the ground do flie by swarmes into the ayre ... [The symptoms are] a fever going before, noisome and lothesomenesse of stomacke, wambelying of the harte, pulse not equall, urine stinking, desirous of sleep, perilous dreams ... and then a little pushe will creep forth like a scabbe ... and shine like pitch or Bytumen ... and then it will have a crust like unto the squames or flakes of iron when thei fall of when the Smith doth worke ...

The cure was uncertain, but Bullein gives a number of medicinal remedies, some of which were put in Latin as formal prescriptions for the use of apothecaries. Prevention included the obvious one of moving as rapidly as possible from the infected area, controlled diet, no fresh fruit, and avoiding

> anger and perturbations of the mynd, specially the passion called feare, for that doth drawe the spirites and blood inwards to the hart ... [Music is beneficial and pleasaunt tales] ... Forget not to keepe the chamber and clothying cleane, no Priuies at hand ... Shifte the lodging often time, and close the Southeaste windows, specially in the tyme of mistes, cloudes, and windes ...[1]

Three other books on the plague deserve to be mentioned. The earliest is by Thomas Phaer, who added a section on the plague to his *Regiment of Lyffe*.[2] The second is Simon Kellwaye's *Defensitive against the Plague;* and the third, Thomas Lodge's *A Treatise of the Plague*, actually associated the disease with rats. The period also saw the publication of a number of other specialised works. Early books on psychology included Timothy Bright's *A Treatise on Melancholie*, published in 1586, which may well have influenced Shakespeare; Edward Jordan's work on hysteria *A Brief discourse of the disease called the Suffocation of the mother;* and Thomas Wright's *The Passion of the Minde*, published in 1601. Another important work which appeared in translation was Juan Huarte's *An Examination of Men's Wits*. The first book in English on pediatrics was Thomas Phaer's *The Boke of Chyldren*. Phaer recognised smallpox and measles as different diseases and knew them to be highly contagious. His work is both humane and practical. 'The best and sure helpe is not to meddle with any kinde of medicines, but to let nature work her operation'.[3] Gynaecology was covered by

[1] W. Bullein, *A Dialogue against the Fever Pestilence*, E.E.T.S. 1888.
[2] This is regarded by Duffy as the most definitive of the plague pamphlets.
[3] Thomas Phaire, *The Boke of Chyldren*, ed A. V. Neale and H. R. Wallis, E. and S. Livingstone 1955, p56.

The Byrth of Mankynde, translated from Roesslin. Among a group of recipes for potions to ease the pain of labour, Roesslin gives one containing twelve grains of opium.[1] Taken as a whole these books widened the general knowledge of medical theory and practice. With the increase in literacy this meant that although most medicine remained home medicine, it was at least better informed.

Development of surgery in England

The development of surgery followed a course parallel to medicine. The surgeons improved in knowledge and skill, and showed the same tendency towards increased professionalism. Unlike the physicians, the Barber-Surgeons had emerged as a City guild in the fifteenth century, and had acquired privileges, which eventually included exemption from military service and from serving on juries. In 1540 they were incorporated by Royal Charter as the Company of Barber Surgeons under the Mastership of Sargeant-Surgeon Thomas Vicary. The constitution was similar to that of the earlier College of Physicians and the original group (painted by Holbein at the presentation of their Charter) includes two physicians, Dr John Chamber and Dr William Butts. Sir George Clark suggests that it was the influence of Dr Chamber which secured the incorporation Charter.[2] In 1543 the surgeons obtained disciplinary rights over their own members, and the right to dissect four bodies each year.[3] The bodies were those of executed criminals, and this not infrequently led to the bribing and counter-bribing of the hangman between the relatives of the victim and the representatives of the doctors. The education of surgeons was based on the system of apprenticeship, common to all the craft guilds. A boy became bound to a practising surgeon at the age of about twelve and was trained for a period of seven to nine years. The applicant had to be of good health and have basic grammar school education. At the end of his apprenticeship he was examined by the Masters in the Barber-Surgeons' Hall. Even after qualifying, a young surgeon would be required to attend lectures on anatomy and even to perform dissections himself. Apart from these lectures, the surgeon like the physician, had to learn from experience. The sixteenth century was a period of rapid advance in anatomical knowledge and surgical techniques. The general study of anatomy was part of the Renaissance, equally valid for the scientific as for the artistic world. But the techniques of surgery developed under the direct stimulus of war. The invention of gunpowder caused wounds of greater severity, and different in character from anything seen before. They required new methods

[1] Roesslin, *The Byrth of Mankynde, otherwise named the women's boke. Newly set forth, corrected and augmented,* Thomas Raynald Phisiton 1552, Fol 113.
[2] Sir George Clark, *A History of the Royal College of Physicians,* p85.
[3] This right also existed in the provinces.

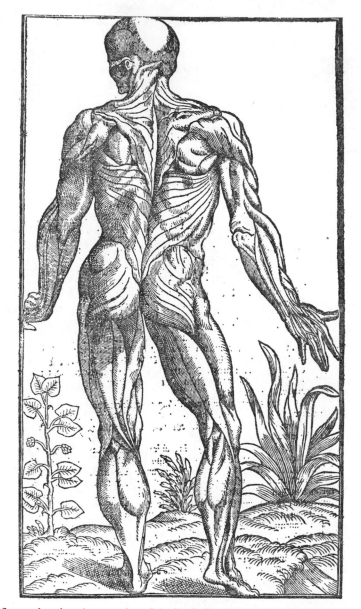

9. Male figure showing the muscles of the back. Based on an illustration from
Vesalius' *De Humani Corporis Fabrica* in John Bannister's *The Historie of Man* . . . ,
London, 1578. *(By courtesy of the Wellcome Trustees)*

of treatment and undoubtedly increased the number of amputations. Initially all gunshot wounds were regarded as poisoned by the lead from the bullet, but even when this theory was abandoned, the high incidence of gangrene often required drastic surgery. In addition to the stimulus of actual warfare, the rise in the standard of living meant that more people could afford surgical treatment. The surgeon was expected to live in the house of his patient until a cure was effected, the number of cases a distinguished surgeon could take in one year was therefore limited, and the surgeon's fees proportionately high. Surgical treatment of the poor was normally in one of the charitable hospitals for the sick, and it was here, and on the battlefield, that the young surgeon got his practical experience.

The period saw the publication of a number of surgical text books in English, the first was by the founder member of the College, Thomas Vicary, whose *A profitable treatise upon the Anatomy of a Man's body* and *The Englishmen's Treasure* appeared in 1548.[1] In 1563 *Certaine workes of chirurgerie* by the surgeon Thomas Gale, who had served with the army in France, was published. It was followed in 1575 by John Bannister's *A needefull new and necessarie treatise of Chirurgerye*, and in 1578 by his *The Historie of Man, sucked from tho sappe of the most approved Anathomistes*. In 1588 William Clowes published *A prooved practise for all young Chirurgians, concerning burnings with Gunpowder, and woundes made with Gun shot, Sword, Halbard, Pyke, Launce, or such other*. Clowes' book included a translation of a Spanish treatise on syphilis, and 'a commodious collection of Aphorismes both English and Latin taken out of an old written copy'. The book was published 'for the benefyte of his Countrey'. A second edition appeared in 1591, and this was followed in 1596 by *A Profitable and Necessarie Booke of Observations, for all those that are burned with the flame of Gun powder, etc. and also for curing of wounds made with Musket and Caliver shot, and other weapons of war commonly used this day both by sea and land*, ... William Clowes himself was a distinguished and capable surgeon. *The Profitable and Necessarie Booke of Observations* . . . contains the first description of the tying of arteries when amputating a leg, a practice which was gradually superceding cauterisation by hot metal or boiling pitch.[2] Clowes describes some extremely successful cases of compound fractures, and in one instance of the cure of a soldier who was run through by a sword in battle, the sword entering the front of the chest and protruding between the shoulder blades. In another case, that of a man with severe head injuries, Clowes' description is particularly interesting since it shows the survival of traditional theory in an age of rapid anatomical advance. The wounded man 'was in the more danger, for that he received his hurt very near the full of the moon

[1] The first known edition is that of 1577. See F. N. L. Poynter, *Selected Writings of William Clowes*, Harvey and Blythe 1948.
[2] F. N. L. Poynter, *Selected Writings of William Clowes*, Ch VIII.

10. Patient being treated for a chest wound. From Thomas Gale's *Certaine workes of chirurgerie*, London, 1563. *(By courtesy of the Wellcome Trustees)*

whereby this evil followed, that the Dura Mater did rise and thrust itself out of those places of the skull that I did perforate or pierce with the trepan, the which I did safely bring down again.' He quite rightly remarks that to be a successful surgeon needed 'a Lion's heart, a Lady's hand, and a Hawk's eye'.[1]

Clowes, who was born about 1540, served in both the armed forces. In 1563 he accompanied the Earl of Warwick's army to Normandy, and then served in the navy till about 1570, and rejoined to take part in the Armada. He was made a Barber-Surgeon in 1569 and in 1575 he was appointed to the staff of St Bartholomew's Hospital in London; in 1576 he became visiting surgeon to the children of Christ's Hospital. Clowes became a recognised expert on syphilis, and published a book on the disease which went through several editions, and which included a detailed description of the treatment with mercury. In the edition of 1585, Clowes states that while working at St Bartholomew's Hospital, ten out of every twenty patients admitted had the pox, and that during his ten years of office he had cured or attempted to cure over a thousand cases. This can have been only a small portion of the total number in London let alone the rest of the country, and indicates the serious nature of the problem. The treatment with mercury was often worse than the disease, since it was given in enormous amounts and frequently poisoned the patient. The great French physician Fernal wrote in his *De Curatione* that in one case on lifting a piece of dead bone he found actual droplets of quicksilver quivering underneath it.

Clowes was clearly both an excellent surgeon and independent and inventive as a man. He was jealous of the dignity of his profession and pointed out in his writings that the classical writers such as Homer indicate that surgery existed before Physic was even thought of. He was also in advance of his time in being ready to use whatever methods he could for the benefit of his patient, regardless of accepted dogma. After listing all the classical authorities, including Galen, he continues

I had here likewise thought good to have spoken somewhat of Paracelsus, but I must confess his doctrine has more pregnant sense than my wit or reach is able to construe; only this I can say by experience, that I have practised certain of his surgical inventions, the which I have found to be singular good and worthy of great commendation. Howbeit I know there is much strife between the Galenists and the Paracelsians, as was in time past between Ajax and Ulysses for Achilles armour. Notwithstanding for my part, I will here set up my rest and contention, howsoever impertinent and unseemly it may be. That is to say, if I find, either by reason or experience, anything that may be to the good of the patients, and better increase of my knowledge and skill in the art of Surgery, be it either in Galen or Paracelsus, yea Turk or Jew or any other infidel, I will not refuse it, but be thankful to God for the same.

[1] F. N. L. Poynter, *Selected Writings of William Clowes*, pp35-7.

In another context he wrote:

> Truth is truth, from whomsoever it come, be it from Hippocrates, Galen, Paracelsus or any other learned man.[1]

Clowes was clearly a successful and presumably a well-off man. The portrait in the Wellcome Historical Institute which Dr Poynter uses as evidence for this, since it shows Clowes wearing a furred gown with a jewel in his cap, a gilded chain, and a ring on his hand, closely resembles the Holbein portrait of Sir Richard Southwell, now in the Uffizi, and must therefore be either a copy or a standard pose.[2] The furred gown, however, is distinctive in the Clowes portrait, and the fact that he was painted at all is a proof of a certain wealth and status. Clowes's face (in marked contrast to that of Southwell) is that of a sensitive and thoughtful man, and confirms the impression made by his writings.[3]

The marked difference in standing between physicians and surgeons is shown by the Household accounts of Henry VIII. The salary of his physician, Dr William Butts, was a basic £100 per year, increased to £126.13.4. He also received £20 per year for attending the Duke of Richmond, and livery, consisting of blue and green damask for himself and two servants, and a length of cloth for his apothecary. In contrast, the King's surgeon, Thomas Vicary, got a basic £20 per year, increased to £26.13.4. when he was made Sargeant Surgeon.[4]

Apothecaries

The third branch of the medical profession, the apothecaries, until the end of the century were included in the Grocers Company which controlled the spice trade. In 1540 the College of Physicians was given the right of inspecting and testing apothecaries' drugs. This was important, for it was the apothecaries who 'provided the bulk of the day-to-day doctoring for the general population', and here more than anywhere else there was real need for control and for the suppression of quacks and ignorant practitioners. If Dr Poynter is right in his estimate of one fully qualified physician for every 25,000 people, the so-called Quacks Charter, the Acts of 1542–3, which allowed anyone with a knowledge of herbs to treat minor ailments, becomes a rational and intelligible decision, but it added to the need for supervision of drugs and medicaments.

[1]F. N. L. Poynter, *Selected Writings of William Clowes*, pp46–7.
[2]For a comparison of the two paintings see F. N. L. Poynter, *Selected Writings of William Clowes;* and K. T. Parker, *The Drawings of Hans Holbein . . . at Windsor Castle,* Phaidon Press, 1945, p47.
[3]The practice of having ready-made poses prepared in a studio, was a normal one. The comparison is only interesting in linking the Clowes portrait with the Holbein studio – since Holbein himself died probably of the plague in 1542.
[4]H. A. Colwell, 'Andrew Boorde and his medical works', *The Middlesex Hospital Journal,* July 1911, p34.

Dr William Bullein, a Fellow of the College, had warned the apothecary that he should 'meddle only with his own vocation, and that he doe remember that his office is onely to be ye Physicians cook.' Nevertheless the increasing knowledge of drugs and the widening variety of remedies both herbal and mineral, meant that apothecaries needed more extensive and more accurate knowledge, and this in turn led to an improvement both in skill and status. The Apothecaries first petitioned for separate incorporation free from the Grocers in 1588. They did not succeed: and it was not until 1617 that, with the help of Sir Francis Bacon, they became the Worshipful Society of the Art and Mistery of the Apothecaries.

The sixteenth century therefore saw a steady advance towards organised professionalism in all three branches of medicine. If the physicians and surgeons were not yet considered members of a single profession, it was because the theory underlying the practice of medicine was still unreformed, and because the vested interests of the senior group, the physicians, prevented it.

The publications of Elizabeth's reign were a mixture of new works and reprints of medieval treatises. As long as the underlying theory of medicine remained unchanged traditional expositions were in demand and men could buy Lanfranc, Guy de Chauliac, John of Vigo or Galen himself on surgery, and John Gaddesden's *Rosa Anglica*, the *Regimen Sanitatis Salernitanum*, and other medieval texts on medicine.

Paracelsian ideas in England

Yet the College of Physicians could not prevent the spread of new ideas even though it rejected them in its official teaching. By the end of Elizabeth's reign there was a small group of Paracelsians in England, some of whom had penetrated the College itself. When in 1585 the College of Physicians was planning the production of a much-needed pharmacopoeia, one section was to be devoted to chemical medicines. This section was put in charge of three physicians, one of whom, Thomas Moffet, (see also chapter 9 for Moffet's importance as a naturalist) was an open Paracelsian, and who nevertheless was a Fellow of the College and had considerable influence at Court. The section on chemical medicines was not printed, but it indicates that the Fellows of the College were not as rigidly pro-Galen as is sometimes thought. A letter from Stephen Bredwell in the front of Gerard's *Herball* in 1597 actually suggested setting up a lectureship in chemical medicine at the College to supplement the study of herbal remedies of disease, although Bredwell himself was an anti-Paracelsian. The main fear was clearly against the unauthorised use of these medicines by untrained quacks, and the obvious remedy was the study of the new methods of treatment by the doctors themselves. As long as the humoral theory was accepted and taught as dogma, there was the possibility of a dangerous rift between theory and practice. The fact that this did not happen to any great extent in England, was due to the commonsense of the medical profession, and in part to the revival of science, particularly chemistry, among highly placed members of the Court and aristocracy.

Moffet himself boldly asserted that 'the body of men consists of sulphur, mercury and salt alone, not because we know this as perfectly as Adam, but because the resolution of all kinds of natural as well as artificial bodies show it to be so'.[1] An important defence of Paracelsus appeared in 1585 with R. Bostocke's *Difference betwene the auncient Phisicke . . . and the latter Phisicke.* Bostocke, who was not a doctor, seems to have been the first person to see the ideas of Paracelsus as part of the whole revolution of European thought. In an interesting passage he compares Paracelsus with the religious reformers, from Wyclif to Calvin, and with the work of Copernicus in astronomy, as a thinker who had restored knowledge to its original truth by rejecting the theories of Aristotle and the medieval schoolmen. It was as a reversion to pristine knowledge rather than a revolution that he welcomed Paracelsian medicine. By this curious irony Bostocke linked Paracelsian iconoclasm and humanism as different aspects of the same reappraisal of accepted thought.

Another influence leading to the acceptance of chemical remedies as a useful addition to the resources available to the physician and surgeon was that of the great Swiss naturalist Conrad Gesner. Gesner, through his contacts with nearly all the leading naturalists in England, was clearly an important indirect influence on the whole of English scientific thought, and Gesner, while avoiding Paracelsus' Hermeticism, was well aware of his theory of chemical remedies. And it is interesting that Turner, Moffet, and the surgeon George Baker (1540-1600), all of whom were prepared to use chemical remedies, were all directly influenced by Gesner.[2] Baker again is linked with one of the most interesting of the Elizabethan background figures in the field of science, the printer and publisher Thomas Hill. Hill specialised in the compilation and translation of scientific books ranging from gardening to palmistry, but he was far more than a mere purveyor of current ideas, he translated and interpreted the new scientific developments in European thought for the ever-widening circle of interested laymen. His books were all remarkable for their accuracy and lucidity. He helped to inform and therefore to mould the outlook of the average educated Elizabethan, and has with some justice been described as the 'Elizabethan Huxley'.[3]

Baker saw through the press Hill's last book, a translation of Gesner's *Treasure of Euonymus,* under the title of the *Newe Jewell of Health,* 1576, and

[1]Quoted by Allen G. Debus, *The English Paracelsians,* p37.
[2]See Allen G. Debus, *The English Paracelsians,* Chs. 2 and 3.
[3]F. R. Johnson, 'Thomas Hill. An Elizabethan Huxley', *Huntington Library Quarterly,* August 1944.

added a preface on 'the virtues of medicines by Chimicall distillations are made more viable, better and of more efficacie than those medicines which are in use and accustomed.' Another friend of Hill's, John Hester also a Paracelsian published a smilar translation *A Joyfull Jewel,* 1579, and continued to advocate the use of chemical medicines throughout his life, particularly in the treatment of new diseases, such as syphilis, for which there existed no traditional cure. Hester's many translations were undoubtedly of the greatest importance in the introduction of chemical remedies into England, and through them many English physicians must have become aware for the first time of the different aspects of the new movement on the Continent. The attitude of the College of Physicians remained non-committal the projected pharmacopoeia of 1585 was never completed, and without any such work of reference the way was wide open for the sale of universal remedies of doubtful value such as the gold remedies (aurum potabile) of Francis Antony. A number of doctors and surgeons such as John Bannister had compiled their own lists of remedies which included chemical compounds, and herbal recipe books were numerous, but none were complete, and none were official.

The College of Physicians made another attempt at compilation in the seventeenth century, this time with more success. The *Pharmacopoeia Londinensis* was published finally in 1618, under the double stimulus of the incorporation of the Apothecaries and Sir Theodore Mayerne, a convinced but moderate supporter of chemical medicines, who remained Royal Physician until 1655.[1]

Public health

While the sixteenth century saw the steady progress of scientific knowledge in the whole of medicine, the question of public health and hygiene remained regrettably static. On a national level any solution required state intervention, at local and individual level it was a question of education and convention. The most advanced minds of the century were well aware of the dangers of infection and pollution. Dr Dee violently attacked the growing filth of the Thames and proposed alternative methods of the disposal of sewage.[2] Erasmus noted with disgust that the floors of English houses were 'covered with rushes that are now and then renewed, but not so as to disturb the foundations which sometimes remains for twenty years nursing a collection of spittle, vomits, excrements of dogs and human beings, spilt beer and fishbones, and other filth which I need not mention.'[3] A description which is confirmed by the writings

[1] It is from Mayerne's accurate notes of the periodic illnesses of James I that it has been possible for modern doctors to prove the existence of porphyria in the royal family. A full discussion of the *Pharmacopoeia Londinensis* and its contents can be found in Allen G. Debus, *The English Paracelsians,* Ch 4.

[2] I. R. F. Calder, 'John Dee studied as an English Neoplatonist', p694.

[3] W. S. C. Copeman, *Doctors and Disease,* p165.

of Andrew Boorde. Various attempts were made during the century at regulating hygiene in towns. Statutes in 1488 and 1495 prevented slaughterhouses from being too near inhabited buildings, and regulated the activities of upholsterers in an attempt to prevent the spread of vermin. Marshes were to be drained of all standing water before any new building. The commissioners for sewers throughout the country were technically responsible for refuse disposed in their areas, but sanitation outside London and the major provincial towns was virtually non-existent. Thomas Cromwell, in 1532, attempted reforms which included the setting up of public standpipes with running water in most towns, and imposed penalties for water pollution. But, as always, the difficulty was effective enforcement. Sir Thomas More, in *Utopia*, laid considerable stress on public health. The cities were built with broad streets, gardens, open spaces, public water supply, drainage and cleansed streets. Abattoirs were outside the city limits, and there were public hospitals for the sick. More is known to have improved London's water as Commissioner for Sewers in 1514, and it is possible that Cromwell's legislation of 1532 may reflect his advice. It is certain that Cromwell's papers include projected reforms with increased medical care for the poor, but they were never implemented.

The use of sea coal for fires in London was regarded as a danger to health, but this did not stop the steady increase in shipments from Newcastle: between 1560 and 1592, the amount of coal shipped from Newcastle to London increased from 35,000 tons to 100,000: by 1625 it had risen to 400,000 tons.[1]

The precautions necessary against the plague are outlined in Simon Kellwaye's treatise of 1593, and lazar hospitals for cases of leprosy had existed since the Middle Ages. The contagious nature of disease was recognised but this is not the same as understanding the nature of infection, the panic remedy of isolation of victims and families therefore remained the only practicable solution. After the dissolution, a proportion of charitable bequests went to the care of the infirm and sick throughout the country, but nothing like a national system existed. Personal hygiene varied with social status. The great houses of the later Tudor period were built with primitive sanitation provided by running water in conduits under the house, and wooden floors and glass windows led to improved comfort and cleanliness by the end of the century. But there was little or no improvement in the housing conditions of the poor, and the increasing overcrowding in the towns aggravated the problem.

Nothing has been said about childbirth because there is little constructive to say. The incidence of infection was appallingly high. The fourth Duke of Norfolk lost three wives in childbed. Until the invention of the forceps in the seventeenth century little could be done to help a woman in a difficult labour. Midwives were supposed to be licensed by the Bishop but, according to Andrew Boorde, many were not. Until serious demographic studies are under-

[1]J. U. Nef, *The Coal Industry in the Sixteenth Century.*

taken from the parish registers of the period, no firm conclusions can be drawn. The increase in population which is an important factor in the sixteenth century was due rather to improved diet and general living standards, than to any improvement of the care of women in childbed or of the infant during the first crucial months of life. Suckling by wet nurse was the normal practice among the upper classes, and it is of interest to note that even adults in case of severe illness were often nourished by this means.[1]

The provision of hospitals for the sick had originally been the duty of the Church. The existing hospitals in England were therefore directly affected by the dissolution of the monasteries. In London five out of eight hospitals were closed, leaving, as the Mayor complained in 1538, 'the poor, sicke, blind, aged and impotent persons . . . lying in the street, offending every clean person passing by with their filthy and nasty savours'.[2] As the result of this pressure from the City, Henry refounded St Bartholomew's in 1544, and in 1547 made an agreement with the citizens giving them a measure of control over the hospitals within the City. In 1552 a further act ratified that of 1547, and the City raised considerable sums of money for rebuilding and drew up a comprehensive system of relief by which the sick were cared for at St Bartholomew's, the infirm at St Thomas', children at Christ's Hospital, the insane at Bethlehem, and vagabonds at Bridewell.

Elsewhere in the country the situation after the Dissolution was serious, and it was only gradually that local hospitals were founded or refounded by private charity.

[1]A. G. Dickens, The Clifford Letters of the Sixteenth Century, Surtees Society, Vol CLXXII 1957, p149.
[2]Sir A. MacNalty, 'The Renaissance and its influence on English medicine, surgery and public health', The Vicary Lecture 1945, Christopher Johnson.

9. The naturalists

In botany and zoology the process of change was accelerated by the new discoveries in America and the Far East, which added a totally unknown flora and fauna to a picture of the natural world already shaken by the work of the humanists. The botanical work of Dioscorides was soon found to be inadequate even for Northern Europe, and naturally gave no description even approximating to the plants of India and America.

Traditional knowledge

The need to collate and examine all the traditional lore on natural history, and to combine this with the new discoveries produced the important and encyclopaedic works known as 'pandects' which consisted of extracts from earlier scientific writers together with all available new knowledge in a defined field. The most famous compilation covering zoology and botany was that of Conrad Gesner of Zurich, whose work appeared during the middle of the century, and was left unfinished.[1] Gesner had, in his own words, 'an infinitely questing spirit', he was an almost universal scholar, a humanist, encyclopaedist, philologist, bibliographer, zoologist, botanist, alpinist, linguist, and an M.D. The enormous scope of his learning was only possible during the Renaissance when one world system was in the process of transformation into another, and when Latin as an international language made communications between scholars a simple matter of writing letters. Gesner, during his lifetime, acted as a sort of receptacle for all the new discoveries in natural history and used the work of others (which he freely acknowledged) together with his own research. He persuaded all his friends to contribute and exchanged information and specimens with naturalists all over Europe.[2]

In England the only scientific writer to produce a work of this category in the sixteenth century was Dr Edward Wotton, who graduated in medicine at

[1]For a short account of Gesner, see H. Fischer, 'Conrad Gesner 1516–1565 as Bibliographer and Encyclopedist', *The Library*, 5th Series XXI, No 4, 1966.
[2]Marie Boas, *The Scientific Renaissance*, pp56–8. Gesner's works included a complete survey of the animal world in *Historia Animalium*, but he was also interested in plants, fossils and geology. His English friends and correspondents include Dr Caius, Dr William Turner, and Dr Thomas Penny. A similar comprehensive work on plants was Leonhard Fuchs' *De Historia Stirpium*.

Padua in the early 1520s, and who eventually became physician to Henry VIII and President of the College of Physicians in 1541–3. His book *De Differentiis Animalium* was printed in Paris in 1551 and dedicated to Edward VI.[1] It really should have been dedicated to the ubiquitous Sir John Mason, the diplomatist and courtier, since it was through his encouragement that it was even printed. It consisted of ten books, which according to Gesner contained nothing new, but was a useful digest of previous works on the subject. Wotton did, however, show a slightly new approach. He was more critical of his authorities, and although he gives no indication that he ever tried to make deductions about animal behaviour and species from direct observation, he did reject the more outrageous myths and improbable descriptions. He refused to believe that the osprey had one webbed foot and one claw, and felt some doubts about the story of the Phoenix.[2] Yet the most popular of all these compendiums of natural science was the *De Proprietatibus Rerum* of Bartholomaeus Anglicanus written in the thirteenth century. It was printed three times in translation before the end of the sixteenth century; the last edition of 1582 was edited and brought up to date by Stephen Batman, chaplain to Archbishop Parker. *Batman uppon Bartholome* was the most comprehensive scientific work in Elizabeth's reign and the most influential. Batman incorporated as much as he could of new research for, as he says in his Preface, the book

was held in great estimation among the learned as well beyond the seas as at home, untill within 60 years past there sprung up famous and worthy persons, of singular perseverance and learning: which from the course of ancient beginings, set forth the same that was formerly written of, with additions aunserable to time present, using new titles, whereunto is added so much as hath been brought to light by the travaile of others as Conradus Gesner of Tygure, Phistion, writing of the nature of beasts, birds, fishes, & serpents, Fuchius, Mathiolus, Theophrastus Paracelsus, and Dodenous, these wrote of the natures, operations and effects of Hearbs, Plants, Trees, Fruits, Seeds, Metals and Minerals. Sebastian Munster, Henry Cornelius Agrippa, and others of Astronomie and Cosmographie. Abraham Ortelius of Antwerpe for maps & descriptions: all of whiche woorkes hath done great good in diverse commonwealths. I have therefore as an imitator of the learned, for the good will I bare to my countrie collected forth of these aforesaid authors, the like devises, which they in times past gathered of their elders, and so renuing the whole book as is apparent by additions . . .

In spite of Batman's editing the *De Proprietatibus Rerum* is essentially a medieval work. Its popularity confirms the view that the Elizabethan world picture was in general that of the Middle Ages.

[1] C. E. Raven, *English Naturalists*, p137.
[2] C. E. Raven, *English Naturalists*, pp40–42.

Botany and zoology

Advances were made not on a wide front, but in specific areas of knowledge. In both botany and zoology, the sixteenth century produced men whose careful and accurate work marks the beginning of a new technique of scientific observation.

The first English printed herbal is anonymous and was produced by Richard Bankes in 1525. It had no illustrations and was probably based on a medieval manuscript. It had no claim to originality but it was popular and continued reprinting throughout the century. A number of herbals are derived from it: Ascham's *Herbal* of 1555, Copland's *Herbal,* and *A new Herbal of Macer* are all based on Bankes. The *Grete Herbal* printed by Peter Trevesis in 1526 and 1529 was a translation of a French work illustrated with woodcuts made for the German *Herbarious zu Teusch.* The practical side of plant collecting was covered by *The vertuose boke of Distyllacyon of the waters of all maner of Herbes* published in 1527 by Lawrence Andrews.

The first scientific naturalist producing genuinely original work was William Turner. Turner was born at Morpeth in Northumberland in 1508, and educated at Cambridge during the 1520s and early 1530s. This affected his whole life. He was at the University during the most brilliant and formative period in the sixteenth century, and was a contemporary of all the great scholars of the mid-Tudor period: John Cheke, Thomas Smith, William Grindal, Roger Ascham, John Aylmer, William Bill, Thomas Cranmer, and of the strongly protestant group led by Nicolas Ridley and Hugh Latimer. The younger men at the University included both Matthew Parker the future Archbishop of Canterbury, and William Cecil. It was during this time at Cambridge that Turner's strongly protestant religious views were formed. His religious convictions directly contributed to his development as a scientist, for they forced him into exile on the Continent during the Catholic reaction at the end of the reign of Henry VIII and again during the reign of Mary, and so enlarged his experience. Interspersed among his botanical works are a splendid series of vituperative polemical attacks on Stephen Gardiner such as *The Hunting of the Romyshe Foxe of 1543.* Canon Raven has pointed out that Turner's religious opinions and his scientific works are connected; they both involved a drive towards an exact interpretation of words, and the meaning of words. His purpose was to learn 'what St Paul and the Gospels had to say about Christianity, or Aristotle and Pliny about ornithology, or Theophrastus and Dioscorides about herbs'.[1]

Turner's first book on plants was printed when he was a young graduate before he went into exile. It was the *Libellus de re Herbaria* published in 1538. It is simply a list of 144 plants with their names in Latin, Greek and English, with occasional comments. Its importance lies in the fact that it reveals

[1] C. E. Raven, *English Naturalists,* p57.

Turner's early interest in exact identification; and the Preface, in which he excuses himself for writing, gives a list of eminent doctors including Dr Clement (son-in-law of Thomas More), Dr Wendy, Dr Owen and Dr Wotton, all of whom were clearly interested in botanical identification but who, except for Wotton, never got as far as publication. Canon Raven also thinks that Turner must have known Sir Thomas Elyot from internal evidence between Turner's *Names* and Elyot's *Dictionary*. It is from Turner, therefore, that we can infer the existence of a small but influential group of men having a common interest in botanical identification.

Turner left England for his first period of exile in 1540, and did not return until the end of the reign of Henry VIII. During this time he took his M.D., probably at Bologna, and more important, came under the influence of the great Italian botanist Lucas Ghini, from whom he first learnt the art of drying plants between pieces of paper and producing a 'hortus siccus'. Turner then left Italy and spent some time in Switzerland where he met the naturalist Conrad Gesner, with whom he kept up a life-long correspondence, exchanging specimens and information. He then travelled slowly through Germany, and in 1544 published his second scientific work, the *Avium*, a study of European birds based on the descriptions of Pliny and Aristotle. Like all Turner's works, when he gave actual descriptions based on his own observation, they were accurate and detailed and perfectly correct.[1] Later in the same year he was in East Friesland, where he dissected two porpoises and earned his living as a doctor. He continued his interest in the identification of plants and began to collect information and specimens for the *Names*. He also met the Polish divine, John à Lasco, an event of considerable importance for the Anglican Church, since it was through Turner that à Lasco came to England during the reign of Edward VI, and influenced Cranmer, and therefore the Book of Common Prayer.

In 1548 Turner returned to England and published in English his *Names of Herbes*. This was a more exacting and far-reaching work than the *Libellus*. It consisted of the Latin name followed by the name in English, Greek, German, French, and Low German (where Turner knew it). Turner also gave a description of the flower and an identification with the classical name where he could. He also noted its medicinal properties – whether it was hot, cold, moist or dry, and in what degree. In many cases Turner added where he had found it, and its normal habitat. For example:

> Papauer corniulatum is called in greke mecoon ceratites, in englishe horned poppy or yealow poppy, in duch Gaelma. It groweth in Douer clyffes, and in many other places by the sea syde. It is cold in the furth degree.[2]

In 1551 Turner managed to get appointed Dean of Wells through the

---

[1] An English translation of this work exists: *Turner on Birds*, ed A. H. Evans, CUP 1903.
[2] Both the *Libellus* and the *Names* are printed in facsimile by The Ray Society, 1965.

influence of Cecil, and continued his scientific studies in the West Country. Here he began *The New Herbal* dedicated to Protector Somerset, but not destined to be completed for many years. At the same time he was corresponding with Gesner about fishes and identifying as many varieties as he could. An example of his accurate and informative style in compiling early zoological information can be quoted from a letter to Gesner who had sent him a picture of a lump fish.

> The Lump has its name from the shapeless mass which we call a lump. It may be Pliny's Orchis but it cannot be Belon's Orb, for our Lump is edible, scaleless and cartilagineous. It has no true bones or spines inside but cartilages. It tastes like skate. It has only two fins below the gills. It has on each side three rows of spines from head to tail and on the back a single row. These are not continuous but set at intervals. They resemble the thorns of a bramble. Under its chin is a round hollow like a wheel: by this it seems sometimes to fix itself to the ground or the rocks . . .[1]

During Mary's reign Turner was again in exile. He settled at Cologne for a time but moved about Germany, and was certainly at Frankfurt at the time of the Knoxian Coxian dispute. In 1557 he wrote the long and valuable letter to Gesner on English fishes which suggests he may have himself contemplated a work on this subject. He returned to England at the accession of Elizabeth and resumed his post as Dean of Wells, where his puritanism annoyed the Bishop, who complained that he was 'much encombred with Mr Doctor Turner Deane of Welles, for his indiscrete behaviour in the pulpitt: where he medleth with all matters and unsemelie speaketh of all estates, more than is standinge with discressyon.'[2] Before his death in 1568, he wrote a short medical treatise on baths and finished the *Herbal*. This was an extended version of the *Names*. It contains an interesting discussion of the problems of accurate identification of plants and has a considerable amount of medical knowledge added to the text, including actual cases of treatment disastrous or otherwise. Turner recorded a total of 238 new native plants. The illustrations are far superior to anything seen in England earlier, and are taken from the blocks cut for the *De Historia Stirpium* of Leonard Fuchs. These illustrations were in themselves revolutionary and belong to a new school of botanical drawing first seen in the work of Hans Weiditz for Otto Brunfels *Herbarum Vivae Eicones* in 1530. Weiditz drew directly from life with such accuracy that from the scientific point of view his illustrations are superior to the accompanying text. In Turner's *Herbal* the text itself was original but the illustrations enhanced and increased its impact The *Herbal* was published in three parts. The first in London in 1551, the first and second at Cologne in 1562, and the complete work in 1568.

[1]Quoted by C. E. Raven, *English Naturalists*, pp113–4.
[2]Agnes Arber, *Herbals: Their Origin and Evolution*, p120.

Turner was the first of a long line of observational naturalists and remains one of the greatest of them. His work broke new ground and where it relies on Turner's own observation it is full and accurate. The fact that Turner wrote in English had the effect of limiting his influence to England and he never achieved European fame, but he remains the first naturalist of real stature in this country. 'In his own day he stood alone as a sceintific botanist in England and it is largely due to him that no one has ever been in this position again.'[1]

Turner's exact contemporary Dr. Caius never seems to have worked with him although their interests overlapped. The fact that Turner was a vehement Protestant and Caius a crypto-Catholic meant that they were in exile on the Continent at different times. Their common link was therefore through their mutual friend Conrad Gesner. Caius' major work in natural history was *De Rariorum Animalium atque Stirpium Historia*, published in 1570. The zoological entries are more original than those on plants, and many of them were desscriptions from life of animals in the Tower menageria, for instance those of the Cheetah, Lynx, and Hartebeeste. His limitations as an observer are shown in his description of an animal he called a Hippelaphus. It had been brought from Norway and although Caius describes it with great accuracy and notes that in Norway it was called an Elk or Eland, he refuses to accept the identification on the grounds that Caesar in his *Gallic War* had explicitly stated that Elks had no kneejoints and had therefore to sleep leaning up against a tree. Caius, unlike Turner, accepted the ancient lore, and for him its verdict was final. Gesner, in reply, bluntly told Caius that no-one nowadays believed Caesar's story. The relationship between the two scholars seems to have been close, Caius evidently sent to Gesner not only actual specimens, such as an osprey's foot, and shells and bones of animals, but also beautiful and accurate drawings of those he had seen and described. Unfortunately his treatise on British dogs, arrived too late for inclusion in Gesner's *Historia Animalium*. It was published separately in an English translation in 1576.

The triple connection of strong religious convictions, medicine and scientific interests is seen in the next generation of English pioneers. Thomas Penny was born in 1536 and educated at Cambridge, becoming, in 1564, Senior Bursar of Trinity. Archbishop Parker described him as 'ill-affected towards the establishment', because he was a puritan, and although he had been ordained in 1561, Penny swung away from a career in the Church towards one in medicine and science. He left England and went to meet Conrad Gesner at Zurich. This was fortunate for he was able to exchange knowledge and specimens with Gesner in the few months before the latter's early death at the age of forty-nine from bubonic plague. Penny began his scientific career as a botanist. He had started a 'hortus siccus' before leaving England, and was in correspondence with de L'Ecluse in France, to whom he sent a description and drawing of the creeping

[1]C. E. Raven, *English Naturalists*, p137.

Knotberry (*Rubus chamaemorus*). Canon Raven thinks highly of Penny's descriptive powers. 'There is perhaps no other of the early botanists who had his command of terse and exact phrasing, who employs technicalities so precisely, or who can give so clear and vivid a classification of the chief points in any species. His pictures, which must surely have been his own work, are worthy to stand alongside the . . . illustrations by professional artists which decorate the Herbals of the period and were collected by the great publishing house of Plantin'.[1] Twenty-two of Penny's botanical drawings survive among the papers of Conrad Gesner and some specimens from his 'hortus siccus'. In return Canon Raven suggests that Gesner may have given Penny his notes and illustrations of insects for Penny to prepare for publication.[2]

While he was on the Continent, Penny made another important and life-long friendship with the Flemish botanist Mathias de L'Obel. He studied at Montpellier, and visited Majorca, then botanically unexplored, and brought back plants, one of which, *Myrtocistus pennaei*, was named after him. Penny then went to France, and continued on to Germany, where he met Peter Turner (the son of the botanist William Turner) and William Brewer. He travelled with them as far as the Baltic, still collecting and identifying plants. He returned to England in 1569 and settled in London, where he was twice examined and refused a licence to practise by the College of Physicians, possibly because he was not a sufficiently orthodox believer in Galen. In spite of this, he became a well-known and successful doctor. During the last years of his life he concentrated on the study of insects, in which he had been interested since his visit to Gesner. Penny published nothing in his lifetime, but his importance is great. He clearly had a gift for friendship and became one of the circle of European botanists and naturalists. He was generous in giving descriptions of plants, specimens and drawings for other men to use. In England he has a special importance in that he introduced the first Alpine plants into this country and acted as a link between the scholar botanists and the new class of practical experimental gardeners now emerging in London. He left his medical and botanical papers to Peter Turner, and his entomological ones to Thomas Moffet.

Thomas Moffet or Mouffet, the Paracelsian, had, like the other naturalists, been educated at Cambridge. He was at Caius and Trinity and took his M.A. in 1576. He then travelled on the Continent and studied under Felix Platter at Basel.[3] Moffet was incorporated as M.D. at Cambridge in 1584. His Paracelsian views soon made him one of the interesting group of experimental chemists and alchemists round Dee and the Sidney family. In later life he lived under

[1]C. E. Raven, *English Naturalists*, p155.
[2]C. E. Raven, *English Naturalists*, p157.
[3]Platter was a naturalist and the maker of an early herbarium. An interesting account of him can be found in Thomas Platter, *Journal of a Younger Brother*, ed Sean Jennett, London 1963, which also has a first hand description of the medical school at Montpellier.

the patronage of Lady Mary Herbert. Lady Mary Herbert is herself interesting since she not only patronised scientists but was herself a chemist. According to Aubrey:

> In her time, Wilton House was like a College, there were so many learned and ingeniose persons. She was the greatest Patroneses of witt and learning of any Lady in her time. She was a great Chymist, and spent yearly a great deale in that study. She kept for her Laborator in the house Adrian Gilbert . . . halfe brother to Sir Walter Raleigh, who was a geat Chymist in those dayes and a Man of excellent naturall Parts; but very Sarcastick, and the greatest Buffoon in the Nation . . . She also gave an honourable yearly Pension to Dr. Mouffet, who hath writt a Booke *De Insectis* . . .[1]

Moffet's originality as a naturalist seems to have lain in his approach. He wrote a book called *Health's Improvements*, which contains a list and description of birds and fishes – but from the culinary rather than the scientific standpoint. The lists themselves are entirely derivative from earlier authorities, and bear no evidence of first-hand investigation except as a cook. Moffet soon became a fashionable physician, settling eventually on the Pembroke estates near Wilton. He made some sort of effort at getting Thomas Penny's entomological papers in order, but only spasmodically and with considerable rewriting. He died before he could publish, and his widow sold the rights to Sir Theodore Mayerne. It was not until 1834 that the *Theatrum Insectorum*, the first English book on entomology, was printed; and even then it was a composite work with Penny's more precise scientific observations, overlaid by Moffet's own discursive passages, and comments often lifted from other authors. In any case it had its genesis in Conrad Gesner's notes. Yet in the chapter on bees, scarabs, flies, butterflies and moths, the idea of spontaneous generation of insects is gently edged aside, and the process of identifying the exact complicated stage of the metamorphosis of the various genera was begun. While Gilbert in *De Magnete* argued that soil produced plants and that therefore the earth contained life, the superstructure of such ideas in the animal world was patiently being dismantled.[2]

By the last quarter of the century the work of Continental botanists was being assimilated in England. Turner used Fuchs' blocks to illustrate his *Herbal*. In 1578 Henry Lyte published an English translation of L'Ecluse' version of Dodoens' *Cruydeboeck* of 1554 which he brought up to date with references to de L'Obel and Turner. Lyte was himself a collector of rare plants.[3] The Flemish botanist de L'Obel was himself a refugee working in London.

[1]'Lady Mary Herbert', in Aubrey, *Brief Lives*, ed O. Lawson Dick, Penguin Books 1962.
[2]Illustrations for the *Theatrum Insectorum* were done by John White and given to Penny in 1587. They exist in manuscript in the British Museum, Sloane 4014.
[3]Agnes Arber, *Herbals*, p126 and E. S. Rohde, *The Old English Herbals*, Longmans 1922, p95.

His *Adversaria* was published in 1570 and dedicated to Queen Elizabeth. It has some claim to be one of the first scientific botanical works since de L'Obel abandoned the alphabetical method of listing plants and classified them according to leaf structure dividing the straight veined from the net veined leaves, thus in effect separating the monocotyledons from the dicotyledons. De L'Obel supervised the London garden of Lord Zouch and later became official botanist to James I. His other botanical works were printed on the Continent. De L'Obel's botanical papers were used by John Parkinson.[1]

One result of the increasing interest in natural history was that the fauna and the flora of a country had become once more an integral and expected part of its description. The clearest example of this new attitude of mind is in Thomas Harriot's concise and admirably scientific description of Virginia, and in the illustrations by John White which accompanied his report on Ralegh's voyage of 1585.[2] But the same thing was being done in England. Leland gave a description of the places he visited during his search for monastic books. William Lambarde wrote his *Perambulation of Kent* with notes on the climate, products, geography, and an account, hundred by hundred, of the towns, villages and anything of interest. John Stow wrote a similar *Survey of London* which included details of the history and customs of the city as well as descriptions of its monuments and buildings. Richard Carew wrote a *Survey of Cornwall* divided into two books, one of topographical description, and the second a perambulation of the hundreds from East to West. Similar accounts were compiled of Pembrokeshire, Staffordshire, Warwickshire, Durham, Cumberland, and of the Principality of Wales and Chester.[3] A more general account was William Harrison's *Description of England* published as a supplement to Holinshed, the edition of 1587 having considerably more detail of the natural resources of the country than that of 1577. The most important as well as the most ambitious was William Camden's *Britannia*. Camden was a scholar of European stature, a friend of Ortelius and a correspondent of men like de Thou and Casaubon. His *Britannia* has been described as 'the crowning achievement of Tudor and Early Stuart antiquarianism'.[4] Camden himself describes the effort that went into its compilation:

> I got some insight into the old British and Saxon Tongues for my assistance; I have travell'd almost all over England . . . I have diligently perus'd our own Writers; as well as the Greek and Latin who mention the least tittle of Britain. I have examined the publick Records of the Kingdom, Ecclesiastical Registers, and Libraries, and the Acts, Monuments and Memorials of Churches and Cities.

[1]R. T. Gunther, *Early English Botanists*, Oxford 1922, p246.
[2]Thomas Hariot, *A Briefe and True Report of the New Found Land of Virginia*, 2nd ed, 1590.
[3]May McKisack, *Medieval History in the Tudor Age*, chapter 6.
[4]May McKisack, *Medieval History in the Tudor Age*, p152.

The result was one of the most informative, the most detailed and the most scholarly books of its generation although a description of the natural resources of the country was only a minor part of the whole. Dictionaries, like the *Thesaurus Linguae Romanae et Britannicae* of Thomas Cooper, also began to contain descriptions of common birds and fishes.

Farming and husbandry

A number of books appeared during the century on farming techniques and husbandry. Wynkyn de Worde printed Bishop Grosseteste's *Boke of Husbandrie* in 1510, but the first new work was Fitzherbert's *The Boke of Husbandrye* printed by Pynson in 1523 which went through eight editions during the century. It dealt with all the obvious problems of estate management, the equipment needed, the capital required, and the most profitable methods to use. The text shows that the principles of manuring were understood and that drainage was practised. Fitzherbert recommended enclosure in order to increase productivity. An equally popular work along the same lines was Thomas Tusser's *A hundred points of good husbandrie* which appeared in 1557. In 1573 it was expanded into *Five hundred points*, and *united to as many of good house wifry*. In this somewhat encyclopaedic form it was re-issued in 1576, 1577, 1580, and 1593. Tusser advocated a three crop and fallow rotation, and like Fitzherbert advised enclosure. With the diversification of publishing to meet demand, books were produced dealing with specific subjects such as Leonard Mascall's three works: *A boke on The Art and Manner of how to graft and plant all sorts of trees* published ?1569, *The husbandrie ordering and government of poultrie*, published in 1581, and *The first book of Cattel . . .*, published in 1596. Mascall's book on poultry is the first on the subject in English, his book on cattle included information on the care of sheep, goats and horses. Mascall also wrote a book on fishing which is largely taken from the *Boke of St. Albans*. Books appeared on hop farming and bee keeping, and foreign works on husbandry and home economy were translated.[1] Riding and the care of horses were covered by the books of Thomas Blundeville, *The Arte of Ryding and Breaking Great Horses*, published in 1560, *The fower chiefyst offices belongyng to Horsemanshippe*, published 1565-1566, and *The Order for curing Horses disease*, published 1566, and *The Discourse of Horsemanshippe* by Gervase Markham published in 1593. Both authors were reprinted several times before the end of the century. Hunting and falconry were covered by two books by George Turberville based on French works on the same subject. A more important and original work on sport was Roger Ascham's *Toxophilus* which was first published in 1545 and twice reprinted.

[1] G. E. Fussell, *The Old English Farming Books from Fitzherbert to Tull 1523-1730*, Crosby Lockwood 1947.

Growing interest in the natural sciences

The extent to which the natural sciences were gaining in general popularity can be seen in the list of translations and compendiums undertaken by Thomas Hill in the *Shorter Title Catalogue*.[1] The Catalogue lists twenty-two works by Hill, all of them scientific, and the majority on gardening or grafting trees. Hill was an active leader in expounding mysteries of science in simple terms for the unlearned layman. His manuals of practical scientific lore range from treatises on physiognomy and on gardening to a text book on astronomy and a short account of bees. Hill's great merit was his accurate and clear prose. In this respect he was far in advance of the earlier translators and can be said to have done in print and over a wider range of subjects what Robert Recorde accomplished in his Muscovy Lectures and mathematical text books. 'After the confusion and nonsense of these earlier handbooks, Hill's lucidity comes like a refreshing breeze after a sultry day . . . To Thomas Hill, as much as anyone, belongs the credit for raising the level of books designed as easy and pleasant introductions to the mysteries of applied science.'[2] Another writer who produced a series of books on crops and horticulture at the end of Elizabeth's reign was Sir Hugh Plat.

The growing interest in science is also reflected in library lists. Lord Arundel and his son-in-law Lord Lumley both bought scientific works and these are listed in the catalogue of the Lumley Library by Sears Jayne.[3] Another interesting library is that of the Knyvet brothers at Ashwellthorpe in Norfolk which is now in the University Library Cambridge. The medical books alone occupy ten folio pages of the list, and include Gesner's *Historia Animalium* and his *De Fossilium Genere*, Georgius Agricola's *De Subterraneis* and *Ortus Sanitatis*, Brunfels *Simplicium Liber*, Fuchs *De Historia Stirpium*, Ruel *De Natura Stirpium*, Dodoens *Frumentorum leguminum etc Historia*, and Petro Pena and de L'Obel *Stirpium Adversaria*.[4] The Knyvet Library does not seem to have been kept fully up-to-date after the middle years of the century, although it contained Gilbert's *De Magnete* and Ralegh's *History of the World*.

The development of the Tudor garden and of Tudor parkland was one aspect of the Renaissance and as such it was influenced by Italian mannerism and the classical revival. The development of the scientific garden was another matter.

By the middle of the sixteenth century it is clear that a small group of botanical gardeners existed in London. The bias was medicinal and the more

[1]See Appendix B for this list.
[2]Francis R. Johnson, 'Thomas Hill, An Elizabethan Huxley', *Huntington Library Quarterly*, August 1944, p329.
[3]See Chapter 4.
[4]For a complete list, see C. E. Raven, *English Naturalists*, pp173–5.

important of these men, for example Hugh Morgan and John Rich, were apothecaries and had experimental gardens with new varieties of herbs and plants. Hugh Morgan was twice censured (without much effect) by the Royal College of Physicians for dispensing medicines without a licence.

The most important of these practical botanists was John Gerard, whose famous *Herball* was published in 1597.[1] Gerard was born at Nantwich in Cheshire in 1545. After he left school, he apparently travelled in Eastern Europe since he states in the Preface to the *Herball* that he has travelled 'from Narva to Moscovia, and in Denmark, Swenia, Poland, Livonia or Russia'. In 1562, he was apprenticed to Alexander Mason, a Barber-Surgeon. In 1569, he was admitted to the Company and became its Master in 1607. Gerard was, therefore, successful and intelligent in his own profession, and rose to the top of it. But it must be remembered that surgery was still primarily a craft, not an intellectual profession, and this does not in itself mean that Gerard was a man of scientific learning. It may, however, explain why he was such a successful gardener, since both callings require patience and manual skill. Another point to note is the fact that surgeons unlike physicians mixed their own drugs. Gerard had his own experimental garden in Holborn, and he was given charge of Burghley's gardens in London and at Theobalds. Gerard published a *Catalogue* of his own garden in 1596 dedicated to Burghley, and issued an expanded version in 1599. The *Herball*, intended as a comprehensive summary of plants, was published in 1597 by Thomas Norton. The *Catalogue* appeared with a commendation by the great Flemish botanist de L'Obel, who was in temporary exile in England.[2] De L'Obel emphatically did not recommend the *Herball*, which he knew to be both pirated and inaccurate. But, plagiarised or not, it became a best seller, and was expanded and corrected by Thomas Johnson in 1636, and continued reprinting throughout the seventeenth century. The *Herball* consisted of an alphabetical list of plants each with a woodcut illustration. The descriptions are partly scientific – like Turner Gerard gives the medicinal degrees of the humoral theory where he knew them – and partly topographical. Thomas Johnson noted in his Preface to the seventeeth century edition that Gerard was heavily indebted to de L'Obel for his method, and to the manuscript notes of a Doctor Priest for much of his material. 'For the author Mr. John Gerard I can say little . . . His chief commendation is that he out of a propense goodwill to the publique advancement endeavoured to perform therein more than he could well accomplish.' Canon Raven's verdict is that Gerard 'was not only a rogue, he was, as has been indicated, a comparatively ignorant rogue.'[3] In point of fact, this judgement is too harsh. Gerard may

[1] *Gerard's Herball*, ed Marcus Woodward (from 1636 edition), Gerald Howe 1927.
[2] The possibility that de L'Obel later regretted this is indicated by the copy in the British Museum, which has 'haec esse falsissima' signed by de L'Obel written on the flyleaf. See C. E. Raven, *English Naturalists*, p206.   [3] C. E. Raven, *English Naturalists*, p208.

have been credulous, but so was Caius; he certainly made mistakes, some of them careless, and some as a result of his poor knowledge of Latin and lack of university education; he undoubtedly borrowed largely from other men's work without acknowledgement, but in the sixteenth century such 'borrowings' were common, and all men stand on other's shoulders. But all these sins are out-weighted by the fact that Gerard's *Herball* is a tremendous attempt to synthe-sise a vast amount of knowledge, and by the majestic beauty of its prose. Gerard's dedicatory Preface addressed to Lord Burghley and 'To the Courteous and well-willing Reader' is a minor masterpiece.

The study of plants, Gerard claims, is the study of the beauty of Creation 'what greater delight is there to behold the earth apparelled with plants, as with a robe of embroidered worke, set with Orient Pearles and garnished with great diversitie of rare and costly Jewels?' The well-willing Reader is urged to enjoy the book as knowledge well worth having for its own sake, and for the use to which the *Herball* could be put. He finished with an interesting contrast between the search for gold and the search for herbs:

> Yet behold in the compassing of this wordly drosse, what care, what cost, what adventures, what mysticall proofs and chemical trials are set abroach, when as not withstanding the chiefest end is but uncertaine wealth. Contrari-wise in the expert knowledge of Herbes, what pleasure still renewed with variety? What small expense? What security? and yet what an apt and ordinary means to conduct man to that most desired benefit of health . . . who would therefore look dangerously up at Planets that might safely look down at Plants.[1]

In his description of the scope of the *Herball* Gerard makes it clear in the Preface to Burghley that the book is not only English flora but as wide as he could make it:

> To the large and singular furniture of this noble island I have addressed from forreine places all that I might in any way obtaine, I have laboured with the soile to make it fit for plants, and with the plants that they may delight in the soile, that so they might live and prosper under our clymat, as in their native and proper country. What my success hath beene, and what my furniture is, I leave to the report of they that have seene your Lordship's gardens, and the little plot of myne own especial care and husbandry. But because gardens are privat, and many times finding a negligent successor come soone to ruine, there be that sollicited me, first by my pen, and after by the Presse to have make my labours common, and to free them from the danger where unto a garden is subject. . . .[2]

The *Herball* was illustrated by 1800 woodblocks which included the drawing of a potato plant. In the original edition many of these wood blocks were

[1]*Gerard's Herball*, ed Marcus Woodward, pp4–5.   [2]Ibid, p3.

misplaced in the text which naturally caused considerable confusion: these errors were corrected in the 1636 edition. It is interesting to compare the crude woodcuts of the *Herball* with the perfect pen and wash drawings of the sixth century manuscript of Dioscorides.[1]

Gerard gives first-hand descriptions of plants in the London area and in the home counties, the kidney vetch for example 'I found growing upon Hampstead Heath neere London, right against the Beacon, upon the right hand as you goe from London, neere unto a gravelle pit. They grow also upon black Heath, in the high way leading from Greenwich to Charleton, within half a mile of the towne.'[2] Gerard could be critical, he included two hyacinths with the note that they are 'generally holden to be feigned or adulterine.'[3] He could also be credulous and reinforced the theory that Barnacle geese were hatched from mussel shells on pieces of dead tree, by the statement that he had actually seen them half out of the shells. A possible alternative to Canon Raven's theory that Gerard is simply lying in this passage, is that he did actually see dead and half open mussels with the soft interior part hanging out, and was misled as were his predecessors by the superficial resemblance to a chick embryo, and did not investigate further. It is, however, impossible to explain away Gerard's assertion that he had personally seen down-covered chicks inside the shells. His entry on the foxglove is also interesting in that it shows that the medical properties of digitalis were totally unknown in the sixteenth century. 'The Foxgloves', he wrote, 'in that they are bitter, are hot and dry, with a certain kind of cleaning quality jointed there with: yet are they of no use, neither have they any place among medicines, according to the antients.'[4] Gerard, if not a great scientist, was at least a great populariser.

In addition to the professional gardeners, a growing number of amateur botanists were listing the names of local plants, often writing their records in the margins of botanical books. An anonymous botanist, probably Dr. Walter Bayley of New College, Professor of Medicine at Oxford from 1561 to 1582, annotated a copy of du Pinet's *Historia Plantarum* with lists of plants and their localities, he also wrote a short medicinal treatise on peppers. A similar list was made in a copy of de L'Obel's *Icones Stirpium* by the Kentish clergyman and physician William Mount covering the area round East Malling. Mount listed a total of thirty-three new plants (Gerard only listed eight) and his contribution is therefore of some importance. Sir John Salusbury of Lleweni made a list of

[1]Agnes Arber, *Herbals.*   [2]*The Herball,* ed Thomas Johnson, 1636, p1241, Ch 521.
[3]*Gerard's Herball,* ed Marcus Woodward, p107.
[4]*Gerard's Herball,* ed Marcus Woodward, p182.
It is worth noting that at the same time William Mount allowed the foxglove medicinal properties. 'Foxgloves. Hereof Loniceros writeth fol 74 that yt doth attenuate, clense, purge, loase, cut flegme or grosse humoures: and all virtues and qualities which Gentiane hathe, yt allso hathe.'

local plants round Denbigh in a copy of Gerard's *Herball*. Salusbury was a poet with literary connections in London and a man of some wealth, he had an extensive garden at Lleweni of which some lists survive. His cousin William Salusbury was the compiler of a herbal in Welsh based on extracts from Fuchs, Dodoens, and Turner. In Yorkshire a gentleman called Richard Shanne seems to have had another interesting garden since it is recorded of him that:

> his chefest delite was in plantinge and grafting all maner of herbes trees, and had growinge in his gardinge a great number of rare and straunge plants, there was not allmost anie herbe growinge but he did knowe the severall names thereof, and the nature and opperation of the same, he did practise both in physicke and specially in Chirurgie and did cure verie manie daungerous wounds and ulcers. He made three bookes of the Nature and operations of herbes and Trees and drew with his pen the trew picktures of everie plante, set downe in what ground everie herbe and tree was to be found and the tymes of their springinge, florishinge and sedinge.[1]

Shanne was also a keen naturalist and recorded the first description in English of the ruff.

Another important development was the introduction and naturalisation of a growing number of plants from abroad. The American voyages resulted in the successful acclimatisation of the tobacco plant and the potato, but less well known species were also cultivated. Richard Garth, who was by profession a clerk of Chancery, is described by Gerard as 'a worshipful gentleman and one that greatly delighteth in strange plants'. He had connections with South America and was instrumental in introducing some Brazilian plants into England.[2] Garth was a friend of the Flemish botanist L'Ecluse and in return for some South American specimens L'Ecluse gave him a root of Solomon's Seal which Garth in turn gave to Gerard.

In 1577 a translation of Nicolas Monardes' account of the plants of America by John Frampton was published as 'Joyful newes out of the Newe founde world' thus giving added publicity to the expansion of botany.

One thing is common to all these early naturalists: with the possible exception of de L'Obel, they did not yet conceive of a scientific grouping by characteristics except within the broad division they were investigating. They surpassed and above all extended the knowledge of the ancient world. They rejected mythology and substituted direct observation. In so doing they began the laborious but necessary process of exact identification. They found out a number of new facts as well as increasing the number of animals and plants known. But they did not create, nor could they create anything more.

[1] Add Mss 38599. 17, quoted in R. T. Gunther, *Early English Botanists*, p264.
[2] Including *Papyrifera arbor, Juni-pappeeywa Brasiliorum* and *Phaselous Brasiliorum*; R. T. Gunther, *Early English Botanists*, p237.

10. Conclusions

A number of forces lie behind the achievements of the Elizabethan age, which help to explain the sudden and prolonged upsurge of genius in so many and varied fields. The first was the continuous interaction of humanist thought in England with similar thought on the Continent. England had never been isolated intellectually, and if anything she was more affected by continental ideas in the sixteenth century while Latin was still an international language, than from the seventeenth century onwards. The effect of Erasmus on the English church and on education, of Castiglione and Machiavelli on the Court, the amount of Italian material in Shakespeare, are obvious examples and illustrate the general community of idea and the European background. The mid-century expansion of education, and perhaps more particularly the social changes in education, meant that the generations that came to maturity under Elizabeth were equipped mentally to absorb more sophisticated values, and to produce from their own ranks men of creative ability and genius. At the same time the increasing prosperity of the country as a whole, and the overall increase in private wealth with its corollary of cultivated leisure, created a class which could patronise and enjoy new ideas: a courtier class, which by its very existence stimulated development, and which under Elizabeth produced from among its own ranks an impressive amount of talent. Finally the use of print gave to the individual artist, to patrons, and to the state, a medium through which new ideas could spread and policies be formed. The subtle shift in emphasis at the centre helped to increase this diversity and brilliance. Where Henry VIII used scholars trained and controlled by the state to justify the Reformation and to argue his case before international opinion in Europe, Elizabeth used her courtiers and ministers to encourage a wide range of individual scholars and writers and to focus the emergent nationalism, speed up technological advance, and ultimately to create a legend which still exists.[1] The Queen evoked but did not create the intellectual achievements of her reign. In this respect England differed from the rest of the Continent, and the divergence is significant. In other countries the release of creative forces in art and learning produced by the impact of humanism on wealth was financed and to a large extent directly controlled by individual rulers. The sixteenth century Papacy, the Medici in

[1]The Tudor use of the press for propaganda purposes is well covered for the first half of the century by W. Zeevelt, *Foundations of Tudor Policy;* and for the reign of Elizabeth by E. Rosenberg's, *Leicester, Patron of Letters,* Columbia University Press 1955.

Florence, the Sforza in Milan, the Kings of France, were all magnificent and prodigal in their patronage. But Elizabeth, although she became the focal point of much of the genius of her age, did little to sponsor it herself. She chose the more subtle role of recipient rather than patroness. The same men who served the Queen as chiefs of state became the principal agents of royal patronage. She preferred to have others perform for her the sordid task of buying flattery, of employing patriotism. Through their efforts public opinion was controlled and directed so that she could in fact make good her claim to rule by popular will. Their protégés – not her own – exhorted the reader to regard with wonder the virtues of his Queen. Their followers produced the works which supported her policies and controverted those of her enemies. She delegated patronage in the same way as she delegated authority, preferring to seem uncommitted, although ultimately she controlled both the policies and the propaganda of her government. Her reign was the high point of Renaissance culture in England, but it was not the Queen who paid.[1]

Leicester had 100 works dedicated to him ranging from books on technology and science such as Cunningham's *Cosmographical Glasse* or the surgical treatises of Gale and Clowes to major historical and literary works: Stow, Holinshed and Grafton sought his patronage. As Chancellor of the University of Oxford, Leicester received dedications of works on education such as Mulcaster's book on the writing of English; he sponsored a number of translations as part of a programme for the encouragement of both scholars and learning. As a protector of puritanism he gave his support to a large number of religious polemics. At the end of his life when he had emerged as the leader of the radical anti-Spanish group, he had a varied selection of dedications, nationalistic, military and religious. The study of these dedications (even if some were unsolicited) gives Leicester considerable importance as a patron of learning and as the focus of a radical pressure group. Besides his personal connections with the friends of his nephew, Philip Sidney, such as Fulke Greville and Edward Dyer, Leicester actually employed such men as Dyer, Gabriel Harvey, Edmund Campion and Edmund Spenser.

Burghley received 92 dedications, some shared, equally as varied as Leicester's, which included important scientific works such as Digges' *Alae seu scalae mathematicae*, Blagrave's *Mathematical Jewell* and Gerard's *Herball*, both Ascham's *The Scholemaster*, and Robinson's translation of More's *Utopia*, historical works by Grafton, Holinshed, Stow, and Camden, and Spenser's *Faerie Queen*.

Ralegh had twenty-three dedications of which six were concerned with exploration, a fact which is used as evidence for a certain amount of court planning of dedications as a means of propaganda. 'In at least two such fields – the anti-Jesuit campaign of the early 1580s and the publicity campaign for the new

[1] E. Rosenberg, *Leicester, Patron of Letters*, pp8–10.

world ventures in the latter part of the decade, we can find evidence of official delegation either by the Queen herself or by the Privy Council with the Queen's approval. Leicester and other members of the Council seem to have been selected for patronage of the former and Ralegh of the latter; in both cases Walsingham probably provided the plan and organisation.'[1] The younger Hakluyt was also possibly concerned with this orientation of dedications to Ralegh.[2] Professor Hill sees Ralegh as the inheritor of Leicester's influence, at least in regard to science and foreign policy, and through him of Northumberland's and to a certain extent of Philip Sidney's. Certainly after the deaths of Sidney and Leicester and the execution of Essex, Ralegh was left as the obvious man to-wards whom the explorers and scientists could look for protection and encouragement. He shared and improved on many of the ideas of the Sidney circle with regard to overseas expansion combined with the protestant ethic and a Dutch alliance against Spain. The ramifications of Ralegh's influence read like a catalogue of the major scientists, explorers and poets of the late Elizabethan age.[3]

Ralegh's foreign policy, which may have been deliberately fostered by a group of the Privy Council, involved an expansion of England's maritime empire at the expense of Spain and had the backing of an influential section of the merchant community. Ralegh, like Bacon, had a clear vision of potential power and economic expansion. 'Whosoever commands the sea, commands the trade, whosoever commands the trade of the world, commands the riches of the world, and consequently the world itself.'[4]

While the government influenced ideas at one remove by its manipulation of patronage, the new generation were themselves moulded by the schools and

---

[1] E. Rosenberg, *Leicester, Patron of Letters*, p11.

[2] E. Rosenberg, 'Giacopo Castelvetro. Italian publisher in Elizabethan London and his patrons', *Huntington Library Quarterly*, No 2 Vol VI, 1943.

[3] It is interesting that the scandal of 'The School of Night' and the charges of atheism arose out of a dinner table conversation on cosmology between Ralegh and a clergyman called Ralph Ironside. They were investigated by a Commission at Cerne Abbas in 1594, but were not sustained. An account is given in C. Hill, *Intellectual Origins of the English Revolution;* M. C. Bradbrook, *The School of Night*, CUP 1936; *Willobie his Avisa*, ed G. B. Harrison, Bodley Head 1926; this book includes the whole of the Cerne Abbas proceedings. The notable exception to the Ralegh group was the Earl of Southampton and his protegé William Shakespeare.

[4] Ralegh, *Works*, ii 80, quoted C. Hill, *Intellectual Origins of the English Revolution*, p168. The heirs of Ralegh were the founders of the Virginia Company, Hakluyt, Bacon, Sir Edward Coke, Fulke Greville, Viscount Lisle and Briggs, together with leading merchants and the Livery Companies of the City. The heirs to the Virginia Company were its Secretary Sir Edwin Sandys, and the New Providence Company in the 1630s which included the Earl of Warwick, Lord Saye and Sele, John Hampden, Oliver St John and John Pym, all of whom were leaders of the political opposition to the first two Stuarts. There is a convincing link between an expansionist mercantile policy and hostility to the prerogative of the crown.

universities. The gentry consolidated their position by infiltrating the educational system, but the learning they acquired there remained curiously static and was based almost entirely on a knowledge of the classics. The humanist revolution of the early sixteenth century became the accepted norm, ceased to be revolutionary, and in its final form became a restrictive and not an enlarging influence. There is no evidence that the advances in scientific thought penetrated the educational system. The reaction against Ramism in the universities reinforced the hold of classical studies and stifled the earlier humanist encouragement of science.[1]

'Mathematicks at that time, with us were scarce looked upon as Academical Studies, but rather Mechanical: as the business of Traders, Merchants, Seamen, Carpenters, Surveyors of Lands, or the like, and perhaps some almanac makers in London . . .'. Dr. John Wallis was writing in the seventeenth century, but the process had begun in the sixteenth. Sidney, Dyer, Fulke Greville, Hariot, Ralegh and Northumberland, were as exceptional as they were brilliant. The curricula of schools and universities did not reflect the changing ideas of the scientific world and the real interest of the Elizabethan age is not found in the conventional centres of learning but outside them.

The development of scientific thought had two facets. The idea that all knowledge was now open to reason and the mind of man was balanced by a growing awareness of the limitations to human knowledge. In this way the potential conflict between religion and science was side-stepped and a direct confrontation avoided. John Bannister's confident assertion – that 'In fine, there is nothing so hie in the heavens above, nothing so low in the earth beneath, nothing so profound in the bowels of Arte, nor anything so hid in the secrets of nature, as that good will dare not enterprise, search, unclose or discover' – was balanced by Fulke Greville's conviction that all science was based on probabilities, and the pessimism of Sir John Davies in his 'Nosce Teipsum':

> What can we know ? or what can we discerne ?
> When Error chokes the windows of the minde,
> The Divers formes of things how can we learne
> That have been ever from our birth day blind . . .

> The wits, that dived most deep and soared most high,
> Seeking men's power, have found his weakness such.
> Skill comes so slow, and life so fast doth fly;
> We learn so little and forget so much . . .

[1]For the whole question of the influence of Peter Ramus and the government sponsored reaction against it, see H. Kearney, *Scholars and Gentlemen. Universities and Society in Pre-Industrial Britain, 1500–1700*, Faber and Faber 1970.

We that acquaint ourselves with every zone,
And pass both tropics and behold the poles,
When we come home are to ourselves unknown
And unacquainted still with our own souls . . .[1]

Slowly, accepted scientific thought was shaking itself free of magic and at the same time demoting or elevating the religious element to a point outside scientific observation. It was part of the general reluctance to deal with first causes which were impossible to define except in terms of God, and to concentrate on the more surely demonstrable second causes. The process is clearly illustrated in the practical observational books of Edward Wright, John Blagrave, Robert Norman and Robert Hues among the mathematicians and of men like Juan Huarte and Timothy Bright among the doctors.[2] The significance of this process is described by Dr. Kocher: 'It was not irreligious, but non-religious. They merely took religion for granted. But this point itself was ominous of a future divorce between religion and science, once so closely wedded. The quiet indifference of the scientists was to work worse mischief to religion in the long run than the conjuring of a John Dee or the blaspheming of a Christopher Marlowe. It was one of those massive almost imperceptible movements that change the shape of the World while everyone is looking the other way.'[3] The same process is seen at work in Ralegh's view of world history. 'Ralegh secularized history not by denying God as the first cause, but by concentrating his vision on secondary causes and insisting that they are sufficient in themselves for historical explanation.'[4]

In science the division between experimental thought and the ideas and values of ordinary men was increased by a linguistic development of considerable importance. The introduction of technical terms into English scientific texts led to a specialized vocabulary which in turn prevented the ordinary reader from a full understanding of the subject matter.

By the end of the century, any writer had a choice of language. He could write in Latin, and appeal to a European audience, or in English, and reach a wider group within national boundaries. Many writers wrote in both languages depending on the subject: Thomas Digges, for example, wrote *Alae seu scalae Mathematicae* in Latin but the *Prognostication* and the *Caelestiall Orbes* in English. John Dee deliberately wrote the famous *Preface to Euclide* in English

---

[1] *The Oxford Book of Sixteenth Century Verse,* Clarendon Press 1955. Extracts from the poem only, p773.
[2] Huarte wrote *An Examination of Men's Wits,* published 1594. Bright, *A Treatise on Melancholie* in 1586. Both books were early observational studies in psychology.
[3] H. Kocher, *Science and Religion in Elizabethan England,* San Marino California 1953, pp53–4, 160.
[4] C. Hill, *Intellectual Origins of the English Revolution,* p181.

so that it could be read by craftsmen, but his works on the occult and on number were often in Latin. In general important works such as Gilbert's *De Magnete* continued to be in Latin, while popular works were written in English and an increasing number of works were translated from Latin and other European languages into English.[1] These translations and popular technical works in English raised the important question of the translation of terms for which no direct English equivalent existed.

Initially, when this problem first became apparent in the first half of the century, the general opinion of scholars was that all technical terms should if possible be 'Englished' either by simply adapting the term and giving it an English ending, or by direct translation, for example 'endsay' for 'conclusion'. Sir Thomas Elyot, Ralph Laver and Roger Ascham all tried to adapt and translate Latin terms and incorporate them in the language. Sir John Cheke summed up this whole school of thought. 'I am of the opinion', he wrote, 'that our own tongue should be written clean and pure, unmixt and unmingled with borrowing of other tongues, wherein if we take not heed in time, ever borrowing and never paying, she shall be fain to keep her house bankrupt.'[2] Cheke was supported by all the literary scholars of the day; the only group which did not agree were the scientists, and their disagreement was to have far-reaching consequences. 'Yet during this very period, after experimenting with neologisms compounded from native English roots, the scientists were the first group openly to defy the prevailing literary opinion, and to come out flatly in favor of drawing freely upon Latin and Greek, the traditional language of science, in coining new English words.'[3] The scientists more than any other group of writers were faced with a real difficulty in translating specific technical terms, and if they borrowed the term and 'incorporated' it into English, they were forced to define it and give it a precise meaning. This in itself produced a greater flexibility and an ever-widening vocabulary in English itself. Robert Recorde provides a clear example of this for in his attempts to popularise mathematics he was forced either to translate or to incorporate technical terms. In his earlier works he tried to incorporate and define 'by coining new words from native English roots' as, for example, 'perpendicular or plumme line', 'touch line' for 'tangent', 'cinkangle' for 'pentagon', and 'straight line' instead of 'right line' for 'linea recta'. Recorde's knowledge of Anglo-Saxon undoubtedly helped him in these early attempts at adaptation. In his later works, Recorde abandoned all attempts at translation and, knowing that English was in any case a composite language, he began to use the classical term in its classical form with a simple explanation of its meaning. Thus, by the end of the century, English

[1] For a discussion of translations see H. S. Bennett, *English Books and Readers 1558–1603*.
[2] Quoted by F. R. Johnson, 'Latin versus English: the sixteenth century debate over scientific terminology', *Studies in Philology*, Vol XLI, 1944, No 2, pp109–135.
[3] F. R. Johnson, *Studies in Philology*, Vol XLI, p117.

was being enriched by the bodily incorporation of untranslatable technical terms which it soon absorbed.

The surgeons and anatomists did exactly the same: in Bartholomew Traherne's *The most excellent worckes of Chirurgery made and set forth by Maister John Vigor*, 1543, which is described by Professor Johnson as 'the first example in English of a painstaking scholarly translation of a comprehensive medical treatise.' Traherne simply took over the Latin words and added a glossary of definitions at the end of the book. This method of adding a glossary soon became the general practice in all scientific works and clearly facilitated the absorption of foreign technical terms. A parallel example of the process can be found in the works of William Turner. In the *Names of Herbes in Greke, Latin, English, Duch and Frenche wyth the commune names that Herbaries and Apothecaries use*, published in 1543, 'Turner deliberately coined many new words, for he systematically noted each instance where he could find no English term in current use and then proceeded to suggest a word . . . In his skilful coining of new words Turner nearly always used native material, but sought to make the term either a literal translation of the Latin or one descriptive of the plant itself.'[1]

This coining of new words from English roots was common to both Recorde and Turner, but while the botanists found themselves able to draw upon herb and folk law, the mathematicians and surgeons, who were breaking new ground in any case, found themselves forced to take over the Greek or Latin terms unchanged, and to give English explanations and definitions. Andrew Boorde adopted this practice in the *Breviary of Healthe*, 1552, and Nicolas Udall did the same in his translation of Thomas Gemini's version of Veselius' *De Humani Corporis Fabrica*. Udall often included the Arabic terms as well, and when dealing with a Latin or Greek word which he intended should be absorbed into the English vocabulary, he gave it 'a form compatible with the structure of the English language, thereby facilitating its adoption into the vernacular'.[2] In the same way Thomas Digges, in the addition on regular geometrical solids added to the *Pantometria* in 1571, used both English terms such as 'straight line', 'ground line', but kept a number of technical words in Greek and Latin:

> let no man muse that writing in the English tongue, I have retained the Latin or Greek names of sundry lines and figures as chords, Pentagonal, lines diagonal, Icosahedron, Dodecahedron or such like. For as the Romans and older Latin writers, notwithstanding the copious and abundant eloquence of their tongue, have not shamed to borrow of the Grecians these and many other terms of art: so surely do I think it no reproach, either to the English tongue, or any English writer, where fit words fail to borrow of them both . . .[3]

[1] F. R. Johnson, *Studies in Philology*, Vol XLI, pp120–1.
[2] F. R. Johnson, *Studies in Philology*, Vol XLI, pp129–30.
[3] Quoted by F. R. Johnson, *Studies in Philology*, Vol XLI, 1944, No 2, p133.

All the scientists, but especially the doctors, were accused by the conservative element of prostituting their knowledge by making it available to all. The more intelligent pointed out that since Greek and Latin had been the normal everyday language of the classical authors, there was no difference in writing in English for an English-speaking public in the sixteenth century. The trouble was that scientific knowledge ceased to be available to all. The infiltration of classical terms into English texts gradually created a language of mathematics and science, and the process was re-inforced by the development of symbols. As scientific thought increased in precision and complication, it became progressively more specialised and less comprehensible to the ordinary man.

Throughout the whole of science the forces of change were too strong to be resisted. It was becoming no longer sufficient to repeat the views of the past or to write in classical Latin. The sixteenth century was a century of change, a change which it was impossible to halt or to confine within the limits of accepted learning. This point was realised and forcefully expressed by the great French scientist Jean Fernel. His words apply equally to England and the rest of Europe:

Many tell us that the art of healing, discovered by the labours of our fore-fathers, and brought to completion by Reason, has now attained its goal. They would have us, who come after, tread in the same footsteps as did the Past. It were a crime, they tell us, to swerve a hairs breadth from the well established way. But what if our elders, and those who preceded them, had followed simply in the same path as those before them? . . . Nay, on the contrary, it seems good for philosphers to move to fresh ways and systems . . . In that way each age produces its own crop of new authors and new arts. This age of ours sees art and science gloriously re-arisen after twelve centuries of swoon. Art and science now equal their ancient splendor or surpass it. This age need not, in any respect, despise itself, and sign for the knowledge of the ancients. Once again music, geometry, the handicrafts, painting, architecture, sculpture and many other kinds of skill display themselves in such measure as in no wise to fall short of the achievements of antiquity . . . Our age to-day is doing things of which antiquity did not dream . . .[1]

Sir Walter Ralegh made the same point in *The History of the World*:

But for myself I shall never be persuaded that GOD hath shut up all the light of learning within the Lanthorn of Aristotle's braines. That God hath given invention but to the heathen; and that they only invaded Nature, and found the strength and bottom thereof; the same nature having consumed all her store, and left nothing of price to after ages.

The final example of this conviction that a new age had indeed come for mankind was Sir Francis Bacon. Many of Bacon's ideas were derivative, and he

[1]Quoted by Sir Charles Sherrington, *The Endeavour of Jean Fernel*, CUP 1964, pp16–7.

cannot be taken seriously as an experimental scientist.[1] But as a thinker he grasped more clearly than any of his contemporaries the nature and magnitude of the changes brought about by new technologies and by the discovery of the New World. He saw immediately that it was through these discoveries and inventions that the whole of European civilization had been altered, the work of craftsmen rather than the ideas of philosophers had brought in the new age. The significance of this fact dominated his thought. 'For myself', he wrote, 'I found I was fitted for nothing so well as for the study of Truth; as having a mind nimble and versitile enough to catch the resemblences of things (which is the chief point), and at the same time steady enough to fix and distinguish their subtler differences . . . .' It was not for nothing that he wrote to Burghley that he had taken all knowledge for his province. His mind was too large, too comprehensive for his age, and his vision of King Solomon's House as a centre of academic learning and experimental science where men could discover how to control and manipulate nature, was only half-realised in the Royal Society and still remains a dream.[2]

Bacon had two basic ideas. He thought that philosophy divorced from practical observation of nature was dangerously unrealistic; and he wanted to restore 'the commerce of mind with things', in order that men should apply their knowledge for the 'relief of man's estate'. The Greek philosophers Plato and Aristotle had by their concentration on metaphysical speculation prevented the constructive application of knowledge.

> This kind of degenerate learning did chiefly reign among the schoolmen: who having sharp and strong wits, and abundance of leisure, and small variety of reading (their wits being shut up in the cells of a few authors, chiefly Aristotle their dictator, as their persons were shut up in the cells of monasteries and colleges), . . . did, out of no quantity of matter, and infinite agitation of wit spin out unto us those laborious webs of learning, which are extant in their books. For the wit and mind of man, if it work not upon matter, which is the contemplation of the creatures of God, worketh according to the stuff and is limited thereby; but if it work upon itself, as the spider worketh his web, then it is endless, and brings forth indeed cobwebs of learning, admirable for the fineness of thread and work, but of no substance or profit.[3]

Philosophy of this sort, without a study of nature and a knowledge of the mechanical inventions of man, was sterile; it was only when it was combined with experiment and applied to the purposes of mankind that it could act as a constructive force. This is, or should be, the greatest end of knowledge.

[1]For the view that Bacon was intellectually corrupt as a naturalist, see Lynn Thorndike, *History of Magic and Experimental Science,* Vol VII.
[2]For Bacon's influence in the seventeenth century, see C. Hill, *Intellectual Origins of the English Revolution;* For King Solomon's House, see the appendix in B. Farrington, *Bacon: Philosopher Founder of Industrial Science,* Lawrence and Wishart 1951.
[3]F. Bacon, *Of the Advancement of Learning,* Macmillan 1900, p192.

But the greatest error of all the rest, is the mistaking or the misplacing of the last or farthest end of knowledge: for men have entered into a desire of learning and knowledge, sometimes upon a natural curiosity and inquisitive appetite; sometimes for ornament and reputation; and sometimes to enable them to victory of wit and contradiction; and most times for lucre and profession; and seldom sincerely to give a true account of their gift of reason, to the benefit and use of men: as if there were sought in knowledge a couch, whereupon to rest a searching and restless spirit; or a terrace for a wandering and variable mind to walk up and down with a fair prospect; or a tower of state, for a proud mind to raise itself upon; or a fort or commanding ground, for strife and contention; or a shop for profit or sale; and not a rich storehouse, for the glory of the Creator, and the relief of man's estate.[1]

Bacon's view of the purpose of knowledge as a sort of applied technology is too narrow but it has validity. If the sixteenth century saw an intellectual revolution then it is arguable that its most significant aspect was scientific. It was no accident that in cosmology, geography, medicine and the allied fields of botany and zoology the century saw basic solutions put forward which have lasted until our own time.

The part played by printing was to ensure that these solutions once achieved were not lost but acted as the basis for further advance. The knowledge of new discoveries spread more widely and with greater rapidity through the printed book, but this is not the same thing as saying that they were accepted. The Copernican theory took more than a century to overcome the alternative theories of Ptolomy and Tycho Brahe in the minds of the general public, but because it was known and accepted by a few, the advance continued. The wide dissemination secured by print made it certain.

Bacon's idea of a centre of scientific experiment and learning was echoed in a similar plan for the education of the wards of the crown put forward by Sir Humphrey Gilbert, and in Dr Dee's vain hope that he might combine the Mastership of St Cross with a laboratory and experimental school conveniently situated near the glass makers of Sussex. If Dee, Digges and Harriot had been able to pursue their optical experiments with the encouragement rather than the indifference of the crown, they might have placed England in the forefront of the scientific advance of Europe a century before Newton. As it is their experiments are tantalisingly undocumented and incomplete.

When the sixteenth century is viewed as a whole certain salient facts become apparent. The mid-century period was crucial. This applies to all aspects of development, the political and social as well as the intellectual. It was then that the new educated administrative class came to maturity; it was then that the dispersal of the monastic lands widened the basis of wealth; it was then that the infiltration of the educational system by the monied classes began in earnest; it

[1]F. Bacon, *Of the Advancement of Learning*, p201.

was then the Cromwellian reforms took on their final shape. The remaining years of the century merely closed the political options, and hardened the lines. The final result of the social changes was a more static society with the land-owning class as a self-perpetuating oligarchy. The chance to implement the ideas of social justice put forward by the humanist reformers had been lost. The opportunity to reform the administration had been lost as well. The political corruption of the reign of James I had its origin in the quagmire of patronage under Elizabeth. Elizabeth's reign was one of conservative consolidation not of enlightened evolution. The only change was a shift in power away from the crown; but that in itself was enough to destroy the Tudor state.

Yet in England and in Europe the century was the point of take-off. The impact of printing on society was decisive and irreversible. It forced the pace of change in every field of learning. The widening of education, the proliferation of ideas, the rise of experimental science would all have been impossible without the use of print. It altered the world.

APPENDIX A

Books printed in England, 1480-1640[1]

	Philosophy* and Religion	History	Social Science†	Govern- ment and Politics	Science	Literature	Arts	Sports	Total
1480	10	2	2	—	—	—	—	—	14
1490	6	—	1	1	2	—	—	—	10
1500	15	—	10	5	2	14	—	—	46
1510	29	2	7	16	2	11	—	—	67
1520	26	3	18	29	4	17	—	—	97
1530	51	3	14	44	16	17	1	1	147
1540	38	1	12	18	13	9	—	—	92
1550	126	4	12	25	13	21	—	1	202
1560	54	5	7	27	17	36	1	2	149
1570	62	17	8	26	8	56	1	1	179
1580	111	11	20	19	21	44	—	2	228
1590	111	41	11	23	28	46	3	3	266
1600	94	25	12	24	11	84	7	2	259
1610	173	33	10	29	20	47	10	1	323
1620	193	48	26	37	18	87	11	—	410
1630	212	31	21	48	29	117	5	1	464
1640	251	30	30	78	30	156	—	2	577
Total	1,562	256	221	449	234	762	29	17	3,530

*Pure philosophy was rare, 8 titles in 1640 being largest.
†This term is used to cover commerce, economics and education.

[1]This analysis is taken from Edith L. Klotz, *Huntington Library Quarterly* 1938, p418.

APPENDIX B

A list of the publications of Thomas Hill (From the *Shorter Title Catalogue*, 13480-13502)

The arte of vulgar arithmetic, 1602

A brief and pleasant treatise intituled Natural and Artifical conclusions, 1586

The contemplation of mankinde, 1571

A pleasant history declaring the whole arte of physiognomy, 1579

A contemplation of mysteries, 1571

The gardeners labyrinth, 1577, reprinted 1578, 1586, 1594, 1608

A most briefe and pleasant treatise, teachynge how to dress a garden, 1563, reprinted 1568, 1572

The profittable arte of gardening now the third time set forth whereunto is added the arte of grafting trees, 1574, reprinted 1579, 1586, 1591

The arte of gardening, 1608

The most pleasant arte of the interpretation of dreams, 1576, reprinted 1601

A necessary almanack and kalender, 1560

A new almanack for 1572.

A prognostication for the year 1572

The schoole of skil, containing two books: the first, of the spheres of heaven etc, the second of the spherical elements, 1599

Bibliography

Agnes Arber, *Herbals: Their Origin and Evolution, 1470-1670*, CUP 1938

M. Aston, 'Books and Belief in the Later Middle Ages', Paper presented to *Past and Present* Conference 1966

John Aubrey, *Brief Lives,* ed Oliver Lawson Dick, Penguin 1962

R. Bacon, *The Opus Majus,* R. B. Burke, University of Pennsylvania Press 1928

Frier Bacon, *His discovery of the miracles of Art, Nature, and Magick faithfully translated out of Dr Dee's own copy by T. M. and never before in English,* Printed for Simon Miller at the starre in St Paul's Churchyard 1659

G. Baskerville, *English Monks and the Suppression of the Monasteries,* J. Cape 1958

G. R. Batho, 'The Library of the "Wizard Earl": Henry Percy 9th Earl of Northumberland, 1564-1632', *The Library* 5th Series Number 4, December 1960
'The Household Papers of Henry Percy Ninth Earl of Northumberland', *Camden Society*, XCIII 1962

Stephen Batman, *Batman upon Bartholome,* T. East 1582

F. le van Baumer, *The Early Tudor Theory of Kingship,* Cambridge Mass. 1938

H. S. Bennett, *English Books and Readers, 1475-1603* 2 volumes, CUP 1952

W. Blunt, *The Art of Botanical Illustration,* Collins 1950

Marie Boas, *The Scientific Renaissance,* Collins 1962

Andrew Boorde, *The fyrst Boke of the Introduction of Knowledge,* ed F. J. Furnivall, E.E.T.S. 1870
Breviary of Helthe, W. Middleton 1547
A compendius Regyment or Dyetary of Helth, London (?) 1542.

William Bourne, *A Treatise on the Properties and Qualities of Glasses for Optical Purposes,* Ms Lansdowne 121. 13.
A Regiment for the Sea, ed E. G. R. Taylor, CUP for the Hakluyt Society 1963

V. J. K. Brook, *Archbishop Parker,* Clarendon Press 1962

Otto Brunfels, *Herbarum Vivae Eicones,* John Schott, Strasbourg 1530

W. N. Bryant, 'Matthew Paris Chronicler of St Albans,' *History Today*, November 1969

Curt F. Buhler, *The Fifteenth Century Book,* University of Pennsylvania Press 1960

William Bullein, *A Dialogue against the Fever Pestilence,* E.E.T.S. 1888

Douglas Bush, *The Renaissance and English Humanism,* Toronto 1956

C. C. Butterworth, *The English Primers, 1529-1545,* University of Pennsylvania Press 1953

J. Buxton, *Sir Philip Sidney and the English Renaissance,* 1954

I. R. F. Calder, 'John Dee studied as an English Neoplatonist', Unpublished thesis, London University 1954

John Caius, *The Boke of John Caius against the Sweating Sicknesse*, C. G. Gruner; ed H. Haeser, *Scriptores de Sudore Anglico*, F. Maukii, Jena 1847

E. M. Carus Wilson, *Medieval Merchant Venturers*, Methuen 1954

T. F. Carter, *The Invention of Printing and its Spread Westwards*, revised by L. Carrington Goodrich, Ronald Press, New York 1955

F. Caspari, *Humanism and the Social Order in Tudor England*, University of Chicago Press 1954

Ernst Cassirer, *Language and Myth*, trans Langer, Harpers, New York 1946
   The Platonic Renaissance in England, trans J. E. Pettegrove, Nelson 1953

William Caxton, *Prologues and Epilogues*, ed W. J. B. Crotch, E.E.T.S. 1928

Owen Chadwick, 'The Case of Philip Nicols', *Cambridge Bibliographical Journal*, Vol I, part V, 1953

R. W. Chambers, *Sir Thomas More*, Penguin 1963

K. Charlton, *Education in Renaissance England*, Routledge and Kegan Paul 1965
   'The Professions in sixteenth century England', *University of Birmingham Historical Journal*, Vol XII No 1. 1969

G. Chaucer, ed Nevill Coghill, *Canterbury Tales*, Penguin 1951

Sir George Clark, *A History of the Royal College of Physicians*, Clarendon Press 1964

L. A. Clarkson, 'English Economic Policy in the Sixteenth and Seventeenth Centuries', B.I.H.R. 1965

R. M. Clay, *The Medieval Hospitals of England*, Methuen 1909

William Clowes, *Selected Writings*, ed F. N. L. Poynter, Harvey and Blythe 1948
   Profitable and Necessarie Booke of Observations ed Starres and Leake, New York 1945

Thomas Cogan, *The Haven of Health*, Melch Bradwood for John Norton 1612

D. C. Coleman, *The British Papermaking Industry*, Clarendon Press 1958

H. A. Colwell, 'Andrew Boorde and his medical works', *The Middlesex Hospital Journal* July 1911

John D. Comrie, *A History of Scottish Medicine*, Wellcome 1932

G. Connel Smith, 'English Merchants trading to the New World in the early sixteenth century,' B.I.H.R. Vol XXIII 1950

W. S. C. Copeman, *Doctors and Disease in Tudor Times*, London 1960.

Sir Alexander Croke (ed), *Regimen Sanitatis Salernitanum*, Oxford, Talboys 1830

A. C. Crombie, J. V. Pepper, D. B. Quinn, J. W. Shirley, R. C. H. Tanner, 'Thomas Harriot (1560–1621): an original practitioner in the scientific art', *Times Literary Supplement*, 23 October 1969

Courtney Danton, *The Story of England's Hospitals*, Museum Press 1961

H. S. Darby, *Hugh Latimer*, London 1953

Richard Deacon, *John Dee: Scientist, Geographer, Astrologer, and Secret Agent to Elizabeth I*, Frederick Muller 1968

Allen G. Debus, *The English Paracelsians*, Oldbourne 1965

John Dee, *The Private Diary of Dr John Dee and the Catalogue of his Library of Manuscripts*, edited J. O. Halliwell, Camden Society 1842
   Mathematical Preface to Billingsley's Euclide, London 1570
   Autobiographical Tracts, ed James Crossley, Chatham Society Miscellany 1851

A Supplication to Queen Mary . . . for the recovery and preservation of Ancient Writers and Monuments. Together with The Compendius Rehearsal, Thos. Hearnius Johannis confartris & monarchi Glastoncensis Oxford 1726

De L'Obel, *Plantarum seu Stirpium Historia,* Plantin 1546

M. Dewar, *Sir Thomas Smith: an Intellectual in Office,* Athlone Press 1964

Hugh. C. Dick, 'Thomas Blundeville's *The true Order and Methods of wryting and reading Hystories,* (1574)', *Huntington Library Quarterly* 1940

A. G. Dickens (ed) *The Clifford Letters,* Surtees Society CLXXII 1957
     The English Reformation, Batsford 1964

A. G. Dickens and D. Carr (ed), *The Reformation in England to the Accession of Elizabeth I. Documents of Modern History,* Arnold 1967

Leonard Digges, *A Prognostication of Right Good Effect,* T. Gemini 1555, and T. Marsh 1579
     A Boke named Tectonicon. Briefle shewing the exact measuring and speedie reckonong all manner of Land, Squares, Timber, Stone, Steeples, Pillars, Globes etc . . . With other things pleasant and necessarie most conducible for surveyors, Landmeaters, Ioyners, Carpenters and masons, T. Gemini 1556
     A Geometrical Practical Treatise named Pantometria . . . with sundry strange conclusions both by instrument and without, and also by Perspective Glasses . . . lately finished by Thomas Digges, Henrie Bynneman 1571
     A Prognostication Everlasting . . . With a Perfit Description of Caelestiall Orbes. T Marshe 1576

Thomas Digges, *An Arithmetical Warlike treatise named Stratioticos,* London 1579 (for Digges' other work see Leonard Digges).

P. H. Duffy, 'Medicine in Elizabethan England as illustrated by certain dramatic texts', Harvard, unpublished thesis 1942

P. Duhamel, 'The Oxford Lectures of John Colet', *Journal of the History of Ideas* 1953

G.R. Elton. 'The Political Creed of Thomas Cromwell', *Transactions of the Royal Society,* 5th Series Vol 6. No. 19
     'King or Minister. The man behind the Henrician Reformation', *History* 1964
     'State Planning in Early Tudor England', *Economic History Review,* 2nd Series Vol 13, 1960–1961
     'Sir Thomas More and the opposition to Henry VIII.' B.I.H.R. Vol XLI No 103, May 1968

Sir Thomas Elyot, *Castel of Helth,* 1541, New York 1937
     The Boke named the Governour, Everyman edition, Dent 1909 and 1937

A. B. Emden, 'Donors of books to St Augustine's Library Canterbury' *Oxford Bibliographical Society Occasional Publications,* No 4, 1968

F. G. Emmison, *Tudor Secretary: Sir William Petre at Court and Home,* Longmans 1961. 'A Plan of Edward VI and Secretary Petre for re-organising the Council', B.I.H.R. XXXI 1958

Erasmus, *The Essential Erasmus,* ed J. P. Dolan, Mentor Omega Books, New American Library 1964

A. H. Evans (ed), *Turner on Bird*, CUP 1903

B. Farringdon, *Francis Bacon: Philosopher of Industrial Science*, Lawrence and Wishart 1951

Lucien Febvre and H. J. Martin, *L'Apparition du Livre*, Editions Albin Michel, Paris 1958

E. W. Fowler, *English Sea Power in the Early Tudor Period 1485–1558*, Folger Booklets on Tudor and Stuart Civilisation, Cornell University 1965

John Foxe, *Acts and Monuments*, John Daye 1563

R. W. Freeman, *English Emblem Books*, Chatto and Windus 1967

H. Fischer, 'Conrad Gesner (1516–1565) as Bibliographer and Encyclopedist', *The Library*, 5th Series XXI, No 4, 1966

Leonard Fuchs, *De Historia Stirpium*, Basel 1542

Thomas Fuller, *The Church History of Great Britain*, London 1655

G. E. Fussell, *The Old English Farming Books from Fitzherbert to Tull 1523–1730*, Crosby Lockwood 1947

F. Smith Fussner, *The Historical Revolution. English Historical Writing and Thought 1580–1640*, Routledge and Kegan Paul 1962

Thomas Gale, *Certaine Workes of Chirurgie*, Thomas East, London 1586

C. H. Garrett, *The Marian Exiles*, CUP 1938

P. Gaskell, 'Henry Justice: A Cambridge book thief', *Cambridge Bibliographical Journal*, Vol I Part 4, 1952
Morvern Transformed, CUP 1968

C. Gesner, *A Newe booke of destilatyon of waters called the Treasure of Eounymus*, trans by Peter Morwyng, John Day 1565
The Newe Jewell of Health, trans by Thomas Hill and George Baker, London 1576
The Practise of the new and old Phisicke, translated by Thomas Hill and George Baker, London 1599

W. Gilbert, *On the Magnet*, ed Sylvanus P. Thomson, Gilbert Club Translation, London 1900

H. Cameron Gilles, *Regimen Sanitatis, The Rule of Health from the Vade Mecum of the famous MacBethes*, University Press, Glasgow 1911

Giraldus Cambrensis, *Itinery through Wales*, Everyman edition No 272, 1935

P. Goldschmidt, *The Printed Book of the Renaissance*, CUP 1950

E. H. Gombrich, 'Botticelli's Mythologies: a study in the Neoplatonic symbolism of his circle,' *Journal of the Warburg and Courtauld Institutes*, VIII 1945

R. T. Gunther, *Early Science in Oxford*, OUP 1923
Early Science in Cambridge, OUP 1937
Early English Botanists, OUP 1922

P. M. Handover, *Printing in London*, Allen and Unwin 1960.

Thomas Harriot, *Additional Manuscripts*, 6782–6789.
Leconfield Manuscripts, 241–242.
Harley Manuscripts, 6001–6002 and 6083

Sir John Harrington, *Regimen Sanitatis Salernitanum, the English Version of Sir John Harrington*, Ente provinciale per il Turismo Salerno.

G. B. Harrison (ed), *Willobie his Avisa*, Bodley Head 1926

Gabriel Harvey, *Letter Book of Gabriel Harvey*, ed E. J. Scott, Camden Society 1884

Hirem Haydon, *The Counter Renaissance*, Charles Scribner and Sons, New York 1950

G. Heron (ed), *De Docta Ignorantia*, London 1954

J. H. Hexter, *Reappraisals of History*, Longmans 1961
> *More's Utopia. The Biography of an Idea*, Princeton 1952.
> 'The Loom of Language and the Fabric of Imperatives. The Case of *Il Principe* and *Utopia*', *American Historical Review* 1964.
> *The Complete Works of Sir Thomas More*, ed with Edward Surtz S. J., Yale 1965

Christopher Hill, *Intellectual Origins of the English Revolution*, Clarendon Press 1965

R. Holinshed, *Chronicles of England, Scotland and Ireland*, 6 Vols, London 1808

J. Huizinga, *Erasmus of Rotterdam*, Phaidon 1952

R. Hunt, 'Medieval Inventories of Clare College Library', *Cambridge Bibliographical Journal*, Vol I Part 2 1950

Dard Hunter, *Papermaking: the History and Technique of an Ancient Craft*, Cresset Press 1947

Raymond Irwin, *The English Library*, Allen and Unwin 1966

Sears Jayne, *John Colet and Marsilio Ficino*, OUP 1963
> *The Lumley Library Catalogue of 1609*, ed with F. R. Johnson, British Museum 1956
> *Library Catalogues of the English Renaissance*, University of California Press 1956

Sean Jennett, (ed and trans), *Journal of a Younger Brother. The Life of Thomas Platter as a Medieval Student in Montpellier at the Close of the Sixteenth Century*, London 1963

W. K. Jordan, *Philanthropy in England 1480–1660*, Allen and Unwin 1964
> *The Charities of Rural England*, Allen and Unwin 1961
> *The Chronicle and Political Papers of Edward VI*, Allen and Unwin 1966

F. R. Johnson, edited with Sears Jayne, *The Lumley Library Catalogue*, see above.
> *Astronomical Thought in Renaissance England*, John Hopkins Press 1937
> edited with S. V. Larkey, 'Thomas Digges, the Copernican System and the idea of the Infinity of the Universe', *Huntington Library Bulletin* No 5 1934
> edited with S. V. Larkey, 'Recorde's Mathematical Teaching and the Anti-Aristotelian Movement', *Huntington Library Bulletin* No 7 1935
> 'Digges and the Progress of Astronomy in England', *Orisis* 1936
> 'Latin versus English: the sixteenth century debate over scientific terminology', *Studies in Philology*, Vol XLI No 2 1944.
> 'Thomas Hill: An Elizabethan Huxley', *Huntington Library Quarterly*, August 1944

C. H. Josten, 'An unknown chapter in the life of John Dee', *Journal of the Warburg and Courtauld Institutes*, Vol XXVIII 1965

H. F. Kearney, 'Puritanism, Capitalism and the Scientific Revolution', *Past and Present*, No 28 1964

N. R. Ker, *Medieval Libraries of Great Britain*, Royal Historical Society, 2nd edition 1964

'Medieval Manuscripts from Norwich Cathedral Priory', *Cambridge Bibliographical Journal*, Vol I Part I 1949

'Oxford College Libraries in the Sixteenth Century', *Bodleian Library Record*, Vol VI 1957–1961

'Introduction to Oxford College Libraries in 1556', *Bodleian Library Catalogue of the Exhibition of 1956*

G. Keynes, *Timothy Bright 1550–1615*, Wellcome 1962

E. L. Klotz, 'Table of Early Printed Books', *Huntington Library Quarterly* 1938

P. H. Kocher, *Science and Religion in Elizabethan England*, San Marino, California 1953

Thomas Kuhn, *The Structure of Scientific Revolutions*, University of Chicago Press 1968

Brian Lawn, *The Salernitan Questions*, Clarendon Press 1963

Stamford E. Lehmberg, *Sir Thomas Elyot*, University of Texas 1960.

Sir Walter Mildmay and Tudor Government, University of Texas 1964

H. Lehmann–Haupt, *Gutenberg and the Master of the Playing Cards*, Yale 1966

Leland Miles, *John Colet and the Platonic Tradition*, Allen and Unwin 1962

John Lohne, 'Thomas Harriot 1560–1621. The Tycho Brahe of Optics', *Centaurus*, Vol 6 No 2 1959

W. MacCafferry, *The Shaping of the Elizabethan Regime*, Jonathan Cape 1969

L. G. Matthews, *The History of Pharmacy in Britain*, E. and S. Livingstone, London 1962

J. K. McConica, *English Humanists and Reformation Politics*, Clarendon Press 1965

M. McKisack, *The Fourteenth Century*, Clarendon Press 1959

Medieval History in the Tudor Age, Clarendon Press 1971.

Marshall McLuhan, *The Gutenberg Galaxy*, Routledge and Kegan Paul 1962

F. W. Maitland, *English Law and the Renaissance*, CUP 1901

H. A. Mason, *Humanism and Poetry in Early Tudor England*, Routledge and Kegan Paul 1959

G. Mattingly, *Catherine of Aragon*, Jonathan Cape 1963

H. Maynard Smith, *Pre-Reformation England*, Macmillan 1938

A. J. O'Hara May, 'A study of English Dietary Advice in the Second Half of the Sixteenth Century,' unpublished thesis, London 1969

Hope Mirrlees, *A Fly in Amber. Being an Extravagant Biography of the Romantic Antiquary Sir Robert Cotton*, Faber 1962

R. J. Mitchell, *John Tiptoft*, Longmans 1938

Sir Thomas More, *Utopia*, Everyman edition, Dent 1916

Stanley Morrison, *Black Letter Text*, CUP 1942

'Early Humanistic Script and the first Roman Type'. *The Library*, New Series XXIV 1943

English Prayer Books, CUP 1949

German Incunabula in the British Museum, Gollanz 1928

A. N. L. Munby, *Phillipps Studies*, CUP 1951–1956.

J. U. Nef, *Cultural Foundations of the Industrial Revolution*, CUP 1958
M. Nicolson, 'English Almanacs and the 'New Astronomy', *Annals of Science*, Vol 4 No I 1939

J. C. T. Oates and H. L. Pink, 'Three Sixteenth Century Catalogues of the University Library', *Cambridge Bibliographical Journal*, Vol I Part 4 1952
O'Malley *English Medical Humanists*, Kansas Press 1965
J. F. Osborn, *The Autobiography of Thomas Whythorne*, OUP 1962
Charles Singer, E. J. Holmyard, A. R. Hall, T. I. Williams (eds),
Oxford History of Technology, 4 Vols, OUP 1954

J. V. Pepper, 'Harriot's Unpublished Papers', *British Journal for the History of Science*, Vol 6 1967
'Harriot's calculation of the Meridional Parts as Logarithmic Tangents', *Archive for the History of the Exact Sciences*, IV 1967–1968.
'A Letter from Nathaniel Torporley to Thomas Harriot', *British Journal for the History of Science*, Vol 3 1966–1967
F. N. L. Poynter, *Selected Writings of William Clowes*, Harvey and Blythe 1948

D. B. Quinn and J. W. Shirley, 'A Contempory List of Hariot References', *Renaissance Quarterly*, No I 1968

Sir Walter Ralegh, *The History of the World*, Constable 1820
C. E. Raven, *English Naturalists from Neckham to Ray*, CUP 1947
Robert Recorde, *The Grounde of Artes*, R. Wolfe 1542.
The Castle of Knowledge, R. Wolfe 1556
The Whetstone of Witte, John Kyngston 1557
Jaspar Ridley, *Thomas Cranmer*, Clarendon Press 1962
E. Roesslin, *The Byrth of Mankynde, otherwise named the womens boke newly set forth, corrected and augmented . . . by Thomas Raynald Phisition*, London 1552.
E. S. Rohde, *The Old English Herbals*, Longmans 1922
E. F. Rogers, *Sir Thomas More Selected Letters*, New Haven, Conn. 1961
E. Rosenberg, *Leicester, Patron of Letters*, Columbia University Press 1955
'Giacopo Castelvetro, Italian Publisher in Elizabethan London and his Patrons,' *Huntington Library Quarterly*, VI 1942–1943
E. Rupp, *Studies in the Making of the English Protestant Tradition*, CUP 1947

G. Sarton, *The Appreciation of Ancient and Medieval Science During the Renaissance, 1450–1600*, University of Pennylvania Press 1955
J. W. Shirley, 'The scientific experiments of Sir Walter Ralegh, The Wizard Earl, and the Three Magi in the Tower, 1603–1617', *Ambix* 1951.
'An early Experimental Determination of Snell's Law', *American Journal of Physics*, Vol 19. 1951
'Binery Numeration before Leibnitz', *American Journal of Physics*. Vol 19 1951
F. S. Siebert, *Freedom of the Press in England, 1476–1776*, University of Illinois 1952
Joan Simon, *Education and Society in Tudor England*, CUP 1966
Charles Singer, *Galen on Anotomical Procedures*, OUP 1956

C. A. Sneyd (ed), *The Italian Relation*, Camden Society Ist Series, XXXVII

S. H. Steinberg, *Five Hundred Years of Printing*, Faber 1959

Henry Stevens, *Thomas Hariot, the Mathematician, the Philosopher, and the Scholar*, London 1900

L. Stone, *Social Change and Revolution in England 1540–1640*, Longmans 1965
Thr Crisis of the Aristocracy, OUP 1967
'The Educational Revolution in England 1540–1640', *Past and Present*, No 28 1964
'Social Mobility in England 1500–1700', *Past and Present*, No 33 1966
'The Political Programme of Thomas Cromwell', B.I.H.R. 1951

John Strype, *Life of John Cheke*, Oxford 1821
Ecclesiastical Memorials, Clarendon Press 1822
Memorials of Thomas Cranmer, London 1694

C. H. Talbot, *Medicine in Medieval England*, Oldbourne 1967
'Simon Bredon 1300–1372: Physician, Mathematician, Astronomer', *British Journal for the History of Science*, Vol I 1962–1963
The Medical Practitioners of Medieval England, a Biographical Register, Wellcome 1965

R. C. H. Tanner, 'On the role of equality and inequality in the history of mathematics', *British Journal for the History of Science*, Vol I No 2 1962–1963
'Thomas Harriot as a Mathematician', *Physis. Revista Internazionale de storia della scienza*, Vol 9 1967

E. G. R. Taylor, *Tudor Geography*, Methuen 1930
The Mathematical Practitioners of Tudor and Stuart England, CUP 1954
'The doctrine of Nautical Triangles Compendius', *Journal of the Institute of Navigation*, Vol 6 1953 with D. H. Sadler

Lynn Thorndike, *A History of Magic and Experimental Science*, 8 vols, New York 1929–1958
Science and Thought in the Fifteenth Century, Columbia University Press 1929

H. Trevor Roper, 'The Decline of the Mere Gentry', *Economic History Review* 1953
Collected Essays, OUP 1957

W. Turner Berry and H. Edmund Poole, *Annals of Printing*, Blandford 1966

W. Turner, *On Birds* ed A. H. Evans, CUP 1903
Libellus de Re Herbaria, The Names of Herbs, fascimile edition by the Ray Society 1965
A New Herball. On Baths, Arnold Birkmann Collen 1568

D. B. Updike, *Printing Types: their History, Forms, and Use*, Harvard 1922

Thomas Vicary, *The Anatomie of the Bodie of Man*, edited Furnivall, E.E.T.S. Extra Series LIII, London 1888

John Ward, *The Lives of the Professors of Gresham College*, London 1740

D. W. Waters, *The Art of Navigation in England in Elizabethan and Early Stuart Times*, Hollis and Carter 1958
The Rutters of the Sea, Yale 1967

R. Weiss, *Humanism in England during the Fifteenth Century*, Basil Blackwell 1941

Franklin B. Williams, *Index of Dedications and Commendatory Verses in English Books before 1641*, The Bibliographical Society, London 1962

Neville Williams, *Thomas Howard, Fourth Duke of Norfolk*, Barrie and Rockliff 1964

J. A. Williamson, *The Voyages of the Cabots and the English Discovery of North America under Henry VII and Henry VIII*, London 1929

C. E. Wright, 'The Dispersal of the Monastic Libraries and the Beginnings of Anglo-Saxon Studies. Matthew Parker and his Circle', *Cambridge Bibliographical Journal*, Vol. I No. 3 1951

L. B. Wright, *Middle Class Culture in Elizabethan England*, North Carolina 1935

Winifred Wulff, *Rosa Anglica*, Simkin Marshall 1929

George Wyat, *Extracts from the Life of the Virtuous Christian and Renowned Queen Anne Boleigne*, written at the close of the sixteenth century and printed in London, 1817

Francis A. Yates, *Giordano Bruno and the Hermetic Tradition*, Routledge and Kegan Paul 1964
The Theatre of the World, Routledge and Kegan Paul 1968

W. G. Zeeveld, *The Foundations of Tudor Policy*, Harvard 1948

Index